HINDU FESTIVALS

IN A

NORTH INDIAN VILLAGE

Stanley A. Freed
Curator, Department of Anthropology
American Museum of Natural History

Ruth S. Freed
Research Associate, Department of Anthropology
American Museum of Natural History

ANTHROPOLOGICAL PAPERS OF
THE AMERICAN MUSEUM OF NATURAL HISTORY
NUMBER 81, 336 PAGES, 86 FIGURES, 8 TABLES
ISSUED NOVEMBER 5, 1998

ABSTRACT

This monograph is the tenth of a series devoted to the description and analysis of life in Shanti Nagar, a village in the Union Territory of Delhi. Our research is based on holistic fieldwork carried out in 1957–59 and 1977–78. Previous monographs, all published in the *Anthropological Papers of the American Museum of Natural History*, have dealt with social organization, economics and technology, rites of passage, fertility and sterilization, sickness and health, enculturation and education, politics and elections, ghosts in the context of a woman's psychomedical case history, and a functional and historical analysis of ghost beliefs based on case studies.

The present monograph is the pendant of *Rites of Passage*. Such rites take place when a person passes through a change of status. Rites of passage can occur at any time. In contrast, the festivals described here are set by the calendar and often concern society as a whole. They are basically rites of intensification, for they honor and propitiate the deities, celebrate great events in Hindu mythology, reinforce basic interpersonal relationships, and give people opportunities to enhance their merit by performing pious acts. They reaffirm the attachment of individuals to the basic beliefs, uniqueness, and unity of a society.

The description of each festival is placed in ethnographic context. The analysis is supplemented by reference to Indian history and to Hindu mythology, astronomy, and astrology. Differential participation in festivals by caste, sect, age, and gender is described. The study covers a period of two decades. Although the festivals were overwhelmingly stable from the 1950s to the 1970s, differences between the observances of festivals during the period are noted. Comparisons are made with practices in other villages and cities.

COVER ILLUSTRATION
An altar for the festival of Dassehra is on the ground in front of a representation of the goddess Sanjhi that is plastered on the wall. The altar and the figure have no connection, but their juxtaposition recalls that the festivals of Dassehra and Sanjhi are celebrated simultaneously. A tree branch that partially obscured the small figure to the left of Shanji has been removed from the photograph. The empty area was repaired with part of a similar photograph taken from a different angle.

TITLE PAGE ILLUSTRATION
Mural of Hoi Mata, Brahman's house, 1977; see fig. 21.

Anthropological Paper no. 81 is distributed by the University of Washington Press
P.O. Box 50096
Seattle, WA 98145

CONTENTS

TABLES

ILLUSTRATIONS

INTRODUCTION

THE 3000-YEAR-OLD HINDU tradition is a religious, philosophical, and literary masterpiece. It has given rise to an ethical system of unsurpassed sophistication, has produced epics—the Ramayana and the Mahabharata—that are on a par with the epic literature of the West, has elaborated six systems of philosophy, and, as perhaps its crown jewel, has given the Bhagavad Gita to the world. Although one can learn a great deal about classical Hinduism by studying its voluminous sacred literature, that approach has its limits, for it cannot fully take into account the Hinduism that is currently practiced by the people. To understand modern Hinduism, one must go to everyday people in the villages.

Festivals are the most visible feature of village Hinduism. All common ritual practices are on display. The relationships of festivals to family life, the agricultural year, and the ordinary concerns of people are clearly seen in offerings to deities, gifts exchanged between relatives, songs, drama, and storytelling. Hinduism loses richness and relevance when studied only at the literary level, and, in turn, village life cannot be understood without an appreciation of the depth of the villagers' attachment to Hindu belief and practice. Festivals are the best point of entry into the study of Hinduism in ethnographic context.

TYPES OF FESTIVALS

All societies have a roster of festivals, that is, repetitive ritualized activities usually with a religious aspect. They fall into two broad categories, distinguished chiefly by their different purposes and contexts. Those that are precipitated by an individual's change of status are called rites of passage. They take place principally at birth, marriage, and death. Their purpose is not only to confirm a person's change of status but also to establish new social relationships as may be necessary, such as between in-laws.

Festivals of the other category, which are the subject of the present work, revolve around the concerns of a society as a whole. Almost all of them are celebrated on specific lunar or solar dates. They are often connected to the agricultural year, taking place during the harvest and sowing seasons. They may be related to epidemic diseases that make their appearance at particular seasons and against which

1

the whole society seeks protection. They often celebrate events in the lives of deities, episodes from sacred literature, or astronomical moments such as equinoxes, solstices, eclipses, and the phases of the moon. They give individuals opportunities to enhance their merit by performing pious acts. Many of them are occasions for reinforcing basic interpersonal and familial relationships.

Such festivals are called rites of intensification to emphasize their purpose, or calendric rites when the focus is on their dates in the annual ceremonial cycle. In practice, the two phrases are generally used interchangeably. Rites of intensification reaffirm the attachment of individuals to the basic beliefs, uniqueness, and unity of a society. Most of these rites are religious and hence are usually limited to believers. Modern heterogeneous nations need secular rites of intensification with which all citizens can identify, such as independence days, the birthdays of national heroes, or days honoring soldiers or workers. Festivals that are basically religious can assume a quasi-secular aspect that broadens participation, for example, the gift-giving and exchange of greeting cards at Christmas.

In this monograph, we deal with rites of intensification, or calendric rites, as they were observed in 1958–59 and again in 1977–78 in Shanti Nagar (a pseudonym), a north Indian village. We have previously described and analyzed the rites of passage practiced in this village (R. Freed and S. Freed, 1980, 1985, 1993). The two works are complementary. Although calendric rites differ from rites of passage in many ways, we follow the same general analytical outline for treating calendric rites as we used for rites of passage. We describe each rite, recount its mythological charter when there is one, and place the rite in its socioreligious context. The dominant themes of each rite are pointed out as they are manifested in behavior and symbolism. The rites as practiced in 1958–59 are compared to their celebration in 1977–78.

The definitions and use of terms in this work generally follow the style of our earlier study of the rites of passage. A rite includes many ceremonies, rituals, and events. A ceremony is a complex of ritual acts. For example, the ritual of circling the pyre is part of the ceremony that takes place at the Holi bonfire, which in turn is part of the Holi festival. Rituals often occur within a ceremony but may exist by themselves. For example, the fulfillment of a vow, as when an offering is made at a shrine for the welfare of a child or for the protection of a departing traveler, is a ritual independent of a ceremony. Some actions that are part of a rite are not sacred. They are events—for example, the collection of fuel for the Holi bonfire. Although such events take on some of the characteristics of rituals because of their predictability, they generally are not sacred acts and are best classified as events rather than rituals or ceremonies (R. Freed and S. Freed, 1980: 333–334).

When treating both rites of passage and rites of intensification, one needs a term covering both categories. "Festival" may serve this purpose. However, we deal here only with rites of intensification (or calendric rites) and so use "festival" in place of these more cumbersome phrases. Although we try to use our terminology consistently, all the terms have popular and general meanings, and there is much overlap. On a few occasions, nomenclature may be more in tune with common usage than with our classification. In such cases, the meaning of a term will be clear from the context.

A conspicuous difference between rites of passage and rites of intensification is that in rites of passage the protagonists are members of the community. Birth ceremonies, for example, star the mother and infant with the adult women of the household as the supporting cast. Bride and groom are featured in the marriage rite. Calendric rites lack such personae. Their protagonists are deities, not local people. Thus, Shiva has his special night, the birthday of Krishna is celebrated, and various goddesses are worshipped in several rites.

Other differences between rites of passage and rites of intensification involve complexity and variety. Rites of passage are much more intricate than any calendric rite, and so priests and other specialists are needed to conduct them properly. The calendric rites as celebrated in Shanti Nagar do not require ritual specialists, with the exception of Sat Narayan's Katha. Also, because rites of passage are complex, they are lengthy. Calendric rites vary in this regard. Some calendric rites require a fair amount of time when they selectively include storytelling, processions, the creation of representations of a deity, and feasting. Others are over quickly, as when water is offered to the moon.

On the other hand, rites of intensification are much more varied than rites of passage, necessarily so because there are so many of them compared with basically only three rites of passage. The worship of a variety of deities is the dominant feature of calendric rites. Most festivals feature a specific deity and a unique mythological charter. In some festivals, the religious aspect is greatly reduced or even suppressed to the point where the festival is effectively secular—Tijo, for example. The rite of Charm Tying seems to have no religious aspect in Shanti Nagar. Shraddha (or Kanagat) is held to honor ancestors. Some calendric events are entirely secular: Republic Day and Independence Day. When the rites that are celebrated weekly, monthly, and annually are taken into account, one or another festival is observed almost every day of the year. However, no individual takes part in all the rites, and some rites attract relatively few participants.

The strengthening of ties with kin, friends, and family retainers is a feature of both rites of passage and calendric festivals. Most of this ceremonial interaction takes the form of quasi-mandatory presents, mainly food, money, and clothing, given and received. During calendric rites, much such activity is between families united by marriage or between sister and brother, which, after a sister's marriage, also involves relations between in-laws.

People give gifts on ceremonial occasions to members of other castes as well as to kin. At calendric rites, the recipients are Brahmans, Barbers, and Sweepers. For example, Brahmans are fed at Shraddha and Nirjala Ekadashi. Sweepers receive food and other gifts at Sili Sat and eclipses. Most such gifts, however, are basically payments under the jajmani system: that is, they are payment for services. Nonetheless, they function to strengthen traditional relations between families of different castes, just as gifts to relatives help maintain the kinship network (S. Freed and R. Freed, 1976: 120–131).

A major festival theme concerns the general well-being of the individual and family. Well-being has several aspects: protection from illness, enhancement of fertility, finding a good husband, preventing widowhood, assuring the welfare of children, and increasing prosperity. Of the 28 calendric festivals in Shanti Nagar that take place only once a year as contrasted to festivals that recur weekly or monthly, 14 have as their major purpose the well-being of the family.

Health, fertility, and general family welfare are closely connected. Without health and fertility there can be no family welfare. Women are the principal participants in most of these festivals. The blame for a sterile marriage is always placed on women. Consequently a woman might be returned to her parents or, at least, her husband would be likely to take a second wife. The death of a son is a tragedy for a family, especially for women, who sometimes may die or commit suicide after such a devastating loss. The high rate of infant mortality and a relatively short life expectancy (less than 50 years in the 1960s) make the untimely death of a son or a spouse a distinct possibility. The early death of a husband affects women much more than the loss of a wife affects men. Hanchett (1988: 71) observed, "The woman who is a wife today may be a widow tomorrow, her social status as degraded as that of a married woman is glorified." The anxiety of women is apparent in many annual festivals.

The 14 festivals where family welfare is an important theme attribute misfortune, illness, suffering, and evil to natural and supernatural causes. These causes are conceptually distinct but are sometimes closely connected in village curing practices. The deaths of cattle, for example, seriously affect family prosperity and welfare. Cattle may die from, among other causes, snakebite or disease. Cattle disease, like infectious human disease, has a supernatural persona and can be treated both by an exorcist and by medicine (R. Freed and S. Freed, 1966). Snakebite would seem to be almost as mechanical as accidental death, and yet it too is amenable to a supernatural approach, for snakes have a divine aspect and may be propitiated (R. Freed and S. Freed, 1993: 98, 179). The great epidemic diseases, such as smallpox (until recently) and typhoid, are sent by mother goddesses to whom offerings must be made. An individual's choice of how to treat disease tends to be pragmatic and may combine exorcism, supplication, and remedies from Ayurvedic and Western medicine.

Misfortune and evil do not involve the concept of individual sin. The idea of personal repentance, common in Western religions, as a way of avoiding punishment and misfortune is rare in modern rural Hinduism, if it exists at all. Immoral individual actions find their consequences in the doctrines of karma and rebirth. Villagers know that evil people abound who harm others, but the wrongdoers themselves are not necessarily harmed, at least not usually in this life although surely in later lives. An individual's evil acts are balanced by good acts, not by repentance, as is common in the West. We go into these matters very briefly only to point out that none of the unique festivals for family welfare shows any trace of misfortune as punishment for individual sin, which therefore requires repentance. Confession is prominent in Christianity, and Yom Kippur (Day of Atonement) is the most sacred day in the Jewish calendar. Such ideas and festivals are foreign to the Hinduism of Shanti Nagar.[1]

The festival year in Shanti Nagar is replete with rites honoring, or beseeching, the great deities of modern Hinduism: Vishnu and his avatars, Shiva, and the mother goddesses (Shakti, the female energy of a deity, especially of Shiva). Vishnu, particularly in his avatars of Krishna and Ram, and the mother goddesses receive more attention than Shiva. The strong influence of the Arya Samaj in Shanti Nagar has probably led to the relative suppression of the worship of Shiva, for the founder of the Arya Samaj, Swami Dayananda Saraswati (1824–1883), abandoned the worship of Shiva when he was 14 years old. His father, a devout follower of Shiva, insisted that his son observe a fast for Shiva worship in a temple. Forcing himself to stay awake, he saw a mouse creep onto the image of Shiva and nibble at the offerings. This called into question the power of the deity, for obviously the mouse was not afraid and the deity did nothing (Rai, 1967: 8–11).

Rites of passage are concerned with status transitions rather than with devotion to the great deities. Vishnu plays almost no role. Mother goddesses are important because of their protective functions. The Chamar Leatherworkers worship the Shiva Lingam for fertility in one of the wedding rituals; otherwise Shiva is inconspicuous. Ganesh, the son of Shiva, receives attention in his role as Remover of Obstacles at the beginning of important undertakings. He is essential to the success of all marriages. However, in rites of passage, emphasis is on the protagonists who are villagers, and not on the great deities.

ARYA SAMAJ AND SANATAN DHARMA

There are two outstanding religious groups in Shanti Nagar: the Samajis, who are followers of the Arya Samaj, and the Sanatanis, who believe in traditional Hinduism, Sanatan Dharma (the Eternal Religion). The Arya Samaj sect of Hinduism was founded by Swami Dayananda Saraswati in the last half of the 19th century. Swami Dayananda was influenced to some extent by monotheism and other Western values (Farquhar, 1915: 115). According to village informants, the Arya Samaj was active in Punjab in the 1890s and in the Shanti Nagar region in the 1920s. The sect is active today in the Union Territory of Delhi, Punjab, and Uttar Pradesh.

The chief doctrinal differences between Sanatanis and Samajis involve different interpretations of Sanskritic literature, particularly the Vedas. The Sanatanis are more in accord with the generally accepted understanding of the Vedas than are the Samajis, who follow the exegesis of Swami Dayananda. Although he was emphatic about returning to the Vedas as the source of all knowledge, his interpretation of them does not follow orthodox tradition or the generally accepted translations and interpretations of Sanskritic scholars (Farquhar, 1915: 113–118).

Monotheism was perhaps Swami Dayananda's most important doctrine. He taught that Vedic mantras mention only one deity and that various names of deities are only ways of describing one god. "Light is one but it has many flashes," a maxim that the villagers sometimes quoted to us, summarizes this basic principle. Swami Dayananda denounced the belief in ghosts and spirit forces and all forms of magic and sorcery, claiming that their practitioners (bhagats) were frauds. He declared that sickness should be cured by cleanliness and by fumigation with fire and incense and that curing should be practiced only by those with scientific medical knowledge. He opposed shamans and exorcists, the vested interests of Brahmans, alms, and cults of deities. In particular, he argued strongly against the cult of Krishna worship (an avatar of Vishnu), as described in the Bhagavata Purana, saying, "Each *Purana* vies with another in humbuggery" (Saraswati, 1956: 489). Although he believed in the efficacy of prayer when coupled with Vedic mantras and the fire ceremony, he disapproved of fasting and the repetition of mystic syllables, including the various names of deities (Saraswati, 1956: 46, 469–567, 853–857).

The Sanatanis, on the other hand, conceive of a spirit world inhabited by many spirit forces and a number of deities. They believe that intrusive spirits, such as ghosts, can cause disease. Intrusive spirits can be exorcised by bhagats who know the appropriate rituals. Sanatanis accept the domination of Brahmans over prayer and ritual, the giving of charity to Brahmans, fasting and the repetition of mantras and Sanskritic words to propitiate the deities, and the efficacy of the fire ceremony (*havan*) as a potent protection from malevolent forces. In Shanti Nagar, the disinclination of Samajis, mainly Jats, to give gifts to Brahmans is phrased in terms of "equality" between the castes.

Members of the Jat caste are the principal followers of the Arya Samaj in Shanti Nagar. The single family of the Merchant caste (1950s) also adhered to the Arya Samaj. Most Brahmans follow Sanatan Dharma, as do the Potter, Barber, Leatherworker, and Sweeper castes. The other castes may follow either doctrine but tend to favor Sanatan Dharma, for most of them look to Brahmans for the performance of their life cycle ceremonies and other religions activities. Although generally the Jats are Samajis and the Brahmans are Sanatanis, these identifications have exceptions. Some Jats hold beliefs that characterize the Sanatanis, and a few Brahman men profess to be Samajis but have retained Brahmanical caste customs. The Arya Samaj is anti-Brahmanical, but the Jats were in some measure against the Brahmans before the introduction of the Arya Samaj (Temple, 1883–1887, 1: 134).

SHANTI NAGAR, A SKETCH

In 1958, Shanti Nagar was located in the Union Territory of Delhi about 11 mi (18 km) northwest by road from the city limits of Delhi, a distance that has decreased slightly since that time because of the gradual spread of the city. Several villages are situated between Delhi and Shanti Nagar. Travel between Shanti Nagar and Delhi was relatively easy in 1958. Except for about 1 mi (1.6 km) the road to Delhi was paved. A bus made four round trips daily; during the rainy season, the bus traveled only to the end of the paved road and passengers had to complete the journey on foot through flooded fields. By 1977, the paved road had been extended to Shanti Nagar, and bus service was more convenient.

The village is west of the Grand Trunk Road. The habitation site and about half the agricultural land are on land (called *bangar*) high enough above the Yamuna River to avoid flooding during the monsoon season. Flooding is a serious problem for the *khadar* (riverine) zone east of the Grand Trunk Road and also for some village land, classified as *khadar*, that lies east of the principal north-south road that passes through the village (fig. 1). The area designated *bani* in figure 1 is relatively poor land overgrown with shrubs and trees. All village shrines are in the *bangar* area. Part of the village land is irrigated by the Delhi Branch of the Western Yamuna Canal. In the 1950s, Persian wheels mounted on masonry wells provided a small amount of additional irrigation. In the 1970s, private tubewell irrigation was probably of greater importance than canal irrigation, and Persian wheels were no longer used.

The climate of the Shanti Nagar region has four seasons. Three are sharply marked: a dry hot season from March to June, the monsoon from July to September, and a dry, cold winter from December to February. The fourth season, October and November, is less distinctive than the other three. The Indian Meteorological Department calls it the "[S]eason of the Retreating South-West Monsoon" (Mamoria, 1980: 42). The fading monsoon in September is followed by a brief hot spell. About 74% of the annual rainfall comes during the monsoon months, and if the pre-monsoon rains of late June are taken into account, the figure increases to about 80% (Gazetteer Unit, Delhi Adm., 1976: 33; Maheshwari, 1976: 3).

The climate influences ceremonial life. Because weddings involve considerable travel, none takes place during the monsoon season when travel is difficult. During this period, the gods are said to be sleeping. An annual festival just before the monsoon season marks the day when the gods go to sleep; another festival takes place in the first fortnight of November, when they awake.

Shanti Nagar conforms to a type of village, common in northern India, often described as nucleated. The houses are crowded together, sometimes sharing one or more walls with adjacent houses. The compact habitation site still has a little undivided common land at its edges, especially to the east where the school and the cremation grounds are located. Beyond this tract lie the cultivated fields. The shared

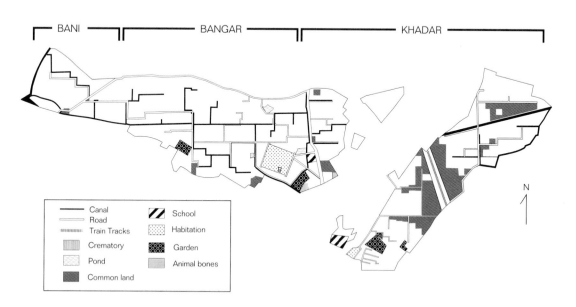

FIG. 1. Map of Shanti Nagar. Adapted and simplified from the cadastral map as revised after land consolidation in the 1970s. The area of the village is 1037 acres (420 ha), which is the average of the slightly different figures from the 1950s and the 1970s. See text for definitions of *bangar, bani,* and *khadar.*

architecture and geographic arrangements of nucleated villages are matched by similarities of culture patterns concerning domains such as caste, family life, ceremony,
and economy. The population of Shanti Nagar had increased by 66% in the 20 years
between our two studies and was crowding the village. Of the 799 villagers in 1958
–59, 392 were females and 407 were males; of 1324 persons in 1977–78, 629 were
females and 695 were males (S. Freed and R. Freed, 1985: 238–239, tables 1 and 2). As
the population of Shanti Nagar has grown, the habitation site has been expanded at
the expense of the common land (figs. 2, 3).

Caste plays a role in ceremonial life. Castes are named endogamous social
groups in which membership is acquired by birth. The castes of a village form a hierarchy based on social esteem and precedence. A caste has a combination of attributes, prominent among them a traditional occupation. However, many members of a
caste do not follow the traditional occupation. Representatives of 13 castes lived in
Shanti Nagar in the 1950s; there were 14 castes in the 1970s (table 1). Some festivals

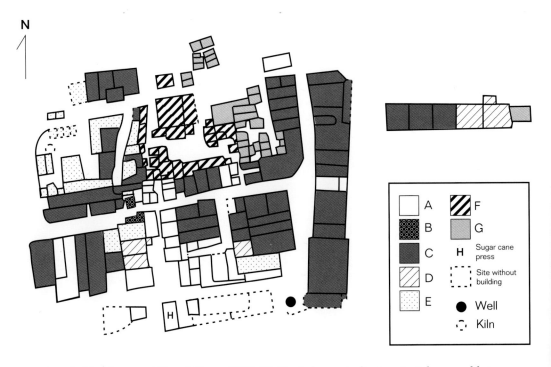

FIG. 2. Sketch map of Shanti Nagar, 1958–59. Shaded areas indicate privately owned lots
with a building that covers all or part of the site. A broken line represents a site claimed
as private property but without a building. It may be enclosed by a wall or unenclosed.
Unshaded areas are lanes available to everyone and courtyards used principally by members
of families whose houses surround them. The different shaded areas denote the location of
caste blocs as follows: A, Brahman Priest; B, Baniya Merchant; C, Bairagi Mendicant Priest
and Jat Farmer; D, Jhinvar Watercarrier, Lohar Blacksmith, and Mali Gardener; E, Gola
Potter, Mahar Potter, and Nai Barber; F, Chamar Leatherworker; and G, Chuhra Sweeper.
A caste bloc is a caste or group of castes that occupies a particular rank in the caste
hierarchy (S. Freed and R. Freed, 1976: 100–101). The Chhipi Dyer was a tenant and
owned no house site. Therefore, that family is not represented on the map.

FIG. 3. Sketch map of Shanti Nagar, 1977–78. The code is the same as in figure 2. A family of Khati Carpenters, which arrived in Shanti Nagar after our departure in 1959, owned no house site. Like the Chhipi Dyer family, it is not represented on the map.

are of greater interest to some castes than to others. For example, Sakat is celebrated chiefly by Brahman women, but not all of them observe the day. In some festivals, members of one caste fulfill a ceremonial role for people of other castes. For example, Brahman women traditionally tell the story of Hoi for women of other castes.

In the interval between our two periods of research in Shanti Nagar in the 1950s and 1970s, a number of social and economic trends had become more firmly established or newly introduced: the educational level rose dramatically; health services improved; there was a substantial increase in salaried urban occupations; a few women worked for salaries outside the home; the technological level of agriculture was considerably improved by the introduction of tractors and tubewells; the villagers were deeply involved in markets outside Shanti Nagar, owing to the construction of an immense vegetable market just north of Delhi within easy reach of the farmers of Shanti Nagar; electricity was introduced; radios were commonplace; there were a few television sets and automobiles; and newspapers were delivered daily. The village had a somewhat different appearance: it had been expanded to accommodate the increased population, and houses made of dried chunks of mud, common in 1958, had almost entirely been replaced by structures of brick. The village was more modern, better informed, and more prosperous in 1977–78 than in 1958–59. Despite such changes, many cultural values, chiefly in the domain of family life, kinship, ideology, and proper conduct (dharma), persisted relatively unchanged.

RETURN TO SHANTI NAGAR

"All happy families are alike but an unhappy family is unhappy after its own fashion" (Tolstoy, 1978: 13). With appropriate adjustments, Tolstoy's famous observation applies to ethnographic fieldwork. The constant element in "happy" fieldwork is the early and full cooperation of the host society. Full cooperation and, of course, a good deal of luck will result in a successful study no matter how troublesome are the problems of research and the trials of day-to-day living. Cooperation means much more than just the absence of hostility or the tolerance of the outsider. It means that almost everyone will be available for an interview, that people will call you for ceremonies, that little effort will be made to conceal information, and that at least some people will sense what might interest you and will volunteer information without being asked.

We enjoyed the cooperation, hospitality, and eventually the friendship of the people of Shanti Nagar from the day that we arrived in the village in 1958. Our good fortune was no accident. Government of India officials contacted the leading men in several villages to find one that would accept us. The men of Shanti Nagar were willing to take us in, a commitment, we later realized, that involved certain responsibilities on their part. We noticed that the villagers acted is if it were a matter of village honor that we be properly treated. We were protected from exploitation and overcharging, and nothing of value was ever stolen from us. When we attended ceremonies, especially those out of the village, the people of Shanti Nagar made sure that we were well treated and tried to prevent us from doing anything gauche. We found at times that some people quietly and intelligently worked behind our backs to assist us.

That our entry into Shanti Nagar was under the auspices of the government and at the invitation of the leading men of the village greatly eased our way. We did not have to go through a difficult period of penetrating a wall of indifference, suspicion, and hostility. The villagers selected us before they had even seen us. When we arrived on the first day, villagers swarmed to greet us and offered us warm milk, the token of village hospitality. But even under favorable circumstances, village life is no bed of roses, and research adds special problems to those of daily living. We have previously described in great detail our adjustment to Shanti Nagar and the conduct of our fieldwork in 1958–59 (S. Freed and R. Freed, 1976: 17–28). We shall not repeat that account, even though almost all of it is pertinent to our work in the 1970s. Rather, we shall describe the second research period in 1977–78, emphasizing how it differed from the 1950s.

We returned to Shanti Nagar in 1977, twenty years after the beginning of our first sojourn in India. We expected the second trip to be less difficult than the first one, and in some ways it was. We were better financed the second time, which was a great blessing. Our affiliation with the University of Delhi had been arranged before our arrival. The worry of finding a village for fieldwork was no factor, for we could return to Shanti Nagar and live in the same quarters as in the 1950s. Friends in Delhi found translators and assistants for us. We had a cook who saved us no end of time and energy. At maximum strength, our staff consisted of four translator-assistants (one woman and three men), a cook, sweeper (outside and latrine), cleaning woman (inside), and watercarrier.

In the 1950s, we could do almost all the interviewing ourselves. The village was of a convenient size for a husband-wife team, and we were not pressed for time. We lived in Shanti Nagar for 13 months. We then moved to Delhi to interview people from Shanti Nagar who had moved there and to read systematically over our fieldnotes—looking for gaps, weaknesses, and ambiguities. However, we continued to maintain our village residence and made frequent trips there chiefly to attend ceremonies and to gather information on subjects that were not clear in our notes. While we were living in Delhi, one of our young research assistants, Satish Saberwal, who went on to a long distinguished career of research and university teaching, remained in Shanti Nagar to finish some surveys.

The village population was 66% larger in the 1970s than in the 1950s, and our time was shorter, 30 weeks as compared to 17 months in the 1950s. Thus, in the 1970s, we had to make greater use of assistants working independently. We did this with confidence, because we could daily check their data against information that we ourselves were collecting. Moreover, we could compare their interviews with our data from the 1950s. For example, the census of a family from the 1970s could be compared to the census of the same family from the 1950s. Mistakes and dubious information were quickly spotted and corrected.

TABLE 1.

SHANTI NAGAR POPULATION BY CASTE IN 1958–59 AND 1977–78

CASTE	1958–1959	1977–1978
Bairagi Mendicant	27	48
Baniya Merchant	6	13
Brahman Priest	187	319
Chamar Leatherworker	98	188
Chhipi Dyer	5	7
Chuhra Sweeper	96	140
Gola Potter	58	125
Jat Farmer	260	385
Jhinvar Watercarrier	13	21
Khati Carpenter	0	3
Lohar Blacksmith	11	23
Mahar Potter	3	1
Mali Gardener	10	7
Nai Barber	25	44
Total	799	1324

The first day back in the village was exhausting. Many people came to see us from the moment we arrived, and we had to unpack and organize while trying to greet and talk to old friends. Within the first hour or so, two conversations impressed us, for they never would have happened early in our first field trip. Out of a clear blue sky, one visitor enumerated the murders that had taken place in the village since we departed in 1959. Another visitor, without being asked, recounted the history of his family since last we saw him.

These conversations illustrate something about fieldwork that is important. In the course of fieldwork, not only does the investigator learn how to study his hosts, but they in turn learn how to be studied. This reciprocity is the fundamental aspect of "rapport," about which so much has been written. Rapport is not just acceptance or even friendship. It is cooperation in a joint enterprise. We reached a high watermark in this regard late in our first field trip when one of our best informants, a well-educated village man, remarked at the end of an excellent interview, "I never realized that you wanted to go into things so deeply." Wax makes the point somewhat differently:

> The great feat in most field expeditions, as in life, is to find the areas in which a mutual or reciprocal trust may be developed. That these areas will be new or odd to both hosts and fieldworker is very likely. But it is in these areas of mutual trust and, sometimes, affection, that the finest fieldwork can be done . . . [Wax, 1971: 372–373].

Toward evening of the first day, we managed to take a walk in the fields to have a little rest from all the commotion. We were visibly tired, and at the invitation of a farmer, we sat down beside his tubewell. We were talking of nothing in particular, when unexpectedly he said, "When you were here last, there were many trees in the fields. Now they have all been cut down." Later we realized that many other villagers recalled events and conditions during our first trip. We were surprised at how well they remembered us and the village of twenty years earlier. They picked up the thread of our joint lives almost as if there had been no intermission.

In the course of this conversation, the tubewell owner made a comment that revealed another aspect of our relationship with the villagers. They never stopped evaluating us. We were bemoaning our failure to pay more attention to some feature of village life, perhaps ecology in accord with the decline in the number of trees, and the farmer said, "You did the best you could under the circumstances." Fieldworkers have a tendency to dwell on their oversights, the more so since they may be thousands of miles from their hosts when the gap in their information is discovered, and corrective measures may be difficult. The farmer's comment advised us to use a little common sense.

Another bit of sage advice came from a sophisticated village man early in our first field trip. Observing our ineffectual efforts to do something or other, he said, "Don't try to be perfect villagers after just two weeks." One point of not trying to be perfect villagers is that the villagers were interested in typical Americans and not in Americans trying to be Indians. They wanted to see, and hear, something different and exotic, not an imitation of themselves. One of the jackets that we sometimes wore during the cold weather was warm but shabby. The villagers did not like it and made remarks. They wanted "their" Americans to be prestigious, which meant, among other matters, dressing properly. They were pleased when a high official in the Delhi government visited us one day to see how we were managing. It was conceivable that the village could derive some benefit from our presence.

Of course, we adjusted to village life in many ways, especially in trying to avoid giving offense; for example, our diet was strictly vegetarian. In matters of diet, cleanliness, and respectful behavior, villagers did expect us to meet village standards, always cutting us some slack for our errors due to ignorance, for our need for more comfort and privacy than are common in village life, and for the demands of our research. They allowed us liberties that they themselves would hesitate to take. The men of our team routinely attended women's ceremonies and were welcome. In case of need, the women could be present during meetings that were strictly the province of village men. Although we were somewhat vaguely "high caste," we enjoyed free relations with people of the lower castes. In fact, in 1958 a high-caste village man cleverly arranged an event that made us "people of the whole village" (S. Freed and R. Freed, 1976: 20–21).

Adults did not find us quite the curiosity in the 1970s that they did in the 1950s. People still came regularly to see us, often more visitors than we could manage, but they were no longer interested in watching us eat, for example. Modern communications had made the world smaller, people were better educated and more sophisticated, and many Westerners passed through Delhi. Moreover, the features of Western life that were of greatest interest to villagers, certainly to young men, had changed markedly. In the 1950s, the principal topics of conversation when villagers asked about the United States were the treatment of cows, which are sacred to Hindus, the eating of beef, and the care of old people. In the 1970s, people rarely mentioned those topics. Instead they wanted to talk about marriage and courtship, in other words, illicit premarital sexual activity, smoking, and drinking. Young men mentioned the Westerners whom they had seen in Connaught Place (Delhi). Hippies, both American and European, infested the place and in all probability created an unfortunate impression. Young village men told us that 50% of American women drink and smoke. A conservative couple such as the authors would not generate the same interest for young men as did the young Westerners in Delhi.

As in the first trip, children were a significant nuisance, often following us about, mobbing us, and sometimes making enough commotion so that interviews were impossible and householders were annoyed. There was a slight but noticeable decline of manners among children and adolescents. It was a general feature of Indian life, even rural life, but it also affected us from time to time. There were several teenagers in the village who were nothing but trouble. After one brief unpleasant episode, we wrote in our notes, "There simply is no question that children and teenagers cannot be controlled nearly so much as formerly. Adults other than family members can do relatively little, and authority even in the family is weaker than formerly." This scenario was to be played out at Holi when unruly teenaged boys prematurely lit the Holi bonfire, an event described later.

Some developments were most welcome. The extension of a paved road between Delhi and the village made transportation much easier. The village had electricity in the 1970s, which was lacking in the 1950s. We no longer had to deal with kerosene lanterns, had a refrigerator, and could use our electric typewriter. Our bedroom had ceiling fans. Heat can be almost unbearable in North India, and ceiling fans offer some relief. They also keep mosquitoes away. Although we had metal nets installed in our windows, mosquitoes could still enter, including the dangerous Anopheles mosquito, the female of which carries malaria. After an effective governmental campaign using powerful insecticides had almost eliminated malaria in the Delhi region in the early 1960s, it had come roaring back by 1965. Anopheles mosquitoes had developed resistance to insecticides. Increased irrigation from tubewells and canals resulted in more standing water in the fields as potential breeding sites for mosquitoes. From 1974 to 1978, malaria was present in epidemic proportions.

We thought that we suffered less illness during the second trip. Only after we returned to New York and had a chance to read through our notes did we realize the toll that illness had taken, not only on us but also on our assistants. A serious bout of hepatitis and intestinal maladies troubled us during the first trip, but during the second trip, we were able to avoid hepatitis, and intestinal troubles were considerably reduced. Instead, respiratory illness was the major problem. The villagers themselves expected colds and fever in the winter. In the densely populated village and crowded Delhi, there was no escaping them. Our assistants were not spared. All of them were repeatedly sick and sometimes out of action for up to a week. In addition, one assistant was bitten by a dog and missed several days. By mid-January, we noted that health had become a serious problem, not that any of the illnesses (aside from an episode of severe food poisoning) was particularly dangerous but that the work routine was upset. In fact, it became rare to have all our assistants available in the village at one time.

Most people of the older generation of the 1950s had died by 1977. The day after our arrival, we were walking along the main lane when an elderly woman asked us into her house to greet a once important elderly man whom we had known in the 1950s. He was dying, but he stirred himself to smile and welcome us. Later the same day, we chanced on another elderly man resting on a cot. Although feeble, he sat up to greet us. Some of our best informants were among the missing, especially our landlord's late mother. We saw her every day during our first visit. She was always great company and full of reliable information about the village. Another of our best informants, a man who visited almost daily, was also no longer available, although still alive. He lived on a farm at some distance from Shanti Nagar. We were sure that he would return home for a visit to see us, but he never did. Most likely, a family tragedy kept him away from Shanti Nagar. We greatly missed all these people.

The change of generations takes place gradually, and a permanent resident adjusts to the normal slow attrition. We were absent for 20 years and then suddenly were back in a familiar village that lacked many familiar faces. We should have expected it and braced ourselves emotionally, but we were caught off guard and experienced a bit of a shock. It took us a while to shake off the feeling.

ACKNOWLEDGMENTS

We thank the Social Science Research Council and the National Science Foundation for supporting our fieldwork in 1957–59; and the American Institute for Indian Studies and the Indo-U.S. Sub-Commission for Education and Culture, the Indo-American Fellowship Program for fellowships that supported our work in 1977–78.

During our fieldwork in Shanti Nagar in 1958–59 and 1977–78, we were aided by many individuals and organizations. Their indispensable assistance and hospitality are acknowledged with thanks in S. Freed and R. Freed (1976: 28–29) for the work in the 1950s and in S. Freed and R. Freed (1982: 200–201; 1985: 232) for the 1970s.

Specifically for this monograph on festivals, we thank the current and former staff of the American Museum of Natural History: Geraldine Santoro and Vera Perrone for their invaluable library research; Laila Williamson for her assistance with research, proofreading, and checking details; Petica Barry, Paul Goldstein, Diana M. Salles, Stacey Symonds, and William Weinstein for computer assistance; Salles for drawing the figures and maps, Salles and Barry for the cover design; and Brenda Jones, Manager of Scientific Publications, for handling the production. The book was designed by Lynne Arany, Ink Projects, New York, and Manjit Misra, Aegis Editorial Services, Mineola, NY, prepared the index.

We thank Wendy Doniger O'Flaherty, University of Chicago, for answering our questions about the Mahabharata, Jeffrey P. Bonner, Indianapolis Zoological Society, for information about the solar eclipse at Kurukshetra on February 16, 1980, Neil de Grasse Tyson, Princeton University and Frederick P. Rose Director of the Hayden Planetarium at the American Museum of Natural History, for astronomical calculations and checking parts of the manuscript, and Edward O. Henry, San Diego State University, for his informative letter about musical performances in North India.

We extend our heartfelt thanks for the comments, criticisms, and suggestions of the prepublication reviewers who undertook the arduous task of reading the whole manuscript: Lawrence A. Babb, Amherst College; Doranne Jacobson, International Images, Springfield, Illinois; Sunalini Nayudu, Kasturba Gandhi National Trust; and Susan S. Wadley, Syracuse University.

Finally, we thank the people of Shanti Nagar for admitting us to their village and for treating us with unfailing kindness and hospitality. Nothing would have been possible without their acceptance and cooperation. That we were able to take their darshan[2] for two long periods is one of our most cherished memories. We have tried to protect their privacy by using a pseudonym for their village and for each individual whom we have occasion to mention.

A NOTE ON TRANSLITERATION AND NOMENCLATURE

For ease of communication with non-Indologists, proper names of persons, castes, organizations, places, festivals, and geographical features, and all words of Indian origin contained in Webster's *Third New International Dictionary of the English Language, Unabridged* have been reproduced in roman type. Other Indian words, many of which frequently appear in English publications, have been italicized and spelled in their customary romanized form without diacritics. English plurals and posses-sives have been used. Although alternative spellings are common, we have general-ly tried to maintain a consistent orthography except in the case of direct quotations, where the original spelling is retained.

We have used binomial names for castes. The first word is the usual Hindi des-ignation for the caste; the second is an English word that denotes the traditional occupation of the caste and/or translates the Hindi term. For example, the English translation of Nai is "barber," the traditional occupation of the caste, thus the name, Nai Barber. Although Jat does not mean "farmer" in English, the Jats are tradition-ally farmers, hence, Jat Farmer. We often shorten the caste name after its first use either to the Hindi or English component. In such use, the English word is capital-ized. Words such as potter, farmer, and sweeper when not capitalized refer to occu-pations and not to castes.

1   DATING THE FESTIVALS

... Time, no matter how accurately or beautifully it may be presented on our wrist, is first and foremost humanity's reconciliation of the movements of the spheres. The sun regulates our life, and our most precise timing devices are adjusted to stay in synchronization with astronomical events [Garver, 1992: 11].

The calendar situation in India before 1957 has been described as chaotic. From 25 to more than 30 calendars were in use according to estimates of various authorities (Watkins, 1954: 227–229). In an effort to reduce the complexity, the government of India issued a reform solar calendar, the Indian National Calendar, to take effect on March 22, 1957. Also, the prime minister then in office, Jawaharlal Nehru, wanted India to take her distance from English institutions while at the same time having a "scientific" calender corresponding to the Gregorian calendar. It seems that few people pay much attention to the Indian National Calendar (Shastri, 1979: 3–5). The Gregorian calendar remains the solar calendar of India.

The Indian National Calendar has 12 months—5 months consisting of 31 days, and 7 months consisting of 30 days, a total of 365 days. An extra day is added to the first month in a leap year. The days are numbered consecutively for the entire month rather than separately for each of two fortnights, as in the lunisolar calendar. The year begins the day after the vernal equinox. The months bear the traditional Sanskrit names that are used in the lunisolar calendar. The date of the current year is reckoned from the beginning of the Shaka era in 78 C.E. (The two most popular Indian eras are the Vikrama and the Shaka, each dating from obscure historical events.) To find the corresponding date of the Common Era for a Shaka date, one adds 78 (or 79 after December 31) to the Shaka date. Thus, 1 Chaitra 1879 Shaka era is March 22, 1957. The Gregorian calendar is the other solar calendar used in India. A few festivals are dated by these solar calendars, for example, Baisakhi, Republic Day, and Christmas, which is a religious festival for the Christian community and otherwise a civil holiday.

The dates of most festivals, however, are set by the ancient lunisolar systems. Units of time in the lunisolar systems correspond neither to those of the Gregorian system nor to those of the Indian National Calendar. Moreover, the correlations of lunar and solar days, months, and years in the lunisolar systems are complex and can lead to what seem to be anomalies, as when a rite is celebrated a day in advance of what appears to be its proper date. The basic concepts of the lunisolar calendric system used in Shanti Nagar (and generally in India) that are necessary for understanding the dating of festivals are presented below. The presentation is a summary of the extensive explanation given in R. Freed and S. Freed (1964), which in turn is based chiefly on Sewell and Dikshit (1896) and secondarily on Underhill (1991).

Lunar Elements

The two fundamental lunar elements of the lunisolar calendar are the lunar day and the lunar month. They are based on the revolutions of the moon around the earth and the earth around the sun. Important astronomical events are the full and new moons, which divide the lunar month into fortnights, and an increase of an average of 12° in the angular separation of the moon and sun along the ecliptic, which determines the beginning of a new lunar day.

The Lunar Day

Viewed from the earth, both the sun and the moon move from west to east relative to the background stars. The sun moves eastward about 1° per day, while the moon moves about 13°. The lunar day (*tithi*) is the time required for the angular separation of moon and sun to increase by 12°. Since the moon passes through 360° during a synodic revolution, a lunar day is 1/30 of a lunar month. Because of the elliptical orbits of the earth and moon, the plane of the moon's orbit at an angle to the plane of the ecliptic, and other factors, the lunar day varies in length from a minimum of approximately 21.5 hours to a maximum of approximately 26 hours, with a mean of 23 hours and 37 minutes.

The Lunar Month

The lunar month (*chandra masa*) is the time required for the moon to complete one series of its successive phases. This is known as the synodic period of the moon and requires roughly 29.5 solar days. Twelve lunar months compose one lunar year of 360 lunar days, approximately equal to 354 solar days. In northern India, the moment of the full moon ends the lunar month. Thus, the first fortnight of a month, which lasts approximately 15 days until the moment of the new moon, is known as the dark fortnight because the moon is waning. The time following sunset is dark until moonrise, which occurs after sunset. During the second fortnight the moon is waxing, and time following sunset is illuminated because the moon is above the horizon. In Shanti Nagar the first (waning) fortnight is called *badi*, a popular form of *vadya* (black) or may be called *krishna* (dark). The second (waxing) fortnight of the month is called *sudi*, a popular form of *shukla* (bright).

Lunar months have names that are taken from 12 of the 27 lunar mansions (Nakshatras). As the moon revolves through the heavens, it passes near 27 stars or groups of stars that were recognized and named in ancient times. Table 2 presents the names of the months and the associated Nakshatras.

TABLE 2.

LUNAR MONTHS AND ASSOCIATED NAKSHATRAS

LUNAR MONTH	ASSOCIATED NAKSHATRAS AND THEIR SERIAL ORDER
Chaitra	14 *Chitra*, 15 Svati
Baisakh	16 *Visakha*, 17 Anuradha
Jyesth	18 *Jyeshtha*, 19 Mula
Asharh	20 *Purva Ashadha*, 21 Uttara Ashadha
Shrawan	22 *Sravana*, 23 Dhanishtha
Bhadrapad	24 Satataraka, 25 *Purvabhadrapada* 26 Uttarabhadrapada
Ashvin	27 Revati, 1 *Asvini*, 2 Bharani
Karttik	3 *Krittika*, 4 Rohini
Margashirsh	5 *Mrigasiras*, 6 Ardra
Paush	7 Punarvasu, 8 *Pushya*
Magh	9 Aslesha, 10 *Magha*
Phalgun	11 *Purva Phalguni*, 12 Uttara Phalguni 13 Hasta

Sources: Sewell and Dikshit, 1896: 25; Underhill, 1991: 18.
The Nakshatra that gives its name to a lunar month is italicized. There is a short interposed interval, known as Abhijit, between the 21st and 22nd Nakshatras, that is necessary for astronomical reasons (Sewell and Dikshit, 1896: 21; Underhill, 1991: 17).

In northern India the new lunar year begins with the first day of the bright fortnight of the month of Chaitra, that is, in the middle of the month rather than at the beginning. This anomaly comes about because different calendric systems are used in northern and southern India. In northern India under the *purinmanta* system, the month ends with the full moon. In southern India under the *amanta* system, it ends with the new moon. The *amanta* system alone is recognized with regard to naming months. The names of the *purinmanta* months are derived from the *amanta* system by the following rule: the bright (first) fortnight of the given *amanta* month becomes the second fortnight of the same *purinmanta* month; and the dark (second) fortnight of the given *amanta* month becomes the first fortnight of the succeeding *purinmanta* month. In the *amanta* system the new month begins a fortnight later than it does in the *purinmanta* system. Under both systems the year begins with the bright fortnight of Chaitra, that is, just after the same astronomical event, the new moon. But because this event occurs at mid-month in the north and at the beginning of the month in the south, there appears to be a difference of a fortnight, when in fact the event takes place on the same day in both regions.

Except the last day of each fortnight, lunar days have numerical names that are ordinal numbers. A specific lunar day is designated by its ordinal number in either the *badi* or *sudi* fortnight reckoned from the full or new moon respectively. The fifteenth or last day of the dark (*badi*) fortnight is called Amavas (new moon), and the last day of the bright fortnight is called Purinmashi (full moon). Dates are given by the month, fortnight, and day. For example, the second day of the dark fortnight of the month of Chaitra is called Chaitra *badi duj* (Chaitra dark second). The eleventh day of the bright fortnight of Karttik is called Karttik *sudi gyas*. Chaitra Amavas and Chaitra Purinmashi mean respectively the new and full moon days of Chaitra. The date on which a festival is observed is often part of its name. For example, Karva Chauth (Pitcher Fourth), Guga Naumi (Guga's Ninth), and Sili Sat (Cold Seventh).

SOLAR ELEMENTS

The solar elements of the lunisolar calendar are the day, month, and year. The day, from sunrise to sunrise, is based on the rotation of the earth. Although there are traditional units of time associated with the solar day, as described below, the international system of hours and minutes is used everywhere in India. The solar month is 1/12th of a solar year. Sewell and Dikshit (1896: 7) indicate that the Indian solar year has been sidereal for at least 2000 years. The sidereal year is slightly longer than the tropical year owing to the precession of the equinoxes, which means that without periodic adjustments, calendar months would advance slowly through the seasons. An important astronomical event is the passage of the sun from one sign of the zodiac to the next. This moment is known as a Sankranti.

The Solar Day

The solar day (*divasa*), which is the civil day in India, begins at sunrise and ends at the following sunrise. Unlike the lunar day, which is further subdivided only into half-days (*karana*), the solar day is subdivided into a series of units that increase in multiples of 60 from the *prativipala* (which is not used) to the *vipala* (0.4 seconds), the *pala* (24 seconds), the *ghatika* (24 minutes), and to the day (24 hours). The solar day is also divided into eight watches (*prahara* or *pahar*) of about three hours each (Underhill, 1991: 25; Forbes, 1861: 331, 360).

Solar days take their names from lunar days by the following rule: the lunar day that is current or begins at sunrise of a solar day gives its name to that solar day. Thus, if lunar day Chaitra *badi* 2 is current at sunrise on a Tuesday, then the solar day from sunrise Tuesday to sunrise Wednesday will be called Chaitra *badi* 2. The solar day is not named according to its position among the days of the solar month.

TABLE 3.

WEEKDAYS

HINDI NAME	ENGLISH NAME	HEAVENLY BODY
Itvar	Sunday	Sun
Somvar	Monday	Moon
Mangalvar	Tuesday	Mars
Budhvar	Wednesday	Mercury
Brihaspat or Guruvar	Thursday	Jupiter
Shukravar	Friday	Venus
Shanivar	Saturday	Saturn

Solar days also bear the names of weekdays. The Western solar calendric system, with the seven-day week, has been known in India since about 320 C.E. Although the Western calendar never superseded the Hindu lunisolar system for dating festivals (Jones, 1792: 257–259), the week became a feature of the Indian calendar. The days of the western week are named after seven heavenly bodies that "wander" against the background stars—the sun, moon, and the five planets visible to the naked eye (Mercury, Venus, Mars, Jupiter, and Saturn). The weekdays in northern India use the Hindi equivalents of the Western names. Table 3 gives the names of the Hindi and Western weekdays and the associated heavenly bodies. Certain weekdays are considered inauspicious, although opinion seems to vary as to which (Williams, 1883: 345; Underhill, 1991: 25).

The seven heavenly bodies that serve as names of the Indian weekdays are members of a set of nine *graha*s, or "planets." They are considered to be deities, both benign and evil. The two *graha*s not used as names of weekdays are Rahu and Ketu, the ascending and descending nodes of the moon, that is, the two points at which the orbit of the moon crosses the plane of the ecliptic. In Hindu mythology they are demons that pursue the sun and the moon and cause eclipses (Williams, 1883: 344; Underhill, 1991: 28–29; Majumdar, 1958: 241–242). All eclipses are inauspicious. People cease work and give alms, and a marriage should never occur at the time of an eclipse.

The nine *graha*s are represented at festivals by drawings, generally nine squares or dots in a three-by-three pattern or by a swastika. The swastika is an ancient symbol in Hinduism.[3] It is often drawn as an auspicious sign by housewives to replace another symbol that had been drawn on a house wall during a festival. The replacement is to prevent a ghost or any evil spirit from occupying the empty space. It is also drawn by Brahman priests to represent the nine *graha*s for ceremonies marking a beginning, such as birth and marriage (R. Freed and S. Freed, 1980: 336–337; S. Freed and R. Freed, 1980b: 87, 95–101).

Representations of the *graha*s may form part of the design drawn on the ground to serve as an altar on which a fire ceremony is conducted to forestall the evil effects of the Mula Nakshatra. Some Nakshatras are auspicious, some, inauspicious. Rural north Indians believe that the Mula Nakshatra has the most evil influence. We attended one such ceremony held for a male infant and photographed the altar (fig. 4). The *graha*s were represented both by a swastika and by nine small squares in a three-by-three pattern. The double appeal to the *graha*s was appropriate in this case, for it is believed that a male child born under the Mula Nakshatra either dies or, if he lives, could bring ruin to his family (see also S. Freed and R. Freed, 1980a: 73–75; 1980b: 98–101).

The Solar Month

A solar month is the time required for the sun to pass completely through one sign of the zodiac. The Indian zodiac is divided into 12 parts of 30°. The moment the sun leaves one zodiacal sign and enters another is called a Sankranti. A Sankranti is named after the sign of the zodiac whose beginning it marks. The solar year begins with the Mesha Sankranti, the vernal equinox, which is the moment of the sun's

TABLE 4.

LUNAR AND ZODIAC-SIGN NAMES FOR SOLAR MONTHS

LUNAR NAME	ZODIAC-SIGN NAME [a]
Chaitra (March–April)	Mesha (Aries)
Baisakh (April–May)	Vrishabha (Taurus)
Jyesth (May–June)	Mithuna (Gemini)
Asharh (June–July)	Karka (Cancer)
Shrawan (July–August)	Simha (Leo)
Bhadrapad (August–September)	Kanya (Virgo)
Ashvin (September–October)	Tula (Libra)
Karttik (October–November)	Vrishchika (Scorpio)
Margashirsh (November-December)	Dhanus (Sagittarius)
Paush (December–January)	Makara (Capricorn)
Magh (January–February)	Kumbha (Aquarius)
Phalgun (February–March)	Mina (Pisces)

[a] The Sankrantis also take their names from these zodiac-sign names.

passing the first point of the constellation of Aries. Because the Indian system does not take into account the precession of the equinoxes, there has been a gradual loss of correspondence between the Sankrantis and the equinoctial points. The true vernal equinox is now in Pisces.

The months have two sets of names. Common practice in India is to use the names of lunar months for the solar months as well. These names are based on the Nakshatras. The zodiac signs are also used as the names of solar months, but in Shanti Nagar they are used only by astrologers to cast horoscopes at birth and to fix auspicious times for weddings. Table 4 lists both the names for lunar and solar months based on the Nakshatras and the zodiac-sign names for the solar months.

Like the days of the week, the zodiac was borrowed from European astronomy and astrology, which were known in India from the early centuries of the Common Era. A combination of the occult and science, astrology was born in Mesopotamia and reached its full development in Greece. It diffused to all the civilizations of the ancient world, eventually spreading from Europe to China. It had great influence everywhere. In India, this knowledge was, and is, used chiefly for prognostication. Character analysis, a prominent feature of Western astrology, plays little part in Hindu predictive astrology. In earlier times, Indians foretold the future from dreams, omens, physiognomy, birthmarks, and other such signs. These older beliefs were retained, but astrology became preeminent and today almost all Hindus believe in it. Indian astrology allows an individual to avoid dangers arising from his or her nativity by selecting astrologically favorable times for important activities, for example, a wedding. Indians also believe that fate can be altered by ritual activity, for the celestial bodies are conceived of as deities amenable to supplication (Basham, 1954: 490; Braha, 1986: 2; Encyclopedia Britannica, 1992: 25, 82).

Foreigners who consider astrology to be only a pastime or a superstition put themselves at a disadvantage in trying to understand India. After working in the village for about 10 months, we were reprimanded by a Brahman, one of our good informants. He said, "You are always asking about things but you never ask about astrology. India moves by astrology. In America you have science; in India we have astrology." He took out an almanac that he praised highly. He said that it was a year old and had correctly predicted everything during the past year. He read 20 or 30 predictions about India, the United States, England, and Russia, but only two or three had the vaguest resemblance to what had happened during the past year. He then asked us about the correctness of the predictions. We politely said that they were about 80% correct. He said with great assurance that the discrepancy was because our information from the United States was not complete.

CORRELATING THE LUNAR AND SOLAR ELEMENTS

The celestial motions involved in the lunar and solar elements of the lunisolar calendar are largely independent of one another. The solar day is based on the rotation of the earth. The lunar day is defined in terms of the revolutions of the moon around the earth and the earth around the sun. The solar month, which refers to the path of the sun around the ecliptic, depends on the earth's revolution. The lunar month is defined by the moon's revolution with the eastward movement of the sun taken into

FIG. 4. Altar to be used in a fire ceremony (*havan*) to forestall the harmful influences of the Mula Nakshatra.

account. The time durations required for the various celestial motions do not correspond exactly. The lunar month is shorter than the solar month, and the lunar day
varies in duration; it may be longer or shorter than the solar day. The combination
of these disparate elements into a single integrated system requires precisely defined
rules. They are outlined below.

Lunar and Solar Days

Since a lunar year of 360 lunar days is equal to about 354 solar days, six lunar
days must be deleted so that the correspondence of one lunar day to one solar day
can be maintained. It is useful to keep in mind that one deletes the names for days
and not astronomical time. Most lunar days begin on one solar (civil) day and end on
the following day. However, lunar days vary in length so that occasionally a lunar
day may begin and end on the same solar day. Other times, a lunar day may touch
three solar days, beginning on the first, encompassing all of the second, and ending
on the third.

A lunar day beginning and ending on the same solar day is expunged. It is
known as a deleted day (*kshaya tithi*). For example, if the fourth lunar day began on
Wednesday after sunrise and ended before sunrise on Thursday, it is dropped.
Wednesday is called the third day of the fortnight and Thursday, the fifth. There is
no fourth day. If a ceremony should occur on the fourth day of the fortnight, it would
be celebrated on the third. The weekday of a deleted lunar day is considered to be
the solar day on which it begins and ends although it does not give its name to that
day.

A lunar day on which the sun rises twice is repeated. For example, if the third
lunar day began just before sunrise on Wednesday and ended just after sunrise on
Thursday, both solar days are called the third day. The lunar day current at sunrise
gives its name to the weekday, and in this case the third day was current both on
Wednesday and Thursday. The second of two days with the same name is called an
added lunar day (*adhika tithi*). When a festival falls on a lunar day that is repeated,
it may be celebrated on either day, but usually on the first day. Underhill (1991: 27–
28) states that it is not uncommon to find wealthy people observing the festival on
both days. There are commonly 13 deleted lunar days and 7 added lunar days in a
lunar year.

Lunar and Solar Months

The lunar year of 354 solar days is brought into accord with the solar year of
365 days by adding and deleting lunar months. Lunar months vary from 29.31 to
29.81 solar days. Solar months vary from 29.32 to 31.64 solar days. The mean solar
month is 0.92 solar days longer than the mean lunar month. Therefore, an occasional
lunar month will lack a Sankranti; rarely, a lunar month will contain two Sankrantis. In the former case a lunar month is added, and in the latter, a month is deleted.
A month is added every two-and-one-half to three years. Deleted months occur in
periods ranging anywhere from 19 to 122 years.

The rules for adding and dropping lunar months are more complicated in northern than in southern India because different calendrical systems are in effect: the

amanta system in the south and the *purinmanta* system in the north. Added and deleted months are first calculated in the *amanta* system and then translated into the *purinmanta* system. Under the *amanta* system, when a lunar month contains no Sankranti, it is called an added (*adhika*) month and is given the name of the following lunar month, which is known as the true (*nija*) month. A typical sequence would be Chaitra, added Baisakh, true Baisakh, and Jyesth.

Under the *purinmanta* system, the added month is reckoned according to the *amanta* system. Then, the dark fortnight of the month preceding the added month is given the name of the following true month. Then come the bright and dark fortnights of the added month, and finally the bright fortnight of the true month. The added month comes between the fortnights of the true month. A typical sequence would be Chaitra, true Baisakh (*badi* fortnight), added Baisakh (*sudi* and *badi* fortnights), true Baisakh (*sudi* fortnight), and Jyesth. Popularly, the first two fortnights of Baisakh may be called first Baisakh, and the last two, second Baisakh. This usage was customary in Shanti Nagar, although the second month was called *laund* (added).

When a lunar month is deleted, the procedure is similar to the method for adding a month, that is, the name of the month is determined under the *amanta* system. A lunar month has to be suppressed when two Sankrantis occur in the same month. In such a case, the lunar month corresponding to the second Sankranti is dropped. For example, suppose that the Sankrantis of Dhanus and Makar occur in the same *amanta* month. Then Paush, the month associated with the second Sankranti, Makar, is dropped. The *amanta* sequence is Karttik, Margashirsh, Paush deleted, and Magh. In the *purinmanta* system, the name of the month to be deleted is taken from the *amanta* system. Then the remaining months are named according to the *purinmanta* rule that the second (dark) fortnight of the *amanta* month becomes the first fortnight of the following *purinmanta* month (Sewell and Dikshit, 1896: 25–26, 30–31; R. Freed and S. Freed, 1964: 77–80).

Underhill (1991: 20) presented evidence indicating that festivals are not celebrated in added months because they are considered to be unpropitious. We did not interview people on this point, but we have some evidence suggesting that the belief that added months are inauspicious, if held at all in Shanti Nagar, is not strong enough to bar the celebration of festivals at such times. When we were in Shanti Nagar in 1958, an added month of Shrawan occurred. A festival called Tijo (Third) is celebrated on Shrawan *sudi* 3. Although people could have waited to observe the festival during true Shrawan, they celebrated it during added Shrawan, that is, the first of the two possible dates. On the other hand, the festival of Raksha Bandhan (Charm Tying) was held on Purinmashi in true Shrawan, the second possible date. Since both Tijo and Raksha Bandhan take place in the bright fortnight, the villagers were aware that one of the fortnights was added. Yet they were not deterred from celebrating a festival during a period that Indians allegedly presume to be inauspicious.

2 CLASSIFICATION OF THE FESTIVALS

FESTIVALS CAN BE CLASSIFIED and described from several points of view, the choice depending on the feature or features of ceremonial life to be selected for emphasis. A chronological exposition is unambiguous in the sense that problems of classification are avoided. Another advantage is that it highlights the ceremonial rhythm of the year. However, important themes that are prominent in several chronologically disparate ceremonies may not receive appropriate emphasis. For example, Hoi and Sili Sat are separated by months and yet are united by the worship of mother goddesses and their underlying theme of the welfare of children. Almost everyone who writes about festivals provides a chronology, but analysis requires an additional classification according to some principle or theory.

One way to analyze village festivals derives from the ideas of Srinivas, Redfield, and Singer in the early 1950s. Although Srinivas on the one hand and Redfield and Singer on the other began from different bases, their work effectively merged into a single point of view. Srinivas contrasted Sanskritic Hinduism and village-based nonsanskritic Hinduism. The dichotomy reflects the hierarchical caste system. Sanskritic Hinduism is the domain of the higher castes, especially the Brahmans. Nonsanskritic Hinduism is found among the lower castes. Low castes try to raise their status by emulating the festivals and rites of high castes, a process known as Sanskritization, which tends to erode local traditions in favor of literate Sanskritic Hinduism. Srinivas's focus was more on caste differences and mobility than on the movement of religious belief and concept between Sanskritic and nonsanskritic Hinduism (Srinivas, 1952: chapt. 7).

Redfield and Singer's point of departure was the folk-urban continuum (Redfield and Singer, 1954), a bipolar model given its definitive anthropological treatment more than a decade earlier by Redfield (1941). In this view, an urban class of literati develops a literate tradition that diffuses to rural areas. This literate, or great, tradition serves as the standard or core culture that unites the members of an indigenous civilization. The dichotomy of Redfield and Singer was urban versus rural or great versus little tradition, as opposed to Srinivas's high-low caste distinction that he correlated with Sanskritic versus nonsanskritic traditions. Although the concepts of Srinivas and of Redfield and Singer are by no means identical, they have generally fused into a single theory in Indian anthropology, which effectively recognizes higher and lower strata of Hinduism and is in accord with the sharp indigenous distinction of *shastrik* (scriptural) and *laukik* (popular) belief and practice (Fuller, 1992: 24–28).

Marriott (1955) used this point of view in an analysis of the festivals of Kishan Garhi, a village in Uttar Pradesh. His analysis of detailed data collected in the field both highlighted features of village festivals that might otherwise escape notice and at the same time improved the theory, chiefly by pointing out the circular movement of ritual and mythological elements between the two presumed strata of Hinduism. He scotched the implication that the prestige of the great tradition confers the power to displace the little tradition at the village level.

Marriott's approach used the concepts of an indigenous (primary) civilization, the great (literate) tradition, and the little (folk) tradition. The great tradition of an indigenous civilization (as opposed to a heterogenous, or secondary civilization) grows out of its folk culture. The process involves the intellectual activity of a class of literati who develop a sacred literature, a sophisticated philosophy, and elaborate ritual activities, all of which derive from folk practices and, in turn, are available in Sanskritized form to the folk for local use. A primary civilization absorbs foreign material by syncretism. Muslim saints and ghosts, for example, are absorbed into village Hinduism without noticeable disjunction (R. Freed and S. Freed, 1993: 56, 94). In the case of strong philosophical impulses, such as the monotheism of Christianity, accommodation can come about through the creation of sects, the Arya Samaj and the Brahma Samaj, for example. Such sects are important and can produce significant changes in village religious belief and practice. However, analysis in terms of an indigenous civilization hews closely to a two-fold orthogenetic process: first, the development in a straight line from the folk tradition to the great tradition by a process of universalization, and second, a devolution or parochialization of elements from the great tradition to the little tradition.

The advantages of such an analysis are, first, a broadened appreciation of the complex connections of literate and folk traditions and, second, considerable insight into processes of cultural change and development within a single tradition. There is a circular flow of material from the little tradition to the great tradition and back again in Sanskritized form. However, the great tradition, having developed from the little tradition, does not replace it on the local scene. The traditions merge to the point where it is often difficult to tell which tradition is represented by a specific ritual element. Marriott's approach underscored the fact that a knowledge of Indian civilization and history is indispensable for understanding village life. It is perhaps less apparent but equally true that a genuine feel for Indian civilization will prove elusive without familiarity with village life.

The disadvantage of this approach is that the effort to classify festivals and rituals as belonging to one or the other tradition soon takes on such erudition and sophistication that it tends to focus on matters at some distance from the concerns of village life. In fact, it may prove a considerable intellectual challenge for field-workers whose interests are more mundane than literary. Moreover, as literary erudition increases, the number of festivals or their elements that can be assigned to the great tradition also grows (Marriott, 1955: 203, fn. 8). Thus, Marriott found only four of nineteen festivals to be without great-traditional sanction in Kishan Garhi.

The next step in an analysis of the great and little traditions is to shift from the festivals to the elements within festivals, searching for rituals, myths, folklore, or deities unconnected with the great tradition. Such an analysis involves speculation as to the Sanskritic literary origins of this or that mythological or ritual element and, as Marriott noted (1955: 206), ". . . goes beyond what is conscious or relevant to villagers today."

Reiniche warned that an analysis of the great and little traditions may give the impression of a sharp dichotomy between two structures that lack a common basis.

> . . . The distinction . . . reduced a complex ensemble to the simple juxta-position of two universes. From this point of view, the religious practices of the largest part of the Hindu population are implicitly understood as superstitions and survivals. It is thus forgotten that if the practice of the elite is still distinct from that of other social categories, that does not imply two systems of values. . . . The same values . . . govern the whole [Reiniche, 1979: viii].

Far from being simple, Marriott's analysis is complex and subtle, successfully avoiding the trap of placing too much emphasis on the distinctiveness of the two traditions rather than on their unity. The circular flow of material between the two traditions emphasizes their intimate connection. There is nothing pejorative about the "little tradition," as Marriott uses the term.

Toffin also was critical of the "excessive" opposition of the great and little traditions.

> On the contrary . . . the Hindu world is *one* and Hinduism is defined more in terms of relations between its different levels than in terms of the opposition of disjointed poles isolated from social reality . . . . Today, it is difficult to think that the anthropology of a complex society with a written tradition and a very high level of civilization like India could do without this double approach, of which one is the complement of the other [Toffin, 1982: 8].

Marriott's analysis seems to do just as Toffin suggested: the relationship of the two facets of Hinduism, local practice and ancient written tradition, is at its center. Their analytical separation enhances understanding but is not to be taken as a disjunction.

However, there are a few peripheral cavils that might be mentioned. Although Indian culture and Hinduism are adept at absorbing outside influences, nonetheless the concept of a primary civilization becomes increasingly uncomfortable in modern India with television, radio, state schools, strong representation of important non-Hindu religions (e.g., Islam, Sikhism, Christianity), and influential sects. Marriott (1955: 211) alluded to this point: "A newly standardized great tradition is thus externally available [from state schools, etc.] to the people of Kishan Garhi as a transformed, now heterogenetic criticism of the indigenous religious order of the village . . . ." One result of this development is that festivals can jump from the little tradition to the great tradition when a little traditional deity is identified with a deity of the great tradition. Although in times past this process may have been gradual, today with modern communications it can take place quickly. There is no need for a slow diffusion of a literate tradition from centers of intellectual activity into the countryside. Radio and television effectively eliminate time and distance.

Babb views modern media as a system for transmitting information in the form of religious symbols. He makes the important point that mass media attenuate social barriers: ". . . The new media have not only given religious symbols greater spatial mobility but have significantly enhanced their social mobility as well. That is, new media have increased the capacity of religious symbols to penetrate social barriers and to bypass social bottlenecks that have inhibited their propagation in the past . . . . This has probably been [their] most important effect on South Asian religion" (Babb, 1995: 3–4). In the 1950s in Shanti Nagar, mass media meant principally books, pamphlets, and lithographs. In the 1970s, films became important. Since the 1970s, the mass media have burgeoned. Films, television, cassettes, and comic books with religious themes flood the country. This development is a major subject of study and lies outside the scope of our inquiry. Babb and Wadley (1995) offered an extensive survey of the various aspects of the media revolution in India.

Despite recent developments, the classification of great and little traditions has undeniable intellectual attraction. It has a strong, necessary historical aspect, is in accord with the Indian distinction of scriptural and popular Hinduism, and helps to make sense of a bewildering assortment of ritual detail. It must always be kept in mind, if only to supplement another approach.

Wadley's classification of yearly festivals was based on the *power* of the deity involved in each festival and, secondly, on the associated dominant ritual. Wadley suggested that "power," not usually recognized as a dominant principle, is fundamental in Hindu ideology and society, much more so than is the principle of the "pure" and the "impure," which has received so much attention (Wadley, 1975: 186). The power of deities is reflected in the ritual appropriate for their worship.

Wadley identified two major rituals, namely, *vrat* and puja. The usual meaning of *vrat* is a fast or a vow to perform some meritorious act of devotion. Wadley broadened the meaning of the term to include a series of events: fasting, worship (puja), a ritual story (*katha*), and singing; it may also be reduced just to fasting and a puja. *Vrat* is performed when dealing with powerful deities. Puja, the worship of deities, is more common than *vrat* and is performed without *vrat* for deities of lesser influence than those supplicated by *vrat*. The deity is treated as an honored guest. Its image is usually bathed, dressed, and given offerings, such as flowers and food. The food offering, known as *prasad*,[4] is distributed in the community.

Puja is prevalent in village life. In addition to festival use, it is a daily rite in many houses, often taking the form of an offering to the household fire and feeding a piece of bread to a cow. All *vrats* involve a puja, but not all pujas occur with a *vrat*.

According to Wadley, there is a third category of festivals, those involving mutual exchange, which cover auspicious beings of less power than those that merit either *vrat* or puja. The "mutual exchange" category contains only three festivals and overlaps the puja category. One important festival, Dassehra, is not included in any of the categories (Wadley, 1975: chap. 8, tables 13, 14, 15, pp. 210–213, table 16).

This classification calls attention to the forms of worship, such as singing, offerings, and the telling of stories. Because *vrat* is a more elaborate series of rituals than puja, fewer festivals require it. Among them are at least two festivals of the great tradition, Krishna's Birthday and Shiva's Night, but also Pitcher Fourth, which Marriott identifies as a festival of the little tradition. Festivals with puja but not *vrat* include several great festivals, such as Holi and Diwali, but also minor observances, such as Eternal Fourteenth (Anant Chaudas). There does not seem to be a clear connection between ritual complexity and the great- or little-traditional category of a festival. As concerns the dominant theme of festivals, there is no apparent distinction between festivals characterized by *vrat* and those by puja. The theme of family welfare, for example, appears indiscriminately in the two categories (Wadley, 1975: 156, 164, tables 1 and 2).

Wadley used the term *vrat* to mean, basically, a fast. *Vrat* also means "vow." Perhaps her classification would be somewhat altered if both meanings of *vrat* were taken into account. Another mildly troublesome aspect of her classification concerns the relationship of power to particular situations. For example, Shiva and Durga are more powerful than Kanti Mata, the Goddess of Typhoid, but when one has typhoid one supplicates to Kanti Mata. Wadley (1975: 138) explicitly made this point: "A deity with only a few powers is . . . more recognized and in some senses more powerful than a higher-level deity with many powers. . . . The . . . more powerful deity is acknowledged, but men first approach . . . the deity specifically concerned with their present trouble." Crooke (1968, 1: 213) quoted a proverb that makes the same point: "Which is the greater, Râma or Gûga [a regional saint with power over snakes]?" The reply is "Be who may be the greater, shall I get myself bitten by a snake?" That is, "Though Râma may be the greater . . . I dare not say so for fear of offending Gûga."

Wadley's approach is valuable in the context of this report because it focused attention on distinctive and important ritual activity and also called attention to the question of power. Her novel analysis made clear that Hinduism has more festivals and rites than rituals and that therefore one encounters considerable similarity in ritual activity from festival to festival. Thus, the apparent lack of congruence of the two categories, *vrat* and puja, with either themes or the classification based on the great and little traditions indicates that *vrat* and puja function as general elements in religious activity and are not affected by the purpose of a festival or its degree of Sanskritization.

Hanchett took a point of view different from those of either Wadley or Marriott. Instead of using the ritual elements of *vrat* and puja as a point of departure as they are for Wadley, Hanchett focused on the family as the basic operating unit of a class of festivals, namely, the "family festivals." She was not particularly interested in the Sanskritic tradition or its relations to the folk tradition, as was Marriott. Folklore itself and symbolic activity were her keys to understanding the practices and drama that are played out in the course of a festival. The great tradition cannot be ignored, but it is more manifest in the Hindu world view, which villagers rarely express in words but which permeates their ritual activities (Hanchett, 1988: 274). Hanchett proposed the principle of "danger," instead of Wadley's "power," as dominant in the South Indian family festivals that she examined.

Choice among these three modes of analysis, each designed by an investigator with intensive experience in village India, depends more on personal interests than on any alleged advantage of a particular approach. The great-tradition little-tradition method covers all festivals in the sense that every festival can be placed in one of the categories. The *vrat*-puja approach supplemented with a small third category, mutual exchange, encompasses most but not all the festivals. Hanchett's choice of the family as the defining criterion of a category of festivals excludes festivals in which the family is not the basic operating unit while including rites of passage, for such rites are basically family concerns.

These three classifications by no means exhaust the possible analytical approaches. Sivananda (1993) used a three-fold classification: festivals, birthdays (*jayanthi*s), and *vrat*s (vows). Dube (1955: 96) proposed three major types of ceremonies and festivals: family, village, and caste ceremonies. Jacobson (1970: 386) classified the festivals as major, medium, and minor. Gnanambal (1969: 2–3) offered two classifications. One is based on the extent of the area over which a festival is observed: all-India, state, and local. The second is based on "central theme": festivals for agriculture, for propitiating malevolent goddesses, for family welfare, and for obtaining spiritual merit.

Bouillier (1982: 91–92) outlined a classification of festivals from two points of view. She classified them by what may be termed their style or basic activity into fairs, processions, and *vrat*s (vows). it is noteworthy that fairs and processions (*jatra*s) are represented as categories only in Bouillier's classification. A fair is a great assemblage around temples or places of pilgrimage. A *jatra* is a solemn procession transporting the image of a deity. Bouillier also looked at festivals from a second point of view, that of women. This perspective led to a three-fold classification of festivals: those from which women are excluded and this rejection is emphasized, those in which they participate as the wife of the master of the house, and most importantly, festivals from which men are entirely excluded or where they play only very minor roles.

Some classifications are intended to do little more than organize an inconviently large roster of festivals into smaller categories more easily managed and understood. Sivananda's classification was of this type. On the other hand, some classifications reflect a basic theory, as do those of Marriott and Wadley. The classifications of Bouillier and Hanchett were basically designed to isolate and analyze a category of festivals to reveal, in Bouillier's words (1982: 92), ". . . the principal relations around which social life crystalizes."

We have chosen to present the festivals from two chief perspectives: 1) by successive date, beginning with Chaitra *sudi* 1, the New Year, and 2) by dominant theme or concern. A chronological list is a basic point of orientation. It locates each festival in relation to the calendar, astronomical events, seasons, and the agricultural year. Important features of the festival year are evident in a chronological list. For example, the lumping of festivals at harvest time in autumn is clearly seen in a calendric list. This obviously useful approach is employed by all authors who deal with the yearly festivals. The chronological sequence is given in table 5.

TABLE 5.

ANNUAL FESTIVALS IN CHRONOLOGICAL ORDER

DATE	FESTIVAL
Chaitra (March–April)	
sudi 1	New Year's Day. Recognized but not celebrated
sudi 8	Devi ki Karahi (The Cooking Pot of the Goddess)
Baisakh (April–May)	
April 13	Baisakhi (Vernal equinox) *a*
Jyesth (May–June)	
sudi 10	Jyesth ka Dassehra (Tenth of Jyesth)
sudi 11	Nirjala Ekadashi (Waterless Eleventh)
Asharh (June–July)	
sudi 11	Dev Shayani Ekadashi (Gods' Sleeping Eleventh). This is a major eleventh but the only observance is the usual fast that takes place on bright elevenths
Shrawan (July–August)	
badi 1	Swings are hung from trees prior to celebrating Tijo
sudi 3	Tijo (Third)
Purinmashi	Raksha Bandhan (Charm Tying), also known as Salono
Bhadrapad (August–September)	
badi 8	Janamashtami (Birth Eighth), birth of Krishna, avatar of Vishnu
badi 9	Guga Naumi (Guga's Ninth)
sudi 2	Budh ki Duj (Old Man's Second)
Purinmashi	See Ashvin *badi* 1 below
Ashvin (September–October)	
badi 1	Akhta, a cattle curing festival, which began in the evening of Bhadrapad *sudi* 14 and continued for the next two days, Purinmashi and Ashvin *badi* 1. It is held from sundown on a Friday to noon of the following Sunday only when an epidemic of cattle disease occurs (see text)
badi 1–*sudi* 1	Shraddha (Ancestor Worship). Also known as Kanagat
sudi 1–*sudi* 9	Sanjhi
sudi 10	Dassehra
Karttik (October–November)	
badi 1	From the first to the end of this month, girls rise early in the morning and go singing to the well where they bathe. By the late 1970s when girls had more freedom, they went to the Yamuna River for a dip
badi 3	Karva Chauth (Pitcher Fourth)
badi 7	Hoi

TABLE 5. *(Continued)*

DATE	FESTIVAL
badi 13	Dhan Teras (Wealth Thirteenth)
badi 14	Girhi or Choti Diwali
Amavas	Diwali (Festival of Lights)
sudi 1	Gobardhan (Cowdung Wealth)
sudi 2	Bhai Duj (Brother Second)
sudi ll	Dev Uthani Gyas (Gods' Awakening Eleventh)
Purinmashi	Ganga Nahan (Bathing in the Ganges)
Margashirsh (November–December)	No annual festivals are observed
Paush (December–January)	Makara Sankranti
Magh (January–February)	
badi 4	Sakat
sudi 5	Basant Panchami (Spring Fifth)
Phalgun (February–March)	
badi 14	Shivaratri (Shiva's Night)
Amavas	Phalgun Khelna. Pre-Holi skits begin on Amavas and continue nightly until Holi
sudi 11	Amla Sinchan Gyas (Amla Watering Eleventh)
Purinmashi	Holi
Chaitra (March–April)	
badi 1	Dulhendi
badi 7	Sili Sat (Cold Seventh)

In addition to the festivals that the villagers celebrate, a few dates and/or festivals have been included for purposes of orientation or completeness. New Year's Day is an obvious landmark. Basant Panchami, Phalgun Khelna, and Shrawan *badi* 1 mark preliminary events or the start of preparations for later festivals but are not the occasion for ritual activity. Gods' Sleeping Eleventh (Dev Shayani Ekadashi) is not celebrated but is the known pendant of Gods' Awakening Eleventh (Dev Uthani Gyas).

a Baisakhi is also the first day of the Sikh year (Buttar, 1988: 3).

Our second perspective on the festivals involves classification. Our criteria for classifying festivals are three themes that dominate the festival year. These important, pervasive themes are

1) Welfare, fertility, and protection. Goddess worship is a subordinate criterion in this category. The festivals that fit this category are given in table 6 (pp. 38–39).

2) Honoring the Sanskritic deities. Table 7 (pp. 146–147) lists the festivals of this category.

3) Interaction, especially among relatives. Honoring the dead, a form of interaction with relatives, is included. Table 8 (p. 241) lists the festivals of interaction.

Each of the three themes can strongly characterize specific festivals but may play a minor role, or even be absent, in others. Despite some inevitable ambiguity, all the religious festivals can therefore be fitted into this threefold scheme, except Holi, Dulhendi, and Baisakhi.

The festivals of the first category are dominated by the theme of family welfare. These festivals involve mainly the mother goddesses, who collectively are one of the three great deities of modern Hinduism. It might be argued that Diwali and its associated festivals, Dhan Teras and Girhi, ought to be placed among the honorific festivals (category 2) with Dassehra rather than in the welfare category. Diwali is closely connected to the story of the Ramayana and hence to Dassehra. Dassehra recalls the victory of Ram over Ravan, and Diwali celebrates Ram's victorious return to his capital.

However, family welfare clearly dominates the ritual of Diwali, and Lakshmi, the Goddess of Wealth, is the most prominent deity despite the fact that several other Sanskritic deities are also worshipped. Moreover, there is a strong undercurrent of worship of non-Sanskritic goddesses. The new moon day of Karttik, the date of Diwali, is auspicious and has in all likelihood accumulated layers of diverse beliefs and practices. That the worship of Sanskritic deities has been added to an older base of sacred belief is suggested by Majumdar's (1958: 275–276) description of the Diwali ritual in his village. It is basically exorcism, much like Akhta in Shanti Nagar. Men carry burning torches of maize stalks out of the village and deposit them on waste land. Formerly, no deities were worshipped, but now Lakshmi is venerated. Marriott (1955: 195–196) listed five rituals practiced on Diwali in Kishan Garhi that have no connection to the great tradition. Two of them involve propitiating non-Sanskritic goddesses for family welfare.

The festivals of the second category honor the deities of the great tradition and recall great events from Hindu sacred literature. Shiva and Vishnu (in his various avatars) are two of the major deities prominently honored. The welfare aspect, so central to the festivals featuring the mother goddesses, plays a small role in most honorific festivals. They are primarily rites of intensification. In Shanti Nagar Vishnu and Shiva do not receive equal attention. Vishnu, especially in his avatars of Krishna and Ram, is celebrated in several ceremonies. Shiva has but a single festival that honors him, Shivaratri (Shiva's Night), which is a minor festival in Shanti Nagar. However, Shiva's son, Ganesh, receives some attention, and Shiva's wife, Durga, has her place among the mother goddesses.

Interaction, the third category of festivals, differs strikingly from the other two. All the festivals of the first two categories have associated deities. On the other hand, four of the six festivals in the "interaction" category had no apparent connection to any deity in 1958. Moreover, the presence of a deity in the other two festivals was weak and subordinate to the dominant theme of recognizing or strengthening ties of kinship. The tie of sister and brother is prominent in the interaction category, stronger even than the ties of husband and wife or mother and child. The latter two relationships are highlighted in festivals of welfare and in rites of passage. For example, in one marriage ritual a son renders homage to his mother by kissing her breast.

As the foregoing discussion makes clear, our classification of Hindu festivals imposes a structure on a fluid situation. How stable is this structure? Will it continue to be useful beyond a few decades or does the disparate behavior of the current villagers foreshadow changes that will soon render it obsolete? The variation that we observed in Shanti Nagar does not appear to suggest a trend. Some people or families observe or fail to observe specific festivals owing to individual personalities and interests or to particular family events, for example, a death. There are differences between castes and sects. Not every festival is observed by members of every caste, and people who follow the Arya Samaj often have a point of view different from that of more traditional villagers. However, caste and sect differences appear to have been stable for decades, and, in any case, classification would not be affected if a caste began to observe a festival previously ignored.

The potential sources of significant change are probably the schools and modern media, which can suggest a mythological background for a festival that previously lacked one or can identify a local god or goddess with one of the great traditional deities. The direction of change would thus be progressive Sanskritization. Such a development would blur our categories only slightly, if at all, because their defining criteria are largely independent of Sanskritization.

There are other possibilities for overriding the current sharp demarcation of our categories. For example, gift exchange might become a feature of Janamashtami, opening the possibility of classifying the festival as one of exchange instead of, or in addition to, its current placement in the category of honoring a deity. Nevertheless, our classification works well for the period 1958–78 and should continue to be useful in the foreseeable future.

The classification that we suggest here is not intended to be a replacement for the other systems described above. It basically offers a different perspective. When used in conjunction with the analytical approaches of Marriott, Wadley, Bouillier, and Hanchett, it serves to deepen and enrich our understanding. Solidly grounded in ethnography, it reflects the daily concerns of the villagers, makes clear their basic religious doctrines, and lends itself well to historical, symbolic, and functional analysis.

Festivals of Welfare, Fertility, and Protection

THE GENERAL THEME of the festivals of "welfare, fertility, and protection" is family welfare. Fertility comes into the picture because without it there can be no family welfare. "Protection" involves chiefly goddesses, for they can either offer protection or be extremely dangerous. Thus, Wadley's "power" and Hanchett's "danger" are two sides of a coin. In any case, goddesses are to be propitiated. That Devi (Goddess), or Shakti, in her many forms is the dominant deity of this category of festivals is clearly seen in table 6 (pp. 38–39), where 7 of the 14 festivals involve goddess worship exclusively, and in still another festival, Hoi, one of two deities is a goddess.

Themes based on the concerns of villagers rather than deities are basic to our classification. Therefore, the deities are not partitioned among our categories so that a particular deity appears in only one category, but there is some overlap. A particular deity may appear in festivals of more than one category. However, the deities rarely appear across categories, tending to frequent a single category and to take a minor role in others. For example, Shiva does not appear in the "welfare" category. Vishnu, in the avatar form of Krishna, is invoked in only two welfare festivals, both of which concern cattle, which is appropriate given the connection of Krishna with cattle.

Women more than men are involved with the festivals of welfare, for fertility, children, and husbands are their special concerns. Thus, women play the major roles in the propitiation of mother goddesses. Karva Chauth is for the long life, thus the welfare, of husbands. The participants are women. Although children take part in Hoi, which is for their welfare, women play the major roles. Sili Sat, when the goddesses of dreaded infectious diseases are worshipped, is for women. Men play prominent roles in only two ceremonies of the welfare category: Akhta and Gobardhan.

The basic information for the festivals of each category is given in tabular form by date. Table 6 lists the festivals of the "welfare" category. The accompanying text elaborates the aspects of the festivals that serve as the headings of columns, namely, Deity (God/Goddess), Theme, Ritual Group, Gift Exchange, etc. The use of an image and the place of worship are covered in a single column (Image/Place), for sometimes the place serves as the image, or symbol, of the deity. For example, worship at a river is equivalent to worshipping the image of a goddess in one's home. The bare ligaments of the festivals as presented in the tables are augmented in the text by descriptions of ritual, interviews with villagers, songs, stories, and comparison with descriptions of comparable festivals in other towns and villages. Generally, the festivals were celebrated similarly both in the 1950s and in the 1970s. However, a few differences are noted in the text.

DEVI KI KARAHI

The worship of Devi on Chaitra *sudi* 8 is chiefly for the welfare of children. In Shanti Nagar, the festival is called Devi ki Karahi (The Cooking Pot of the Goddess). Celebrated in mid-April in the midst of the wheat harvest, a busy time, it is a minor festival in the sense that many families completely ignore it. Of those families who observe it, some limit themselves to a relatively simple ritual at home while others may make a pilgrimage to a shrine for Devi, often to fulfill a vow (*vrat*). At important shrines, fairs may be held in conjunction with the festival, which add a recreational element to the religious aspect. In addition, the fairs are occasions for business, especially the buying and selling of animals. The Kumhar Potters trade horses, donkeys, and mules at the fair at Beri.

The festival is known by various names in other villages and generally in India. Commonly, the name of the goddess Durga is incorporated into the name of the festival. In Wadley's village in Uttar Pradesh, the festival occurs on Chaitra *sudi* 9 and is named Devin ki Puja, or Goddess Worship (Wadley, 1975: 210). In Kishan Garhi, also in Uttar Pradesh, the villagers have two names for the festival, Durga Naumi (Durga Ninth) and "Stony One Worship" (Marriott, 1955: 192). Channa (1984: 119) called the day Durga Ashtami (Durga's Eighth), as did Underhill (1991: 136). The name used in Shanti Nagar appears to be a regional variant, which is reported also for two other villages in Delhi Union Territory (Lewis, 1958: 203–204; Bhatia, 1961: 64). In Lewis's village of Rampur, the festival is observed on the eighth.

Villagers usually called the goddess honored at Devi ki Karahi simply Devi. Some named Durga as the deity, and other villagers cited other names, often Beriwali Mata (the Goddess of Beri). Kalkaji (Goddess of the Cremation Grounds), which is not a term for Durga, was frequently mentioned. After the release of a popular film about a goddess called Santoshi Ma (or Mata), some women in 1978 identified her with the goddess worshipped on Devi ki Karahi. Chatterjee (1953: 257) summarized the question of nomenclature in terms of a supreme goddess with many names: "The Supreme God is conceived in the Tantra as one, universal spiritual power (shakti) and is called the Divine Mother (Devi). The Divine Mother is variously named as Kali, Tara, Durga, Chandika, and so on." The local name involving *karahi* may allude to two of the festal foods (puri and halva) prepared for the occasion, which are cooked in ghee in a *karahi* (a cooking pot).

Another festival for Durga, known locally as Sanjhi, takes place six months after Devi ki Karahi on Ashvin *sudi* 8. Babb (1975: 126) noted a general association between the eighths of a month and goddesses. The bright eighths are for the worship of Durga. The villagers' capricious observance of Devi ki Karahi may be a consequence of a rather weak interest in Shiva, for Durga is his consort. Although generalization is uncertain as families and individuals may change their behavior from year to year, we suggest from our fieldwork that Durga worship is strongest among the Brahmans and the lower castes, the Kumhar Potters, Chamar Leather-workers, and Chuhra Sweepers. However, the Potters were less observant in 1978 than in 1958. Many Brahmans, the highest caste, observe the day, but most families of high-caste Jats, the largest village caste, ignore the festival. The influence of the Arya Samaj in general and a relative disinterest in Shiva in particular may account for the fact that few Jats participate in Devi ki Karahi. Regardless of caste, obser-vance of the festival was a matter of individual choice.

The basic ritual for Devi ki Karahi begins the day before the festival. The house is freshly cleaned. On the eve of the festival (the seventh), women start to fast and light a lamp for the goddess. Fasting in village terms means to abstain from grains, especially wheat bread. It does not always mean the avoidance of all nourishment. In practice, the morning meal is skipped. Afterwards, some people may eat a little fruit during the day, or take tea at noon or at the normal time in the late afternoon.

TABLE 6.

ANNUAL FESTIVALS OF WELFARE, FERTILITY, AND PROTECTION

FESTIVAL	GODDESS/GOD	THEME	RITUAL GROUP
Devi ki Karahi	Devi, Durga	Honor goddess, welfare	Family, mainly women
Jyesth ka Dassehra	Yami, Ganga	Thanksgiving, honor goddesses	Individual, men, women
Guga Naumi	Guga Pir	Family welfare	Family
Budh ki Duj	A saint	Family welfare, pleasure	Individual, men, women
Akhta	Krishna	Exorcise cattle disease	Village
Karva Chauth	Sun, Moon	Husband's welfare	Married women, mostly Brahman and Baniya
Hoi	Hoi, Sun	Children's welfare	Mothers
Dhan Teras	Lakshmi	Preparation for Girhi, Diwali	Family
Girhi	Lakshmi	Welcome Lakshmi to household	Family
Diwali	Lakshmi	Welfare, fortune	Family
Gobardhan	Gobardhan, Krishna	Welfare	Family
Ganga Nahan	Ganga	Gain husband like Krishna	Individual, women, men
Sakat	Sakat Mata, Ganesh	Welfare, children	Mothers
Sili Sat	Mother goddesses	Welfare, protection	Women

TABLE 6. *(Continued)*

FESTIVAL	GIFT EXCHANGE	IMAGE/PLACE	RITUAL
Devi ki Karahi	Housewife gives food to kin, neighbors	Lithograph	Fast, light lamps
Jyesth ka Dassehra	None	Ganges, Yamuna	Bathe
Guga Naumi	Women give food to lineage	Drawing	Light lamp
Budh ki Duj	Women give sweets, cash to children	Fair, pond	Offer food, clean pond
Akhta	Village gives feast for old Brahman men, children, Chamars, Chuhras	Altar	Exorcism, procession, havan
Karva Chauth	Women give food, pots to husbands, in-laws	Decorated pot	Fast, story, offer water
Hoi	Mothers give headcloth to mother-in-law	Drawing	Fast, story, offer water
Dhan Teras	None	Household	Buy dishes, light lamp
Girhi	None	Household	Prepare food, light lamps
Diwali	Family gives money, food, clothes to married daughters, sisters	Lithograph	Light lamps, procession, singing, fireworks, havan
Gobardhan	Family gives money, food to Nai, cowherd	Cowdung sculpture	Men circle image, light lamp, fireworks
Ganga Nahan	Returned pilgrim distributes *prasad* to all	Ganges or Yamuna	Bathe at Ganges, procession in village to well by women
Sakat	*Prasad*	Drawing, household	Fast, story, water to moon
Sili Sat	Women to their Sweeper woman servant, food, clothes	Mother goddesses, Bhumiya, shrines	Procession to shrines, offerings of food and water

Village tea with gur and buffalo milk is delicious and quite nourishing. Rice pudding (*khir*) seems to be the special food used to break the fast.

Women who have a lithograph of Devi light their lamp in front of the picture and worship the image. On the morning of the eighth, women again light a lamp and worship Devi. Then women cook the special foods, puris (deep fried bread), halva, and *khir* (rice pudding), which are eaten at the close of the festival by family members, especially children, and which may be distributed as *prasad* to children and other families of the *biradari* (the local resident members of a specific caste) and to Brahmans. Before the family eats, a bit of food may be offered to a cow. If the family uses a picture of the deity, the food is placed before it as *bhog* (food offered to an icon).

This basic ritual is subject to considerable variation. Pilgrimages and vows may be added, and some features, such as fasting, feeding a cow, and the distribution of *prasad*, may be dropped. Even the date of the festival can be ignored. People regard Devi worship as a general activity that can be scheduled at any time. Sometimes when we interviewed people about the festival, they mentioned, instead of individual worship, a communal caste feast for Devi that took place approximately at Devi ki Karahi. They thought in terms of Devi worship in a generic sense and were little concerned with the precise date of Devi ki Karahi.

Our interviews show ritual variation but nothing that would suggest a trend. Caste differences are not particularly evident in ritual detail but rather in the proportion of families that participate in the festival. However, the rate of participation within a caste can vary from decade to decade just as much as does the rate of participation between castes.

The Kumhar Potters may be the best example of differences in observance of the festival over time. In 1958, the Kumhars had developed a strong interest in the worship of Durga, probably because a young married man had gone to Durga's shrine at Beri and brought back a stone which he set up as a shrine in his house. By 1978, the man and his family no longer celebrated Devi ki Karahi. One woman alleged that only a single Potter family observed the day. Another Potter woman, who kept no fasts, said that it is not necessary to worship Devi on the eighth. However, she showed us a picture of Devi before which she claimed to light a lamp every evening. This apparent decline of interest in Devi ki Karahi probably does not represent a secular trend. The rate of observance could quickly recover. A simple event such as a family's setting up a shrine could lead to increased observance among the Potters.

As befits the Brahmans' role as priests and their position at the top of the caste hierarchy, an elderly Brahman man in 1958 invoked something of Hindu philosophy in trying to make us understand about Devi ki Karahi and mother goddess worship in general. He said, "Shakti, Devi, Maya, and Girja are all names of the goddess. Sometimes I celebrate this day and sometimes I don't. It depends on how I feel. Without Shakti (the power to create) and Maya (the energy to create) how can a woman have a son? Girja, also known as Parvati, was the wife of Shiva. She has the power to do everything. God is one and has various representations."

This informant expressed the family welfare aspect of Devi ki Karahi in terms of fertility. Although he was not an Arya Samaji, his final statement is one of the main tenets of the Arya Samaj. It is also a feature of traditional Hinduism (Sanatan Dharma, the Eternal Religion). Like other villagers, he felt no compulsion to observe the festival. Only people who made a vow felt any obligation to propitiate Devi.

A middle-aged Brahman man commented, "Devi ki Karahi is not celebrated by everyone these days [1958]. Durga is the goddess and the cooking pot is put on for her. Then if one wants to eat something nice, one may." Brahman women who observed the festival fasted and lit lamps. At least one group of Brahmans went to Gurgaon for Devi ki Karahi. Many mother goddesses (matas) and devis have shrines at Gurgaon, including Gurgaonwali Mata and Beri Devi.

The Baniya Merchants rank just below the Brahmans in the local caste hierarchy. The head of the only Baniya family in Shanti Nagar in 1958, a thoughtful elderly man, told us:

> Some people celebrate Devi ki Karahi on the eighth day following the new moon every month; others, only on this day in Chaitra and Ashvin. I celebrate in the latter manner. We make *khir*, halva, and puris, light a lamp, bow before it, and say to Devi, "Help us," and then feed the children. Some people distribute food to others. What one does depends on the individual. There are temples at Kalkaji in Delhi, Beri near Rohtak, near Narela, and others. Some people go there every six months, others may not go for many years. I used to go previously, but I haven't gone for many years.
>
> In ancient times, it is said, Devi became very powerful and helped all her disciples. Now people in trouble go to Devi and vow to distribute *laddu*s [sweet coconut balls the size of a billiard ball] and to offer a few coins if the trouble passes. If successful, the goddess has a new devotee; if not, it is still all right.

Although the Baniya man mentioned the distribution of *prasad* at the end of the feast, we learned of only one family that distributed *prasad*, or at least did so with some forethought. In the evening when the lamp was lit, a Potter woman made eight heaps of food near the lamp and then distributed them to eight Potter households with which her family was on good terms. She claimed that she would receive a return gift of food from each of the households.

The Chuhra Sweepers and the Chamar Leatherworkers worshipped Devi, but not necessarily on Devi ki Karahi, although they knew the date of the festival. A Chuhra man said that Devi worship took place to fulfill a vow. He himself gave such a feast to fulfill a vow when he sold a cow for a good price. Another Sweeper man, in thanks to Devi, fed members of his caste when his wife recovered from illness. On the other hand, an elderly Sweeper man explained that he did not celebrate Devi ki Karahi because God gave nothing to him. Therefore, he gave nothing to God.

The Leatherworkers reported holding a communal feast for Devi near the date of Devi ki Karahi. Our knowledgeable informant claimed that such a feast could be held whenever one wished. There was no need to hold it on Devi ki Karahi. The feast of the Chamars was paid for by the caste panchayat, not by an individual, as among the Sweepers.

Despite such communal feasts, individual families of Chamars and Chuhras might observe the day with the traditional family ritual, if they wished. Men representing five families of Chamars went to the fair at Kalkaji where they lit a lamp and offered flowers and five pice (1.25 annas in the older currency, see note 32) to Devi. Offerings to Devi usually contain a quarter, thus five pice, or possibly Rs. 1.25. The Chamar men did not fast, but the usual sweet dishes were prepared in their households. The Chamar men made offerings to the mother goddess because she benefits them. In case of illness, she brings about a prompt recovery. One of the men made an offering in the hope of obtaining a job.

Few, if any, Jat families participated in the ritual in 1958. One Jat informant said that his group of four families did not observe the festival. However, when participation depends on individual choice, it becomes impossible to make statements about castes, especially castes as large as the Jats and Brahmans, that admit no variation. Thus, the Jats were nonparticipants, although a complete survey of the caste in 1958, which was impractical, would probably have turned up a few women who practiced the traditional ritual. In fact in 1977, we interviewed a Jat woman who cooked festal food on Devi ki Karahi.

Most Brahman families observed the festival in 1958, but a few informants stated that they "did not accept Devi." The Bairagis denied participating. We gathered no information from the Jhinvar Watercarrier, Nai Barber, Mali Gardener, and Lohar Blacksmith castes.

In 1978 we took a survey, interviewing one or two people from almost all castes about the festivals. The basic ritual of Devi ki Karahi had not changed, although, as in 1958, some individuals dropped one or another element, especially the fasting. Lighting a lamp for Devi and cooking and eating special food were the aspects of the festival that people liked most. Participation by members of a particular caste varied quite a bit from 1958 to 1978. Some Bairagis, who denied participation in 1958, observed the festival 20 years later. They cooked the special food and lit a lamp, but no one fasted. The Potters, who were quite active in 1958, did little in 1978. The Lohar Blacksmiths and Jhinvar Watercarriers did nothing, but the Mali Gardeners, Baniya Merchants, Nai Barbers, and Chhipi Dyers observed the festival. The Dyers made a pilgrimage to Beriwali Mata. Our Mali informant mentioned making a pilgrimage to Beriwali Mata and getting a haircut for a son who had been born to the family in the preceding year and was about eight months old on Devi ki Karahi. Writing of Rampur village, Lewis (1958: 204) described a custom involving a child's first haircut: "Children born subsequent to a vow made to Devi are taken by their parents to Beri for their first haircut. The first lock of hair cut off is buried in the pond; a few hairs are placed in the shrine." In Shanti Nagar, there was no mention of communal feasts among the Chamar Leatherworkers and Chuhra Sweepers in 1978. Individual participation among the Chamars varied. Our Sweeper informant said that the Sweepers did nothing that year (1978).

For all castes but the Jats, whether or not one observed the festival was a rather casual decision in the absence of a vow. People were not particularly concerned. Only Jats who were devoted followers of the Arya Samaj had strong feelings about the festival. Their sentiments were generally hostile. When one such Jat man was asked about Devi ki Karahi, he replied, "Why do you ask us? We are Arya Samajis. We don't worship all these devis [goddesses]. We have only one God and our guru is Swami Vivekananda. Other castes like Brahmans, Chuhras, Chamars, and Kumhars may have it." Jats who were not so strict about Arya Samaj beliefs might observe the festival. One elderly widow claimed to do so, adding that she cooked *khir* on every eighth. Not all followers of the Arya Samaj were Jats. The Jhinvars had become Arya Samajis by 1978, which is probably the reason that they no longer observed the festival.

JYESTH KA DASSEHRA (GANGA FESTIVAL)

Jyesth ka Dassehra (Jyesth Tenth), takes place on Jyesth *sudi* 10 after the wheat harvest. It is of little importance in Shanti Nagar. Few people observe the day, which honors the river goddesses Yami and Ganga, and no one had much to say about it. This lack of interest is shown not only by our informants' sparse descriptions of the festival but also by some confusion about dates. In 1958, A Brahman correctly placed the festival in the *sudi* fortnight, but a knowledgeable Nai Barber reported that it was celebrated in the *badi* (first) fortnight. In 1978, only the *sudi* fortnight was mentioned. Almost every other source, for example, Channa (1984: 121) who called the festival Ganga Dussehera, Mukerji (1916: 63), Imperial Record Department (1914: 31), and Wadley (1975: 165), dated the festival in the *sudi* fortnight. The only exception is Bhatia (1961: 64) who cited the first (*badi*) fortnight.

In 1958, our informants reported only that people might go to the Ganges or Yamuna for a bath and might cook special food. It was an individual matter. People who went for a bath did not always prepare special food for the festival. In any case, no one mentioned the performance of any rituals. One informant explicitly denied that any worship took place. The comments of a Nai Barber were typical: "One may go to Delhi for a bath at the Yamuna, but this is nothing special. If you have the money, you may go for a bath. Otherwise you stay at home. That is all." A Brahman confirmed these comments, adding, "Not many are enthusiastic."

People had more to say about the festival in 1978, probably because we made an extensive survey of the festivals. A Brahman woman said that her family celebrated the day only when something good had happened in the family, for example, the birth of a son. For many years they did not observe the day because of a death in the family. Then the engagement of a son was held on Jyesth ka Dassehra, and the family began to observe the festival (see also, Opler, 1959b: 275).

A Jat woman said that her family distributed sugar water, fans, money, and melons to passersby. Bathing was optional. An elderly Blacksmith woman reported the distribution of sweetened water, melons, and fans, denied fasting, and reported cooking the festal foods of *khir*, rice, and halva. Other informants confirmed these details. Several informants said that their families did nothing for the festival. A Chamar woman said that Brahmans and Jats, the better off castes, distributed, food but that her family was too poor to do that. Only one of our informants volunteered a motive for the festival, the Brahman woman cited above, whose family celebrated the day in thanks for a blessing.

Descriptions of the festival in other villages add a few features not mentioned in Shanti Nagar. Since the festival takes place after the spring harvest, bathing in the Ganges or Yamuna is thought to offer shelter and rescue by removing the sin incurred in agricultural work when insects may be killed and oxen beaten (e.g., Lewis, 1958: 205; Srivastava, 1961: 67; Wadley, 1975: 165). Thus, the festival is properly classified under welfare and protection. Also, flowers and small coins on leaves are floated downstream as ritual offerings to the river, and food is given to beggars. Growse (1883: 179) noted that kites are flown in the evening. The descriptions of the festival in four of the studies of Delhi villages carried out under the Census of India in 1961 by Bhatia, Nautiyal, Ratta, and Srivastava are very brief and quite similar to one another and to the account in Lewis (1958). The fifth of these studies, by Luthra, made no mention of Jyesth ka Dassehra.

Underhill (1991: 101–103) called the festival Dashahara (Destroyer of Ten) or Gangotsava (Ganga Festival). It is observed for 10 days from the first to the 10th of the bright fortnight of Jyesth. "Ten" in the festival's name refers to the 10 chief sins (harsh speech, lying, slander, clamor, theft, injury, adultery, covetousness, evil thoughts, and foolish obstinacy) that the proper observance of the festival will destroy. The devotee bathes at dawn for 10 days in a sacred river, if possible the Ganges, recites mantras, and gives grain to 10 Brahmans and 10 cows. Images of riverine creatures are made of flour and floated downstream. "It is unmistakably an ancient festival to the river goddess, and takes place immediately before the rainy season, when it is hoped she will be replenished" (Underhill, 1991: 102). The myth offered to explain the festival involves the power of Ganges water to restore the dead to life. Underhill commented that the festival is exceptional: if it occurs in a year with an added Jyesth, then it is celebrated in the added month and not in the true one.

Mukerji (1916: 63) pointed out that the word "Dasahara" is an abbreviation of the Sanskrit *Dasa-bidha pap hara*, which means "the destroyer of ten kinds of sin." It is the birthday of the goddess Ganga, a destroyer of human sins. The birthday denotes the day on which the river, originally a celestial stream, descended from heaven to flow on earth. A bath in the Ganges not only removes past sin but also bestows spiritual merit for future rebirths. Mukerji (1916: 63–69) and Dowson (1891: 108) recounted the legends that underlie the festival.

The festival as described by Underhill and Mukerji suggests a devolution of a great traditional festival to a simpler one of the little tradition. Thus, an observance of 10 days is shortened to one day, and the 10 chief sins are reduced to the inadvertent ones that attend agricultural operations. In the Sanskritized version, mantras are chanted, and cows and Brahmans are fed. On the other hand, villagers dispense with mantras and feed beggars. The images of riverine creatures offered to the river, which may represent the animal sacrifices that were sometimes made (Imperial Record Department, 1914: 32), are replaced in the village version by flowers and coins floated on leaves. Supplicating the river goddess specifically for water in the great traditional form becomes a plea for general welfare or thanks for any kind of good fortune in the village version. Villagers appear to be unaware of any mythological charter for the festival.

GUGA NAUMI

Nothing is known for certain about a famous regional saint known as Guga Pir (Saint Guga) or Zahir Pir (Saint Apparent), whose festival, Guga Naumi (Guga's Ninth), is celebrated on Bhadrapad *badi* 9 during the monsoon season. Some people, chiefly Chamar Leatherworkers, call him Jhar or Jhar (Zahir) Pir. Guga Naumi is very important in Shanti Nagar. Members of all castes and most families observe the festival, even some Arya Samajis, who may do so surreptitiously. Many villagers are familiar with elements of the various legends of Guga Pir. There are shrines to Guga Pir in Haryana, one in particular where some families have made pilgrimages. A fair is held there on Guga's Ninth.

According to Crooke (1968, 1: 211), the tales told about Guga Pir are wild legends. He is said to have been a ruler, perhaps a Chauhan Rajput, in Northern Rajputana in the middle of the 12th century. However, he may have lived early in the 11th century and have been a contemporary of Prithvi Raj, fighting with him in battles against Mahmud of Ghazni, the Islamic invader. He is said to have been killed in one of these battles or, on the other hand, to have embraced Islam. His grave, that is, the place where the earth opened to swallow Guga and his stallion, is near Dadrera (Dadrewa) Khera in the former princely state of Bikaner in Rajasthan. A shrine still stands to mark the spot (Blackburn et al., 1989: 227). Temple (1884–1900, 1(6): 121) wrote, "The whole story of Gugga is involved in the greatest obscurity."

Guga Pir has innumerable devotees in Punjab, Haryana, Delhi, Rajasthan, and western Uttar Pradesh (cf., Blackburn et al., 1989, map 1, p. 19). However, Growse (1883: 268) made no mention of a festival for Guga Pir in his list of festivals for Mathura district, just a short distance from Delhi. Farther east in Uttar Pradesh in Karimpur, the village studied by Wadley, Zahir Pir is known but apparently no festival for him is celebrated on Bhadrapad *badi* 9 (Wadley, 1975: 137–142, 211). Lapoint (1978: 283) noted that the cult of Guga has not penetrated farther east than western Uttar Pradesh.

An elderly Baniya Merchant man narrated in detail the version of the myth of Guga Pir that is widely known in Shanti Nagar. The Baniya was an Arya Samaji. Mindful of the sect's position against the worship of deities such as Guga Pir, he commented at the end of his recital that what he had told us was just a legend, implying that Guga's sanctity was tenuous, although he was ambiguous on the point. He said, "Perhaps people worship Guga as a matter of imitation [tradition] or because they admire him or because he granted their wish." His account is similar to those of Temple (1884–1900, 1(6): 121–209), Lewis (1958: 211–212), and Crooke (1968, 1: 211–213). We have annotated his version mainly by adding the names of the personages:

A man [Raja Vasta, according to Crooke, or Raja Jewar, according to Temple] had two wives [sisters]. The senior wife [Bachchal] was good but had no children. She learned about a wise old grandfather [Guru Gorakhnath[5]] and went to serve him. He was pleased with her and granted her a boon. When she said she wanted a child, he answered that he would give her medicine [*gugal*, incense used in exorcism, hence the name Guga Pir] the next time she visited him. The younger wife [Kachchal] who was jealous wanted to know where Bachchal had gone. Bachchal, a trusting woman, told her about the wise man and the boon. So Kachchal went to Gorakhnath. He could not see very well and gave the medicine to Kachchal instead of to Bachchal. When Bachchal returned to Gorakhnath, he said, "I've already granted your boon; you will have two sons." Then Bachchal guessed what had happened, told the wise man, and said, "But both sons will also be mine." "No," said Gorakhnath, "I will give you something else. I will give you one son more powerful than the other two and he will kill them." Kachchal and her sons schemed to kill Bachchal and her son, Guga, without success. Then years later when Guga was fighting a war he inadvertently killed both of Kachchal's sons. After he had killed his two [half] brothers, he took their heads to his mother, who was quite startled. He said he didn't know they were his brothers. She scolded him and told him to get out of the house so he went to the jungle, but he would sneak into the house every night to see his wife [Siriyal] whom he loved very much. She would dress up for his visits so Bachchal accused her of having relations with other men. Siriyal then told Bachchal the truth. Bachchal told Siriyal that she must tell her the next time Guga comes. When he next came, his mother scolded him, and he was so ashamed that he went down into the earth.

Other informants recounted their usually brief versions of the myth, which often were somewhat different, sometimes very different, from the Baniya's account. For example, a Sweeper woman said that Guga, a Muslim, had great power because he was a disciple of Guru Gorakhnath and defeated a wealthy man in war. A Brahman man said that Guga was a Brahman who lived in the Age of Truth (Satyayuga or Kritayuga). He and his horse were entombed in the earth, so now he is worshipped. A Brahman woman said that in the Age of Truth someone killed a horse named Guga, so now the horse is worshipped. Another Brahman woman said that Guga is the god of serpents, and people worship him for the sake of snakes. Two informants said that Guga was swallowed by the earth because he was truthful, just as the truthful Sita, the wife of Ram, was swallowed. A Jat man said that Guga was a Hindu exorcist who was forced to read Muslim scripture and so he became a Muslim. He was swallowed by the earth, so now everyone accepts him.

A Chamar man narrated a story rather like that of the Baniya except that the end was different. Instead of scolding Guga so that he went down into the earth, Bachchal seized the tail of Guga's horse as he was leaving Siriyal, and both Guga and his horse turned to stone because he could not show his face to his mother. A Jat woman told a variation of this ending. After being swallowed by the earth, Guga returned nightly to visit his wife. His mother wondered why Siriyal dressed so nicely every evening, since her husband was dead. Siriyal finally had to explain to Bachchal that Guga came to visit her. As Guga was leaving one night, his mother went to meet him. To avoid the meeting, Guga cried out that the house was on fire.

As his distracted mother turned to look at the house, Guga buried himself alive and never returned.

Although the Baniya's recital of the myth omitted one of its most important elements, namely, the connection of Guga Pir and snakes, several of our informants did mention it in various ways. Guga's power over snakes is prominent in Temple's version of the myth summarized below. The worship of Guga by most devotees emphasizes this power. Before a senior woman recited the myth of Guga Pir on Guga Naumi, she first drew on the wall above her stove a sketch of Guga on horseback surrounded by snakes.

Guga Naumi takes place during the monsoon. Snake rituals occur throughout North India during the rains. The important festival of Nag Panchmi (Snake's Fifth) is celebrated during the monsoon in Shrawan, the month before Bhadrapad. Nag Panchmi is not observed in Shanti Nagar. Lewis (1958) and the four Delhi village studies from the 1961 census also make no mention of it.

Guga received power over snakes from his guru, Gorakhnath. Wadley (1975: 136–138) posited a tie of Guga through Gorakhnath to Shiva, the primary god of fertility who controls snakes and may perform other good deeds. Shiva delegates these powers to his disciple, Gorakhnath. Guga is related to Gorakhnath in two ways. In addition to the guru-*chela* (disciple) relationship, Guga owes his birth to Gorakhnath, who granted the boon of fertility to his mother, Bachchal.

A synopsis of Temple's full treatment of the legend, a Punjabi version with an English-Punjabi text in poetic form, is given here (Temple, 1884–1900, 1(6): 121–209). In this account, replete with miraculous feats attributed to Guga, Raja Jewar and Queen Bachchal anxiously want a son, so Queen Bachchal beseeches Guru Gorakhnath, with his miraculous powers, to help her bear one. Bachchal's sister, Kachchal, also a mate of Raja Jewar, disguises herself as Bachchal and visits Guru Gorakhnath, too, in order to obtain sons. The guru does not realize she is not Queen Bachchal and promises her that she will bear two sons. Then she and a sister of Raja Jewar spread gossip about Queen Bachchal being in the royal garden at midnight with a yogi, implying that she has ruined her reputation and become pregnant. They repeat this gossip to the Raja, who then banishes Queen Bachchal from the palace.

Although Bachchal is 12 (sic) months pregnant, she begins her travels to her natal family in transport pulled by bullocks. When the coachman stops to water the bullocks, a snake bites them and they die. While Queen Bachchal bewails the bullocks, Guga miraculously speaks from his mother's womb and tells her how to bring the bullocks back to life by using a branch from a nim tree, calling on Guru Gorakhnath, making an offering for the Guru, repeating eight charms for snakes, and then praising the Guru. This is the first step in establishing Guga's miraculous power with snakes. Bachchal follows Guga's directions, and the bullocks stand up immediately. After examining the stars, a Brahman priest determines that the eighth day of Bhadon (Bhadrapad, August–September) would be a propitious time for Guga's birth, and other favorable omens are seen—a partridge and a snake. With these omens, Raja Jewar and Bachchal are reconciled and happy with the birth of their son.

In Temple's version, Guga's betrothal and marriage also illustrate Guga's power over snakes. This power accounts for the worship in Shanti Nagar of the drawing of

Guga Pir on horseback surrounded by snakes. Shortly after Guga's betrothal, his father dies, so the engagement is broken. Guga then goes into the forest and calls on Guru Gorakhnath to put him in touch with the Chief of Snakes, Basak Nag, who in turn sends his servant, Tatig Nag (a snake), to Guga. The Chief of Snakes tells Tatig Nag to do whatever Guga orders because Guru Gorakhnath is known to have special power over snakes. Then according to Guga's instructions, Tatig Nag disguises himself as a Brahman and visits the garden of Guga's former fiancée's father, where she is sitting. When she sees Tatig Nag after he resumes his snake form, she faints. He then has another plan. When she goes to the lake to bathe, he enters the lake in his snake form, bites her toe, and she dies. Guga, known for his power with snakes and snake bites, is then called. By using the same procedure that he told his mother to use for the dead bullocks, he revives the girl. They are again engaged and soon wed.

After the wedding, the twin sons of Kachchal, Surjan and Urjan, ask for a share of Guga's property. He refuses, so they plot to kill him while hunting together. When they try, Guga draws his sword to defend himself, kills each of them with one stroke apiece, and cuts off their heads with a second stroke. He next places the heads on the pommel of his saddle and takes them to his mother. She curses him, saying that he is no longer a Hindu, and tells him to go down into the earth to die. He then asks Mother Earth to take him, but this goddess tells him that to be buried he will have to become a Muslim. He seeks a Muslim teacher, learns the creed, and goes down into the earth to die, for Muslims are buried. This legend reflects the influence of Islam in North India.

A later version of the legend from Meerut District, western Uttar Pradesh (Blackburn et al., 1989: 225–227), incorporates some of the above features and adds that Queen Bachchal nurses the twin boys because their own mother is unable to do so, thus accounting for Bachchal's feelings about their death. This version also highlights the love of Guga for his wife, Siriyal (Lado Serial), and his surreptitious visits. The theme of romantic love ending in tragedy is popular in North India, for example, the Marriage of Hir and Ranjha (Temple, 1884–1900, 2: 507–580). One of our informants said that Bachchal caught the tail of Guga's horse as he was leaving after a visit to his wife. In Blackburn's version of this episode, Guga escapes rather than being turned to stone, as in our villager's version.

Many details are different in various versions of the legend. For example, Crooke identifies the medicine that Guru Gorakhnath gives to Bachchal as *gugal* (an incense used in exorcism), while in the accounts of Blackburn et al., (1989: 225–226) and Lapoint (1978: 289–290), the medicine given to Kachchal is two barley seeds and Bachchal's medicine is the soul of one of Guru Gorakhnath's disciples obtained by boiling him in water until his body disintergates. Exorcism is a theme in the legend, first implicitly by the use of *gugal* and then explicitly in the ritual used to revive Siriyal (Temple, 1884–1900, 1(6): 189). There is an echo of the exorcism theme in the testimony of one of our informants, a Jat man and an Arya Samaji, who called Guga Pir an exorcist (bhagat).

Warfare is emphasized in Blackburn's and Lapoint's versions but is absent in Temple's. In the version of Blackburn et al., Prithvi Raj sides with the sons of Kachchal in the dispute over inheritance and sends an army of nine *lakh*s (900,000) against Guga's 500 soldiers. He is saved by Guru Gorakhnath's disciples. After failed negotiations, the twin brothers attack Guga and then try to flee, but he catches and beheads them. In Temple's version, the twins invite Guga to go hunting, try to kill him, but are themselves killed and beheaded. Guga is both a romantic and a martial hero although he did not die in battle, which Blackburn regards as a basic criterion for a military hero.

Lapoint (1978: 281–308) published a detailed version of the epic of Guga as recited by devotees (bhagats) in the North Indian village of Garvpur, Meerut District, Uttar Pradesh. The text is accompanied by an analysis of the principal themes expressed in the epic and their relation to Sanskritic classics, chiefly the Ramayana and the Mahabharata. In Garvpur, three bhagats play the leading role in the cult of Guga. They recite the myth during a nightlong ceremony on Guga Naumi. Villagers come to the recitation bringing offerings of food and money, which are an important source of supplementary income for the bhagats. In return for their alms, the donors receive Guga's blessing, conferred verbally or with a touch on the head with an iron whip, a symbol of Guga. Lapoint's description resembles those of Lewis (1958: 211–212) and of our Baniya informant (see below), noteworthy features being the role of the bhagats and the iron whip. Lapoint did not mention flagellation or spirit possession. The myth itself conforms in all important details to those cited above.

Lapoint identified several themes in Guga's myth that correspond to those of the Sanskritic great tradition: karma, reincarnation, exile, filial loyalty, family conflict, and the martial hero. He emphasized the treatment given familial and extended kin relationships. "The characters in the epic are people with whom villagers can identify. The realistic description of family conflict [especially daughter-in-law and mother-in-law, and between the brothers] affords individual listeners a dramatic vehicle on which they may project their own anxieties and aspirations" (Lapoint, 1978: 292, 305).

The legend of Guga Pir illustrates the movement of material between little and great traditions. A Rajput warrior, Guga Bir (Guga the Hero), wins local fame. A myth develops featuring the hero's death, his power to cure snakebite, and a birth with supernatural elements. The hero is deified, becoming a saint, Guga Pir. The next step is the identification of the hero with a god of the great tradition, Shiva, which comes about through an intermediary, Guru Gorakhnath. Ideally, the movement is from local hero to identification with a deity of the great tradition, followed by loss of the hero's earthly origin. However, in Guga's case, the process has not yet reached that point. Guga is deified, but his earthly persona has not been forgotten (Blackburn et al., 1989: 26–27).

Instead of universalization from the little tradition to the great tradition, the Guga Pir myth can also be interpreted as a process of parochialization. Crooke (1968, 1: 206) suggested that five Rajput heros known as Panch Pir, Guga among them, represent at the regional level the five Pandavas of the Mahabharata. That is, the assumed worship of the Pandavas devolved into the worship of the Panch Pir. Muslims also have a group of saints known as the Panch Pir. The five Pandavas merge with the five Rajput pirs and the five Islamic pirs, making them popular deities for both Hindus and Muslims. In any case, both Hindus and Muslims worship the Panch

Pir. In Shanti Nagar, there is a shrine to the Panch Pir that is worshipped on Sili Sat and other occasions, especially by the Chamar Leatherworkers.

Guga's Ninth takes place the day after Janamashtami (Birth Eighth), the birthday of Krishna. The two days are not related, but their proximity, the connection of both Krishna and Guga with snakes, and the sharing of food creates some confusion. Villagers who fast on Janamashtami break their fast with festal food at approximately midnight, moonrise, when Krishna was born. Some of the food prepared for the occasion may be carried over to Guga Naumi. This overlap, along with observance on successive days and the involvement of snakes, led a few villagers to confuse the meaning of the two days. A Watercarrier woman connected Guga and Krishna by quoting a saying: "On Guga Naumi it definitely always drizzles. When it rains, they say that Guga has washed Lord Krishna's clothes." However, most villagers recognized that Guga Naumi and Krishna's birthday are separate festivals.

The ritual of Guga Naumi is generally similar throughout Shanti Nagar. Early

FIG. 5. Guga Naumi, 1958. An elderly Brahman woman celebrates the festival of Guga Naumi in her kitchen. She has drawn the image of Guga Pir on horseback near her stove where she is cooking bread for the morning meal. Guga holds the horse's reins in his right hand. A lighted lamp and an offering of food are below the drawing. See the sketch above the photograph for a clearer image.

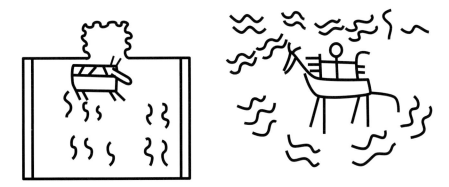

FIG. 6. *(above)* Guga Naumi, 1958. Drawings of Guga, horse, and snakes by two Brahman women.

FIG. 7. *(below)* Two versions of Guga on horseback drawn by Leatherworker women, 1958. The sketch on the left shows the horse and rider but no snakes. Four of the ten sketches, reproduced here, lacked snakes. The artist of the sketch on the right said that the horseman and snakes have no relationship.

in the morning, women prepare festive food, some of which was cooked the previous day. A senior woman draws a sketch of Guga on horseback surrounded by snakes on the kitchen wall near the stove. Soot from the stove serves as paint. The woman sets a small clay lamp under the drawing and places food beside it. After the woman lights the lamp, family members fold their hands and pray for the good health and welfare of the family. Then they eat some of the food and distribute the rest as *prasad* to lineage and caste members (figs. 5–12).

Although the ritual itself varied only slightly among families, the associated explanations and comments showed a few noteworthy differences. Four respondents said they observed the festival for general family welfare, while three noted that its purpose was specifically either for the sake of snakes or for protection from them. One woman, unusually afraid of snakes, saw them in her dreams, believing them to be the souls of ancestors. She maintained that worship on Guga's Ninth, especially the distribution of *shrini* (offerings of sweetmeats to saints), afforded considerable protection. Anytime she saw a snake, she distributed *shrini*.

All devotees worshipped before the sketch on the wall, but in addition, two informants offered water to the sun, and one, to the moon. In 1958, the distribution of *prasad* was mainly to family, lineage, and caste. In 1977, people claimed to give *prasad* to Brah-

FIG. 8. (*left*) Guga (Jahar) on horseback and snakes sketched at the home of a Leather-worker, 1958. Guga and two snakes are drawn in charcoal; the two snakes at the far right are done in ghee.

FIG. 9. (*below*) Sketches of Guga by two Jat women, 1958. The small drawing on the left was hidden in a back room. The sketch on the right lacks snakes.

mans and cows. A distribution to relatives was not specifically discussed, although informants may have taken such a distribution for granted and felt no need to mention it.

As Arya Samajis, the Jats had problems reconciling their observances with their beliefs. One Jat woman said that she observed the festival, but another Jat woman, present at the interview, claimed that the myth of Guga was an old one and that no one believed it any longer. Women and children of another Jat family hid their drawing. First saying that they had not made a drawing, they then led us into a back room where a small sketch was hidden behind trays and sacks of grain (fig. 9). The family had performed the ritual. The head of this family, an elderly man, was quite willing to relate the myth, but the other household members were reluctant. The senior woman said that it was the "day of the snakes" and connected somehow

FIG. 10. Unusual sketch of Guga Pir on horseback, drawn by a Potter boy for Guga Naumi, 1958. View from the front depicts Guga on horseback under a *jati* tree (possibly *janti, Prosopis spicigera* [Maheshwari, 1976: 145]). The Potter boy said that the lines to the left and right form the image of a horse. He said that Guga rode through a forest of *jati* trees and in this context is sometimes called Gugajati.

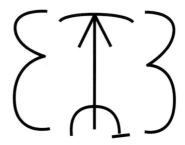

to Krishna's birthday the day before. This notion is not too farfetched. In Karimpur, where Guga Naumi is not observed, the relationship of Krishna and snakes is emphasized on his birthday (Wadley, 1975: 138–142).

Several informants mentioned shrines to Guga in Haryana, but only a Sweeper woman told of her family's having made a pilgrimage to a distant shrine. Her son was ill, and the family vowed to make a pilgrimage to Guga's shrine if the boy was saved. He recovered, and several family members went to the shrine to fulfill the vow. They considered Guga so important that family members who stayed at home observed several taboos to protect the pilgrims and themselves. They swept the house with a cloth instead of a broom. They put chapatis on a cold griddle (*tawa*) and then heated it. If they first heated the griddle, they believed that they would get big blisters on their backs. Probably for the same reason, to avoid blisters, they did not use frying pans. They did not quarrel or beat dogs or cats. If they beat one of these animals, a pilgrim would be beaten. Two other informants noted a connection between Guga and boils. A Jat woman said that failure to worship Guga could result in big yellow boils. A Baniya man said that if one does something wrong after worshipping Guga, boils will break out all over the body. However, they are not painful. Boils are usually associated with one of the mother goddesses, Phul ki Mata.

FIG. 11. Guga Naumi, remains of the ritual at the Potter boy's house, 1958. A lamp, some coals, a goblet with water, a pile of wheat, and a sprig of the *jati* bush are visible. The family lit the lamp, put some burning coals in front of the lamp, and fed the lamp with ghee. They put 16 puris on one side of the lamp and 16 *pura*s on the other. (A *pura* is fried bread that is thicker than a puri.) When the lamp burned out, people who had been fasting ate the puris and *pura*s. Then the devotees went into the lane and offered water to the sun. The family head lead the ritual. The drawing on the wall is not for Guga Naumi but for Salono, which took place only nine days before Guga Naumi.

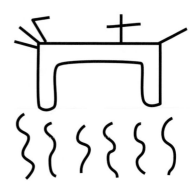

FIG. 12. Sketch of Guga, horse, and snakes at a Sweeper's home, 1958. Informant said that the horse was included so that no one would ever be without a horse.

Flagellation and spirit possession used to be traditions on Guga Naumi. Our Baniya informant said:

> Thirty years ago, lots of people who worshipped Guga stood holding a heavy chain. Suddenly they would start shaking [spirit possession] and then would whip their backs with the chain.[6] If they were simple good people, the chain would leave no marks. If they were guilty of bad actions, there would be marks. No one does this in Shanti Nagar or in Delhi today. The Arya Samaj came here and held open discussions about beliefs. If there was no basis for a belief, why celebrate? So people gradually began to give up [observances]. As a result of modernization and education, people believe less and less in these things.

Lewis recounts a similar custom. At one time, there were four bhagats (exorcists, or devotees) in Rampur (near Delhi). They performed a ritual in honor of Guga, were possessed by the saint, and prophesied.

> On these occasions . . . Bhangis [Chuhra Sweepers] and Camars [Chamar Leatherworkers] beat small drums . . . and sang songs about Guga. The *bhagat* was then considered to be possessed by Guga's spirit. After shivering and shaking, which indicated Guga's advent, the devotee would get up, jump about, and beat himself with an iron rod. People would then ask questions about future marriages, births, or the coming of rains. The *bhagat*'s self-administered blows were supposed to cause no bruises, although he kept it up throughout the night [Lewis, 1958: 212–213].

Guga Naumi illustrates three basic features of Hinduism: the eclecticism of popular Hinduism, its protean nature, and the absence of an impermeable distinction between gods and humans. A mythology and a cult develop around a Rajput prince who is worshipped by both Hindus and Muslims as a powerful protector throughout a large area in northwestern India. This history is not particularly unusual. Because humanity and divinity are not separate spheres in Hinduism, a person who becomes a deity represents no departure from traditional Hindu polytheism (Fuller, 1992: 3, 49–50). Some informants in Shanti Nagar remarked that Mahatma

Gandhi would eventually follow a similar trajectory. On the other hand, a relatively recent Hindu sect featuring a monotheistic doctrine, the Arya Samaj, has managed to suppress the worship of Guga Pir among its followers and is alleged to have successfully eliminated some of the rituals, flagellation and spirit possession, once generally associated with Guga Naumi.

Not only does popular Hinduism change through time, but it also exhibits considerable regional variation, even from village to village. Although researchers simply may have overlooked the festival or possibly decided that it was too insignificant to report, nonetheless three of the five village studies that are part of the 1961 Delhi census make no mention of it (Luthra, 1961; Nautiyal, 1961; Srivastava, 1961). Concerning regional variability, Marriott (1955: 194) made the telling point that of a roster of 35 presumably all-India Hindu festivals, only 9 occur in Kishan Garhi.

Budh Ki Duj

Budh ki Duj (Old Man's Second), a festival for the worship of an anonymous holy man who achieved local renown for his good deeds and piety, takes place on Bhadrapad *sudi* 2, the Old Man's birthday. The festival is celebrated in mid-September, just after the monsoon season and at the beginning of the kharif harvest (the summer-autumn crop). The festival has many similarities to Guga Naumi. Both Guga and the Old Man were humans who became deities worshipped for protection. The ritual in both cases involves cooking and distributing special food. Each deity has shrines to which devotees may make a pilgrimage for the festival. Fairs, held at the shrines, offer entertainment and various goods for sale. Neither festival finds favor with the Arya Samajis.

However, the differences between Guga and the Old Man are as instructive as are the similarities. Guga is more ancient, is worshipped over a much larger territory, and has more shrines than the Old Man. In fact, none of the other studies of Delhi villages (Lewis, 1958, and the five village studies from the 1961 census) mention Budh ki Duj, but again, the census investigators may not have considered the festival worth reporting. The worship of Guga takes place in the home, for his shrine is far from Shanti Nagar and few people make the pilgrimage. People who worship the Old Man usually go to his shrine in a nearby village. The fair is more of an attraction than the ritual for the Old Man. The persona of the Old Man is vague and no myth has developed around him, as compared to Guga whose legend, miraculous deeds, and connection through Guru Gorakhnath to Shiva are recounted in an elaborate myth. The Old Man remains at the beginning of the trajectory from revered human to deity whereas Guga is near the end. If Guga's human origins are forgotten, he may become a deity with full-fledged great traditional status.

Celebration of Budh ki Duj was a matter of individual choice. Nai Barbers, Chuhra Sweepers, and Kumhar Potters were most active in the ritual. In general, observance was so limited that many individuals were ill-informed as to which castes and, indeed, which families in their own caste participated. Two informants surprisingly named the Baniya family as a participant, which the elder Baniya denied, pointing out that he was a follower of the Arya Samaj. Almost all the Arya

Samajis ignored the ritual aspects of Budh ki Duj, but unbelievers nonetheless went to the village where the Old Man lived and died to attend the fair for amusement. They often took a number of children with them. People claimed that the fair was mainly for children, with its small wooden Ferris wheel and stalls for selling sweets and trinkets. However, there was professional wrestling, the wrestlers arriving in automobiles, which in the 1950s was a clear sign of wealth and status. The wrestling appealed to the men, who smiled as they invited Stanley to participate, offering even to procure an Englishman as an opponent.

The ritual had two basic features: at the pond that served as the Old Man's shrine, women first offered a very thick piece of bread (roti) called the Old Man's bread (rot); second, devotees helped to clean the pond. Women who made the rot sometimes collected flour from other families. Three informants, one an Arya Sama-ji, noted that Chuhra Sweepers collected flour from them. The families in question had a jajmani relationship, the Sweeper family serving their high caste patrons and, in turn, receiving donations. Thus people, participated indirectly in the festival, the offering being made by a surrogate. Two informants who made an offering of bread on behalf of other families said that they collected flour from seven families to make the rot. Seven is an auspicious number in Hinduism. One informant described the offering as a cooperative group effort among the seven families. However, a Barber woman claimed only to collect flour for the rot from any seven families of Jats and Brahmans and to take it to the shrine where she gave it to a beggar. Rot could also be left beside the pond or buried there. Sometimes it was broken into pieces and distributed, especially to children. Women not wanting to make the journey might leave their rot near the pond at Shanti Nagar or distribute it within the village. Sometimes people did not make rot but simply scattered some flour while taking the name of the Old Man. In addition to the rot, a few families cooked, ate, and distributed halva, puris (fancy wheat bread deep-fried in ghee so that it puffs), and khir.

Devotees almost always removed a bit of mud from the pond to clean it, an action believed to prevent blisters, boils, and eczema. A Barber woman described a connection between cleaning the pond and the offering of rot. She said that a low-caste beggar sits by the pond. An elderly Barber man called this man a priest (pujari) rather than a beggar. In any case, one gives the bread to him and he takes mud from the pond, a handful for each family member. A Brahman woman said that a lock of hair from a child's first haircut could be offered at the Old Man's shrine, just as could be done at one of the shrines for Devi on Devi ki Karahi. A Brahman man sketched the outlines of a myth that one day could be woven around the Old Man. He suggested that the Old Man "took mercy on cattle and introduced the custom of cleaning ponds so that cattle may have good water to drink." The Old Man might eventually be connected to Krishna because of their mutual concern for cattle.

The villagers participated mainly as customers in the commercial aspects of the fair. Several people said that they gave small sums of pocket money to children. We learned of only two villagers who operated shops. A Chamar Leatherworker said that he set up a shop at the fair to sell sweets. He did not sell all of them, even when he reduced prices. He claimed to have lost Rs. 9 and had sweets left over, which he ate. He commented that it was just bad luck.

One of the village potters, the other vendor at the fair, made a batch of about 500 hookah (pipe) bowls for sale. His problem was that Budh ki Duj takes place toward the end of the monsoon season, and it was raining when he hoped to fire his pots. He therefore fired the bowls in his storeroom. The initial firing was unsuccessful: instead of the proper reddish color, the bowls were black. He decided to refire them. If all went well, he would receive about Rs. 37.50 (eight dollars) for bowls which took him about two weeks to produce (S. Freed and R. Freed, 1978: 95–96).

AKHTA

Akhta, a festival for exorcising cattle disease, has four characteristics that set it apart from the other festivals. First, the chief personage is a religious specialist, a Brahman serving as an exorcist (bhagat). No other festival is conducted by a priest or bhagat, except when someone decides to hold a Sat Narayan's *katha* on the day of the full moon, in which case, a Brahman is usually called to conduct the *katha*. Second, although Akhta is celebrated in mid-to-late September at the end of the monsoon when epidemics of cattle disease may strike, it has no fixed date, and is skipped in years when not needed. For practical reasons it is held on a weekend. The village has to be closed during the ritual; that is, no one may leave the village or enter it. This prohibition can be most conveniently observed on a weekend. Moreover, Saturday and Sunday are considered propitious days for cattle. In 1958, cattle disease was raging in Shanti Nagar in mid-September, and Akhta was held on a weekend, beginning on Friday and ending on Sunday. The lunar dates were Bhadrapad *sudi* 14 (evening) to Ashvin *badi* 1 (noon).

Third, Akhta is the one festival of the "welfare" category that is specifically intended to benefit the whole village, even if some villagers do not believe in it. There are a few other festivals in which the ritual group is the village as a whole rather than the family or individual. They are among the festivals for honoring the major deities. Krishna's birthday and Holi may be the clearest cases because, even though some of the rituals are individual or familial, there are others, such as the village bonfire on Holi and the drama of Krishna's birth enacted in the center of the village and open to everyone, that involve participation beyond the family.

Fuller (1992: 129–131) noted a pattern of regional variation with regard to festivals. In South India, there are "collective" festivals explicitly intended to benefit the whole village, which often take the form of a temple festival for a tutelary deity, usually a village goddess. In the Hindi-speaking region, however, temple festivals are rare and collective festivals are few; he claimed that in some places there are none at all. He identified a small elliptical region with Delhi at the northwestern focus and Karimpur, Uttar Pradesh, at the southeastern focus as the area without collective festivals.

Fuller is wrong concerning Shanti Nagar, where at least three festivals have collective aspects, as noted above. Wadley (letter to authors, July 2, 1996) pointed out that Karimpur has two collective festivals, Holi and a curing rite. Thus, the northwestern and southeastern foci of the noncollective ellipse are taken out of the picture. There is really no clear reason why this small region in North India should be without collective festivals. Although it is unlikely that a region of any size without any collective festivals could be found, Fuller's discussion has the merit of fixing attention on the fact that villages are important social units with stable populations whose component groups are integrated by various traditional customs and modes of interaction. In short, there is a strong tradition of village unity.

Although Shanti Nagar has no tutelary deity, its inhabitants think of it as a united, distinctive, and quasi-independent social unit. These qualities are expressed in the villagewide system of fictive kinship, some of the rituals of the marriage rite, the jajmani system and other economic activity, and strong efforts to discourage the meddling of outside govermental officials and police officers in village affairs. On the other hand, there are divisive forces. The presence of over a dozen endogamous castes and the sometimes divergent concerns of landless and landowning villagers, which categories are largely coextensive with the important distinction of high and low castes, give rise to occasional clashes of interest. Factionalism is endemic. Reform Hindus do not always see eye to eye with traditional Hindus in religious and ceremonial matters. While the theme of village unity is generally the dominant sentiment during times of danger and may override these internal divisions, its expression in specific cases is by no means automatic or assured. Usually, skillful political activity is needed to overcome disagreement and bring into play any villagewide cooperative effort.

The possibility of internal village conflict brings us to the fourth feature of Akhta that is unique among festivals. It was the only festival that met with opposition. Some villagers may have been uninterested in other festivals, but no other festival was opposed. Akhta, however, became a bone of contention between reform and traditional Hindus. Members of the dominant Jat caste generally followed the doctrines of the Arya Samaj, a monotheistic reform Hindu sect. The Brahmans, the second most numerous and wealthy village caste, were the principal Sanatanis. Conflict between the Samajis and the Sanatanis was basically between Jats and Brahmans.

The principal opponent of Akhta was the leader of the most powerful Jat faction, a highly respected man and one of the strictest Samajis in the village. He wanted villagers to depend solely on inoculation of cattle. He and his sons, who were well educated by the standards of the time, were modern and progressive. One son told us that his father was against Akhta because, if it were held, we Americans would consider them foolish people. For Akhta to be held, the village council had to approve it. As more and more cattle fell ill and five or six bullocks and buffaloes died within a few days, one of the Brahman leaders in the council suggested to the Jat that if Akhta were not held and more animals died, he would receive the blame. If Akhta were observed, no one could blame him for further deaths. In any case, the ceremony would do no harm. The loss of a buffalo or bullock was a major economic loss for even a well-to-do family, and people were worried. The Jat leader accepted the Brahman's suggestion. The village council then met and decided to hold Akhta the following weekend.

A few days before the festival, young men tour the village, asking for money to pay for a feast and a fire ceremony, the closing events of the festival. The village watchman walks through the village a couple of evenings before the festival to announce that Akhta will be held that weekend. This warning allows villagers to arrange their affairs so as not to enter or to leave the village during the festival. For the ritual to be effective, everyone in the village at the time has to participate and observe the various restrictions.

Many activities are forbidden during Akhta. Because iron cannot be touched, plowing is forbidden, no fodder can be cut, and iron buckets cannot be used to draw water. Wheat cannot be baked on the iron griddle, so none is eaten. Salt is not eaten. To refrain from eating wheat, the major item in the village diet, is equivalent to fasting. Sweeping with a broom is banned. The prohibition of the broom and restrictions on the use of the griddle recall similar taboos associated with Guga Naumi. Villagers explain the various restrictions as necessary rituals, similar to prayer, for banishing the disease and most often refer to them as dharma, that is, right, proper, or ethical action.

At sundown on Friday, the village watchman walks through the village beating a drum to announce that Akhta has begun. After dark, four young men, Jats and Brahmans, visit each house and cattle shed to smoke the animals and buildings. One of them, the Brahman exorcist who is said to be good with cattle, carries a pot with smouldering cow dung and *gugal*, incense used in rituals. The other men make certain that the Brahman does not talk or set the pot down during the ritual. On leaving each house, the attendants of the exorcist shout, "Victory to Saint [pir] Ranjha. Victory to Krishna. Victory to Ranjha and Hir." The villagers speak of the ritual with *gugal* as fumigation and believe that the incense has special cleansing and purifying powers. This concept has its basis in the purificatory fire sacrifice of Vedic times, which origin would appeal to both Sanatanis and Samajis. The fact that it accords with Saraswati's advocacy of daily fire worship and his teaching that scented air and water annihilate sickness would serve to strengthen its attractiveness to Samajis (Saraswati, 1956: 64).

The names of Ranjha and Krishna are shouted because both are believed to possess supernatural powers and were good with cattle. The spoken word or name of a deity or saint has supernatural power, for to know the name of anything is to control it (Edgerton, 1965: 116). Stories about the miraculous powers of Krishna and Ranjha are well known in the Delhi area. Krishna is a popular deity, idealized as a protector of cattle and a romantic hero, owing to his love for Radha. Krishna's role as protector of cattle and his supernatural status provide the rationale for his being called upon during Akhta.

Ranjha and Hir, his beloved, were mortals who lived in Punjab some 400 years ago. They are one of the great romantic couples of India, commonly compared to Romeo and Juliet. Ranjha was a young Ranjha Jat called Didho, but he is known almost exclusively by his caste name. Hir was a Rajput. Although both were Muslims, their love was illicit because of the difference in caste. Ranjha learned (or dreamed) of Hir, became a fakir—a religious ascetic or mendicant monk commonly considered to be a wonder-worker—and went in search of her.

Ranjha and Hir fell in love. Her family arranged Hir's marriage to a Rajput. She told Ranjha that she would spend 12 months with her husband's people and return to Ranjha in the 13th month. In the meantime, Ranjha became a follower of Guru Gorakhnath. Ranjha became a jogi (yogi, an ascetic sometimes credited with supernatural powers, or a saint). The couple eloped and were pursued by Hir's father and his allies. Eventually, she was caught and murdered. Her body was placed in a tomb. Ranjha, transformed into a wonder-working saint, arrived at the tomb and prayed that God either bring Hir to life or slay him. It is said that the grave of Hir opened. Ranjha entered and was sealed in the tomb with his beloved, à la Romeo and Juliet (Temple, 1884–1900, 3: xxi).

Ranjha's name has been popularized by Punjabi bards. According to Temple (1884–1900, 2: 507), the object of the legend ". . . is to give a factitious value to Ranjha by making him out to be a wonder-working *faqir* of the type of the greater saints, and rendering the record of his doings as fabulous as possible." Burial alive was at one time the fate of some fakirs. Like Krishna, Ranjha took care of cattle; and his romantic love for Hir is similar to Krishna's love for Radha. Ranjha's similarities to Krishna and to Muslim and Hindu saints, together with the Punjabi belief that Muslim fakirs have miraculous powers for curing cattle, provide sufficient reasons for calling on him along with Krishna during the rites of Akhta (Temple, 1883–1887, 1: 96, 2: 202; 1884–1900, 2: 177–178, 507 ff.; Singh, 1958: 488).

Villagers say that Akhta is based on the legend of Ranjha and Hir, which they know very well. A Brahman man ended his recitation of the tale by making explicit the connection of the festival and the legend: "One day a *bharat* [wedding party] came for Hir's marriage. She said to Ranjha, 'My heart stays with you. Even if I go with another man, I'll not be defiled and I'll return to you.' Then he became kind of crazy and left his cattle. The cattle said, 'How will we pull on?' Ranjha said, 'When you get sick, you can say victory to Hir and Ranjha.' So on Akhta, when we throw smoke and water on the cattle, we say 'Victory to Hir and Ranjha.'" The village shopkeeper, a Samaji, connected the tale to Akhta through the curing power of Ranjha: "Ranjha was fond of animals and cured them with his own medicine. People believe that if they remember Ranjha on this day, their cattle will always be cured. Akhta is always successful."

In the morning and early evening on Saturday and the morning on Sunday, all the village animals except pet dogs and cats—cattle, a camel, donkeys, mules, horses, pigs, and chickens—are gathered at one place at the edge of the village. Then mainly children, many carrying objects associated with cattle—churns for example, drive them in a complete circle around the village. At two points, they pass under rope gateways where men splash the animals and equipment with water. Spectators line the streets, and as the excited animals run pell-mell through the streets and under the gateways, everyone shouts, "Victory to Saint Ranjha. Victory to Krishna. Victory to Ranjha and Hir." Thus, the procession of animals circles the village three times. Circling the village is equivalent to drawing a charmed protective circle around it. After the first procession, women draw a long horizontal line with cow dung on the wall of a building opposite each rope gateway. These lines also symbolize a charmed circle. (Steel, 1882: 36; Crooke, 1968, 1: 103, 142, 2: 41.)

Each time the animals circle the village, the Brahman exorcist trails them carrying the pot of burning cow dung and smoking incense. On Saturday and Sunday mornings, he runs through the herd after the circumambulation and continues across the fields to the land of another village far enough away from Shanti Nagar so that the people suspect nothing, where he buries the pot, thus removing the disease from Shanti Nagar and burying it in another village.[7] The land on which the pot is buried is near a major irrigation canal and most likely belongs to the government rather than to the other village. An attempt to transfer the disease to another village would lead to trouble if discovered.

On Sunday morning after the pot of dung and incense has been buried away from the village, the festival ends with a fire ceremony and feast at the Brahman meeting house. An elderly Brahman, once a professional priest, supervises the preparation of the altar for the fire ceremony while chanting "Victory to Ranjha and Hir, victory to Lord Krishna." During the ceremony of making offerings of ghee, sandalwood, and incense to the fire, Brahmans and Jats chant hymns from a book. Three Brahman men cook and serve rice pudding. Throughout the ceremony, guests come to the feast in groups organized chiefly by caste: first, old Brahman men and upper-caste children, then Chamars and Chuhras. Donations of food to such recipients is normal behavior for Sanatanis, and the Samajis likewise believe that these acts are beneficial and are not begging.

The Samajis accepted without difficulty those rituals of Akhta that did not violate their principles. The value of the fire ceremony is part of Arya-Samaj doctrine, and the associated concluding feast was also acceptable. Some Samajis reinterpreted and rationalized other rituals that conflicted with Arya Samaj principles in order to reduce the discordance. Thus, intrusive spirits are easily thought of as intrusive germs. The son of the Jat leader originally opposed to Akhta commented, "The smoking of the animals will kill the germs. While the men smoke the animals, they don't even talk. That is so that the germs will not be transferred from the animals to the men." The many proscriptions of Akhta are interpreted as the means of assuring the fumigation of all the animals. Samajis ignored the appeals to Krishna, Ranjha, and Hir and rejected the idea that the collection of alms for the feast was the despised begging. The village shopkeeper, a well-informed and thoughtful Samaji, summarized, "I do not follow [Arya Samaj principles] totally, for I believe in Akhta and it is against the principles of the Arya Samaj. When the animals are sick, one has to believe what is going to cure them, so I believe in Akhta." (See R. Freed and S. Freed, 1966, for a further discussion of Akhta.)

In 1977–78, people told us that Akhta had not been observed for four or five years. Since Akhta is held only in case of need, it is not clear if this relatively long period of abandonment is temporary, needing only a sharp increase in cattle disease for the festival's resurrection, or if Akhta has fallen into permanent desuetude. Although belief and ritual are tenacious, Akhta appears to be vulnerable. Modern medical treatment reduces the danger of cattle disease. The Government of India has a program for providing inoculations for cattle. Often unsure of how to obtain governmental aid or finding the procedures inconvenient, villagers did not always make effective use of governmental programs. However in 1977–78, local assistance was available. A village Jat, a veterinarian, worked for the government and advised villagers how to benefit from the programs for cattle. Thus modern medicine was in competition with exorcism, but this does not necessarily mean that the veterinarian will displace the bhagat and that exorcism will die out. In the case of human disease, Ayurveda (traditional medicine), exorcism, and Western allopathic medicine are all used, often by the same individual or family. People will try anything that appears to work when they are sick. The same reasoning would apply to cattle disease.

It is not so much competition from modern medical treatment that will lead to the demise of Akhta, if indeed it happens, but rather the inconvenience of the festival and the opposition of the Samajis. Closing the village for almost two days in modern times is a great inconvenience. Employment, visits to medical facilities, and other necessary business may mean that people have to leave the village during Akhta. On Sundays, many people like to take advantage of the holiday to visit relatives. And the population of the village was larger in 1977–78 than in 1958–59, which would heighten the difficulty of persuading everyone to observe onerous restrictions.

In such a situation where circumstances may have brought a custom to the verge of extinction or, at least, of drastic change, one determined individual can make a difference. A Mali Gardener told us that Akhta was celebrated for "many years" after we left the village in 1959. Then a Jat man whom we call Reformer (R. Freed and S. Freed, 1993: 113–114), a resolute Samaji, "broke it down" by violating the restrictions. The Mali said that if even one person violates the taboos, Akhta cannot be held. What happened was of course much more complicated than the Mali's brief comment. Reformer himself told us what he did to try to put an end to Akhta, or at least to modify it considerably.

According to Reformer, in 1960 or 1961 the "whole village" attended a meeting at the Jat *chopal* (men's meeting house) the day before Akhta. Discussion focused on the strict requirements of the festival: the closure of the village, the dietary restrictions, and the ban on handling iron. Reformer spoke at some length, pointing out that people lose time from work or may have to consult doctors. When one is sick, eating rice may be harmful.[8] He argued that smoking the whole village was foolish and suggested instead that people stop smoking the hookah, which polluted the air. He denounced the practice of transferring the disease to another village, for one should not harm other people. He offered to let them bury the disease in his own house. Finally, he declared that if the rules were not changed, he would perform every forbidden act on Akhta. People discussed these points and then dispersed without agreeing to Reformer's suggestions.

On Saturday (Akhta), Reformer made good his threat. He drew water from an iron handpump, washed his buffalo with water from an iron bucket, and his wife cooked wheat bread on the griddle. The villagers sent the watchman to summon Reformer to a meeting in front of his house. This step meant that the matter was serious, and Reformer knew it. He commented that "The village is equal to God." However, he was uncowed. He asked, "Why have you come to my house? I am very sad because of it." They replied that he had cooked chapatis (bread) and done other things and was planning to break the prohibition against leaving the village. He replied that anyone who wants to eat chapatis can do so. The villagers asked him questions, he answered and then asked them questions. The villagers conceded that he had taken a useful position and then asked him to accompany them in Ram's (God's) work for the village. He answered that he would cooperate in work that was good but not in bad work. They said that he was very obstinate and a staunch Sama-ji. They dispersed, commenting that talking to him was a waste of time.

As they were leaving, he took his bicycle and followed them down the street on his way out of the village. They saw him, stopped, and asked a strong young Jat to take Reformer's bicycle and beat him. The young Jat abused him in a loud voice and threatened him. Reformer moved his bicycle so that the handle touched his antagonist, thus making him guilty of violating the taboo against touching iron. Reformer said, "If anyone touches me, I'll give him a sound beating." Reformer was a strong young man and capable of giving a good account of himself in any fight. By this time, the crowd was in front of the Jat *chopal*. Reformer said that he would leave his bicycle at the *chopal* for three days and dared anyone to take it. He returned home. The villagers took an oath that if Reformer filed a lawsuit over the bicycle, they would stand united and refuse to say what had happened to the bicycle. The watchman then returned the bicycle to Reformer's house. Reformer mounted his bicycle and left the village for work. He was only a half hour late.

The next day, the villagers again called a meeting and decided that Reformer should be fined. He defended himself on the grounds that he was no liar and had told them what he would do before Akhta was held. He announced his willingness to accept punishment, but said that he would not participate in "misdeeds," as he described Akhta, in the future. We do not know how much Reformer was fined, but the usual fine for violating Akhta was five rupees. Two Jats offered to pay the fine, but Reformer said that he would pay. After these events, villagers all said that Reformer was an obstinate man who heeded no one.

Reformer said that after his one-man protest, Akhta was not held for many years. Even when it did take place, it was a "minor" affair. The cattle were driven around the village and the ritual of exorcism, or fumigation, was carried out. But he said that the taboos were not observed. Villagers told Reformer that if he would cooperate, they would hold Akhta again. He replied that he was with them in doing good deeds. People should pave the floors of the cattle sheds with brick, keep the sheds and their houses clean, have their cattle inoculated, and use latrines. Reformer said, "If you don't do these things and stick to the old system, you will remain underdeveloped."

Reformer was capable of forcing significant changes in a major festival because the restrictions were defined in such a way that violation by a single person could undermine the effectiveness of the festival. Reformer was not working in isolation. He represented the Samaji point of view and thus enjoyed considerable support, as shown by the two Jat Samajis who offered to pay his fine. Although modern times and the Arya Samaj may be against Akhta, exorcism and the theory of disease that it represents retain their hold. Akhta could continue to be held in modified form for the forseeable future.

KARVA CHAUTH

Women, mainly twice-born Brahmans and Baniyas, celebrate Karva Chauth (Pitcher Fourth) for the welfare and long lives of their husbands. In Shanti Nagar, the festival is observed on Karttik *badi* 3, which fell on October 30, near the end of a very busy agricultural season when, among other activities, wheat, the most important rabi crop, is being sown. The inconsistency between the name of the festival (Fourth) and its date (the third) comes to light when one determines the date of observance, the third, by counting from the full moon. The discrepancy is not confined to Shanti Nagar. Marriott (1955: 192, table 1) says that in Kishan Garhi, Uttar Pradesh, the festival is held on the third. However, in Karimpur, Uttar Pradesh, the festival is observed on the fourth (Wadley, 1975: 160; Wiser and Wiser, 1930: 42). Five studies of Delhi villages (Lewis, 1958: 217; Bhatia, 1961: 66; Luthra, 1961: 70; Nautiyal, 1961: 167; and Ratta, 1961: 165) give the festival's date as the fourth. We were told that in metropolitan Delhi, the festival is held on the fourth.

When questioned about the date of the festival, five informants named the third, four said the fourth, and two said that the festival began on the third and ended on the fourth. One caste difference was reported. A Potter boy claimed that his family observed the festival on the fourth, but we have no observational confirmation of his statement. Other Potters did not celebrate Karva Chauth, saying that no Brahman woman would come to recite the story. Except for two or three families of recent Jat immigrants from Delhi and possibly one Chhipi family who celebrate on the fourth, the rest of the villagers of Shanti Nagar who observe Karva Chauth do so on the third.

A few villagers suggested explanations based on astronomy for the apparent inconsistency in dates. One of the astronomical explanations, mentioned by two informants, is that the festival begins on the third but that the final ritual takes place on the fourth. That is, on the weekday of Karttik *badi* 3 when the festival was held, the third lunar day was current at sunrise, hence the solar day until the next sunrise was the third, but the lunar day ended before moonrise. Much of the ritual takes place in the afternoon, but the final and perhaps the most important rituals, an offering of water to the moon and the breaking of an all-day fast, occur after moonrise. If the third lunar day ended before moonrise, then our informants were correct about the festival's overlapping the two lunar days. Another informant speculated that the inconsistency about dates was due to the possibility of a deleted day. If the fourth lunar day happened to be a deleted day, then a festival scheduled for the fourth would be celebrated on the third. The late Thomas D. Nicholson, former chairman of the Hayden Planetarium at the American Museum of Natural History, made the appropriate astronomical calculations to check these two possibilities for 1958, and neither occurred.

Of the astronomical explanations, only the one suggesting that Karva Chauth straddles two lunar days seemed to offer any possibility for explaining, over a period of many years, the discrepancy between the name of the festival and the date of its observance. Neil de Grasse Tyson checked this possibility both for 1958 and 1977. In 1958, the angular separation of the sun and moon along the ecliptic at moonrise on October 30 was 212°. Therefore, all the rituals of Karva Chauth took place on the third. However, in 1977, the angular separation at moonrise was 221°, hence Karva Chauth straddled the third and the fourth.[9] The women offered water to the moon and broke their fasts on the fourth. To extrapolate from these two calculations, it

would seem that the considerable calendric variation from year to year would eliminate an astronomical explanation for the displacement of Karva Chauth from the
fourth to the third.

A possible explanation involves the belief that dark fourths and dark eighths
are inauspicious days. Suffused with menace and misfortune, they are thought to
portend evil. Three festivals of welfare and protection that might be expected to take
place on these days are in fact celebrated on the previous day. Karva Chauth is
observed on the third rather than on the fourth. Hoi and Sili Sat take place on the
seventh instead of on the eighth. The reason for thinking that the fourth and the
eighth would be the appropriate days is that the worship of various forms of Shiva
and of deities associated with him traditionally takes place on bright and dark
fourths and eighths. The three festivals are linked to Shiva either directly or through
a related deity.

Wiser and Wiser (1930: 179) said that the fast on Karva Chauth is in honor of
Ganesh, Shiva's son. At moonrise, the fast is broken and the moon is worshipped.
Underhill (1991: 137) called Karttik *badi* 4, Samkashta Chaturthi (Difficult Fourth).
The name refers to Ganesh as the remover of difficulties or obstacles, hence one of
his names is Obstacle Remover. The worship of Ganesh and the moon have tended
to merge. Worshippers of the moon fast until dark on both light and dark fourths.
Devotees of Ganesh fast on the same days and worship him in the dark fortnight at
moonrise (Underhill, 1991: 69). Thus, the worship of the moon and Ganesh are
merged on Karva Chauth.

Hoi, the name of a festival and of a mother goddess worshipped for the long life
and welfare of children, is celebrated on Karttik *badi* 7. However, one might expect
it to be observed on the eighth, because the goddesses Durga and Kali are worshipped
on bright and dark eights respectively. All goddesses are aspects of Shakti (Power),
the consort of Shiva. Pathak (1976: 1156) gave the date of Hoi as Karttik *badi* 8, the
day set aside for the worship of Kala Bhairava and Kali Bhairavi, Shiva's consort.
They are terrible aspects of Shiva and Kali, which are linked to Yama, God of Death
(cf., Dowson, 1891: 86, 140, 143; Underhill, 1991: 96).

On Sili Sat (Cold Seventh), mother goddesses are propitiated for the protection
of children. These mother goddesses are aspects of Kali and represent various diseases, most prominently the poxes, such as smallpox, that affect children. One
might expect a festival for these goddesses to be held on the eighth. However, the
festival, as the name implies, is observed on the seventh, a day in advance of the
inauspicious dark eighth.

Thus Karva Chauth seems to take part in a general tendency for festivals of
protection and welfare to avoid inauspicious days. This tendency, as suggested by
only three festivals, is by no means confirmed. However, it is worthy of consideration. In any case, it does offer an explanation for the discrepancy between the name
of Karva Chauth and the day of its celebration.

The chief elements of Karva Chauth are a fast, a session when Brahman women
recite the story of Karva Chauth, offerings to the sun and moon, breaking the fast,
and gifts of pots and food to husbands and in-laws. A few days before Karva Chauth,
young married women go to the Kumhar Potters for pots to be used in the festival.

One kind of pot, decorated and filled with water, is the focus of the worship that follows the storytelling session. The other kind of pot has a small spout. Women fill some of these pots with *khil* (popped rice) and sweets and give them to their in-laws. Most of the pots used as gifts are made of sugar (fig. 13). They are purchased from the Baniya's shop. A dozen or more may be given to in-laws or distributed to castemates and neighbors.

The evening before the day of the festival, wives eat a good meal to prepare for the fast. After preparing the pots, nothing is done until midafternoon when groups of fasting wives gather to hear the story of Karva Chauth. The storyteller is usually an older Brahman woman with a living husband. In one instance, a young woman told the story because the senior woman in her family was a widow.

According to an elderly Brahman man,[10] the story of Karva Chauth is part of the Ramayana. Anasuya, the wife of a rishi named Atri, told the tale to Sita, in which were spelled out the duties of a wife to her husband. Although Anasuya does depict the ideal role of a wife for Sita's benefit, she does not recount the myth of Karva Chauth. However, her lyrical description of the wifely role could be taken as the charter for a festival whose purpose is to insure the long life and welfare of husbands. "[A] husband, Vaidehi [Sita], is an unlimited blessing; and vile is the wife who does not pay him reverence. . . . Her one religious duty, her one vow and penance consist in a devotion, in thought and word and deed to her husband's feet" (Growse, 1883: 425).

FIG. 13. Display of *karva*s made of sugar at a Brahman's house, 1977.

FIG. 14. Storytelling session in a Brahman's house on Karva Chauth, 1977. Wives drop wheat and barley shoots into two brass *lota*s, of which only one is visible here.

Marriott (1955: 206) suggested several other Sanskritic sources for the festival of Karva Chauth, or parts of it, but felt that such speculation goes "... beyond what is conscious or relevant to villagers today." He concluded that Karva Chauth is "... an original, if not pristine, contribution of the regional little tradition in its creative aspect." Marriott is clearly correct. However, our literate Brahman informant did suggest a Sanskritic source for Karva Chauth. His way of thinking may have been more common in the 1950s than we suspected, and it probably is even more common today with the great increase in literacy. Nonetheless, the suggested association of Karva Chauth with the Ramayana is an ahistorical conjunction. It is based only on the theme of ideal conjugal roles. There are no details either in the rural myth as told in Shanti Nagar or in ritual practice to support the idea that Karva Chauth represents a devolution from the Ramayana or, in all likelihood, from any Sanskritic source.

In 1958, we attended a storytelling session in a Brahman's house. Present were seven women from four Brahman families and some dozen children. The storyteller was a woman 22 years old. She and the other women sat on the ground around a small metal pitcher or pot (*lota*) containing water, into which they dropped a few grains of bajra (a millet) from time to time to emphasize incidents in the story. In 1977 wheat was often used, as were barley shoots (fig. 14). In this version of the story, the number seven crops up in two episodes. There are seven brothers, and to bring her dead husband to life, the brothers' sister had to remove thorns for seven months. The number seven, usually connected with marriage, is auspicious. The young storyteller's version was the longest that we collected.

There was a king with seven sons and one daughter. After the daughter was married, she fasted on Karva Chauth. She was at the home of her parents and was the beloved of them all so her brothers usually would not eat before her. None of them could eat because she was fasting until the moon came up. They did not know when it would come up, but usually it was late so one brother went into the distance and lit a fire in the bush. Another said to his sister, "Look sister, there's the moon coming up." When she saw the moon, she offered water to it. Then all the brothers and their sister sat down to eat.

The gods became angry because she ate without completing the fast since the moon had not yet risen. As a result, her husband, a king's son, died just as she took one or two morsels. She started crying and began to run toward her marital village. Her mother said, "Press the legs of everybody you meet on the way."[11] On her way she met an old cow and pressed its legs. The old cow blessed her and said, "May your husband live long." She said, "Why give that blessing? My husband is dead. Tell me a way in which the blessing may be fulfilled." The cow said, "Your husband is not quite dead. He is tied up in thorns. Take them out." The girl went to her husband and took out thorns for seven months. Two thorns were left, which held his mouth shut. The girl had grown tired. When a beggar woman came along, the girl said to her, "I'm tired, sit in my place while I rest." The beggar woman did so and removed the two thorns. When the prince regained consciousness, the beggar woman said, "I'm your wife." When the girl returned, she found the beggar woman had become queen. She asked, "Why?" The beggar woman said, "That is that, and I'll be the queen." Then the beggar woman lived as the real wife and had the real wife sent to the palace as a maid.

One day the prince, who had become king, planned to go to a fair and asked the beggar woman, his queen, if she wanted anything. She was a mean person, low and crude reflecting her caste, and asked for onions to eat with bread. [Onions are eaten by *tamoguna*, people who are characterized by the quality of tamas (darkness, dullness, inactivity) (R. Freed and S. Freed, 1993: 47–48)]. Then the king said, "Ask the maid if she wants anything." The beggar woman said, "I can't check with a maid to see if she wants anything." So the king asked. The maid said, "Get me an image or a photograph of Krishna. The king brought back onions and an image of Krishna. The beggar woman ate the onions, and the maid kept the image with her and told her troubles to it every night. The king was curious and eavesdropped. One evening he asked what she told the image every night. She said she only told about her suffering and her husband. Then she told him the whole story, including the beggar woman's taking her place as the queen. The king heard it all and made her his queen and buried the beggar woman half way down into the ground. He was angry with her for taking his wife's place so she finally got her place.

A 40-year-old Brahman recounted another version of the story in 1958. Although the details differ and the incident of the beggar woman replacing the queen is omitted, the plot and motif are similar. She said that the events of Karva Chauth happened in the Age of Truth when wives had only one husband and were devoted to him. She learned the story from wise elderly people, first in her parents' house and later from her mother-in-law. Now she tells the story to younger women.

> A king had seven sons and one daughter. The daughter and her sisters-in-law were fasting. Her brothers went to their mother and asked, "Will our sister eat if she sees the moon"? Their mother replied that she would. So they built a fire and held up a white sheet and a round strainer. They pointed to the light shining through the sheet and strainer and told their sister that the moon had risen. They did this because they had eaten and they wanted their sister to eat. She ate. The first bite had a hair in it. There was a fly in the second bite. With the third bite, the news came that her husband had died. She cried and wanted to go to her husband. Her mother said, "Press the legs of whomever you meet." The first thing that she saw was a tortoise skull with water in it. She put water on her forefinger and little finger, which she pierced so that it bled. She sprinkled water and blood on her husband's corpse.[12] Her husband arose crying, "Hari, Hari [God, God], I've slept a long time." She replied, "You think that you have been just sleeping. I've been slaving here all this time."

In 1977, a 74-year-old Brahman grandmother, a widow, recited a rather chaotic version of the story, which, in many of its details, was like the version presented just above. The woman said that she had been telling the story for 50 years and had learned it from her father's mother and father's sister. The episode of a low-caste woman usurping the queen's role reappears. One detail of this version is particularly noteworthy. Shiva and Parvati make an appearance, and it is Shiva, rather than the wife, who restores her husband to life. The participation of the great god Shiva and Parvati, his wife, directly establishes the connection of Karva Chauth with Shiva rather than by indirectly tracing a link through Ganesh, Shiva's son. Although this version of the legend was told by an old woman, the presence of the two Sanskritic deities may be due to Karva Chauth having become somewhat Sanskritized since 1958. The episode of Lingam worship that we saw in 1977 (see below) also supports this suggestion. However, it is best to be cautious in interpreting variation among a few versions of a myth in terms of change over time, even though 19 years separate the first two versions from the third one.

> A king had a married daughter and seven married sons. The daughter kept the fast for her husband on Karva Chauth. The brothers asked their mother about the fast, and she told them that their sister could not eat until after moonrise. While their sister was fasting, her brothers made a fake

moon so that she broke her fast and started to eat with them. There was a hair in the first bite, a fly in the second, and when she took her third bite, she learned that her husband had died. She then prepared to go to her in-laws to take care of her husband's body. Her mother told her that along the way she should touch everyone's feet. She did. Then she served her husband's body for one year. On the next Karva Chauth, all the other married women kept a fast but she sat in a corner and cried.

Shiva and Parvati had come down to earth. Parvati heard the woman crying and told Shiva to help her. Shiva then cut one of his fingers and sprinkled his blood over the dead body. The king [the woman's dead husband] then rose from his death bed. Parvati told the queen [the wife of the man risen from the dead] to dress up and keep her fast. She did so and prepared *khir* and puris.

No one except the queen knew about her husband's return from the dead. The king's mother and sisters told the maid servant to take some oil to the queen, and they all cursed the queen because she had eaten their son [and brother] away.

When the maid servant went on her errand, she saw that the queen had prepared all sorts of sweets and that the king was sitting beside her. She immediately left and told the whole family that the king was now alive.

The maid wanted to cheat so she started acting as the queen and the real queen was thrown out of the palace. The real queen then served a lame cow for seven years. Married women were not supposed to use needles on Karva Chauth, but the real queen was told to use needles. When she did, they pierced her husband's body so she was very sad. She took the needles out of his body. Then the king knew that the maid servant had acted falsely as his queen and she was thrown out of the kingdom and he got his queen back.

In the versions of the story from Shanti Nagar, only the brothers deceive their sister. In Kishan Garhi, Marriott (1955: 204) collected several versions in which the wife of one of the brothers is involved in the plot. In some of the murals that are drawn on the festival (murals are not drawn for the festival in Shanti Nagar), she is shown hanging by her heels in punishment. Channa (1984: 40, 115) also recounted a version in which crafty husbands' sisters participate in the deceit.

Channa classified Karva Chauth and three other festivals for mother goddesses (Hoi, Sakat, and the fast for Santoshi Mata) as women's festivals. They highlight four important and tension-filled relationships that a woman enters at marriage: namely with her husband, mother-in-law, husband's sister, and husband's brother's wife. In this view, Karva Chauth is for Karva Chauth Mata. In the myth of each festival, the younger innocent woman suffers at the hands of the older one. Thus, Karva Chauth, which is for the welfare of husbands, also has a subtheme of tension between sisters-in-law.

However, in Shanti Nagar the myth focuses only on a woman's husband and

FIG. 15. Ritual after the storytelling session of Karva Chauth, 1977. Two married women are on the left. One covers her head because she is in her husband's village. The younger wife is bareheaded, for she is in her natal village. The older woman pours water over the hands of the younger wife and over a Lingam, a short wooden post, emblem of Shiva.

brothers, who love her. Their duplicity is largely based on their concern for her welfare, for they do not know that her husband will die if she breaks her fast. The beggar or maid who usurps the role of queen is not a relative. In any case, a woman observes the festival in Shanti Nagar solely for the welfare of her husband.

After the storytelling session, the women, who had not dropped all their millet into the *lota* during the session, tied the remainder in the corners of their headcloths. Then all the women went outside into the lane to worship the sun. A 55-year-old woman carried the *lota*. She poured water over her glass bracelets, and the other women held their hands under the stream of water. Glass bracelets are symbols that a woman is *suhagan*—that is, she has a living husband. The women stood together in the lane, mumbled a few words, and looked at the sun while pouring water on the ground as an offering (*argha*). After this brief ceremony, the fasting women could drink water. The women then went back inside the house and pressed the legs of the oldest woman, a Brahman widow, as a sign of respect. Then the group broke up, and women went singing to their homes for additional worship.

We observed a 1977 enactment of this ritual that was significantly different from the 1958 version. We attended the storytelling session at the home of a Brahman family, which was similar to the session that we saw in 1958. After the session, women went into the street to offer water to the sun. The water was poured over the women's hands, as in 1958, but then also over a Lingam (fig. 15). We inferred that the women intended to worship Shiva as well as the sun, but we did not question them on the point. It is possible that the myth we collected in 1977, in which Shiva played a prominent role, and this apparent worship of the Lingam indicate a connection of Karva Chauth and Shiva worship that was not apparent in 1958.

After the offering to the sun in 1958, we accompanied two Brahman sisters, married to two brothers, to their home where they had freshly plastered their kitchen floor with cow dung. In the corner of the kitchen were two pots of water, one for each of the sisters. A red string (nala) was tied around the lip of each pot. Serving as covers were two saucerlike dishes filled with millet (fig. 16). A small tin of turmeric (haldi) was on top of one of the pots. One sister took the tin, moistened the turmeric, and with her finger drew several swastikas around the necks of the pots. Then she put a tilak (dot) of turmeric on the forehead of all present as a form of blessing. Next she circled her own pitcher with millet and water several times. Repeating "Ram, Ram," she alternately touched the pot and her own forehead four times. She said, "When I worship the pitcher, it's like worshipping Ram [God]." She uttered a brief prayer, "As the Karva Chauth has come to me, so may it come to everyone in the world." She said that the pot did not represent her husband.[13]

After attending the ritual in the home of the two sisters, we visited a few other Brahman families. At one home, there was neither a red thread nor haldi marks on the pots. Instead of millet, wheat and also a banana were in the saucers on top of the pots. Both sweets and fruit could serve as gifts on Karva Chauth. At yet another family, the words uttered during the offering to the sun were, "May the number of men in the family increase as the ants increase." During this ritual, all the women touched a silver bracelet. None of our informants named any deity as the object of worship and no one recited mantras. At one house, we asked the senior woman what god they worshipped when they worshipped the pots. She replied, "There is only one God. What shall I say." Trying to be helpful, her son suggested that she say Sat Narayan (Vishnu).

In the evening, we returned to the home of the two sisters, just as the moon was rising. Each sister took a lota of water, faced the moon, and silently poured the water on the ground as an offering. The ritual took no longer than 30 seconds. The women could then break their fast.

None of our informants identified Shiva, Parvati, or Ganesh as the deity of Karva Chauth. Neither Marriott nor Lewis mentioned Shiva worship as a feature of the festival. The four 1961 Census of India studies of Delhi villages that note the observance of the festival say only that it is for the welfare of husbands. No deities other than the sun and moon are mentioned. From these seven cases it would seem that villagers make no connection between Karva Chauth and Shiva (Marriott, 1955: 203–206; Lewis, 1958: 217–218; Bhatia, 1961: 66; Luthra, 1961: 70–71; Nautiyal, 1961: 167; and Ratta, 1961: 165).

In urban Hinduism, however, the connection is explicit. The contrast of village and city becomes clear when one compares a housewife's mural drawn for Karva Chauth in Kishan Garhi with Channa's sketch, in all likelihood based on a commercial lithograph. The village drawing depicts chiefly two moons and episodes from the festival story, such as the portrayal of one of the brothers standing on a ladder to hold up a circular sieve and a Potter woman carrying a load of *karva*s. In addition to the sun and the moon, the urban lithograph represents Karva Mata and a family scene with Shiva, Parvati, and Ganesh, all resting on a Shiva Lingam with lamps on either side, and various episodes from the festival story. Although in the village Karva Chauth is essentially a festival of the little tradition, in the city it is firmly connected to the great tradition (Marriott, 1955: 205; Channa, 1984: 125–126).

Married women observe Karva Chauth to avoid the dread status of widowhood. Brahman and Baniya women are the principal participants in the festival. By caste custom although not by law, they cannot remarry, or suffer considerable disapproval if they do, so their widowhood is usually permanent. Thus, any festival for the welfare of husbands takes on heightened importance for these women. Widows of other castes may remarry.

Participants in Karva Chauth are not limited to Brahman and Baniya women. Any woman may celebrate the festival, and informants told us that a few non-twice-born women observed it. However, we never saw the ritual performed other than by Brahmans. On one occasion (on the third day) when we were told that the women of a non-twice-born family would perform the ritual, we said that we would go to see it, whereupon, an informant quickly said that it would be celebrated the next day (the fourth). Despite never having visually confirmed the participation of castes

FIG. 16. Brahman woman worshipping pots on Karva Chauth, 1958.

other than Brahmans, we think that observance among the Kumhar Potters may have been common and that a few other families, owing to close relationships with Brahmans or to other special family circumstances, may also have held the ceremony.

The wife of the village Chhipi Tailor said she always observed Karva Chauth on the fourth. When she lived in her husband's village (from which they had recently moved), a Brahman woman usually told the story on Karva Chauth. She received half a seer of grain in payment (about half a kilogram). A Bairagi woman celebrated the day in her natal village in Punjab, but in Shanti Nagar, her husband's village, her in-laws would not permit her to do so. Other Bairagis said that they followed the Jats of the Mann *gotra* and did not celebrate Karva Chauth. The Mann Jats, devotees of the Arya Samaj, often set the tone for much of village life.

Four families of Jats of a different *gotra*, Mehlawit, had recently moved to the village from Delhi. They had been influenced by their long urban residence, so much so that perhaps half of this group observed Karva Chauth. One man said that his family celebrated Karva Chauth on the fourth day. Another man denied that his family observed the festival.

A Nai Barber family celebrated the day. This family was very friendly with the Brahmans whom they served and tended to follow their customs, even to the extent of avoiding widow remarriage. Two family members who had been widowed at an early age could have married each other but did not do so, in line with the custom of their Brahman patrons. In this view, the observance of Karva Chauth would be an extension of a pattern of imitating the Brahmans.

At least some of the Potter families in all probability observed Karva Chauth. They furnished pots for the festival, which involved them in it to some extent. In 1958, a Potter's wife said her family observed the festival, but another woman added that although she also celebrated Karva Chauth, no Brahman woman would come to tell them the story. Not all Brahmans were willing to provide ritual services for a caste as low as the Kumhars. However, a storyteller of their own caste could fill the role, which a Brahman man told us was the case. In a survey that we took in 1978, a Potter's wife said that Potters observed the day, and she provided a brief description of their ritual. In Rampur, a village close to Shanti Nagar, Lewis (1958:217) listed the participants in Karva Chauth as Brahmans, Baniyas, and Kumhars.

Gifts from a wife and her family to her husband and his family are a feature of Karva Chauth. The gifts include food, especially sweets in the form of sugar *karva*s, clothes, and cash, perhaps one rupee or Rs. 1.25. The main recipients are the husband, who receives a large cloth (*chaddar*) and a large *karva* filled with *khir* or sweets, and his mother, who is often given a woman's complete costume (*til* or *tirh*) consisting of a skirt, shirt, and headcloth.

In 1958, the family of the two Brahman sisters, whose ritual is described above, received a typical gift from their daughter-in-law's family: two women's outfits and two pairs of glass bangles for the sisters, a large cloth for the husband, a small metal pitcher full of *khir*, cash, and 15 sugar *karva*s that they broke into pieces and distributed to friends, including Jats, Brahmans, Baniyas, Jhinvar Watercarriers, and Barbers. There were two costumes and two sets of glass bangles so that each of the sisters were given similar gifts. A Barber woman brought the gifts, but the daughter-in-law's brother could also have served as messenger. Carrying gifts between families on ceremonial occasions was still one of the traditional occupations of the Nai Barbers.

In this case, the gift was reciprocal. The family of the two sisters sent an even more valuable gift to their in-laws: a large pot, sweets, and considerable clothing. Because they had given more than they had received, they expected to receive a "busload of presents" when next their daughter-in-law returned from her parental home, where she was currently visiting.

The celebration of Karva Chauth in Pahansu, a village in western Uttar Pradesh, resembles the festival in Shanti Nagar (Raheja, 1988: 181–183). However, a few details are different, which led Raheja to inferences about the meaning of the rituals that do not fit the practices that we observed in Shanti Nagar. The key ritual difference is that in Pahansu, a wife touches the end of her garment to a tray of food. Any inauspiciousness afflicting her husband is said to be transferred to the food, which, in turn, the wife gives to her husband's mother or father. To summarize Raheja's highly nuanced discussion, the wife in effect transfers inauspiciousness from her husband to his parents. When Raheja asked the villagers for an explanation of the parents' behavior, they replied only that it was the duty of the parents to accept the offering.

In Shanti Nagar the wife reverentially touches the pot of water rather than a tray of food. She worships the pot. The gesture of touching is honorific and deferential, comparable to pressing the legs or touching the feet of an individual. As for the gifts to in-laws, they are clearly to be understood as gifts from a wife's family to her husband's family. Such gifts are common throughout the year. The transfer of inauspiciousness plays no role at all.

Raheja (1988: 182–183) analyzed the myth of Karva Chauth from the same perspective, that is, as a transfer of inauspiciousness. She presented one version of the myth in which the last four lines represent the key to her interpretation: After the wife's ministrations had restored her husband to life, she returned to her brothers' house. On the way to her temporarily dead husband, she had touched all the men and trees that she encountered. The men had fallen ill and the trees had withered. On her return journey, the trees became green and the men recovered their health when they saw her. However, there are problems with this interpretation. It apparently was the wife's service to her dead husband rather than the transfer of inauspiciousness to the men and trees along the road that led to the husband's recovery. What led to the later recovery of the men and trees is not clear. The inauspiciousness that had been transferred to them was not transferred elsewhere.

We suggest that Temple's concept of the "life index" offered a better interpretation of the myth than did Raheja's transfer of inauspiciousness.

> A corollary also to the idea of temporary death is the notion of the life index, which may be defined as an object very difficult of access existing outside the life of every human being which faithfully indicates his fortunes and the restoration of which, when injured, to its pristine condi-

tion, restores to life. It may be anything, a bird which droops when the
connected life is in danger, loses a wing to an arm, a leg to a leg, feathers
to skin, and so on, and dies when the life dies; or a sword which rusts
when the life is diseased and falls to pieces when the life dies, but when
it is put together the life comes back and when polished up the life is
again healthy [Temple, 1884–1900, 1: xvii].

In this view, the men and trees are the living index of the woman's husband.
When he dies, they sicken or die; when he recovers, they recover. The living index
is chiefly a storyteller's device, which is useful in constructing a myth and adds a
melodramatic touch.

Hoi

Mothers worship Hoi Mata for the welfare of children on Karttik *badi* 7, four days
after Karva Chauth, which is observed for the welfare of husbands. Hoi Mata is
believed to give fertility to women. The ritual and mythology of Hoi closely resemble those of Karva Chauth. Women with children fast, a storyteller recites the myth
of Hoi Mata, the women pray to the Mata, an offering of water is made to the sun,
the fast is broken, and presents are distributed, principally to mothers-in-law. This
ritual sequence is similar to that followed on Karva Chauth.

The myths of Hoi and Karva Chauth emphasize comparable themes. In each
case a taboo is violated, punishment follows, and selfless service restores all losses.
In the myth of Karva Chauth, the chief penalty is the temporary loss of a husband,
restored to life by the devotion of his wife. In the Hoi myth, it is the loss of fertility, which is tantamount to losing a husband. All losses are recovered by service to a
cow. The taboo common to both festivals is the prohibition of digging in the ground.
While this is the key taboo on Hoi, it is merely recognized on Karva Chauth, but
plays no role in the myth. Villagers say that although one must not dig, a man may
still plow. Both holidays take place at a busy agricultural season for men, who must
work in the fields.

The relationship of a mother with her children, phrased in terms of a mother's
concern for her children's long life and welfare, is the reason for worshipping Hoi
Mata. In the myth, this relationship appears as a woman's desire for fertility. Her
womb is taken away and she wants it back. Rather than the mother-child or woman-
fertility theme, Channa (1984: 40) stressed the relationship between husband's sister
and husband's brothers' wives. Channa's analyses of the myths of Karva Chauth and
Hoi emphasized the duplicity of seven brothers' wives who betray their husbands'
only sister. In the myth of Karva Chauth, the sister is the victim. However, in the
Hoi myth, one of the brothers' wives volunteers to endure the punishment in place
of her sister-in-law from fear of, or in consideration of, her mother-in-law. In Shanti
Nagar, deceitful husband's brothers' wives play no role in the myth of Karva Chauth,
but their treachery is an essential element in the Hoi myth.

As in the case of Karva Chauth, the dating of Hoi is somewhat ambiguous.
Almost everyone we questioned in 1977 said that it takes place on the seventh,

although a few informants claimed that some people observed it on the sixth, others, on the seventh. Lewis (1958: 218), Nautiyal (1961: 167), and Luthra (1961: 71), writing about other Delhi villages, reported the date as the seventh. Pathak (1976: 1156) and Channa (1984: 113) dated Hoi on the eighth. We checked the date with a Brahman who consulted his almanac. According to the almanac, the festival was observed on the seventh solar (civil) day, but the seventh lunar day ended at 7:37 A.M., which meant that the ritual in the afternoon took place on the eighth lunar day. In 1977, a comparable situation obtained for Karva Chauth, celebrated four days before Hoi.

Our comments about dates and inauspicious days as they concern Karva Chauth (vide supra) are also applicable to Hoi. In brief, we think that the avoidance of an inauspicious day when it is a question of a festival of welfare is to be preferred to an astronomical explanation. The inauspiciousness of dark eighths is constant, whereas in some years the astronomical explanation may hold good but not in other years. Villagers who celebrated on the sixth solar day probably carried out the ritual on the seventh lunar day. In any case, we accept overwhelming village opinion, supported by our observations, that Hoi is observed on Karttik *badi* 7.

All castes observe Hoi. On the eve of the festival, women plaster their cookstoves and kitchen floors with cow dung and cook festive food for the children. Senior women draw multicolored murals of Hoi Mata on the walls of their houses (fig. 17). A few Jats have the wife of their Brahman *purohit* (family priest) draw their Hoi Mata.

The depictions of Hoi Mata (figs. 17–26) are well drawn as compared to the rough sketches of Guga Naumi (figs. 5–12). The goddess is represented with two arms, two legs, and a square open body surmounted by a head, sometimes realistically depicted, sometimes in the form of a simple triangle. Female figures are always visible inside the body of the goddess. A cow, sometimes with a calf, may also be drawn inside the body. Figures of birds, which resemble peacocks or perhaps parrots, may be inside the square body, attached to the exterior corners of the square, or drawn completely outside the Mata. The sun and moon are depicted outside the Mata. The cow and the sun are included because they play important roles in the myth and ritual.

The woman who drew the Mata in figure 17, Mrs. Fence Sitter, her pseudonym in R. Freed and S. Freed (1993), said that the four figures in her drawing represent her four children. Another woman said that four similar figures in her drawing represented her family's four married women. In 1977, Mrs. Fence Sitter, a reliable informant said that the birdlike figures symbolize a mother goddess named Shau. It is possible that Shau Mata is the Shaod Mata (Mother of Fertility) of eastern Punjab. Crooke (1968, 2: 309) said that Shaod Mata is worshiped in a fertility rite at the wheat harvest. Hoi takes place during the fall when fields are plowed for wheat. The identification of Shau and Shaod is based on similar names[14] and functions, namely, the granting of fertility. Channa (1984: 113–114) named both Hoi Mata and Gau Mata as the goddess of the festival. Gau may be equivalent to Shau.

The artistic drawing of Hoi Mata in Channa (1984: 127) was probably taken from a lithograph. Instead of four female figures, seven female and seven male figures

FIG. 17. Multicolored Hoi Mata drawn by a Brahman mother, 1977. The four human figures inside the body of the Goddess represent the Brahman's children. A cow and two peacocks are depicted below the children. The small female figure at right is offering water to the sun, part of the ritual of Hoi. The sun (with rays) and half-moon are represented at upper left. Written across the top of the drawing are sun (Surya), moon (Chand) and Hoi Mata. A pot covered by a saucer is under the drawing. A paintbrush is on the floor in front of the pot.

are depicted in the body of Hoi, which represent the seven sons and seven daughters-in-law of the myth. The king and queen of the myth are shown as well as the bird figures, which Channa calls love birds representing peace and prosperity. An array of major deities at the bottom of the picture (Saraswati, Ganesh, Lakshmi, and Durga) establish a great-traditional link for the festival, which is absent in the Hoi designs of Shanti Nagar. However, one of our informants, a Brahman man with an urban job who was also a candidate for a master's degree in psychology, said, "Hoi is Lakshmi, the Goddess of Wealth and Good Fortune. She is drawn seven days before Diwali and is worshipped the evening of Diwali." Although the identification of Hoi Mata and Lakshmi was expressed only by this Brahman, a trend of merging non-Sanskritic and Sanskritic deities may in all likelihood develop as the literate proportion of the population steadily increases and television sets become common.

As is done for Karva Chauth, pots filled with water are used in the ritual of Hoi. Each woman is represented by one or two pots, sometimes by a brass *lota* if a pot is not available. A red string is tied around the neck of the pot for ornamentation and auspiciousness. Sometimes, swastikas, symbols of good fortune, are drawn in turmeric on pots. We saw one pot decorated with a necklace that had a pendant with a picture of a cow and seven calves. A saucer is placed on each pot, and gifts for later distribution, usually food and clothing, are on the saucers. The pots are placed on the ground beneath the mural of Hoi Mata (figs. 18–19). Family tradition and events during the year affect the number of pots and the offerings. Two Brahmanis, who were sisters married to brothers, prepared two pots apiece because they said that their mother-in-law had done so. Barley and *batasha*s (a round, white, hollow sugar candy) were on the pots. A Jat woman prepared two pots, one for a daughter and the other for a daughter-in-law, both of whom had children and were with her at the festival. A senior Blacksmith woman decorated one pot for herself; her daughter-in-law prepared two because she had recently borne a son.

The water in the pots becomes auspicious from use in the Hoi ritual and is usually saved for one of the following purposes: to bathe a child; to mix the plaster needed for the festival of Diwali, which takes place eight days later at the new moon; to offer to the sun at Diwali; to mix with the dung used to shape a male figure for Gobardhan, a festival celebrated the day after Diwali; or to make plaster on a day of pilgrimage to the Ganges. An old Brahman woman said that she would wash herself with the water in her own pot.

On the day of the Hoi festival, nothing is done until midafternoon. Then women gather for a storytelling session, often in a Brahman courtyard, for elderly Brahman women are usually the storytellers. Brahmans may be joined by women of neighboring high- or mid-level castes. A few wealthy Jats had the wife of their Brahman priest tell the story after she first drew the depiction of Hoi Mata on the wall. For these services, she was given sweets, or a headcloth or a rupee. One Brahman woman touched a bit of food to all the images in her painting as an offering before an elderly Brahman woman recited the story. Some women place a lighted lamp on the ground beneath the image (fig. 19).

We learned of no storytellers among the lower castes, with the exception of a teenage Sweeper boy who recited a story combining the plot of a film and a story that he had read in his schoolbook. His story had nothing to do with Hoi Mata. One Chamar knew the story but did not recite it. A Kumhar Potter woman said that in her natal village, Brahmanis came to her home to relate the myth. However, in Shanti Nagar it was not the custom for Brahmanis to visit low-caste households as participants in rituals, either in the 1950s or the 1970s.

We attended a storytelling session in a Brahman's courtyard. The floor was plastered and an image of Hoi was drawn on the wall. Four pitchers, two for each of the mothers in the extended family, were on the ground beneath Hoi Mata. Several Brahman women, a Watercarrier woman, and some children were present. A Nai Barber woman later told us that she was there, but we did not see her. Two Brahman mothers, one of them the storyteller, 30 years old, had a glass of water on the ground and grain in one hand. One woman held rice; the other held barley. They dropped grain in the water as the story was recited.

This version of the myth was written down in the heat of ritual activity with all its distractions. Some women interjected comments as the storyteller ran through her version. Because of these circumstances, this version as recorded in our notes may be less coherent, briefer, and less well organized than it was as recounted by the storyteller. It is nevertheless noteworthy for the prominence that it gives to the relationship of mother-in-law and daughter-in-law. The rivalry of husband's sister and husband's brother's wife is minimal. Neither the sister nor the sister-in-law loses any children, although the sister-in-law has to surrender her fertility (womb) to Hoi Mata. Salvation comes through service, but it is not clear to whom, possibly to the mother-in-law. In the end, mother-in-law and daughter-in-law are reconciled and show mutual respect by touching each other's feet.

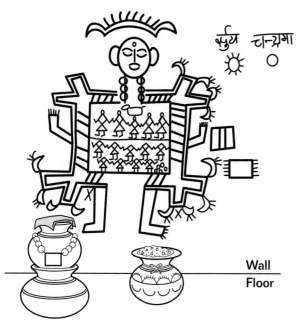

FIG. 18. Mural of Hoi Mata, Brahman's house, 1977. Pots rest on the floor under the mural. On the pot at the right is a plate with millet (bajra), water chestnuts (*singhara*), and sugar candies (*batasha*). A red string (*nala*) is tied around its neck. On top of the stacked pots at the left is a folded cloth as an offering. A necklace of 18 beads is draped over the upper pot. Fourteen figures, probably representing the seven daughters-in-law and seven sons, and a cow are depicted inside the Goddess. Birds decorate her corners. Sun (Surya) and Moon (Chandrama) are written above their respective images drawn near the left shoulder of the Goddess.

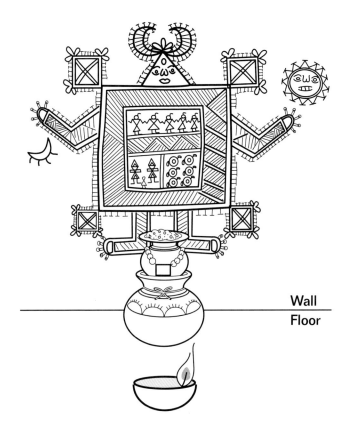

FIG. 19. Mural of Hoi Mata, Brahman's house, 1977. Two stacked pots rest on the floor. On top of the upper pot is a dish with a food offering. A necklace with 16 beads is draped over this pot. A red string (*nala*) is tied around the neck of the lower pot, and a lamp burns in front of it. Female figures, a child, and birds are depicted inside the Goddess. The sun is drawn above the Goddess's left hand, and the moon is shown below her right forearm.

Wall

Floor

Version 1:

A mother-in-law sent her daughter-in-law and her daughter to dig the ground. The daughter did nothing and the daughter-in-law began to dig. The calves of Hoi were cut and buried. Hoi came and wanted to take away the fertility of the daughter. But the daughter-in-law said, "Don't take away her fertility, take mine. Otherwise my mother-in-law will give me no peace. She's an unforgiving woman." Hoi took the fertility of the daughter-in-law, who then went home. Her mother-in-law gave her a hollow rod to keep the crows away [the crow is an inauspicious symbol]. The mother-in-law sent dry bread to her daughter-in-law every day. The daughter-in-law stayed there until the next Hoi. Then she had a son and he was swinging [playing]. The mother-in-law sent her maid with bread for the daughter-in-law. The maid found the child swinging and the place plastered up. She returned and told the mother-in-law, who was surprised. She went and touched her daughter-in-law's feet, and the daughter-in-law touched her mother-in-law's feet [gestures of respect].

Four days before Hoi, we recorded the myth from a 63-year-old Brahman grandmother, one of the women who was present at the ritual described above. Her

FIG. 20. Mural of Hoi Mata, Brahman's house, 1958. A cow and females are represented inside the Mata. Five parrots are sketched to the right. Birds decorate the Mata's corners.

account features service to a cow, which is a standard element of the story. However, a brother's wife becomes the victim directly because she herself violated the taboo against digging, rather than becoming the victim indirectly by taking on the punishment intended for her sister-in-law, the one who broke the taboo. Moreover, the taboo against digging works directly against the violator in that she kills her own children. In other versions, she kills the children of Hoi Mata, who retaliates by taking her womb or by killing her children. The conflict between husband's sister and husband's brothers' wives appears but is overshadowed by an angry, dominant mother-in-law who demands that her daughters-in-law obey her.

Version 2:

Hoi is a goddess. This Hoi gives pregnancy to women. There was a king with seven married sons. The wife of the second eldest son went to the fields on Hoi with her husband's sister to dig earth. You are not supposed to dig earth on Hoi. There was a fight between the sister and the brothers' wives because none of them wanted to dig. The mother-in-law became angry because she wanted the daughters-in-law to dig the earth. So the [second] wife went out and dug and her children [sons] were cut by the spade with which she was digging. That's how they were killed. Because she dug, her sons died. She became possessed in the fields and could not move from there. There was a lame cow she had to serve for 12 years. Her mother-in-law daily sent her one piece of bread made from barley and soaked in oil. She lived off this food every day. Her mother-in-law was still sending it at the end of 12 years. During this time, a palace was built for her, and then a Brahman woman cooked for her. Everything was done on a big scale. When her mother-in-law saw that a palace had been built for her, she came to find out how this happened. The daughter-in-law said that all she had done was to serve a lame cow. Anyhow the palace was there, the sons had been brought back to life, and everything was all right. This is the story of Hoi. This woman was the wife of a king's son and was exiled for 12 years. I think the caste of these people may have been Brahmans, but I don't really know. My grandmother told it to me. I did not learn it in my mother's stomach. Someone taught me.

On Hoi, a Brahman grandmother, 40 years old, told the following version of the myth. The conflict of husband's sister and husband's brothers' wives is prominent. The wives either fight with their husband's sister, as in the preceding version, or deceive her, as in this one. In this version, a wife assumes the punishment—loss of husband and children—intended for her husband's sister. The motive is not clear. The sister violated the taboo, but perhaps the brother's wife felt some guilt about the deception or perhaps wanted to please her mother-in-law. In version 1, mother-in-law and daughter-in-law press each other's legs and are reconciled. In this version, the daughter-in-law tries to press her mother-in-law's legs as a gesture of respect and perhaps expiation, but is repulsed. The mother-in-law remains a hostile and jealous figure. In versions 2 and 3, the restored couple becomes wealthy and lives in a sumptuous palace. This element, common in the versions told in Shanti Nagar, does not appear in other published versions of the myth (Lewis, 1958: 218–221; Luthra, 1961: 71; Channa, 1984: 113–114).

The appearance of the *apsarases* (Indra's nymphs who emerged from the ocean) in this version is unique. The *apsarases* are heavenly charmers who can lure even the most virtuous into misbehavior. Their entry into the myth leads to a general shifting of character and plot. They are blamed for the death of husband and children, but they are also the deities who restore them to life. The benevolent cow in other versions is menacing in this one, sharing to some extent the personality of the mother-in-law.

Fig. 21. Mural of Hoi Mata, Brahman's house, 1977. The personages of the myth are represented in the Goddess: the seven daughters-in-law, the seven sons, the mother-in-law, the mother and her children, and the cow with a calf. Figure 20 was drawn at this same house in 1958. However, figure 21 was sketched by a wife who was not present in 1958. Different compositions in a single family may represent the work of wives from different villages.

Version 3:

A king had seven married sons and one daughter. All seven daughters-in-law and the daughter fasted for Hoi. The king's wife sent them to the fields to dig up some earth, fill their baskets, and return home. The daughters-in-law put their baskets down, making the excuse that they had to go to the jungle [to defecate]. The daughter in the meantime was filling the baskets with earth. While digging, she cut the calves of Hoi Mata. When all of the women were about to leave, Hoi took hold of the daughter. The daughters-in-law said, "What's this?" And Hoi Mata said, "I'll take her fertility." Although the other daughters-in-law went home, the eldest asked Hoi to restore the daughter's fertility and instead take hers. Hoi Mata granted her wish, turning her husband and children to stone. The martyred daughter-in-law then unwound her hair and served a cow 12 years. After 12 years, the mother-in-law said to the family's barber's wife [Nain], "Take a vessel of food for that woman; she has nothing to eat."

At that time the cow came to the martyred daughter-in-law and said, "I'll kill you because you clean me every day." The daughter-in-law said, "Do what you want, but I'll clean you and serve you every day. I've deen doing it for 12 years because my fertility was taken by Hoi Mata." The cow told her "Come to the ocean at midnight. All the *apsaras*es come to bathe then and you can take their clothes." She went there and took their clothes. The *apsaras*es were alarmed and started chasing her, but the cow came and said, "I'll gore all of you; get out of my way." Then the cow said, "You have taken her fertility. Restore it." They agreed, took some water, drew some blood from their little fingers, and sprinkled the stones so that the husband and children were brought back to life [see note 12]. The Brahman woman then began to cook and the Nain worked for her. There was a palace, the restored couple as king and queen lived in it with their children, and everything was all right. Then the mother-in-law sent the Nain with food to the martyred daughter-in-law who hadn't had anything for 12 years. The Nain went back to the mother-in-law and told her that she had been abusing her daughter-in-law and that now the couple was prosperous. The mother-in-law denied any abuse and went to visit the couple. The daughter-in-law ran to press her mother-in-law's legs, but she would not permit the gesture. And everything was all right.

The following version of the Hoi myth was recited by a 35-year-old Brahman mother, assisted by another Brahman woman. The familiar themes of conflict between a husband's sister and the wives of his brothers and between mother-in-law and daughter-in-law are basic to the myth. One of the wives assumes the punishment meted out to the husband's sister, but not voluntarily as in other versions. She is betrayed by the other brothers' wives, and her mother-in-law banishes her to the forest. Although the mother-in-law is unforgiving, referring to the martyred daughter-in-law as a "murderess," she nonetheless sends bread to her for 12 years

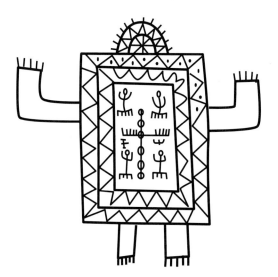

FIG. 22. Mural of Hoi Mata, Brahman's house, 1958.

FIG. 23. *(right)* Mural of Hoi Mata, Leather-worker's house, 1958. Drawing of a woman is inside the Goddess.

FIG. 24. *(below)* Mural of Hoi Mata, Leather-worker's house, 1958. Two peacocks and a woman are drawn inside Hoi Mata; two peacocks are depicted outside the Goddess.

while her daughter-in-law feeds a lame cow. The daughter-in-law's devoted service does not restore her dead children to life, but she has a son after 12 years and builds a palace. The mother-in-law comes to see her, the two women press legs, and the mother-in-law declares that she was mistaken about her daughter-in-law.

Version 4:

A king had seven married sons and one daughter. One day the daughter and all of the brothers' wives went out to dig earth. They were fasting that day. The women argued about who would dig, but only the sister did the digging. While so doing, she cut seven calves of Hoi Mata, who said, "You have cut my seven calves so I will take your fertility." Then the daughters-in-law and the mother-in-law fought because they let her daughter lose her fertility. Six of the daughters-in-law said that it was the fault of the eldest daughter-in-law. The mother-in-law turned the eldest daughter-in-law out of the house. She went into the forest. Then the daughters' children came back to life, but the children of the eldest daughter-in-law died. The mother-in-law then made bread out of gram [chick-pea] chaff and sent it to the eldest daughter-in-law in the jungle. The eldest daughter-in-law met an old woman in the jungle who said, "Take care of a lame cow; feed it and take care of the dung." The eldest daughter-in-law stayed in the jungle 12 years while she served the cow. Then she had a son and fasted again for Hoi Mata. She built a palace there.

The mother-in-law gave her daughter some bread and sent her to her eldest daughter-in-law, saying, "Give the bread to that murderess." The daughter found her eldest sister-in-law living in a palace with her son swinging outside the palace. They had cooked all the nice things usually cooked on this day. The daughter returned to her mother and told her that the eldest daughter-in-law was living in great pleasure in a palace. As a result the mother-in-law visited her eldest daughter-in-law and pressed her legs, and the eldest daughter-in-law pressed her mother-in-laws' legs [signs of respect]. The mother-in-law said, "We were mistaken about you." The eldest daughter-in-law replied, "I stayed here 12 years and served this lame cow and built this palace."

The two storytellers repeated the part about the mother-in-law telling her daughter to give the bread to the murderess and the daughter's surprise at finding her sister-in-law living so well. We asked the two storytellers for their opinion of the myth. They remarked on the injustice of what was done to the daughter-in-law. She had done the right thing in exchanging her fertility for that of her sister-in-law, but nonetheless her mother-in-law turned her out of the house, called her a murderess, and sent her only a piece of inferior bread.

They finished their exegesis with the verse below. The theme of the verse, fertility, fits the purpose of the ritual of Hoi very well. The use of two different trees in the verse represents the different situations of a woman in her natal home and in her marital home—that is, to her roles as daughter and wife, a theme that is highlighted in the myth of Hoi. A wife may fight with some of her in-laws, but she continues to bear children.

> My in-laws are under the tree of *aak*.
> My parents' house is under the tree of *daak*.
> May the two families grow as the ants grow.

When we asked storytellers from whom they had learned the myth, they all claimed to have learned it from their mothers-in-law and said that their own daughters-in-law would learn it from them. This scenario implies a more rigid transmission of culture than actually exists. A woman may be exposed to more versions of the myth than just the one recited by her own mother-in-law. In fact, the storytellers listen to each other. The woman who told version 4 was present when version 3 was recited. Such contact would tend to maintain similar versions throughout the village. Nonetheless there is considerable variety.

The preceding four versions of the Hoi myth were collected in 1958 from nonliterate women. We have two versions from 1977. The first is from a Brahman mother, 41 years old, with a fifth-grade education. Her tale is much like those from 1958 except that Shau Mata replaces Hoi Mata. Our informant identified the birdlike creatures in her drawing as Shau Mata. Although our informant was literate and in the habit of reading, her myth is quite similar to those versions collected from nonliterate women 20 years earlier. In this version, the husband's sister quarrels with his brothers' wives, a common feature of Hoi myths. However, the mother-in-law is a neutral figure, in contrast to her usually domineering persona.

Version 5:

A king had seven married sons and one daughter. The seven wives and the daughter went to dig mud on Hoi Mata day. They argued about who would do the work. The wives made excuses, so the daughter did it. She accidently cut the children of Shau Mata. The Mata came and said, "You have cut my children, so I'll take your fertility." Then the eldest wife interceded, saying "Don't do this because she is the only daughter and we are seven wives. You can take my fertility instead." Shau Mata took her fertility. When the wife returned home, she found that her husband and children had been turned to stone. She asked an old woman what to do and was told to serve a lame cow for 12 years. After 12 years, the cow asked her, "Why have you served me all this time?" The martyred wife told the cow the story. The cow told her to cut her little finger and pour blood on the stones to bring them back to life. Then the mother-in-law had a Nain take food to her daughter-in-law. The Nain returned and told the mother-in-law that the whole family was alive and living very well. The mother-in-law replied, "Why do you joke with me. They're all stone." The Nain said, "Come with me and see for yourself." The mother-in-law did and saw that they were all happy. She asked what the wife had done. The wife replied that she served the cow for 12 years,

हो म्याता

FIG. 25. Mural of Hoi Mata, Barber's house, 1977. Figures of women and cows are inside the square; peacocks are on top. At center-top is depicted a scene from the myth. Two women are above ground and two calves, shown in a box, are below ground. A woman digs in the ground and injures the calves. Ho [Hoi] Mata is written above the sketch.

poured blood from her little finger, and now they were all happy again. There is a typical phrase: "What happened in the beginning should not happen to anyone and what happened at the end should happen to everyone." [Our informant's eyes were moist when she recited this proverb.]

The second version of the Hoi myth from 1977 was recorded in the course of an interview on a different subject with a well-educated (matriculate), urbanized Brahman man in his early 60s. The striking feature of his version, the only one that we collected from a man, is the absence of any mention of conflict in the two relationships that are of great importance to women. When women tell the story, they emphasize the conflicts of mother-in-law and daughter-in-law and of husband's sister and husband's brothers' wives. Our male informant appears to have had no interest in the social and emotional lives of women. The mother-in-law is not even mentioned. The daughters-in-law are present but do not interact with the husband's sister. There is no quarreling, duplicity, or even conversation. Our informant talks mainly of redemption and happiness through selfless service.

His version is noteworthy also in its lack of embellishment and meanders. The story line is clean and direct. There are no palaces, *apsaras*es, daily pieces of bread, or corpses brought back to life. We attribute this sparse plot either to our informant's editing of stories that he had heard from various women or possibly to a printed version of the myth that he had read. As more people become literate and printed versions of popular myths increasingly enter into general circulation, one might expect individual variation among storytellers to diminish. However, this point cannot be established on the basis of the single version presented below.[15]

Version 6:

There was a king who had seven married sons and a daughter. The daughter went into the forest with the wives of her seven brothers. The daughter started digging in the ground for clay while the wives of the brothers strolled in the forest. While digging, she hit Hoi Mata who came up from the ground and wanted to take her womb. The wife of the eldest brother told Hoi Mata to take her womb instead of her sister-in-law's. Hoi Mata agreed to do so. Thereafter the elder brother's wife had no children and was very sad. She met a lame cow and served the cow for 12 years so the cow was very happy. As a result the cow told her that she would grant her any wish. The eldest brother's wife then told the cow that Hoi Mata had taken her womb and she now wanted it returned. The cow then went to Hoi Mata and asked her to return the womb to the eldest brother's wife. Hoi Mata returned it and thereafter the wife had many children.

After the myth is told, women pour water on the ground as an offering to the sun and break their fast with some of the festal foods: *khir*, puris, halva, *malpuras* (a sweet pancake), water chestnuts (*singhara*), and sweet potatoes obtained from the Baniya's shop. Some women prefer to wait for starlight, but generally the fast is broken in the afternoon after the recital of the myth. One woman offered water to the nail used to tie a cow; she offered water to the sun only if there was no nail. In this context, the nail may serve as a Lingam, as did the short wooden peg in the comparable ritual for Karva Chauth (fig. 15). If some grain is left over from the ritual, girls may take it to the Baniya's shop to exchange for sweets. A family might distribute *batasha*s to relatives and neighbors if a son or grandson had been born during the year or a child's marriage had taken place.

Although Hoi is celebrated for the welfare of children, the gifts given at the conclusion of the day emphasize the relationship of mother-in-law and daughter-in-law and, to a lesser extent, that of wife and husband's sister. These are the only two relationships that receive appreciable attention in the Hoi myth. The daughter-in-law gives clothing to the mother-in-law, usually a suit of clothes (*til* or *tirh*) consisting of a skirt, shirt, and headcloth or perhaps a sari and blouse. Since the participants in Hoi are mothers, a childless wife rarely gives a *tirh* to her mother-in-law until she has a child, preferably a son. However, we did record one case of a childless married woman giving *tirh*s to her mother-in-law and to another senior

FIG. 26. Mural of Hoi Mata, Potter's house, 1958. This little stick figure, drawn on the doorjamb, was only about 6 in. tall.

woman. A Sweeper woman summarized, "When a woman has a child, she draws the Hoi Mata on the wall, worships it, fasts, and says, 'If you give me a son, I'll worship you.' Then I give a headcloth or a shirt to my mother-in-law. That's our religion to give to the mother-in-law. To whom else would we give?" However, if the mother-in-law is dead, the husband's sister replaces her as recipient of such gifts. What is more, if a husband's sister is staying with her natal family, his wife gives her a gift of clothing.

A Jat man mentioned a former custom. If a woman had borne a child during the year, a goldsmith in another village who served villagers in Shanti Nagar made silver or gold amulets for the child. Then, on Hoi the mother sent a skirt and headcloth to the goldsmith's wife. Silver, gold, or iron amulets were made to protect newborn children from evil spirits. These amulets were usually sent by the child's maternal grandparents.

It is of some interest that the myth of a festival for the welfare of children has little in it about children and their relationship to parents, dealing rather with two of the relationships with in-laws that are of great concern to women. With regard to the religious sphere, the basic teachings of the Hoi myth revolve around the necessity of proper conduct (dharma). Improper conduct, the breaking of taboos, incurs punishment even in this life, while virtuous service leads to blessing.

DIWALI AND RELATED FESTIVALS

On consecutive days in mid-Karttik (October–November), villagers observe four festivals for the welfare and prosperity of families. The first three festival days form a closely connected series whose heart is the great all-India festival of Diwali on the third day. The two preceding festivals, Dhan Teras and Girhi, are basically preliminaries to Diwali. Our Baniya informant expressed it succinctly, "Diwali is a major festival, and therefore it needs some buildup." The festival of Gobardhan, which is celebrated the day after Diwali, has a weak connection to Diwali through mythology. However, the smooth continuity of ritual, central deity, and village exegesis from the preparatory festival of Dhan Teras through Girhi, known appropriately as "Little Diwali," to Diwali reaches a climax in that great Sanskritic festival. Gobardhan represents a break in the continuity.

Although Gobardhan is essentially a festival of the little tradition, it is not overshadowed by the great-traditional festival of Diwali. In fact, the villagers consider Gobardhan to be more important than Diwali. Marriott (1955: 199–200) sees Gobardhan as an example of parochialization, a devolution of great-traditional elements and their integration into the little tradition. In the case of Gobardhan, this process is open to two interpretations. It may have been a gradual transformation, the passage of Sanskritic elements to the village level, there to enhance a sparse ritual consecrated to some minor local deity. On the other hand, it is more likely that a Sanskritic myth was attached to Gobardhan after the festival had attained essentially its current form and importance. In either case, the observance of Gobardhan on the day after Diwali would be fortuitous. The addition of the myth, however, provides a link between Gobardhan and Diwali.

The four festivals, part of the lively fall festival season, take place between the two crop seasons, the kharif (summer-autumn) crop and the rabi (winter-spring) crop. On Diwali, business people close their accounts and open new ones. The agricultural transition from kharif to rabi and the tradition of closing the old fiscal year and opening a new one give a more intense feeling of beginning a new year than does the official start of the new year in the spring (Chaitra *sudi* 1).

Dhan Teras

Dhan Teras (Wealth Thirteenth) takes place on Karttik *badi* 13, two days before Diwali. It is a minor festival, of which some disclaim knowledge. Most people, even those who know about the day, do nothing. The chief activity is to buy new dishes and utensils, if any are needed. Two informants mentioned lighting a single lamp, perhaps in anticipation of Girhi, when five lamps are lit. One informant said that women whitewash their houses. Another informant called the day Janam Diva (Birthday of the Lamp). Lamps are "born" and people start to light them.

Authors have little to say about Dhan Teras, except Underhill (1991: 59) who described much more elaborate rituals than those of Shanti Nagar. Her comments chiefly concerned merchants who close their accounts on this day, clean their shops and offices, and, having made a pile of their account books and some silver coins smeared with turmeric, worship this assemblage and Lakshmi, Goddess of Wealth. Women clear and decorate the house, prepare festive foods, and draw auspicious designs on the ground. Lamps are lit.

Girhi (Choti Diwali)

Girhi (no translation), or Choti Diwali (Little Diwali), is celebrated on Karttik *badi* 14. Girhi is a festival of welcome for the goddess Lakshmi, the principal deity who is worshipped on Diwali. Choti Diwali and Diwali are closely connected and are essentially a single festival. On Choti Diwali, a few villagers clean their houses in anticipation of Diwali. Many more families light five lamps in the evening. Brahmans and Baniyas commonly observe this ritual. Otherwise, participation varies. Chamars and Bairagis do nothing on Girhi, but Chuhras claim to light lamps. As with all festivals, participation is at the option of a specific family. Most families act as do their castemates, but there are always exceptions.

Descriptions of Girhi written early in this century suggest that the current festival as observed in Shanti Nagar has lost much of its earlier content and meaning. The festival is also called Naraka Chaturdashi (Hell Fourteenth or Naraka's Fourteenth) (Mukerji, 1916: 133–135; Underhill, 1991: 59–61, 116–117). It is associated with various myths, chiefly great-traditional legends whose protagonists are Narakasura and Bali. One legend of Narakasura recounts a war between this demon-king and the gods. A redoubtable voluptuary, Narakasura carries off the daughter of Vishwakarma, the divine architect of the universe, violates her, and adds her to his harem of 16,000 mistresses. He relentlessly pursues the *apsaras*es and the daughters of men and gods. All women live in terror of him. They supplicate Vishnu to destroy the demon and restore their honor. However, Narakasura was a demon of great piety and for a time Vishnu could do nothing. Finally, the sins of the demon outweighed his accumulated merit, and Vishnu sent Krishna to slay him. Since good karma can never be totally erased by subsequent sin, Krishna allowed Narakasura one boon at the moment of his death. The demon asked that the day of his death be forever commemorated as a day of feasting. "So be it," said Krishna, and with one blow of his sword destroyed the demon (Dowson, 1891: 220; Mukerji, 1916: 133–135).

The legend of King Bali depicts a man of such piety, merit, and devotion that he conquered Indra, God of the Heavens, humbled the gods, and asserted his authority over all the universe. The gods appealed to Vishnu, who appeared before King Bali as the Dwarf avatar and asked for a boon. Bali gave away anything that was asked of him, a form of charity considered to be the highest. Vishnu begged for as much land as he could cover in three steps. The king granted the boon, whereupon Vishnu assumed a huge form and in two mighty steps covered the earth and the heavens. With his third step, Vishnu drove Bali down into Naraka (Hell) (Dowson, 1891: 42; Mukerji, 1916: 84–86, 136; Underhill, 1991: 59–61).

This legend is attached to Naraka Chaturdashi because, after Vishnu punished King Bali, he relented and granted him the kingdom of Patala and three days annually to reign on earth wherever no lamps are lit. As a result, during these three days beginning with Naraka Chaturdashi, people put lamps in every building to avoid again falling into Bali's power. The legend of King Bali also has a connection with Diwali through Lakshmi, wife of Vishnu. He had earlier won her good will through prayer and penance. She persuaded Vishnu to release Bali from hell and to grant him the kingdom of Patala, the netherworld. Lakshmi is the Goddess of Wealth and Good Fortune, who is worshipped on Diwali.

According to Underhill (1991: 60, 116), there is a link between Bali, King of Hell, and Yama, Lord of Death. When dead ancestors see lamps, they are released from Yama's clutches and proceed to heaven (Svarga). Offerings are made to Yama so that the souls of the dead may escape suffering. Thus, Naraka Chaturdashi is also known as Bhuta Chaturdashi (Ghost Fourteenth).

Another link between Yama and Bali emphasizes the latter's righteousness. In this version, Bali is Yama's assistant and judges dead souls.

> Yet there, by Yamen's throne,
> Doth Bali sit in majesty and might,
> To judge the dead, and sentence them aright.
> And forasmuch as he was still the friend
> Of righteousness, it is permitted him,
> Yearly, from those drear regions to ascend,
> And walk the earth, that he may hear his name
> Still hymn'd and honour'd by the grateful voice
> Of all mankind, and in his fame rejoice.
> [Balfour, 1885, 3: 585]

The rituals of Naraka Chaturdashi involve special bathing and anointing with oil. New clothes are worn and lamps are lit (Gupte, 1903: 237; Mukerji, 1916: 135; Underhill, 1991: 61). Underhill quoted a saying, "On Naraka fourteenth Lakshmi [i.e., beauty] dwells in oil and Ganga [i.e., cleanliness] in water." Mukerji (1916:

135–136) reported a sumptuous noon meal on Naraka Chaturdashi when 14 different kinds of vegetable dishes are served. In the evening, 14 lamps are lit, the number representing the day of the moon. In Shanti Nagar, only five lamps are customarily lit. Gode (1946: 224) reported that among the Jains, women propitiate "evil spirits." They make offerings of sweets at the crossroads, the site of an important mother goddess, to protect their children during the coming year.

Diwali

Diwali (Lights), or Deepavali (Row or String of Lamps), is a joyous festival celebrated on the new moon day of Karttik. As the climax of the three related festivals beginning with Dhan Teras, it is also known as Bari (Big) Diwali in contrast to the preceding day, Little Diwali. The two outstanding features of the festival are the beautiful display of lamps in the evening almost everywhere in the village and the worship of Lakshmi, Goddess of Wealth. Because the ritual of the festival is essentially a prayer to Lakshmi for prosperity, Diwali is said to be the holiday of the Vaishyas, the commercial castes, just as Dassehra, the celebration of a military victory, is the festival of the Kshatriyas, the martial castes. The festival is a happy day for children, who are home from school because Diwali is a national holiday. They eat sweets, may receive new toys, and have a fine time exploding firecrackers and lighting sparklers. Other prominent features of Diwali, which are common to many festivals, are the special holiday food and gifts to relatives. Patrons (jajmans) make small payments to their clients as customary under the jajmani system (S. Freed and R. Freed, 1976: 120–131).

Men traditionally gamble on Diwali and preceding days. According to Mukerji (1916: 146–147), gambling has received a semireligious sanction as a holy rite that pleases Lakshmi and is required of everyone. Mukerji reports the belief that he who does not gamble on the night of Diwali becomes a disgusting mole in his next life, losing all his accumulated good karma. The traditional gambling game is pachisi (chaupar), a game played with dice (originally with cowrie shells) on a cruciform board. Men told us that they played chaupar at this season, but we did not see much of it. However, card playing was common. A group of men playing cards could be observed many days. More men might have played cards during Diwali than at other times, but we made no note to that effect during the festival. Although none of our informants mentioned gambling as a feature of Diwali, we assume that gambling accompanied chaupar and card games.

Most informants alluded to the story of Ram versus Ravana, as told in the Ramayana, as the reason for celebrating Diwali. Ram defeated Ravana, king of Sri Lanka, a victory marked by the festival of Dassehra, 20 days before Diwali. Ram then returned to his capital, Ayodhya, after an exile of 14 years. The people were happy to see him and rejoiced by lighting lamps. Diwali is the festival of Ram's return, and a display of lamps is its characteristic feature.

Three informants said that there was a connection between Diwali and King Bali; two did not elaborate the point. The third informant apparently traced the connection through the link of Bali to Yama, as outlined above in the paragraphs on Naraka Chaturdashi. However, instead of telling the story of Bali and Krishna in his

Dwarf avatar, as is appropriate on Little Diwali, he recited in detail the story of Savitri and Satyavan from the Mahabharata. In both tales, souls are released from the clutches of Yama; otherwise, they have little in common. The story of Savitri and Satyavan, as recounted by our informant, is as follows:

> Savitri was the daughter of a king called Aswapati [Master of Horses, an epithet for many kings]. The king could not find a husband for her. [She was so beautiful that suitors were hesitant to approach her.] Aswapati told her to find her own husband. She roamed about and found a man [Satyavan] killing a lion. She told her father, but he said that she should marry the son of a king. She insisted on her choice. Although Satyavan's father was blind and in exile, he had once been a king. Manu, a Rishi, told her that Satyavan would die in one year, and so she should not marry him. The couple did marry, and when Satyavan brought his wife to his parents, they were happy. As Manu had foretold, the day of death came. Accompanied by Savitri, Satyavan went into the forest to cut wood. He felt a sharp pain and died. Yama came to take his soul. Savitri tried to stop Yama, but he took the soul anyway. Savitri followed him and would not turn back. Then Yama offered her a boon, anything except the life of her husband. She asked that the father-in-law be given eyes. The boon was granted, but even then Savitri did not turn back. Yama offered another boon. She asked that her father-in-law recover his kingdom. This boon also was granted, but still she did not turn back. Yama offered a third and last boon, after which she would have to turn back. She asked to be the mother of 100 sons. The boon was granted, but it was impossible without the life of her husband. In this way, Satyavan came back to life [see also, Garrett, 1990: 578–80; Underhill, 1991: 127–128].

Savitri is one of the great models of Indian womanhood whose devotion to her husband is so strong that even a god had to yield. Perhaps second only to the tale of Sita, the legend of Savitri is the most beloved by Indian women. The story has led to a festival, Vat Purnima, widely observed in western India (Underhill, 1991: 127). This festival has nothing to do with Diwali and, in any case, is not observed in Shanti Nagar.

A Blacksmith man told a version of the story of Ram and Ravana that ties Diwali to the festival of Gobardhan:

> In the fight between Ram and Ravana, Lakshman [Ram's brother] was wounded. The only thing that would revive him was an herb that grows in the Himalayas. It is boiled in milk over a fire of dung cakes. Hanuman [the Monkey God] brought back the mountain with the herb and the medicine was made. Ram won the war (Dassehra) and returned home (Diwali). Then he remembered that his brother Lakshman was saved by the cows, so he decreed that the day after Diwali was to be dedicated to the welfare of cows and that all the cow dung be examined to see if it is firm, thus indicating that the cows are in good health. This is the festival of Gobardhan.

Families prepare for Diwali on Dhan Teras, Girhi, and Diwali itself. The main preparations are to buy new utensils if necessary, to clean, plaster, and whitewash the house, and to cook the festive foods: *khir*, halva, puris, and vegetables. People buy small clay lamps and candles to light in the evening. Candles were more popular in 1977 than in 1958 because they were cheaper than lamps fueled with the more costly mustard oil. People economized by soaking the lamps in water before use so that they would not needlessly absorb oil. Electric lights, absent in 1958, had also come into use in 1977. Some families buy small statues of Lakshmi and Krishna for use in the family worship (puja) that takes place in the evening. A few women draw an image of Diwali on an interior wall, the drawing serving as a focus of worship.

Some families decorated their family's cattle on Diwali. This practice was widespread in 1958, but we made no note of it in 1977. Necklaces of cord and the quills of peacock feathers were used to decorate cows and buffaloes. One Brahman woman made necklaces of women's hair punctuated with white balls of peacock feathers to decorate bullocks. Feathers are considered auspicious and make a good show. She commented that the black hair looked good against the white bullocks. The Watercarriers also made necklaces of peacock feathers to decorate their buffaloes and cows, and the Potters decorated their donkeys, mules, and horses. A Jat family decorated its camel, the only one in the village.

Diwali means work for the two village potters. A few weeks before the festival, they are busy making the small clay lamps that all observant families use, often by the dozens. The potters sell the lamps in lots of five for which, in 1958, they claimed to receive as much as a pound of grain. This payment appears to be more than the market value of the lamps. Families with whom potters have jajmani relationships make an annual traditional payment in wheat. Under this system, such families pay for most items on delivery, but a few articles, among them lamps for Diwali, are covered by the yearly payment. However, all these articles together are worth less than the annual grain payment. Especially in 1958, Diwali lamps were profitable for the potters, both when sold for cash and also when covered by jajmani payments (S. Freed and R. Freed, 1976: 130). In 1977, candles that could be purchased cheaply at the village ration shop were partly replacing lamps.

After it grows dark and before the ritual, lamps and candles are lit everywhere in the village. Lamps on the roofs, walls, and window frames trace the outlines of buildings, and other lamps are placed everywhere inside them. Lakshmi comes where there are lights. A multicaste group of girls and young women singing devotional songs parades to the village well to decorate it with lamps. Diwali takes place on the new moon and so there is no moonlight to compete with the lamps. The village site is compact with no space between houses, which has the effect of concentrating the lamplight. All families seem to light their lamps at about the same time, and the myriad points of light create an almost magical effect. The side of the village inhabited by the lower castes, the Potters, Leatherworkers, and Sweepers was especially beautiful. The display in 1977 was as spectacular as the one in 1958 despite the electric lights used by a few families to supplement the oil lamps and the light from a few street lamps. The street lights may have been turned off during the display, for none are visible in our photographs. In any case, they were too few to detract from the spectacle (figs. 27–28).

The uniform display of lamps throughout the village suggests a similarity of ritual practice, but in fact the ritual of Diwali varies considerably by caste and by family. Caste differences range from rituals, especially among the Brahmans, where images of major deities are worshipped with offerings, lights, and mantras to the practices of the Sweepers, who sacrifice chickens to an ancestral deity. The Jats do relatively little for Diwali other than to light lamps, and not all families even do that. However, some Jat families conduct a ritual for Lakshmi, and the Jat men's community house, the *chopal*, is decorated with lamps. Some people commented that the festival of the Jats is Gobardhan, not Diwali. The relative disinterest of the Jats in Diwali may partially stem from Arya-Samaj influence with its suppression of Krishna worship.

Family differences within castes vary from lengthy rituals of an hour or more to brief, rather perfunctory observance. Some families do not participate in the festival at all, usually owing to a family death that took place on that day. In such a case, a family may abandon indefinitely the observance of a particular festival. A family that suffers a death during the year preceding Diwali, but not on the festival day, might choose to skip the observance of the festival that year.

We visited as many families as time permitted to watch and participate in the ritual of Diwali. The most elaborate observance took place in a Brahman household. We attended this family ritual both in 1958 and 1977. The same man, the family head, officiated in both years, and so the two enactments were quite similar. The account that follows is based principally on the 1958 ceremony with additions from 1977 to make the description as complete as possible. The Brahman who conducted the rituals was well educated by the standards of the time and, while not a professional priest, knew a number of mantras. In retirement from his urban job in 1977, he was preparing to become a *purohit*, a priest who could conduct such complicated rites as marriage.

The leader began by preparing the altar (*havan kund*) where the fire ceremony (*havan*) would be performed. He sprinkled water to purify a small area upon which he drew a square (*chauk*) with flour. He pointed out that if an insect should head toward the fire, it would eat the flour and not be burned, thus respecting the principle of ahimsa, nonviolence. The altar was furnished with two pictures and seven statues of various deities arranged in a semicircle: Lakshmi, Krishna, Ram, Lakshman, Sita, Hanuman, and Durga. In the Brahman ritual of 1958, Ganesh was represented by a stone wrapped with a red thread, a common representation of Ganesh. The Baniya, however, used small statues for both Ganesh and Lakshmi. In 1977, the Brahman also used a small statue of Ganesh. Ganesh is always the first deity to be worshipped. Other ceremonial paraphernalia included a lamp, a dish of ghee kept fluid on hot dung cakes, incense, a pitcher of water from the Ganges River, a tray with *khir*, *haldi* (turmeric), and money, and two boxes of candy for later distribution as *prasad*. We sat on the floor with the leader on a mat facing the statues and pictures. Children, both girls and boys, sat on a mat to our left.

On the square, the leader arranged sticks of sweet-smelling mango wood, or

FIG. 27. *(above)* Ruth helps her Brahman family decorate the house with burning lamps for Diwali, 1977.

FIG. 28. *(below)* View of Diwali lights from authors' terrace, 1977.

alternatively pipal wood, and lit the lamp. The center of the square had a circular element that represented the earth, around which he placed pieces of wood while praying, "Oh Bhagwan [God] make peace in the world and give prosperity to the world." He placed two small candles in front of a picture of Krishna, waved the lamp around the picture, and chanted Sadhya mantras, which are helpful to human beings, and a Lakshmi mantra (Daniélou, 1964: 337, 342). He told us later that he chanted 27 mantras in all. His mother's brother joined in the prayer. The children watched, listened, grew sleepy, and yawned.

The leader then took some water and touched parts of his face and body in preparation for the *havan*. He sipped water from his right hand four times while chanting the mantra, AUM. He then washed his hands and prayed, "Oh Bhagwan, keep my mouth and cheeks healthy, both nostrils good and healthy, good sight and light in my eyes, power to hear and see everything for 100 years. Oh Bhagwan, give me power in my arms but not so I will hurt anybody, and keep my health good with strength in my feet and body. Keep my whole body healthy."

The leader lit the fire and fed it with ghee and incense, chanting mantras all the while. He put some ghee in the lamp before the picture of Krishna, and worshipped the deity. The remaining combustible material was put in the fire.

After worshipping Krishna, he turned his attention to Lakshmi. We put our currency and coins on a tray in front of the picture of Lakshmi. It contained wheat flour and the stone representing Ganesh. Each bank note was marked with a tilak (an ornamental spot) in turmeric. The leader performed *arati* for Lakshmi, that is, worshipped her by waving a lamp before her picture while everyone sang devotional songs. In 1977, an adult daughter of the family, by that time a schoolteacher, read appropriate selections from the Ramayana. After she read a few verses, everyone sang a verse, treating the verse as a mantra. The children sang a song about Ganesh, also mentioning Parvati. The Ganesh stone was placed before the picture of Lakshmi and again the leader performed *arati*. There was more devotional singing and a final prayer to Lakshmi and Krishna. The ceremony had already lasted one hour. Then the leader tied a red string on the right wrist of all those present, after which

FIG. 29. Mural of Diwali. This drawing was the focus of worship in a Brahman household on Diwali, 1958.

he threw *khil* against the pictures of the deities and offered sweets to Lakshmi and Krishna. *Prasad* was distributed to everyone. Then we had our meal.

In 1977 we attended the ritual of another Brahman family which, although simpler, was generally similar. They displayed pictures of Lakshmi, Ganesh, and Saraswati on the altar, which they decorated with silver plates, flowers, colored paper, and toys. The family head put a tilak on the pictures of the deities. Then his mother put a tilak on all the worshippers. They sang hymns to Hanuman, Ram, Lakshmi, and Ganesh, scattered *khil* on the pictures, and folded their hands. There was no *havan*, *arati*, or reading from the Ramayana. As a final act, a young woman, with a group of her women friends, sang while parading to the well where they left lighted lamps. After returning home, they played with firecrackers and decorated the house with lamps and candles.

Eager to cover the ritual of Diwali in as many castes as possible in 1958, we had no time to visit other Brahman families that evening. However, the next day we called on a Brahman family that had made a drawing of Diwali on the wall (fig. 29). It was next to the drawing of Hoi Mata, which it closely resembled. On the floor in front of Diwali were a *chauk*, lamp, and a dish of turmeric. Family members called the drawing "Diwali." The drawing, the *chauk*, and the remaining ritual paraphernalia show that the drawing was the focus of worship, or at least one of the foci, for the ubiquitous statues and pictures of Lakshmi and Krishna may also have been used. The name of the drawing, Diwali, puzzled us at the time. The question "What gods are you worshipping?" has a meaning similar to "What are you celebrating today?" Thus, Diwali is an appropriate answer to either of those questions. However, family members did not identify the drawing as Lakshmi, which is the response that we rather expected. Channa (1984: 131) reported that ". . . women offer prayers to Diwali which is the image of Ganesh and Lakshmi housed together. Clay idols of Ganesh and Lakshmi, called Diwali, are purchased from the bazar [sic] and are included in the paraphernalia of worship. Figure-drawings representing Ganesh and Lakshmi can also be made on the wall and used." Probably the drawing that we saw represented Ganesh and Lakshmi together, although it was difficult to arrive at that interpretation by studying the crude sketch.

The ritual at a Chamar Leatherworker's house was much less elaborate than the Brahman ritual. The family head claimed not to know the story of Diwali and said that ancestors were worshipped rather than a deity. In this regard, another

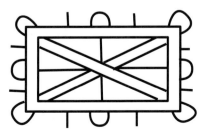

FIG. 30. Square (*chauk*) for Diwali worship drawn with wheat flour on the floor of a Leatherworker's house, 1958. Twenty-one lamps were placed on the square, and *khil* was dropped on it while a mantra was recited.

Chamar man told us that hookah worship, which is guru worship, is usual or compulsory on Diwali and Holi. The Chamars pass the hookah around the ritual fire, offer food to the fire, and turn toward the guru, who lived in another village. In the ceremony that we observed, however, a prayer to God was part of the ritual and we did not see any hookah worship.

The leader's wife cooked festive food and drew a *chauk* in wheat flour on the floor (fig. 30). Family members placed 21 lamps on the *chauk*. They said that any number of lamps could be lit, but there is apparently something special about 21 because a Brahman family also lit that number of lamps. Babb (1975: 129) noted that one of the names of Shitala, the smallpox goddess, is "the twenty-one sisters." In Shanti Nagar, Shitala is one of the Seven Sisters of Disease, but 21 sisters could be an alternative designation, no longer in use but nonetheless leaving ceremonial traces. This ritual with 21 lamps could be an indication of the undercurrent of non-Sanskritic goddess worship that is a feature of Diwali.

There was a large lamp with crossed wicks at the center of the square, and the wicks of the other lamps pointed toward it. The lamps were lit, everyone stood up, prayed for the welfare of the world, recited the Gayatri mantra,[16] and dropped *khil* on the square and lamps. Children threw *khil* into the air to express their happiness. Then a lamp was distributed to each Chamar household. It is the custom of the Chamars to exchange lamps at Diwali. Afterwards the children played with firecrackers and sparklers. One Chamar man had a shrine for Sayyid Pir, a Muslim saint, in his house. He worshipped this deity on Diwali.

We next hurried to the Potters' quarter, but there seemed to be little activity. A few lamps had been lit, but if a ceremony had taken place, we missed it. Four families of Jats who had recently immigrated from Delhi lived in houses near the Potters. We saw no ceremonies there, but a Jat woman told us that the four families exchanged lamps as did the Chamars. She said that it is a Delhi custom. They did not exchange lamps with other Jats. We asked if they made a *chauk* as did the Chamars. She said that a *chauk* was made on the following day, Gobardhan, and not on Diwali. However, the *chauk* was not used in the ritual but rather was drawn on the spot that had been filled by the cow dung figure, the focus of worship, before its removal at the end of the ceremony. Villagers often make a drawing to fill the vacant space that had been occupied during a ritual by a representation of the principal deity. Its removal leaves an empty space that is said to attract evil spirits and is therefore filled with a drawing.

By this time it was too late in the evening to see any more ceremonies, but nonetheless we went to the Sweeper quarter. A Sweeper man said that they neither exchanged lamps nor made a *chauk*, but light only enough lamps for their own use. We saw *khil* in the lamps, and a passing Chamar said that the Sweepers scattered *khil* just as do the Chamars.

A few months later, in the course of an interview about a shrine in the Sweeper quarter, a Sweeper man described the essential part of the Diwali ritual for the Sweepers. The shrine is for Lalbegh, "the Father of all the Sweepers." At Diwali and Holi, the Sweepers sacrifice a cock, furnished by rotation among the Sweeper families, and eat it collectively (fig. 31). The man said that if he prayed at the shrine,

FIG. 31. Small shrine of the Sweepers where they sacrifice a cock on Diwali and Holi.

"Grandfather, if you get me a job, I'll offer you a cock," he would certainly get a job. The Grandfather can fulfill all wishes. In 1977, a Sweeper woman described the Diwali ritual in much the same terms: "We play with firecrackers, wear new clothes, light candles and lamps, and light a lamp and sacrifice a cock to the ancestors. Then we eat meat."

Worship of the deities of the great tradition dominates Diwali, but villagers also propitiate gurus, ancestors, and mother goddesses. The Chamars claim to practice hookah (guru) worship on Diwali. The Sweepers worship at the shrine of their ancestor. At least one Brahman family also worships at an ancestral shrine. One Brahman family drew a depiction of "Diwali" on the wall and used it as a focus for the Diwali ritual. Such drawings appeared to be uncommon, for this was the only one that we saw.

Mother goddess worship, which is for the welfare of children, may be widespread on Diwali. A Chamar woman said that all the mother goddesses are worshipped on Diwali and Holi. A Brahman woman worshipped the Crossroads Mother Goddess. In 1958 the head of the Gardener family said that his family worshipped Kanti Mata, Goddess of Typhoid, on Diwali, Holi, and other festivals. In 1977, however, his son's wife denied that the family worshipped the matas on Diwali, or any other day, because the younger brother of her husband died on a festival for family welfare, either Karva Chauth or Hoi.

Hindu rituals are not constrained by a reigning orthodoxy. The rituals of families that observe the festival have many common elements, but there is also plenty of room for individual initiative, variation among families, and uncommon rituals. When Marriott (1955: 196) found a similar situation, he asked his villagers for an explanation. They replied that the new moon day of Karttik is auspicious, hence all the various rituals are appropriate on this day.

Some of the ritual commonly associated with Diwali is of little note in Shanti Nagar. A few villagers commented that Baniyas and Brahmans traditionally close their accounts on that day and open new ones. In 1958, there was only one merchant (Baniya) family in the village, and the head denied opening new books on Diwali. He had a small business and started a new book only when the old one was filled. There was no ceremony. In 1977, a 28-year-old Baniya woman claimed that this practice was observed on Diwali. However, it did not seem to us that the business had grown very much over the years, and the family was probably acting much as it had 20 years earlier. A Brahman told us in 1958 that the Baniya used to send *khil* and toys to the families of landowners on Diwali, but that the custom had died out. Such gifts would have been part of the jajmani system. Before literacy was common, the landowners summoned the Baniya to keep accounts at weddings, and the gifts may have been an expression of his thanks. This reciprocal relationship had largely disappeared by 1958.

It is a widespread Indian tradition that artisans worship their tools on Diwali. We have little evidence regarding this practice, for only a few families of artisans lived in the village: a blacksmith, two practicing potters, and one basketmaker in 1958, two basketmakers in 1977. An elderly Blacksmith woman said that the Blacksmith men would worship their tools on Diwali. She promised to call us for the ritual, but she did not, so we never saw it. We visited both the Potters and the Watercarriers (who make baskets) on Diwali, but they did not mention the worship of tools, and we did not ask them directly. Although the practice is considered to be traditional, and we have an illustration from a calendar showing a blacksmith worshipping his tools on Diwali, we found no mention of the custom in Channa (1984), Lewis (1958), Marriott (1955), Mukerji (1916), Underhill (1991), or Wadley (1975). Channa's illustration (1984: 129) depicted many deities and a variety of activities, but no one is worshipping tools. All five village studies issued by the 1961 Census of India devote a paragraph to Diwali, but none mentions the worship of tools. It probably does take place in Delhi villages, as stated by our Blacksmith informant, but it should be verified by interviewing and, especially, observation.

The following traditional, or at least common, practices were not noted in Shanti Nagar. Both Marriott (1955: 195) and Wadley (1975: 171) reported that an old basketry winnowing fan is beaten through the rooms of each house in the middle of the night to banish poverty, illness, and evil spirits. Marriott reported that the fans are immediately burned by small boys. These authors also reported the manufacture and use of lampblack, which is put around the eyes of children to protect them from the evil eye and to ward off eye infections. Although we made no note of the practice on Diwali, it is done so commonly at other times that special attention to lampblack on Diwali could have escaped our notice.

In 1977, some older villagers knew about the custom of staying awake all night to protect their money and ornaments from thieves, which was done in the 1950s, but they said that the custom had been abandoned. Channa (1984: 131) took account of this custom: "The night of Diwali is also the darkest night of the year and is referred to as the night of thieves. In which case it is appropriate to sit up the night." Lewis (1958: 222) interpreted the custom from two points of view: "It is the custom to leave a light burning all night in the house, and to leave the doors open, so that Laksmi can come in to bless the household. . . . But since there is a possibility that thieves may enter as well, some people now lock the front door."

Gifts and payments are a feature of Diwali. Patrons (jajmans) make small payments to their clients. Barbers usually receive one rupee. Sweepers are given some of their patrons' festive food and possibly some old clothing. Neither of these castes performs special services for their patrons on Diwali, although a few patron families may use a Barber to carry gifts. The Potters also participate in the jajmani exchange at Diwali, but in their case, they furnish lamps to their patrons.

As in many festivals, a wife's family sends gifts to her and to her husband's family. A wife's brother or a Barber may carry the gifts. Gifts are sent if a wife is at her husband's family; if she is with her natal family, no gifts are presented. The value of the gifts, or whether they are sent at all, depends on the economic situation of a family. The typical gift is food, clothing, and money as circumstances permit. For example, in 1958, a Brahman family gave their daughter's husband's family five seers of rice, five seers of sugar, and one rupee. A Jat family received 1.5 seers of ghee, 1.5 seers of raisins, two seers of *rawa* (a special flour), one rupee, and a suit of women's clothing (*tirh*) from the parents of their son's wife. The clothing was for the wife; the food and money were for the family. A Sweeper family, less well-off than the landowning Jats and Brahmans, sent two seers of rice, 1.5 seers of sugar, and one rupee to the family of their in-laws, which amounted to a significant expense. A Leatherworker man, a landless laborer, told us that he had sent his married sister a gift on Holi but that he could not afford to send anything for Diwali.

The foregoing gifts were recorded in 1958. The gifts in 1977 were similar. We were present when a Brahman man arrived with a gift for his married sister and her family: a sari, clothes for the children, and sweets. The head of this family told us that he had sent Rs. 15 to each of his four married daughters and Rs. 10 to his married sister. He did not use the services of the Barber, claiming that he was too expensive. He sent money orders or else his son carried the gifts.

No description of Diwali would be complete without mentioning liquor. We know that there was some drinking in 1958, but have no way of judging its extent. Prohibition was then in force in the Union Territory of Delhi, but people seemed to have little difficulty in obtaining liquor. Country liquor abounded. In 1958, a low-caste Sweeper couple told us that they drank on Diwali and Holi, adding that "everyone" drank on those festivals, but discreetly in their homes. The couple could buy a bottle, probably country liquor, for Rs. 5 from a vendor in a neighboring village whom they identified as a man from eastern Uttar Pradesh. Five rupees was a considerable sum in those days. An agricultural laborer earned only Rs. 1.50 per day. Some high-caste people also drank, usually in Delhi. When they drank in the village, they did so surreptitiously, because drinking was considered shameful.

Liquor was much more common in 1977 than two decades earlier, and people drank more openly. We have described the prominent role that liquor played in the panchayat election of 1977 (S. Freed and R. Freed, 1987). On Diwali, drinking was not confined to the evening but also took place during the day. Before the display of lamps and the ritual in the evening, the day had been difficult for us, owing especially to an unpleasant encounter with a drunken man. Many of the men who came to the village to visit friends and relatives that day seemed to have been drinking. Informant testimony differed little from that of 1958. A Barber woman told us that, at the end of the evening, her family drank liquor and wine, much like the Sweeper couple whom we interviewed years earlier. A Brahman woman said that "most" people drank, but named, however, only a few well-known drinkers. In any event, it was clear from our observations that drinking had either increased or become less secretive, or both.

Gobardhan

Gobardhan is celebrated on Karttik *sudi* 1, the day after Diwali. The name of the festival may be translated as "Increaser (or Nourisher) of Cattle" (*go vardhana*) or "Cowdung Wealth" (*gobar dhan*) (Marriott, 1955: 200; Vaudeville, 1980: 1). The festival is observed by families with cattle, which in Shanti Nagar includes most families. The characteristic feature of the festival is the worship of cow dung. Women collect dung from the family cattle and either make a small pile of it in the family courtyard or mold it into a crude anthropomorphic representation of the deity called Gobardhan. Men play *chaupar* in the morning. In the evening, the men of the family worship the deity with various offerings and seven (sometimes fewer) *phera*s (circumambulations) around the icon of Gobardhan. Patrons (jajmans) make small jajmani payments to their Barber and cowherd. The festival marks the beginning of the season when dung cakes can be made and stored and also the beginning of the sugarcane harvest. As a rule, dung cakes are not made during the monsoon season, for then they cannot be properly dried.

Some villagers say that there is no story connected to Gobardhan, but we recorded two myths that were offered to explain Gobardhan. One informant told a story from the Ramayana, recounted earlier (p. 94). In the war between Ram and Ravana, Ram's brother, Lakshman was wounded. The herbal medicine that saved his life was boiled in milk over a fire of dung. Therefore, Ram decreed that the day after Diwali was to be dedicated to cows.

In the more common story, the hero is Krishna who saves the people of Gokul from Indra's vengeance. Two informants recited brief versions of this myth from Puranic literature. Their terse accounts are in sharp contrast to the longer legends told at festivals such as Hoi, where a public recital of the legend is part of the ritual. The storytellers know that they will have to recite the legend and make an effort to keep the details in mind. No story is recited on Gobardhan. Although some villagers know the great traditional sanction for the festival, no one is called upon to tell it as part of a public ritual.

A Brahman man summarized the story: "A heavy rain was falling at Gokul [near Mathura, a city about 125 km south of Delhi on the Yamuna River]. Lord Krishna took a bit of cow dung on his finger and created a shed to protect the other people, milkmaids, from the rain. People make this little man of cow dung to remember the day when Krishna saved all of the people of Gokul from the rain." Another Brahman man added the crucial detail that Gobardhan is a sacred mountain near Mathura. "The mountain could not be moved, so it told its devotees that they could worship cow dung, which is also Gobardhan, in their homes. That is the reason for the festival."

A more complete version, taken from Growse, needs to be cited because it is one of the bases for interpreting Gobardhan as predating the Puranic literature. That is, the festival may represent a very ancient religious tradition.

At the end of the rains [monsoon] all the herdsmen began to busy themselves in preparing a great sacrifice in honour of Indra, [God of the Firmament, who controls rain] as a token of their gratitude . . . . [There was rivalry between Indra and Krishna.] Krishna . . . said to Nanda: "The forests where we tend our cattle cluster round the foot of the hills, and it is the spirits of the hills that we ought rather to worship." . . . The people of Braj [a region] were convinced . . . [and] set out for Gobardhan, where they solemnly circumambulated the mountain and presented their offerings to the new divinity. Krishna himself, in the character of the mountain gods, stood forth on the highest peak and accepted the adoration of the assembled crowd . . . . Indra . . . was very wrath, and summoning the clouds from every quarter of heaven, bid them all descend upon Braj in one fearful and unbroken torrent. . . . The ruin was but for a moment; with one hand Krishna uprooted the mountain . . . and balancing it on the tip of his finger called all the people under its cover. There they remained secure . . . [Growse, 1883: 59–60].

The annual ceremony or circumambulation and worship of Gobardhan in Mathura District is still enacted. Gobardhan is currently usually called Giriraj (royal hill). In earlier literature, it was called Annakut, and the festival of Gobardhan is also known as Annakut (Growse, 1883: 300). Vaudeville (1980: 1) said that Annakut refers to the feast, or "mountain of food," offered to Krishna-Gobardhan. Toomey (1990: 165) described a ritual, Annakuta (Mountain of Food), in a temple near Mount Gobardhan where ". . . a large mound of rice, sometimes numbering thousands of kilos, is constructed in the temple courtyard, facing the sanctum where the deity resides."

When villagers connect the Krishna myth to cow dung worship, it is because Krishna was a cowherd and was raised by a cowherd, Nanda, and his wife. However, villagers almost invariably state that the deity who is worshipped is cow dung or Gobardhan, not Krishna. Gobardhan and Krishna are separate deities in the opinion of villagers. As practiced in Shanti Nagar, the festival seems to have only the most tenuous connection to the great tradition. The villagers emphasize that Gobardhan is more important than Diwali, a classic great-traditional festival. The weak great-traditional sanction for Gobardhan contrasts with the importance of the festival, an apparent anomaly that raises the question of the nature and history of the Gobardhan festival.

Marriott (1955: 199-200) interpreted Gobardhan in terms of a devolution or parochialization of the great-traditional story of Krishna, Indra, and the mountain and its intregration with elements of the little tradition. "By the time that this great-traditional story has reached ritual enactment in a festival of Kishan Garhi it has taken on a cruder form and accumulated a number of homely details which have no evident justification in the Sanskritic myth. . . . The sacred hill of the *Purana* has become in each household yard a literal pile of cowdung . . . . [T]he agnates of each family worship it jointly . . . shouting in solemn procession 'Long live Grandfather Cowdung Wealth!'" In this view, the great tradition has historical priority although the little tradition is ethnographically dominant.

Vaudeville reversed the historical sequence. "The Annakut festival, with its primitive ritual, must be anterior to all the Puranic accounts of the *Govardhana-dharana* episode [the lifting of the Govardhana hill], since these accounts presuppose the existence of such a primitive cattle and mountain cult among the pastoral tribes of Braj" (Vaudeville, 1980: 4). In the myth from Growse, cited above, Krishna speaks of the existence of mountain spirits before Indra's revenge forces him to lift the mountain. Thus, these deities were on the scene before Krishna chose to manifest his divine nature in their form.

Cattle rites, which are fertility rites, are also ancient. Vaudeville made this argument from distributional evidence, especially the existence of cattle rites in various aboriginal tribes. The Oraons, a tribal group in Orissa, sacrifice a fowl to the Cowherd-god without apparent reference to Krishna. Vaudeville posited a relationship between cattle worship and snake worship, another fertility rite. "[I]t is clear that both cattle-worship and snake-worship are ancient fertility rites, in which women play a very significant part. In the case of the Govardhana-puja, the connection with snake-worship appears very strong . . ." (Vaudeville, 1980: 3). However, no trace of snake-worship can be discerned in the ritual of Gobardhan in Shanti Nagar.

In Shanti Nagar, Gobardhan is based on the ancient tradition of cattle and mountain worship that predates the Puranas. The Jats, the most numerous and dominant caste in the village, are peasant farmers who keep many cattle. They are not a caste of cowherds, but cattle are an integral part of peasant farming. Thus, the apparent anomaly of the greater importance of Gobardhan as compared to Diwali is explained by its focus on the welfare and fertility of cattle, so important for the cultivator. Many villagers told us that Gobardhan is the festival of the Jats. Diwali is of greater importance to other castes. It is a question of emphasis, not exclusion. Many Jats observe Diwali, and non-Jats, if they own cattle, worship Gobardhan.

Gobardhan and Krishna have not been merged in Shanti Nagar. The Puranic identification of Krishna and the mountain spirits would seem to foreshadow a rapprochement of Krishna and Gobardhan. However, there is a countervailing force, namely, the Arya Samaj. The Arya Samaj opposes strongly the cult of Krishna worship. A well-educated Brahman man, not an Arya Samaji himself but familiar with the doctrines of the sect from having read Swami Dayananda Saraswati's *The Light of Truth*, told us, "Gobardhan is celebrated by everyone and is considered more important than Diwali in Shanti Nagar. A figure of a man is made of cow dung and the men of the family worship him. Men play *chaupar* in the morning. The elements of Krishna worship associated with this day have been repressed because of Arya Samaj influences." In all our interviewing of 25 or so informants, only one person, a Brahman woman, clearly indentified Krishna with Gobardhan.

A Chhipi Dyer man described one means by which Krishna worship on Gobardhan could be suppressed. Speaking of his own family but also in general terms, he commented, "People used to make a man of dung. But most families have stopped now. The Arya Samajis say that you kill a man by making a man of dung and then making dung cakes of that. So my family stopped making a man. We collect dung in a pile." He was referring to the fact that the dung worshipped on Gobardhan is made into dung cakes after the festival. Dung cakes are burned. Therefore, to burn dung cakes that once represented a man is to kill him.

This Chhipi was the only informant who mentioned this belief, but his comment led us to examine the Gobardhans that we saw or that were described to us from the point of view of the Arya Samaj, mostly Jats, versus the more traditional version of Hinduism, Sanatan Dharma. Most Brahmans, the second largest caste of the village, follow the traditional beliefs of Sanatan Dharma.

The image that is worshipped takes two forms: a shapeless pile of dung or an anthropomorphic sculpture. Identification of Krishna with Gobardhan would be more obvious when the image represents a human figure rather than an amorphous mass. Hence, one might expect that the Jats would tend to use a pile of dung; the Brahmans, a sculptured image. We saw or heard about approximately 21 sculptures and 10 piles. The seven Brahman images were all sculptures. The six Jat images included four dung piles and two sculptures. We cannot with certainty characterize the other families as to sect although the Potters, Leatherworkers, Barbers, and Sweepers are best classified as Sanatan Dharma. Nine families representing this group of four castes made sculptures; only one used a pile of dung. Thus, the Sanatanis made sculptures and the majority of our small sample of Jats used just a pile of dung. In short, there is some evidence that the Arya Samajis avoid an anthropomorphic image, which suggests their opposition to multiple deities and Krishna worship. Most other villagers prefer an image, but almost no one identifies it with Krishna.

Festival activities begin early in the morning. After collecting dung from their family's cattle, women make a pile of it in their courtyard or, as is more often the case, mold it into the figure of a man. We watched women of the same Brahman family sculpt Gobardhan in both 1958 and 1977. In 1958, the work started at about 8:30 A.M. The senior woman of the household formed the arms, legs, face, and genitals of the figure, placed a small pot of milk on its genitals, and outlined it with wheat flour (atta). The sculptress interpreted this as feeding the god. Small spots of wheat flour marked the arms, legs, and face of the image (fig. 34). The women covered the figure with a cot to protect it until the evening worship. Before the ritual in the evening, sugarcane, a churn, and a mortar were placed beside the image.

A similar procedure was followed in 1977, the senior woman who made the image now being the wife of the family head instead of his deceased mother (fig. 32). A Jat man, a longtime friend of the family head, was there watching the work. He joked when his friend's wife formed the figure's genitals. The completed figure was outlined with wheat flour. Spots of wheat flour highlighted its arms, legs, and head, and a pot of unboiled milk, water, and sugar was placed on its navel. The sculptress made five small balls of dung, placing two under the figure's left arm and three under its right arm. The balls of dung probably represented the family's three water buffalo and two zebu cattle. A wooden pestle was laid beside the figure on its right (fig. 33). Then a cot covered with a quilt was placed over the image. Children had gathered to watch the activity. Several informants told us that they placed a stick on the cot to protect the image, but we never saw that arrangement. This Brahman family did not do so either in 1958 or 1977. We saw two images with sticks lying beside them, probably the equivalent of sticks placed on the cot.

After watching the molding of Gobardhan in 1958, we visited several other families. A Brahman man told us, "This is dung from the cows, and we are celebrating that happiness. We also worship sugarcane, the churn, and the bullock yoke. We put these beside Gobardhan and worship." In addition to the pot of milk and the wheat flour, another Brahman family placed cotton near the face of Gobardhan and dung cakes on the elbows and knees. They described this as the worship of milk, wheat flour, and cotton. Another Brahman family had two sticks on the image, one on either side of the navel. They represented a man and a woman. Cotton was lying around the image. Under each arm of the figure were two loaflike masses of dung, said to represent tobacco in Gobardhan's pockets. Yet another Brahman family placed bread under the right arm and a pot of *khil* under the left. An elderly woman told us that these items are auspicious for cattle. Little twigs were also stuck in the image.

We visited homes of the three large lower castes. We saw three Gobardhans in the Leatherworker quarter. Two of the images were decorated with cotton and *dub* grass.[17] The grass was gathered together at the top of the image like a canopy. One of the images had a hand-turned flour mill and a spindle under its arm. Another image was encircled with a structure like a house. *Dub* grass serves as fodder for cattle; one of its varieties is said to be an excellent pasture grass. It also has ritual uses (Crooke, 1989: 89, 177; Maheshwari, 1976: 390). The third Leatherworker image was just a pile of dung with a pot of sweetened water on it. A Gobardhan in the Sweeper quarter was undecorated except for three loaves of dung under each arm. A Potter family sculpted a large image decorated with three small pots on it and three large pots on the ground around it. The large pots contained water left over from Hoi. After the ritual, the water was mixed with Gobardhan to make dung cakes.

A family of Barbers protected their sculpture with a cot. The image had a pot on its stomach, a stick in its left hand, and a cloth in its right hand with an image of Krishna under the cloth. The Barbers explained that Krishna was a cowherd, who carried a stick. There were small loaves of dung near the image's right hand. The Barbers were not sure what they represented, but suggested that they might be cows. This image was the only one we saw where Krishna was clearly represented.[18] However, the Barbers did not identify Gobardhan with Krishna. They said, "We worship cow dung every year. This is cow-dung worship, not Krishna worship."

In both 1958 and 1977, we participated in the Gobardhan ritual of the same Brahman family, the one mentioned above where we photographed the molding of the image. The two rituals were sufficiently similar so that they could be partially combined in the following description. The ritual took place just after sundown, about 6:00 P.M. A large brass tray contained *khil*, turmeric, *malpuras*, two chapatis, and halva. A lighted lamp was placed on the little pot on the image's navel. On the ground beside the leader of the ritual was a pot (*lota*) of water. In 1958, the leader was the mother's brother of the family head. He gave each participant a handful of *khil*. While chanting two mantras, he put a *tilak* of turmeric on the image and sprinkled it with water and *khil*. When he scattered his *khil* on the image, the other participants also threw theirs. Reciting the Gayatri mantra, the men of the family then circled Gobardhan three times and bowed to the icon. That was all. A woman said that they would make dung cakes of Gobardhan that same evening which, after drying, would be placed at the bottom of a *bhitaura*, a pile of stored dung cakes protected from rain.

The leader in 1977 was the head of the family. In addition to the lighted lamp, he placed a one-rupee note on the image as an offering. He put a *tilak* of turmeric on all children and participants. He chanted the Shanti Path (Lesson of Peace), scattered *khil* on the image, and sprinkled it with water to bathe it. The men then circled the image seven times. The leader explained, "The purpose of the ceremony is to keep everyone safe, buffalo, grain, and milk, as Lord Krishna did at Gokul." He said, "The family Barber puts *dub* grass on the ears of his jajmans and is given something. [The Barber said that he received a rupee from his jajmans for putting a tilak on their foreheads.] The cowherd gets the food from the ceremony." After the ritual when it was growing dark, we heard firecrackers.[19]

The day after Gobardhan, a teenage Potter boy, who frequently visited our house and was a good informant, described his family's ritual of the preceding evening. The families of three of four brothers united to celebrate the festival. Present were our informant's mother, father, father's brother and his wife, and children. Despite the presence of adult men, our informant's mother and aunt took charge of the ritual, in contrast to the Brahman ceremony where men were the leaders and only men circled the image. Everyone was marked with a tilak of turmeric. However, the image of Gobardhan did not receive one. Lighted lamps were placed on the image, children scattered *khil* on it, and women sprinkled water on and around it. The mother and aunt circled the image once. The women had prepared some bread, probably from millet rather than from wheat, and fed it with some *khil* to their donkeys. They also distributed *khil* to some families in the neighborhood. Finally, the women made dung cakes from the image.

After the ceremony, images were made into dung cakes, almost always an odd number, 5, 7, or 11. Lewis (1958: 223) noted that ". . . even numbers suggest an end, while odd numbers indicate progress." Places where an image had rested did not remain vacant. It was customary to fill such places, for the empty space could attract malevolent spirits. The Brahman family whose ritual we attended in 1958 made 11 dung cakes, plastered the now-vacant site of the image with cow dung, and used wheat flour to outline a square. Two small loaves of dung (they did not have the characteristic shape of dung cakes) and the lamp used in the ritual were placed in the center of the square (fig. 35). The family followed a similar procedure in 1977.

We visited a few other families the day after Gobardhan. Another Brahman family (1958) had drawn a square but omitted the dung and the lamp. In 1977, this family made seven dung cakes from the image, plastered the empty space, and left a small mound of dung surmounted by the small pot that had rested on Gobardhan during the ritual. At a Leatherworker household (1958), the family made dung cakes and left a lamp on the empty space. They drew no square. At a Jat household (1977), there were two loaves of dung and a lamp.

Sugarcane is perhaps the most noteworthy of the many objects placed near or on the image of Gobardhan, for both dung and sugarcane represent the beginning of important activities. Dung cakes are made and stored after Gobardhan. They can be

FIG. 32. *(above)*
Brahman woman
sculpting a figure of
Gobardhan in dung,
1977.

FIG. 33. *(right)*
Gobardhan, the
completed image
shown in process in
figure 32. A pestle lies
beside the figure, in
foreground.

FIG. 34. *(left)* Gobardhan, sculpture of dung made by a Brahman woman, 1958. A small pot of milk rests on the figure. Wheat flour is used to outline the image and to highlight the head, arms, and legs. A stone mortar is beside the figure.

FIG. 35. *(below)* The image of Gobardhan shown in figure 34 was transformed into 11 dung cakes the following day. A square drawn with wheat flour, two small loaves of dung, and a lamp now occupied site of the image.

made to some extent throughout the year, and ten dung cakes are made for Dassehra 21 days before Gobardhan, to be saved and used later in the festival of Dev Uthani Gyas. But the extensive production of dung cakes for storage effectively begins on Gobardhan, when the dung from the image is made into cakes that are placed at the bottom of *bhitaura*s. This practice is different from the disposal of dung from the image in other villages. Both Marriott (1955: 200) and Wadley (1975: 129) reported that in the villages they studied it is made into an "enormous cracker" (Marriott) or into dung cakes (Wadley) that are saved and burned in the bonfire on the festival of Holi several months later.

The sugarcane harvest takes place after Gobardhan, when the long season of cutting and processing it begins. In 1958 sugarcane was by far the most valuable crop grown during the kharif season (S. Freed and R. Freed, 1978: 28–42). A few stalks of

sugarcane were usually placed beside the image of Gobardhan. In 1977 people sometimes specified that the number of stalks should be five. Buck (1917: 105) and Rose
(1919: 238) reported that five whole sugarcanes should be used. The presence of sugarcane with the Gobardhan image meant that it was worshipped just as were the
image itself and the other objects placed near it, such as a plow and a churn. Landless people in Shanti Nagar were traditionally entitled to take some sugarcane from
farmers' fields for use in the Gobardhan festival, so any family that wanted to worship sugarcane could do so. Farmers sometimes disputed the practice and fights
could develop (S. Freed and R. Freed, 1976: 174). By 1977 very little sugarcane was
cultivated, but villagers still claimed to put pieces of it with the image. One Brahman told us that he cultivated a little sugarcane for personal use and that he distributed pieces of it in his lineage. Such small-scale cultivation was probably the
source of much of the sugarcane used in the ritual in 1977.

Although sugarcane is worshipped during the ritual of Gobardhan, the harvest
does not receive priestly sanction in Shanti Nagar. Elsewhere, a priestly pronounce-
ment was part of the ritual. Buck (1917: 105) said, "The Brahman then takes the sugar
cane and eats a bit; and till that time nobody must cut, or press, or eat cane." Mukerji (1916: 152) wrote, "A priest then picks up one of the sugarcanes, crunches a bit
of it at one end, and declares the sugarcane ripe for cutting. How confusedly things
mix up in the hands of the Indian peasant is best instanced in the case of the Gobardhan festival, which, beginning as a celebration in honour of Krishna's cowherd
life, ends as a ceremony preliminary to the cutting of the sugarcane crop."

The confusion that Mukerji attributed to villagers might with more
justification be laid on the doorstep of many scholars. The confusion comes from the
interpretation that Gobardhan began as a festival in honor of an event in the life of
Krishna. However, if one regards Gobardhan as an ancient festival of thanksgiving
for the harvest, with a later Puranic accretion, then the nature of Gobardhan
becomes clear. It is a thanksgiving for the rains, the subsequent harvest, and the
products of the cow. It is also a fertility rite. Its placement after the monsoon and the
kharif harvest may appear somewhat puzzling in terms of the current agricultural
scene, for wheat, the major food crop of the region, is grown during the rabi season.
However, its modern cultivation depends to a great extent on irrigation. The importance of the rabi crop as compared to the kharif crop has greatly increased after irrigation became commonplace. Before irrigation, however, agriculture depended
heavily on the monsoon. Thus, an ancient rite of thanksgiving would logically follow the monsoon season.

Cotton embellishes some of the images of Gobardhan. Cotton was once grown
extensively in Shanti Nagar, but in 1958 it was a relatively minor crop, grown on
only about 11 acres. It had almost disappeared in 1977, occupying less than half an
acre, in all likelihood no longer grown as a cash crop but only for personal use. Sugarcane was not even mentioned in the government's crop chart for kharif, 1977.

Both of the crops honored at Gobardhan, sugarcane and cotton, have lost
almost all their economic importance in Shanti Nagar since the 1950s. However,
they continue to be used for ritual purposes. Rice, an important kharif crop, is ubiquitous in the ritual, but as an offering to the image rather than an object of venera-

tion. Wheat flour (*atta*) is used to draw designs and also to some extent as an offering to the image. Only one informant spoke of worshipping wheat flour. From the point of view of economics, sugarcane and cotton would appear to be ripe for replacement in the ritual. However, the only replacement candidate from the kharif crop would be vegetables, particularly tomatoes, the most important of today's kharif crops. Vegetable farming, while highly profitable, lacks prestige among the Jats. The Jats think of themselves as wheat farmers. A Jat standing beside his wheat harvest feels like a king. This attitude, combined with the conservatism of religion, suggests that sugarcane, and also cotton, will retain their traditional place in the ritual of Gobardhan for some time to come.

GANGA NAHAN

Ganga Nahan (Ganges Bathing), also called Ganga Snan, is observed on Karttik Purinmashi (Karttik *sudi* 15). It is the last of the great fall festivals. The next three-and-a-half months have only two Hindu festivals of note, Makar Sankranti and Sakat. However, two noteworthy secular holidays take place in this interval: Christmas-New Year's Day (secular for Hindus) and Republic Day. Heightened festival activity begins again in mid-Phalgun (February–March) with three important festivals during a fortnight, from Shivaratri to Holi.

Ganga Nahan is the second festival of the year that features bathing. Jyesth ka Dassehra, the first one, takes place after the rabi harvest. A minor festival in Shanti Nagar, it honors Yami, a river goddess. The motive for the villagers' observance of the festival, when one is given, is thanksgiving for a blessing, such as the birth of a son. Ganga Nahan, the second bathing festival, is celebrated in late November after the kharif harvest. Much more widely observed by the villagers than Jyesth ka Dassehra, Ganga Nahan is likewise a festival of thanksgiving for a past blessing, such as the marriage of a daughter or, especially, the birth of a son. People also observe it in hope of future blessings. The festival has particular meaning for unmarried young women and girls, who long for the blessing of marriage to an ideal husband like Krishna. In fact, they practice ritual bathing every day during the entire month of Karttik, when they arise before sunrise and in groups parade singing to the village well where they bathe. The full moon night, the last day of the month, is the climax of this activity. An element of Ganga Nahan noted by other authors (e.g., Lewis, 1958: 226) but not mentioned by the villagers is that bathing in the sacred rivers, the Ganga or the Yamuna, cleanses one from sin. In the village version, the sins in question are the inadvertent ones that accompany agriculture, such as killing insects.

Ganga Nahan honors Ganga, a major river goddess. Only one villager, saying that he took the name of Hari at the river, mentioned any other deity. Hari is an epithet of Vishnu. Ganga is connected both to Vishnu and Shiva, but especially to the latter. The heavenly Ganga, flowing from the toe of Vishnu, was brought to earth by the prayers of Bhagirath, a saint. To save the earth from the shock of Ganga's fall, Shiva caught the river on his brow and checked her course with his matted locks. Thus, Ganga is often represented as flowing from the hair of Shiva.

A Leatherworker man, in the habit of reading religious literature, told us a version of the Bhagirath story, using it to illustrate two Hindu beliefs. The first has to do with the sanctity of the Ganga. After bringing the Ganga to earth, Bhagirath died. His bones and skull were thrown into the river, whereupon he achieved mukti (moksha), release from the round of rebirths. Mukti is the reward of the most pious and virtuous individuals. That one can achieve it by having one's mortal remains immersed in the river is a measure of Ganga's sacredness.

The second belief concerns the distribution of power among the deities, in this case, Bhagwan (God), Shiva, and Bhagirath. The Leatherworker explained, "Shiva is more powerful than Bhagwan. God rules the world but Shivji [-*ji* is an honorary suffix] keeps the world in order, so he's just like a guru and more powerful. All three have the same power, but each has his own domain. Just as a king rules the country, a governor also has powers. They have parallel powers. Bhagirath is a saint, but I don't worship him because he worshipped a higher power [Shiva]. Why shouldn't I also worship the higher power myself?" This explanation justifies either ignoring a lower deity to worship a higher one or, depending on circumstances, imploring a low-ranking deity on the grounds that the particular blessing requested of him lies in his domain. The Leatherworker went to worship Ganga on Ganga Nahan only twice in his life. He personally believes in worshipping the highest-ranking deity when he wants something.

Mukerji (1916: 178–182) considered Ganga Nahan to be a festival that has changed significance in the course of its history while retaining the same date. Both its placement after the kharif harvest and the devotions of villagers mark it as a festival of thanksgiving. In Hindu mythology, the festival celebrates Shiva's victory over the demon Tripurasura. The gods were being subjected to irregular warfare by demons who issued from three towers that served as sanctuaries. Feeling powerless, the gods appealed to Shiva. He showered the demons with so many arrows that not one survived. However, the great magician Mai, who had given the demons their sanctuary, again came to their aid. He threw their bodies into a well filled with nectar, a miraculous fluid that restored them to life. Vishnu drained the nectared well, and Shiva again attacked, finally making an end of Tripurasura (the Triple-towered demon). The victory was won on the full-moon day of Karttik (Mukerji, 1916: 180–181). Underhill (1991: 95) stated that the festival, which she calls Tripuri's full moon, is the second greatest day in the year for Shiva worship.

However, Mukerji (1916: 181–182) noted that the full moon of Karttik has lost its connection to Shiva and has become a Vaishnavite festival commemorating the day of Krishna's Ras Lila, his fabled amorous dance with the milkmaids. Later with the rise of Shaktism, the devotees of Shakti claimed the day as sacred to the river goddess Ganga, and it became one of the most important bathing days of the year.

Ganga Nahan in Shanti Nagar is a day of goddess worship with allusions to the amorous Krishna. We neither heard about nor observed any remnant of Shiva worship. The festival probably has its origins in religious practices older than contemporary Hinduism, namely, in the worship of nature deities and mother goddesses (see also Balfour, 1885, 2: 16). The myth of Shiva and Tripurasura represents a later accretion, as does the Ras Lila. Since the Arya Samaj is hostile both to Shiva worship and the cult of Krishna, one would expect that elements of the festival relating to either deity would be repressed.

Villagers go either to the Ganga or the Yamuna for Ganga Nahan. The Ganga is the most sacred Indian river. Hardwar (Gate of Hari), where the Ganga breaks through the Siwalik Hills onto the Gangetic plain, is one of the most popular places of pilgrimage for Hindus and the favorite of the people of Shanti Nagar. On major bathing festivals, Hardwar becomes an immense camping ground, some 10 mi long and 1 mi or so deep. Villagers often go to Garhmuktesar on the Ganga, which is closer to Shanti Nagar than is Hardwar. People who have neither time nor money for a trip to the Ganga go to Delhi for a dip in the Yamuna. On Ganga Nahan, the buses from Shanti Nagar to Delhi are packed with pilgrims. People of all castes observe the festival.

A 14-year-old Brahman girl described her pilgrimage to the Ganga in 1957. Her grandmother took her, having taken her two older sisters, one at a time, the preceding two years. Her younger sister was in poor health, and her grandmother would probably not attempt to take her on a pilgrimage the following year. The girl said that she and her grandmother were part of a large group that included both Brahmans and Jats. Adult men were well represented. Our informant named four Brahmans and two Jats. Women would not make a pilgrimage without adult men to protect them.

The group took the train to Hardwar and then walked, or perhaps took a conveyance, to the camp ground. They lived in a camp, arose early, lit a holy fire at the river, bathed, and ate. Our young informant offered fruit, flowers, and a small coin, which she claimed was the usual offering. Only a person who had made a vow would offer more. For example, a woman blessed with a son in answer to a vow would offer hair from the infant's first haircut and sweetmeats (*laddus*) worth Rs. 1.25. This pilgrimage was our informant's first. The fair was in full swing, and the youngster enjoyed it. A fair is always held at places of pilgrimage on important festivals. As is customary, the girl brought back a small container of Ganga water. She made no mention of distributing *prasad* after her return, but that is customary.

A 50-year-old Blacksmith woman mentioned distributing *prasad* after her pilgrimage. She had been to the Ganga eight times, the first time when she was a child and also after her wedding. Her offerings were flowers, sweets (*batashas*), and coins. She brought back Ganga water in addition to the *prasad*. She took an aggressive approach to the goddess, saying, "Ganga, you'd better give me some more occasions to come and make offerings to you." She enjoyed the fair and took advantage of the pilgrimage to visit some places of interest.

A Jat woman, an immigrant from Delhi during the decade following Independence, told of a custom that no one else mentioned. In 1977, we were in her courtyard a fortnight before Ganga Nahan and spotted a small plot where shoots of barley were growing. We asked her about them. She said, "We planted the barley on the full moon of Ashvin [a month before Ganga Nahan] and will harvest it on the full moon of Karttik. Then we'll take it to the Ganga and throw it in the river." Barley, the ritual grain in Shanti Nagar, is used in several festivals. The custom of offering barley to the goddess may be a city ritual in view of the woman's previous home. The other villagers do not practice this custom.

A Brahman man, a devout Sanatani about 50 years old, emphasized the role of the *panda*s (or *pujari*s), the Brahmans who preside at the Ganga and assist worshippers. He went to the Ganga the first time when he was 14 and, since Independence, claimed to go every year. As a child, he enjoyed the fair more than the bathing. People sing devotional songs and take part by gender in religious discussions. Devotees vow to abandon various vices, such as alcohol or even hookah smoking. A woman broke into the conversation to emphasize that childless women make offerings. All the pilgrims from Shanti Nagar camp in one location. They make arrangements with the *panda*s and pay for the camp site. *Panda*s may aid pilgrims with pots and other amenities. *Panda*s visit Shanti Nagar and are paid grain, gur (brown sugar), and money. They bring holy Ganga water and *prasad* on their visits. The *panda*s keep records of villagers who have visited the Ganga in former years and recite their names. In this regard, they resemble professional genealogists (*bhat*s), but their lists are limited to pilgrims.

A 70-year-old Potter emphasized the commercial side of pilgrimages. In 1958, he claimed to go to the Ganga every two or three years. He said he stays for seven or eight days, bathes morning and evening, and may spend up to Rs. 50 (the comparable figure in 1977 was Rs. 100). Villagers bring their food, chiefly wheat flour and ghee, from home. The Potter sometimes buys and sells donkeys at the fair. Potters often go to fairs to trade animals, so pilgrimages fit well with their normal business activities. The Potter's wife told us that *panda*s along the banks of the river sell sandalwood paste (*chandan*, made by grinding sandalwood with water) to pilgrims. After bathing, the devotees put a tilak of *chandan* on their foreheads. The fragrant sandalwood is often employed in Hindu rituals, as, for example in Shanti Nagar, at the fire ceremony that concludes the ritual of Akhta.

In our 1958 interviews, three of our informants mentioned the riots and killing that accompanied the partition of the pre-Independence country into India and Pakistan in 1947. Published figures of the number of people killed, both Hindus and Muslims, are only guesses. They range from 200,000 to 2 million. The best Indian and British historians of the period suggest figures from 200,000 to 500,000. In any event, descriptions of the carnage are graphic (R. Freed and S. Freed, 1993: 26). Village children at an impressionable age saw Muslims being killed at Hardwar. Muslims were also killed close to Shanti Nagar, both in a small neighboring village and at a nearby railroad. However, children may not have been present on those occasions. The killings at Hardwar at the time of a religious festival seem to have made a considerable impression.

The account of the killings by a 22-year-old Brahman woman on her first pilgrimage when she was 11 years old specified weapons and their effectiveness. She began by describing her customary ritual during Karttik, beginning with the daily bath at the village well and culminating in a group pilgrimage to the Ganga by train or bus three or four days before the full moon. The pilgrims give alms to *panda*s and beggars, light lamps, and have the scriptures read. She continued, "The first time that I went was the time of the killing. I saw a lot of Muslims being killed at the Ganga. I saw them being cut with a *gandasa* (a heavy cleaver used to cut sugarcane [S. Freed and R. Freed, 1978: fig. 9]). If you hit with it, it goes deep inside the body. I saw their horses and elephants running down the Ganga." Her mother quickly chimed in, "The Muslims started it. They killed Hindu children and pegged them against the wall."

Another Brahman woman went to the Ganga at the time of the killing when she was 12 years old. She had not made a pilgrimage since then. People do not go every year. Long periods may elapse between pilgrimages. However, it seems likely that the shock of witnessing the chaos and killing left unsettling memories that discouraged subsequent visits. A 50-year-old Brahman man, who claimed to visit the Ganga every year, told us that he stayed home during the riots. In his case, it was prudence more than anything else.

A middle-aged Brahman woman described a ritual of human sacrifice practiced by formerly childless women who were granted the boon of a child. She said, "A childless woman goes to the Ganga the first year and begs for a child. Then the second year she comes back and throws the child in the river. If she is sure in her mind that the child was really given by Ganga, the child will be returned to her lap. But if she is afraid that the child will not come back, then the Ganga will swallow the child. Many women from this village have done this." When we asked for names, she could not supply any, and qualified the account by adding "You go and make a promise. Then you fulfill that promise. You may not throw the child in the Ganga but maybe a gourd or something else."

We never investigated the question of whether infants were really sacrificed at the Ganga, as the Brahman woman clearly stated, because such a practice seemed bizarre. After having prayed for a child, why would a mother sacrifice the desired infant to Ganga? There is a parallel in the Bible, the story of Abraham and Isaac, and so the theme is widespread and ancient. Moreover, such sacrifices may have taken place a few centuries ago in India. With regard to a bathing festival conducted on Saugor Island at the mouth of the Ganga in mid-January (Gangasagara Snana), Hopkins (1898: 450) wrote, "Here there is a grand fair and jewels are cast into the river as propitiation to the river-goddess. Not long ago it was quite customary to fling children also into the river, but this usage has now been abolished." Balfour (1885, 3: 474) wrote, "Up to 1802, Hindus drowned their children at the mouth of the Ganges, but the rite was then prohibited." Channa (1984: 105) noted, "Long ago, women threw their infants into the waters as a form of propitiation or sacrifice to the mother river."

This sacrifice in modified form is still practiced. A Brahman woman, who goes with her husband to the Ganga twice every year, probably on Jyesth ka Dassehra and Ganga Nahan, told us:

> When my next child was born after the first died, I went to the Ganga and offered the new baby there.

Asked how this was done, she replied,

> As you have seen, women go to worship the well after the birth of a son, so we go to a place near the River Ganga and buy *karva*s [pitchers] and offer them to the Ganga. My sister-in-law, mother-in-law, and sometimes

other relatives accompany me. We worship near the Ganga, and a priest and my sister-in-law hold a piece of cloth in the water. I drop the infant into the water above the cloth. Immediately my sister-in-law and the priest bring the child up by pulling on the cloth. Then I take the child from them and give them money, as if I am buying the child from them [R. Freed and S. Freed, 1993: 137].

In the above account, the offering of the child to Ganga only symbolized a sacrifice, for the child was instantly recovered. The pitchers offered to Ganga were also a symbolic enactment of human sacrifice.

The modern form of offering a child to Ganga in all likelihood derives from an earlier ritual of human sacrifice, now largely consigned to a distant past. What is startling in the above account of the Brahman woman is her statement that the practice has been recently observed by "many women." She may of course have been referring to the current symbolic form of child sacrifice. On the other hand, cases of sati, a practice strongly suppressed by the government, have cropped up in recent decades (R. Freed and S. Freed, 1993: 34–37). Relatively recent cases of child sacrifice also have been reported, and ritual sacrifices to Ganga cannot be dismissed summarily, especially as the custom would fit very well with the formerly widespread practice of female infanticide. Female infanticide, much less common than formerly, continues today in various forms. As concerns ritual sacrifice of infants to Ganga, it is almost certain that such victims were female. In view of the great value placed on sons, it is almost inconceivable that a family would dispose of a healthy male infant.[20]

SAKAT

Sakat is observed on Magh *badi* 4. The festival is also known as Sakat Chauth (Sakat Fourth). One of our informants said that Sakat is also called Til Kuti ka Vrat, or the fast (*vrat*) for the characteristic festive dish, which is *til kut*, a mixture of sesame seeds and brown sugar. A Dyer man said that the day is also known as Ganesh Chauth. Bhatia, Nautiyal, and Srivastava, authors of village studies for the Census of India, 1961, wrote that Sakat is *sankat* (trouble, difficulty) in the dialect of the Union Territory of Delhi, which would translate the name of the festival as "Difficulty Fourth" (Bhatia, 1961: 64: Nautiyal, 1961: 156; Srivastava, 1961: 68). Underhill designated the festival as Samkashta chaturthi (Difficult Fourth). She commented that the fourth lunar day of each fortnight ". . . is indirectly dedicated to Shiva, being days for propitiating his son Ganesha." She noted that some people worship the moon on both bright and dark fourths, but that the custom is being merged with the worship of Ganesh, whose devotees ". . . fast on these same days, worshipping him in the dark half at moon-rise . . ." (Underhill, 1991: 69, 95, 157). Ganesh is known as Obstacle Remover, in which role he is an appropriate deity for propitiation on Difficulty Fourth.

Bhatia, Nautiyal, and Srivastava gave the date of the festival as the full-moon day of Magh, despite its name, which suggests that it is observed on the fourth. Calling the festival simply Sakat, Marriott (1955: 192) reported its date as Magh *badi* 1–2. Wadley (1975: 212), also naming the festival only Sakat, dated it Magh *badi* 3(4), which in all likelihood means that observance begins on the third and ends on the fourth. Majumdar (1958: 253) said, "The *Sakat festival* is always celebrated in *Magh*, but the date is not fixed, and sometimes it falls before *Makar Sankranti*, and sometimes after . . . ." The date of Sakat is in fact fixed, just as is the date of Makar Sankranti. However, Makar Sankranti has a solar date, and Sakat is dated by the luni-solar calendar, which means that Sakat appears to shift its date with reference to Makar Sankranti.

Sakat is a fast observed by women for the welfare of their children, especially sons. All our information about the day comes from interviews in 1978. We never saw any activity, but there is not much to see. Sakat is not celebrated with processions of singing women or public rituals. Women fast, cook festive food, and may distribute *prasad*. Almost everything transpires in the home. Many women do not observe the festival (some informants thought that it was confined to only a few castes) and a few informants believed that the day was not celebrated at all in Shanti Nagar.

A middle-aged Brahman man described the fast as a very old tradition. Women pound sesame seeds and gur (brown sugar) together to make *til kut*, eat some, and distribute the rest as *prasad*, especially if a son is in his first year. Women with sons (or brothers) bathe and fast during the day. At approximately noon or midafternoon, a woman recites the story of Sakat, after which women may drink water and eat a little sugar. The festive meal is not eaten until evening after an offering to the moon. In terms of lunar days, the fast is broken with the festive meal on the fourth day, but observance begins on the third. Fasting on Sakat is thought to protect a son from misfortune. Underhill (1991: 40) speculated that sesame is believed capable of warding off evil spirits.

A 26-year-old married Bairagi woman said, "I used to keep the fast on the fourth day after the full moon when I was with my parents, but as no one in this village does it, I have also stopped doing it. People who keep it make *til laddu*, offer some to the moon, and then eat it. Then they have their meal." A Brahman woman said, "Sakat is celebrated on the third, but when water is offered to the moon it is on the fourth. Women fast. The fast is said to remove all dangers. Women eat *til* [sesame] and distribute it. I have heard that today is Sakat. However, I [mistakenly] kept the fast on the third of the previous month."

We interviewed three Brahman women who were fasting. One said, "This fast is kept for sons. I will hear the story at about 3:00 or 4:00 P.M. and then will take tea. I will eat my meal at night after about 7:30." Another of these women said, "Anyone can keep this fast, but the Jats don't know much about it. Usually only Brahmans and Baniyas keep the fast." The women said that the fast is observed on Magh *badi* 3. The fourth day begins in the evening (but not every year, of course). Women take their meal after seeing a star in the sky, but one of the women waited until moonrise at about 8:30 or 9:00 P.M. One woman gave us *til kut* as *prasad*.

A Merchant family whose head was a government official (patwari) had been living in Shanti Nagar for three years. The family—husband, wife, and two daughters—came from Gurgaon District, Haryana. There were no sons. Nonetheless, the wife observed the fast on the fourth, claiming that it is for children and not just for sons. She said that only Merchants keep the fast. She consumed nothing during the day, not even tea, and did not eat until she saw the moon. Her husband said, "She went out of the house twice looking for the moon but couldn't see it. She couldn't even feed her daughter [two months old], because she had not eaten anything herself, where would the milk come from. The baby was crying a lot because she was hungry. The third time she went out she saw the moon."

We asked her if she performed a puja. She said "yes." We asked the name of the deity she worshipped. She said, "Before starting to cook, you make Sakat on the *chakla* [the board on which dough is rolled]." This line of questioning often does not yield information in the form that is anticipated. To ask what deity is being worshipped is equivalent to asking for the name of the festival. The woman's reply suggests that an image of a deity called Sakat is drawn on the board. Marriott (1955: 201) encountered a similar situation, that is, informants' replying with the name of the festival when asked about the goddess being worshipped on Nine Nights. (See Diwali and Sanjhi.) The Merchant woman distributed *prasad* of *til kut* to conclude the festival.

The only permanent Baniya family in Shanti Nagar paid little attention to Sakat. The older parents in all likelihood knew a good deal about it, but their strong Arya Samaj beliefs would preclude their observing it. The younger generation seemed to be ignorant of the festival. Their son's 28-year-old wife with two sons and one daughter said, "I don't know anything about this fast. A Brahman woman told me to keep it, and so I asked her about it. But I didn't keep it because I never before kept it and don't know anything about it."

In addition to the interviews recorded in some detail above, we surveyed ten people. All were women except for a Dyer man, who said that his family, the only Dyer family in the village, observed the festival as a fast for sons. One of the two Merchant families, recent immigrants to Shanti Nagar, kept the fast as described above. Otherwise, only Brahmans celebrated Sakat. Informants of the following castes denied celebrating the festival, sometimes disclaiming knowledge of it, or adding that no one in the village observed the day: Barber, Blacksmith, Jat, Leatherworker, Mendicant Priest, Potter, Sweeper, and Watercarrier. Sakat is chiefly a festival for Brahmans.

Majumdar (1958: 253–54) described the observance of Sakat in Mohana, a village near Lucknow, Uttar Pradesh. Women of all castes, but only those who have sons, celebrate the day. Women fast and worship a goddess, Sakat Maharani, for the welfare and good health of their sons. The goddess is believed to help boys in difficulty. Women prepare festive food in the morning. The puja takes place in the evening after moonrise.

Women make an image of Sakat Maharani with flour on a wooden plank. (One of our informants reported a similar practice.) Some foods and a betel nut are also placed on the plank. The figure of a goat is outlined on a metal plate. A lamp with four wicks is lit, and the women recite the story of Sakat Maharani. This ends the puja. The women apparently make no offering to the moon. The women then break their fast. Majumdar does not speak of a distribution of *prasad*, although in all like-lihood it takes place. *Til kut* is not the characteristic festive food. Its place seems to be taken by *laddu*s made of rice flour and jaggery rather than sesame and jaggery (gur).

We never collected the story of Sakat as told in Shanti Nagar and had the impression that very few women knew it. However, Channa (1984: 115–117) offered a full version of the tale. The story of Sakat (Chauth) Mata is told in front of a dia-gram of the goddess sketched on a wall. All offerings are *laddu*s of *til kut*. As in most of the festivals of women, the tale is based on relations within the family, in this case, between brothers' wives, an older sister-in-law (*jethani*), and a younger one (*devrani*).

The *devrani* was very poor and the *jethani* was very rich. The rich wife never helped the poor wife. The *devrani* washed utensils for her *jethani*, who in turn gave her leftover food to eat. The *devrani* and her children barely managed to subsist. On Sakat Chauth, the *jethani* prepared many tasty dishes to break her fast. The *devrani* also fasted but was so poor that she had nothing to cook. After cleaning her *jethani*'s utensils, she asked her for some food. Her *jethani* lied, saying that because she had kept a fast, there was no food, when in fact she had hidden all the delicious dishes that she had prepared. The *devrani* and her children went to bed hungry.

Chauth Mata came in the night. She woke up the *devrani* and asked where she might defecate. The *devrani* said, "The whole house is lying in front of you. Defe-cate where you like." Chauth Mata defecated all over the house and then asked the *devrani* where she could clean herself. The *devrani* said "Do it on my head." The next morning when the *devrani* got up she found the whole house full of gold coins and her hair was filled with pearls.

The *devrani* told her *jethani* what had happened. The *jethani* was very greedy and decided to try her luck on the next Sakat festival. The scenario was repeated but the results were different. When the *jethani* awoke, she found her whole house filled with feces and her hair stunk horribly. Her unsympathetic husband told her that she was a greedy fool and got what she deserved. He ordered her to clean herself and the house. She did as she was told and realized her folly. From then on, the *devrani* and *jethani* lived harmoniously.

Beck et al. (1987: 151–153) recounted a similar version of the tale from Uttar Pradesh. One noteworthy difference is that Sakat is a male deity rather than a god-dess. Lord Sakat comes in the night to the house of the *devrani* disguised as an old man. His feces are transformed into gold. When the *devrani* explained to her *jethani* what had happened, the greedy *jethani* decided to repeat exactly what her *devrani* had done. She said to her *devrani*, "I would now like to work at your house as a ser-vant. Please treat me just as I have treated you" (Beck et al., 1987: 152). Her hopes were disappointed. On the next Sakat, Lord Sakat filled her house with feces rather than gold. Moreover, the two women were not reconciled. Instead of realizing her folly, the *jethani* began to quarrel with her *devrani*. The *devrani* said, "Don't pick a quarrel with me. . . . [Y]ou tried to imitate me because of your greed and envy. So you got your just desert [sic]" (Beck et al., 1987: 153).

Sakat is the third of the four festivals whose myths deal with four important, potentially tense relationships that a woman enters at marriage: namely, with her husband, mother-in-law, husband's sister, and husband's brother's wife. The tale related on Sakat is delightful and engaging, but in comparison with the stories associated with Karva Chauth, Hoi, and the fast for Santoshi Mata, it is sparse, both in character and plot. Aside from the deity, there are only two personages, the *jethani* and the *devrani*. A husband makes a brief appearance at the end of one version. But the roles of mother-in-law, and husband's sisters and brothers, which are usually present, are all absent. As for plot, there is no treachery, broken taboos, exile, or usurpation of roles. The dramatic device is the repetition of the same event but with different outcomes. This contrast illustrates the moral theme of the story: the common Indian maxim that one should act with no thought of reward. Selfless service is rewarded with new riches or with painful losses restored. Actions based on greed lead to unhappiness.

The purpose of Sakat Chauth, the welfare of children, is a minor theme in the myth, which is dominated by the relationship of sisters-in-law. However, the younger sister-in-law endures her suffering at the hands of her elder sister-in-law for the welfare of her children. She lives by the rule of selfless service, first for her family and again when Sakat Mata pays a visit. She and her children are rewarded accordingly.

SILI SAT

Sili Sat (Cold Seventh) is observed on Chaitra *badi* 7. The festival is also known as Basora (Stale Bread Festival), Shitala ki Saptami (Shitala's Seventh), and Mata Rani (Mother Queen). It is strictly a woman's festival, observed chiefly by married woman for the welfare of their children. The festival occurs just one week after Holi and marks the end of the cool weather and the onslaught of the hot season when cooked food is no longer kept overnight. At this season in times past, the dreaded smallpox began to rage through the countryside, subsiding only when the monsoon had well begun. In 1980 the World Health Organization declared that smallpox had been eradicated from the world. Sili Sat has been named after Shitala, the smallpox goddess, who is also called Chechak Mata in Shanti Nagar. Children were especially vulnerable to the ravages of smallpox, for adults, once having had the disease, were immune for life. One of our informants, a teacher of Sanskrit, explained:

> The day is called Sili Sat because it is observed on the seventh day; and Shitala [The Cool One] became Sili [cold] in village language, so now we eat cold food cooked the day previously. The seventh day when Sili comes is for the worship of the seven goddesses [of disease].

Shitala is a complex goddess. In Hindi-speaking northern India, she combines the attributes of two goddesses, the smallpox goddess and Shashthi, a Bengali goddess who is the protector of children. In Gujarat, Shitala entirely loses her connection with smallpox and becomes instead the source of good fortune, husbands, and sons. Shashthi is a variant form of sixth *(chhathi),* hence her epithet, Mother Sixth (Williams, 1883: 229; Bhattacharyya, 1953: 200). She is a deity of classical derivation, the wife of Karttikeya, also called Skanda, the God of War. Shashthi is associated with Shiva worship and appears to be both a malevolent as well as a benevolent deity who can injure or aid newborn infants and their mothers. Tetanus and puerperal fever, both diseases related to childbirth and common in India, occur during the first six days after birth and are blamed on the will of this mother goddess.

A birth rite known as Chhathi (Sixth) is celebrated in Shanti Nagar the sixth day after birth. The mother's midwife, traditionally a Sweeper, or a senior woman of the mother's household, draws the figure of Bemata, Krishna's midwife, on a wall. Holding her infant, the mother faces the drawing, executed in cow dung, and worships. In other parts of India, Sixth, or Mother Sixth, is associated with Shashthi. Thus, a similar rite can be celebrated by devotees of either Krishna or Shiva. In fact, Bemata and Shashthi, the latter as an aspect of the smallpox goddess, have points in common. The connection of a Sweeper midwife and Bemata on Sixth is echoed by the role of Sweeper women with Shitala on Sili Sat (R. Freed and S. Freed, 1980: 372–376).

In Shanti Nagar, where her function is limited chiefly to protecting children from smallpox, Shitala is one of seven goddesses, known as the Seven Sisters, who together control the epidemic pustular diseases, such as typhoid and measles. These diseases are conceived of as mother goddesses; thus smallpox is Shitala Mata, typhoid is Kanti Mata (or Moti Jhara [Pearly Inflammation] or Moti Mata [Pearl Mother]), and so on. A Brahman woman explained, "We worship the matas so that children will not have the matas [diseases]." In Shanti Nagar, the general protective function of Shitala is partly assumed by the other disease goddesses, and, beyond them, by deities, both male and female, who are guardians of the village. These other deities are the Crossroads Mother Goddess, the Panch Pir, who are five Muslim saints, and Bhumiya, a godling who is the founding male ancestor of the village, all of whom are worshipped on Sili Sat. Such merging, extending, and blurring of attributes, functions, and identities is common in village Hinduism, but it seems to characterize Shitala and Sili Sat more than most deities and festivals (R. Freed and S. Freed, 1979: 306–309; Henry, 1988: 80–81; Imperial Record Department, 1914: 74–75; Mukerji, 1916: 49–50; Wadley, 1980).

Wadley (1980: 35) identified "coolness" as Shitala's most compelling attribute, the one which links her various "personalities." In Shanti Nagar, this characteristic also links Shitala with the other goddesses of disease, for all of them are propitiated by devotees who consume only cold leftover food on Sili Sat and make offerings of cold food and water. The common custom of worshipping a deity with a lighted lamp is rarely practiced on Sili Sat. We observed no lamps at all in the ceremonies of 1958 and 1959, and only one group of worshippers used lamps in 1978. The theme of coolness is underlined by the ritual practiced by families, mostly Jats, who claim not to worship the mother goddess or, at least, who avoid participating in the procession of women that circles the village to worship at various shrines. However, the women of these families make an offering inside their houses at the place where they store pots of cool water. Crooke (1968, 1: 130) wrote:

> In her form as household goddess, Sîtalâ is often known as Thandî, or "the cool one," and her habitation is in the house behind the water-pots,

in the cold, damp place where the water drips. Here she is worshipped by the house-mother, but only cold food or cold water is offered to her.

Rose (1919: 351) also noted that women water Shitala's shrine to *cool* her (his emphasis), but that they also worship her with lamps.

The date of the festival of Shitala worship varies throughout northern India, ranging over a period of five months from Chaitra (March–April) to Shrawan (July–August) (Wadley, 1980: table 1). Mukerji (1916: 49) commented, "By many, every moonless Saptami (seventh day of the moon), from the dark fortnight of *Chaitra* to the corresponding fortnight of *Srawan*, is observed as a day sacred to Sitala [which] shows that there is a whole season of five months which is sacred to Sitala. . . ."

In the Hindi-speaking region, Chaitra *badi* 8 is the usual date of the festival. In Delhi, the festival is commonly observed on Chaitra *badi* 7. The four studies of Delhi villages made under the auspices of the 1961 census that mention the festival give its date as the seventh, as does Lewis (1958: 200). Without mentioning a specific locality, Mukerji (1916: 49) also dated the festival on Chaitra *badi* 7. Shitala's festival in some localities may fall outside the five-month smallpox epidemic period. Probably with Bengal in mind, the Imperial Record Department (1914: 74) described the festival of Shitala worship, which they name Citala Sasthi Puja (Shitala Sasthi Worship), as taking place on Magh (January–February) *sudi* 6. (See also Wadley, 1980: 45.)

No single villager gave us a complete list of the Seven Sisters of disease. Usually, an informant would name three or four, sometimes identifying a specific disease with the wrong mother goddess, for example, Kanti Mata (typhoid) might be confused with Shitala (smallpox). We have added an eighth goddess, Chaurahewali Mata (Crossroads Mother). While not one of the Seven Sisters, she was worshipped on Sili Sat for the general welfare of children.

The Seven Sisters are

1. Shitala Mata, also known as Chechak Mata (Pox Mother) or Mata Rani, the goddess of smallpox.
2. Kalka (ki) Mata, also named Masani Mata, goddess of the cremation grounds (*masan*). Kalka in Delhi is the site of a shrine to the goddess. Only Chamar Leatherworkers regularly worshipped Kalka for the welfare of both children and other members of the caste. Inclusion of this mother goddess as one of the Seven Sisters in Shanti Nagar is based on her general protective function, especially as concerns children. Lewis (1958: 238), drawing on sources other than his own fieldwork, also listed Masani Mata as one of the Seven Sisters. No one in Shanti Nagar identified her with a specific disease. However, Rose (1919: 352 –353) said that "Masán is a disease that causes emaciation or atrophy in children, and she is propitiated to avert it. . . . The origin of the name Masáni is not known, but probably it is connected with the disease of *masán* to which children are very liable."[21] Masani Mata is also identified with smallpox.
3. Khamera Mata, the goddess of measles. The difference between measles (rubeola) and German measles (rubella) was not recognized.

4. Khasra Mata, the goddess of itches, scabies, eczema, and similar maladies of the skin. These diseases were usually regarded as minor ailments, but children in particular were frequently afflicted with them. The term also refers to measles. Chicken pox usually fell within the realm of this goddess as a minor affliction, but it sometimes was considered to be in the domain of the Crossroads Mother Goddess.

5. Marsal Mata, the goddess of mumps.

6. Phul ki Mata (The Flower Mother), the goddess of boils and other similar large skin eruptions. This goddess is clearly distinguished from Khasra Mata, for the meaning of *phul*, flower or blossom, in this context is an eruption on the skin.

7. Kanti Mata or Moti Mata or Moti Jhara, the goddess of typhoid. During the second week of fever, a distinctive rash of small rose-colored spots appears on the trunk. It is this rash that is the diagnostic symptom of Kanti Mata in Shanti Nagar. Villagers say that the blisters shine like beads, hence Moti Mata. Rose (1919: 352) noted that the shrines for Kanti Mata ". . . are often to the north of the village, because the disease is supposed to have come from the hills." In Shanti Nagar, the shrine is north of the village.

8. Chaurahewali Mata, Crossroads Mother Goddess. She is propitiated for the welfare of children. She might be worshipped for any illness, if there is no other goddess to propitiate.

The names of the Seven Sisters apparently vary considerably. Ibbetson listed the Seven Sisters, aspects of Devi, as Sítala, Masáni, Basanti (Yellow Goddess), Máhá Mái (Great Mother), Polamde (possibly, She Who Makes the Body Soft), Lamkariá (She Who Hastens), and Agwáni (Leader) (Crooke, 1968, 1: 128; Rose, 1919: 350). Only two names on this list are matched by the goddesses of Shanti Nagar (Shitala and Masani). However, Rose expanded and qualified the basic list. Thus, Chaurahewali Mata appeared as Chauganwa Mata (She of the Four Villages) or Chaurasta Mata (She of the Four Ways). Rose also listed Kanti Mata as the goddess of typhoid, not mentioning the disease by name but remarking the characteristic pustular eruption.

Bubonic plague and cholera are two epidemic diseases that once took frightful tolls and still break out from time to time. Kanti Mata may be worshipped in times of plague, although there is a separate plague goddess, Phúlan Devi, ". . . whose half-completed shrine . . . attests her ill-will or inability to stay the disease" (Rose, 1919: 352). Marí Mái is the cholera goddess. According to Rose (1919: 356), she is in some areas propitiated by animal sacrifice (the *panch-balá* ritual) and, formerly, by the *sat-balá*, ". . . now out of date, as it consisted in the immolation of a pair of human beings, a woman as well as a man, to make up the mystic seven [*sat*]." Neither Phúlan Devi nor Marí Mái is worshipped, or probably even known, in Shanti Nagar.

The following description concerns basically the festivals of 1958 and 1959, enlarged and qualified by our observations of the festival of 1978. Differences between the observances of the 1950s and those of 1978 are not to be taken as indications of significant change. Variation is characteristic of village festivals that are enacted without written guidelines. In all three years, the women of some families worshipped at all the village shrines, others at selected shrines, still others worshipped at home, and some families did nothing. The names of the deities and which goddess was worshipped at which shrine varied remarkably. The more women we questioned, the more the variation seemed to expand. The women were not in the least bothered by the inconstant character of the festival.

Variation among castes was not particularly noteworthy, with two exceptions. The single Gardener family claimed to have the seven goddesses of disease in its garden and worshipped them there instead of at the village shrines. There is a close connection between the Gardener (Mali) caste and the Seven Sisters of Disease, as is evident in several of the songs collected by Henry. A song that paraphrases the explanation of the Gardener of Shanti Nagar is the following:

> Oh, Mali, Mother is spinning around in the swing in your garden.
> All seven sisters at once are spinning around in the swing in your garden. . . .
> With Ganges water in the vessel, the Mali washes her feet,
> Oh Mali, in your garden.   [Henry, 1988: 85]

The second exception concerned the Jats who are followers of the Arya Samaj. Although a few Jat women worshipped at the village shrines on Sili Sat, most of them worshipped at home. Arya Samaj beliefs had modified village Hinduism, a development that affected Sili Sat but was by no means limited to that festival.

On the eve of Sili Sat, women cleaned their stoves and brought fresh water from the well. They prepared the festive foods that would be used as offerings the next day. Women did not cook from the evening of the sixth day until the evening of Sili Sat. Formerly, they did not cook until the morning of the day after Sili Sat. They also purchased one rupee's worth of *batasha*s (white sugar candy) for later distribution as *prasad*, especially to children.

Early the next morning about 6:00 or 6:30 A.M., groups of women, dressed up for the occasion, prepared to parade to the shrines of the goddesses, the Panch Pir, and Bhumiya. The women and children who participated in the procession and the worship did not bathe beforehand. While women waited for their group to form, some of them threw food to expectant dogs, who gulped it down. Kolenda (1982: 235) said that an offering can be transmitted to Shitala through the medium of a black dog. As the women passed through the village, some of them distributed *batasha*s for blessings received during the year: a new bride in the household, a desired pregnancy, the birth of sons, and a son's having found a job. A Brahman man, who would not be permitted to join the procession of women, also distributed *batasha*s because a sick calf had recovered.

The women formed separate groups. The majority of participants in each group represented one caste, but often a few women from other castes, especially small castes, were included. For example, some Barber or Blacksmith women would join a large group of Brahman women who were their neighbors and friends. At least one woman from each family carried a large brass tray holding a dish of turmeric, a small pitcher of water, green gram, perhaps gur (brown sugar), a few coins, and the festive food, chiefly balls of sweet wheat porridge (*daliya*, made with coarse wheat flour, gur, and milk) sprinkled with wheat flour, and kneaded balls of wheat flour, the latter believed to offer protection against large hard boils. On the way to the first shrine, some women plucked wild flowers to use as offerings. Strings of dung cakes were another common offering. They were said to have been left over from Holi, when many such strings were offered to the Holi bonfire. Women sang on the way to the shrines, reciting aspects of the ritual that would follow and praising the goddess, as in the following song:

> Mother, the Gardener [Mali] has made this garden,
>   and the Gardener's wife waters the plants in the garden.
> My mother-queen [Mata Rani] is enjoying a peaceful sleep.
> Oh mother, dig a pond on the way.
> Mother, make a shop on the way.
> Make a storekeeper sit in the shop.
> They will bring coconut sweetmeats from this shop for you.

The song touches on the relationship of the Malis and the mother goddesses and offers praise to the creative power of Shitala (Mata Rani), who can generate a shop and shopkeeper. Offering sweetmeats to the goddess and digging a pond, a service to the goddess, are part of the ritual of Sili Sat.

The women first stopped at a shrine west of the village, a pile of earth and bricks about four feet high. In other ceremonies, women said that the mound was for the Panch Pir. When we asked the women whom we accompanied to the shrine what goddesses they were worshipping, several said that they did not know. Others said that the goddess was Gurgaonwali Mata (Mother Goddess of Gurgaon), some said Kanti Mata (Typhoid), and others said Moti Mata (Pearl Mother or Typhoid). Several informants, both women and men, said that the focus of worship was the Four Directions. Some women identified the directions as the abode of goddesses. A learned Brahman from another village explained the Four Directions as places of pilgrimage associated with a deity or where a deity resides. In the north is Badrinath, a place sacred to Vishnu and also a title of Vishnu (Lord of Badri). Jagannath (Lord of the World) resides in the east. He is a form of Vishnu, or Krishna. Puri, Orissa, is the great seat of his worship. In the south is Rameshwar (Lord of Rama), one of the twelve great Lingams set up by Ram. Dwarka, Krishna's capital in Gujarat (West India), is one of the seven sacred cities (Dowson, 1891: 39, 101, 129, 263).

In 1978, some women explained the directions not as the abode of deities specific to each direction but rather as the direction in which their natal villages (or the villages of their mother-in-law or daughters-in-law or some ancestor) were located. One woman clarified matters by pointing out that the deities being worshipped were the mother goddesses of these other villages. Hence, the directional goddesses are not the same for everyone. They are the mother goddesses located in specific villages related to the worshipper.

It is of interest that no one claimed to be worshipping Shitala or the Seven Sisters. The principal shrine at the spot, the 4-foot mound, is best thought of as a shrine where several deities can be propitiated, as circumstances require. The view is supported by the fact that lamps were lit on this shrine when the Panch Pir were worshipped in a ceremony on another day (fig. 45), but very few were used on Sili Sat, for Shitala is the Cool One.[22] One informant uniquely simplified matters by claiming that the Panch Pir were the Seven Sisters or at least five goddesses (*panch* = five). Another informant ducked the question about names by identifying the deity as "the one who accepts porridge, the one you worship when pox breaks out." Another possibility concerning the main shrine is that on Sili Sat it represented the Seven Sisters and that the Panch Pir were worshipped separately at a nearby spot. In 1978, the shrine was said to be for Moti Mata. No one then spoke of the Four Directions as a set of goddesses.

At the shrine of the Seven Sisters (or the Panch Pir), the women offered water, flowers, food, a small coin, strings of dung cakes, *batasha*s, and a yellow headcloth in some cases, and made tilaks with turmeric at the places of worship and on children (figs. 36, 37). The women removed their shoes when making the offerings. Sweeper women took the headcloths, and dogs ate the food. After the Panch Pir, the women made offerings in an area near the shrine, first to the Goddess of the North, then to the Goddess of the South, and finally, to the Goddess of the West. We did not observe any offerings made to the Goddess of the East. In a few cases, the food offerings were arranged in seven neat piles, probably representing the seven Mother Goddesses of Disease. Dogs quickly devoured the offerings of food. Then the women returned to the Goddess of the North and gestured with their hands, as if they were pressing her legs, a mark of respect. The women next went to a nearby pond, which

FIG. 36. Sili Sat, 1978. Women place their offerings on the shrine: strings of dung cakes, flowers, and the yellow cloth one woman holds in her left hand. The woman in the background has an *indi* on her head, a ring made of fiber cord that women wear when carrying burdens. (See S. Freed and R. Freed, 1978: fig. 66.)

FIG. 37. Sili Sat, 1978. A woman blesses a child with a tilak of turmeric on its forehead. The Brahman woman behind the child was unmarried and need not cover her head.

they called the goddess's pond, and removed lumps of clay to clean it. In 1978, there were two ponds, a small one with a little water and a much larger pond. Women took handfuls of mud from the small pond and threw them, one by one, into the larger pond, while naming each family member and some deities.

Groups of women kept arriving, one after another. The worship was similar for each group. All the women went to three goddesses: north, south, and west. Young women frequently pressed the legs of older women. A surprising observation was that Potter wives touched the feet of Sweeper women, both young and old, and the Sweepers replied with blessings. Because the Sweepers rank lowest in the local caste hierarchy, one would not expect that a higher-ranking caste would make such a gesture. This gesture of respect was recognition of the supernatural power that adheres to Sweeper women on Sili Sat. Kolenda (1982: 232) regarded Sweeper women as mediums of Shitala: "On Mondays, mothers (especially of sons) give flour, oil, and salt to their family's Sweeper woman in order to protect the children from pox. The food . . . is fed symbolically to the goddess."

After worshipping the Panch Pir and the goddesses of the four directions, the women proceeded to the Bhumiya shrine. They poured water on the shrine, offered food, and made marks with turmeric on the front of the shrine near its top. The shrine is relatively large and substantial, made of bricks and mortar (figs. 38–39).

FIG. 38. Bhumiya
shrine, 1958.

Bhumiya is worshipped at marriages or the mating of cows and buffaloes. Although Bhumiya is a male godling, his protective and procreative functions make him an appropriate deity to propitiate on Sili Sat.

The final stop was at the crossroads at the edge of the village where roads point in the four cardinal directions, two roads leading out of the village. This was the site of a simple shrine to the Crossroads Mother Goddess, consisting of just a brick and some sherds. However, the crossroads itself was the shrine, not the brick. The women offered water and food anywhere in the area, generally by the side of a road. The food was quickly devoured by pigs as well as by dogs, for the crossroads is adjacent to the Sweeper quarter (fig. 40). The Sweepers are the only caste that raises pigs.

Most of the activity at the crossroads involved the Sweepers, both men and women. They received whatever food was left after all the shrines had been worshipped. In addition, Sweeper women received gifts from their patrons (jajmans), usually a cloth. A Sweeper woman said that a woman gave a headcloth (*orhna*) to her Sweeper only if she had made a vow to give one to a mother goddess. The Sweeper woman would thus appear to be the surrogate of the goddess.

At the crossroads, Sweeper women released, or passed, a cock over the heads of children as a protective ritual. In Shanti Nagar, this ritual is practiced only on Sili Sat. We did not see the ritual in 1958, although we were at the crossroads. The Sweeper woman who worked for us explained that we missed the ritual because we were with a group of Brahman women but that the Leatherworkers had the ritual performed. She mentioned a Leatherworker woman who had requested the ritual for her children. We visited the Leatherworker woman, who said, "After worshipping

FIG. 39. *(left)* Bhumiya shrine, 1978.

FIG. 40. *(below)* Sili Sat, 1978. Pigs devour the offerings of food that women have left for the Crossroads Mother Goddess.

the goddesses, I asked [so-and-so's wife] to release a cock over my children's heads. I asked her to do it because she works for my family. I gave her a few annas and some grain—one gives what one can. She released the cock over the heads of all the Leatherworker children, and their parents gave her a little money. These other Leatherworkers asked her because she owns a cock." We did not see the ritual in 1959 either, but again we were with a group of Brahman women.

In 1978, we saw this ritual. The Sweeper who worked for us, the same woman as in 1958, was at the crossroads with her cock. She held it over the heads of children but did not release it (fig. 41). She touched the heads of many Brahman women with the cock and also touched it to our heads. She received food and a headcloth (figs. 42–43). After the cock ritual, women put tilaks on their kin and friends, pressed the legs of old women, and distributed batashas and gur as prasad. The women then returned to their homes. A group of women took about one hour to complete the circumambulation of the shrines.

The ritual of the cock appears to be unrelated to the rest of the rituals of Sili Sat. The dominant activity of the festival is to make offerings to the mother goddesses for the protection of children. The cock ritual is not an offering but a ritual of transference. It may partly represent the transfer of ritual pollution from participants to the cock. Although the participants in the circumambulation of the mother-goddess shrines dressed up, they did not bathe beforehand. Thus, they were not as free from pollution as they might have been. This pollution was transferred to the cock.

However, the cock ritual is probably more strongly connected to the concept of an intrusive spirit force as the cause of illness (R. Freed and S. Freed, 1979: 305–306). It may be that a ceremony where participants are brought into close association with potentially dangerous supernatural beings requires a prophylactic ritual at its conclusion. If a participant harbors any spirit capable of causing illness, it is transferred to the cock.

The cock ritual is ancient and widespread in the world. Schauss wrote that on Yom Kippur, Orthodox Jews circle a fowl above the head nine times as a ritual of expiation of sin. The ritual, known as Kaporos, was practiced among the Jews of Babylonia in the 10th century (Schauss, 1938: 150, 164). The New York Post (October 10, 1997, p. 12) published a picture of the Jewish ritual with the caption, "An orthodox Jew swings a rooster over his friends' heads in a ceremony in which their sins are ritually transferred to the bird, which is eaten before the Yom Kippur fast."

Before entering their houses, women splashed water on both sides of the doorway and applied marks of turmeric. Sweeper women were seen going from door to door collecting gifts, probably from their patrons, especially Jats, who had not gone to the crossroads where Sweepers customarily receive gifts. Kanti Mata is located just to the north of the crossroads, and we asked a Brahman woman why this goddess was not worshipped. She replied that Kanti Mata is worshipped all year long, but the other goddesses are worshipped only on Sili Sat.

We saw only a few Jat women at the mother goddess shrines. Although the great majority of Jat women, in accord with Arya-Samaj doctrine, did not participate in the public worship of the goddesses, they worshipped privately. One Jat woman offered porridge, cotton seeds, yogurt, and gram at the place in her house where the

FIG. 41. (above) Sili Sat, 1978. A Sweeper woman circles a rooster over the heads of a mother and her child near the shrine of the Crossroads Mother Goddess.

FIG. 42. (right) Sili Sat, 1978. The Sweeper woman of figure 41 with her rooster over her right shoulder holds a tray of food that she was given by her jajmans. She also received a yellow cloth.

FIG. 43. Sweeper women leave the Crossroads Mother shrine with trays of food and yellow headcloths received from their jajmans.

cool water was stored, the abode of Shitala. She then moved the offerings to the door of the women's quarters, possibly as an invitation to Shitala to leave the premises, thus ushering smallpox out of the house. Then she splashed water on the wall and drew a swastika on it with turmeric. She said that the offering was for the welfare of her children. Another Jat woman followed a somewhat simpler routine. She simply drew a swastika, a good luck symbol, over the ledge where the pots of cool water were kept. Then the women of the family folded their hands in worship. There was no mention of an offering of food. Yet another Jat woman worshipped with a tilak on the ledge where the water was kept, offered food to dogs, and gave rice and *lassi* (a cool yogurt beverage) to the family's Sweeper.

Another Jat woman said that she had given food to dogs but otherwise did not worship as did the rest of the village. No matter where the offerings were made, they were eaten by dogs and, at Chaurahewali Mata, by pigs. It would be appropriate to distinguish between food deliberately fed to dogs, which then serve as mediums of the mother goddess, and food left at shrines. In the latter case, dogs scavenge at shrines on any occasion. For example, offerings left for the Panch Pir, who are male deities, are scavenged by dogs.

A fourth Jat woman described a more elaborate ritual. She plastered a small area with cow dung, offered porridge and yogurt, made a mark with turmeric, and then gave part of the offering to the family's cow and the rest to the dog.

Some Jat women may try to balance Arya-Samaj doctrine and the traditional ritual of Sili Sat. A 56-year-old Jat woman combined a ritual at home with offerings to the Crossroads Mother and to Kanti Mother at their village shrines. For Sili Sat, she said, "I usually cook on the sixth day and we have cold food on the seventh. I put seven piles of porridge, for the seven mothers, in a clean place inside the house. I put a turmeric tilak on all the mothers and then give the food to the dogs. This is Aryaness [*Arya panna*], for we don't worship the *mata*s."

Despite this household ritual, she also worshipped the Crossroads Mother Goddess. She said:

> On Sili Sat, I went to the Crossroads Mother Goddess. I had vowed to offer a headcloth for the birth of a grandson [who was less than five months old on Sili Sat]. So I offered the headcloth [to the family Sweeper whom she had summoned to the crossroads] and distributed two seers of gur and some *batasha*s, five to a child. Only the Brahmans and Bairagis go [on the circumambulation]. They go and worship Kanti Mother when any child has typhoid. If any child from my house has typhoid, then I will also go and offer sweetmeats at [the shrine of] Kanti Mata.

We saw this woman and also the child's mother at the shrine of the Crossroads Mother distributing *prasad*. Although this woman's account seems confusing, for she worships mother goddesses while denying such worship, it actually illustrates a basic tenet of village life, especially concerning sickness. Any or all remedies and rituals may be used if there is any chance of their being effective. In this case, not only had she taken a vow to encourage the birth of a son, but in addition, she worshipped the goddess because the baby had caught malaria. Thus, there were two reason for making offerings at the Crossroads Mother. The role of the Sweeper woman as a surrogate for Shitala is clear in this account.

Consistency is not to be expected from Jat women concerning goddess worship. Another Jat woman told us that she did not worship the goddesses. Then we asked what she did on Sili Sat. She said that she cooked rice and porridge and made an offering to a goddess.

The circumambulation of the shrines in 1978 added two stops that were passed by in 1958 and 1959, namely, the crossroads at the southwest corner of the village and the main village well (fig. 83). The first stop in 1978, as in the 1950s, was the main shrine, called Moti Mata in 1978. Instead of worshipping the goddesses of the Four Directions in the field near the shrine, the women worshipped Gurgaonwali Mata, called Kanti Mata by some of the women. They then proceeded to the southwest crossroads where they made an offering to Chaurahewali Mata. Some villagers called the Crossroads Mother Goddess the strongest of the goddesses. She protected villagers from outsiders who came with evil intentions. Other villagers said that Kanti Mata was the strongest. Next, they went to the Bhumiya shrine, as they had done in the 1950s. Then they made an offering to Gurgaonwali Mata at the village well, which was located at a crossroads. Finally, they went to the main crossroads to worship Chaurahewali Mata, as in the 1950s.

Although the women cheerfully welcomed our company and that of our male assistants during the rituals, they did not permit the presence of village men, because Sili Sat is a women's festival. In 1978 when the women whom we accompanied arrived at the first shrine, the one for Moti Mata, they saw some young men watching them. They sang a song asking the men to leave, and they did without any fuss.

Despite some individual variation in ritual practice and the influence of the Arya Samaj on the Jats, the basic characteristics of Sili Sat are clear. It is a festival where women propitiate the goddess in her several manifestations to protect children from disease, principally the contagious pustular diseases. Women also make vows for various blessings, which often concern fertility. The themes of welfare, protection, and fertility occur in many festivals. The unique feature of Sili Sat is the use of cold, stale bread (*basi* means stale, hence the name of Basora for the festival). The choice of sweet wheat porridge as the principal offering is another noteworthy feature, as are the offerings made in the home where the cool water is stored. Underhill noted yet another unusual particular of the worship of Shitala: "She will accept the prayers and offerings of widows, if mothers, on behalf of their children" (Underhill, 1991: 105).

The role of dogs in the festival bears some discussion. Dogs generally consume the offerings of food left at shrines, not only on Sili Sat but also on other festivals and rituals. However, in all festivals but Sili Sat the participation of dogs is incidental; people do not deliberately offer food to dogs as a religious act, in the way that food is given to cows. However, people deliberately feed dogs on Sili Sat. This behavior is especially noticeable in the worship practiced at home by many Jat women, where the feeding of dogs often assumes a prominent place in what is usually a quick, simple ritual.

Perhaps it is unnecessary to go beyond Kolenda's interpretation that a black dog is the intermediary between a devotee and Shitala except that the connection of dogs and Shitala requires some explanation. A tenuous connection can be established between Shitala and Yama, God of Death. In Tamil country, the smallpox goddess is known as Mariyammai, "Mother Death" (Basham, 1954: 316). If a link between Shitala and a deity representing death can be admitted, then her connection with dogs is clear. Yama is accompanied by two fierce four-eyed dogs ". . . who wander about among men as his messengers, for the purpose of summoning men to the presence of their master . . ." (Garrett, 1990: 746). Thus, feeding dogs could be a way of appeasing both the God of Death and Mother Death.

Marriott (1955: 193) found no evident Sanskritic rationale for Sili Sat in the 1950s. Hence the festival was unambiguously part of the little tradition. Many festivals of the little tradition involve the worship of a local saint. As such, they have relatively little historical depth and are unknown beyond a limited region. There has not been enough time for Sanskritization, and in any case, such deities are of little interest to scholars in the centers of Hindu learning. On the other hand, Shitala is worshipped throughout India. This wide distribution suggests antiquity, as does the nature of the deity. Goddess worship is ancient, most likely pre-Vedic. It would therefore be remarkable if Sili Sat had escaped Sanskritization.

In fact, evidence of Sanskritization is accumulating. In the late 19th century, Crooke identified tendencies in that direction. Because in some places Shitala is identified with Kali, the wife of Shiva, Crooke (1968, 1: 129) commented that "Sitalâ is on the way to promotion to the higher heaven. . . . This has obviously passed through the mill of Brahmanism." Recent support for Crooke's observation comes from songs sung in a north Indian village during a mother goddess festival. The names of Shitala, Kali, Durga, and Mother are used interchangeably (Henry, 1988: 89):

> Riding a lion Shitala comes roaring, villagers.
> You don't know Mother, villagers. . . .
> Riding a lion Kali comes roaring, villagers. . . .
> Riding a lion [her traditional vehicle] Durga comes roaring, villagers.

The currently high level of literacy in the countryside will narrow the distance between Shitala and compatible elements of Sanskritic tradition. Wadley (1980: 34) commented that "the shift from orally transmitted tales to popular printed literature is especially crucial, tied as it is to processes of Sanskritization and standardization." This process is only slightly manifest in the Hindi-speaking region, for, as Wadley noted, ". . . only recently has a literary tradition begun to develop around [Shitala]."

WEEKLY FESTIVALS

Many villagers regularly worship a specific deity on a given day of the week. Such weekly observances can be termed festivals, for their dates are set by the calendar. To be sure, they lack the more spectacular features of other festivals, such as a village wide display of lamps, parades of women circling the village, bonfires, and the

creation of often elaborate images of deities on walls. Nonetheless, the rituals practiced for weekly festivals may be as elaborate as those of some of the annual festivals, even if they usually lack the more public aspects of the latter. Weekly festivals
in Hinduism are similar to the Sabbath in other religions and may be treated accordingly. For example, writing of the Jewish festivals, Schauss (1938: xi) included the
weekly Sabbath in his list of major festivals, all of them annual festivals except the
Sabbath.

The chief difference between weekly festivals and annual festivals may be that
individuals practice the former intermittently. For example, a higher secondary
school student may worship Santoshi Mata every Friday for a few months before an
important examination and then abandon the practice after passing the test, only to
begin again to supplicate the goddess when confronted by another urgent need. By
contrast, people tend to observe the annual welfare festivals, for example, Hoi or Sili
Sat, no matter what may be their current circumstances.

The weekly calendric rites are to be distinguished from various daily pujas, such
as lighting a lamp in the evening for a deity or feeding a piece of bread to a cow. The
weekly festivals are calendric rites, and the daily pujas are not. Moreover, as practiced
by most villagers, the weekly festivals are generally more elaborate than daily pujas.
They involve fasts, reading from scripture, and the distribution of *prasad*.

Sunday's Worship of Kanti Mata and the Sun

Women worship Kanti Mata on Sundays when a family member, usually a
child, has typhoid. One Sunday morning, an elderly Brahman woman showed us
some *gulgula*s (made of wheat flour and gur deep fried) that she had just made as part
of an offering to Kanti Mata. One of her grandsons had Mata (typhoid) for 15 days.
After he recovered, she made an offering on a Sunday, the traditional day. She added
that she would feed seven girls. Girls younger than ten years (*kanya*s, virgins) are rit-

FIG. 44. Brahman
woman making an
offering at the Kanti
Mata shrine, 1977. An
offering of food is on a
brass tray, a pitcher of
water beside it. The
cloth used to cover
the tray on the walk
to the shrine lies on
the ground.

ually pure and may be looked upon as devis (goddesses). Feeding them is equivalent to feeding Brahmans.

The Brahmani prepared a tray with *gulgula*s, *batasha*s, turmeric, ghee, and a lamp and covered it with a cloth. Two or three little girls stood around waiting to be fed. We went with her to the shrine, accompanied by two little boys, the brothers of the victim of typhoid, and a little girl. One of the children carried a small pitcher of water. The Brahmani did not feed anyone on the way to the shrine. When we arrived at the shrine, a woman was already there making an offering. After she finished worshipping, she distributed food to some children, including a Sweeper girl.

The Brahmani then approached the shrine. There are in fact two shrines close together at the spot, one for Kanti Mata and the other for Kali Mata. The Brahmani put her tray on the ground, took the pitcher of water from the child, and washed both shrines (fig. 44). She put a turmeric tilak on both shrines, explaining that when a child has Mata (or Moti Jhara), you have to propitiate both shrines. She offered the *gulgula*s and *batasha*s. Later she told us that she had also offered Rs. 1.25, some rice, and gur to Kanti Mata and Rs. 0.25 to Kali Mata. We did not notice the offerings of money. Next she lit the lamp, folded her hands before it, put tilaks on all the children, and gave them *prasad*. On the way home, she distributed *batasha*s to children, both girls and boys. She told us that when she had the time, she would go to Gurgaon to make an offering to Gurgaonwali Mata.

Sunday is also the day for worshipping the sun. A Chhipi Dyer man told us that he fasts for Suraj Devta (the sun) every Sunday. The fast lasts until 2:00 P.M. He said that salt is not taken that day. The Sunday fast for Suraj seems to be rarely practiced in Shanti Nagar. This Chhipi man, a recent immigrant to the village, was the only person who mentioned it.

Monday's Fast for Shiva

Informants said that many women observe a fast for Shiva on Mondays. Underhill (1991: 70–71) explained that the moon (Monday is the day of the moon) became closely connected with Shiva. Both deities are to be worshipped on Monday, but worship of the moon is dying out while that of Shiva is increasing. Chiefly women perform Monday's fast for Shiva in Shanti Nagar, but men may also do so. Shiva worship was brought up in a general discussion of religion with a group of Brahman and Jhinvar Watercarrier women. These women connected Monday's fast for Shiva and Friday's fast for Santoshi Mata, probably because both are weekly festivals. Also, both fasts are undertaken for individual and family welfare. Other women also paired the two fasts, sometimes including the worship of Hanuman on Tuesdays.

The women were at pains to describe the details of fasting. The key to the fast is grain, which can be eaten at only one meal. Also, liquids, either tea or water, can be taken only once. Fruit can be eaten, and if a woman is in the fields, she can nibble sugarcane.

A Watercarrier woman said that she worshipped Shiva in the morning. She made three *laddu*s (balls of sweetmeats) of *churma* (pieces of bread mixed with ghee and gur). She ate one, offered one to the Lingam (emblem of Shiva), and fed the third to a cow. This was her only meal. She said that the reason women fast is because

Shiva is powerful. Maidens fast to marry a good husband. A Brahman woman chimed in to say that women fast to marry into a good family and so that their husbands will find good jobs.

The Watercarrier woman said that after fasting for 16 Mondays, she terminated fasting by conducting a ritual, Udhyapan,[23] on the 17th Monday. Again she prepared three large portions of *churma*. She offered one portion to her family, one to the community as *prasad*, and one to a cow in honor of Shiva. We note that this woman fasted on 16 Mondays for Shiva and that a Chhipi Dyer man ". . . kept 16 fasts for Shivji many times." The Leatherworker boy described below fasted 16 Fridays for Santoshi Mata.

Thursday's Worship of the Panch Pir

One Thursday in 1977, while watching a man sowing wheat, we saw a large throng of Leatherworker women at a shrine in a nearby field, the same shrine where women worship mother goddesses on Sili Sat. We asked a Jat farmer, an Arya Sama-ji, what the women were doing. He said, "It is superstition. Some women are offering to a mata. There are only two matas, the earth and the mother who gives us birth." A Brahman, whom we encountered after the ceremony, expressed the traditional point of view. He said, "This is an example of Sanatan Dharma [Eternal Religion]. All castes offer at the Panch Pir on Sili Sat. At other times, any person may offer there as an individual. Thursdays of the bright fortnight are auspicious." As the Leatherworker women noted, the Brahman said that the date, which was Karttik *sudi* 7, had nothing to do with the offering.

At first we did not think that we could reach the women in time to talk to them, but when it became apparent that they might remain for some time, we hurried to the shrine. The women told us that it was the shrine of the Panch Pir. Just as with the shrines for Kanti Mata and Kali Mata, this shrine had been moved from its earlier location because of land consolidation.

The woman who had made the principal offering, and apparently had arranged the ceremony, said that she had prayed to the Panch Pir for the welfare of her children and cattle and had vowed to make an offering if her wish was fulfilled. She did not make the vow because of a current sickness. Such offerings always take place on a Thursday during the bright fortnight of any month.

The woman had offered a cloth, which was placed on top of the shrine, and 5 kg of gur, which were distributed to the women and children, both boys and girls, who attended the ceremony. The other women also made offerings, among them *churma*, which was distributed like the gur. At the end of the ritual, the shrine was covered with the offerings: the cloth, burning dung cakes, lamps, water, and several five-paise coins (fig. 45).

Chamar women worship the Panch Pir annually on two occasions—the day before Holi in spring and the day before Diwali in autumn. We saw the ceremony the day before Holi and describe it in conjunction with that festival. The rituals for the Panch Pir before Holi, on Sili Sat and on bright Thursdays are similar. However, while the latter two occasions are welfare festivals, the worship before Holi is to honor the deity. We wanted to verify this point and asked the women engaged in the

FIG. 45. Offerings left by Leatherworker women on the shrine for the Panch Pir, 1977. Note the lamps and compare this ritual with the one shown in figure 36. When the shrine represents Shitala, the Cool One, lamps are not used.

pre-Holi ritual whether the puja marked a happy occasion, such as the birth of a child—that is, a ceremony to fulfill a vow. They replied that Sayyid Puja (or Mata Puja) was customary before Holi and Diwali. The women told us that in this case neither the day, which happened to be Thursday, nor the fortnight was significant.

We saw a similar worship of the Panch Pir on a Thursday in May 1958, but it took place during the dark fortnight. A group of about 15 Leatherworker women and children paraded to the shrine under a *jal* tree. On the way, they sang political and devotional songs. Some of the words from one song, sung to a tune from a recent film, were "Get yourself enrolled in the Congress Party." A line from a more traditional song ran, "The God has come and we fall down at the God's feet."

When the women arrived at the shrine, which consisted of only two stones and a potsherd, they lit a lamp filled with ghee and made an offering of gur, a dung cake, and a burning dung cake, on which they dropped ghee. A woman who took the leading role in the worship blessed the children by touching the burning dung cake and then their heads. The women explained that when someone is ill, they make an offering to the Panch Pir. In this case, a little girl, presumably the daughter of the woman who was playing the principal role, was sick. As soon as her mother made a vow to worship the Panch Pir and to offer them gur, the girl recovered. The ceremony that we saw fulfilled the vow.

After the worship, the mother distributed gur. On the way home, some gur and water were offered to a *jal* tree. We assume that the spot was a shrine to some deity, but we do not know which one. The women told us that "Sometimes we make a vow to offer food to five Brahmans. But they won't take our food [for reasons of caste status], so we give it to five children who are just like Brahmans."

FESTIVALS OF WELFARE, FERTILITY, AND PROTECTION   141

Friday's Fast for Santoshi Mata

In the 20-year interval between our two periods of fieldwork in Shanti Nagar, a new goddess, Santoshi Mata (Goddess of Joy, or Satisfaction), became extremely popular. Her sudden fame is due largely to the commercial success of a film enacting her myth. Many people from Shanti Nagar saw the film, some more than once. In addition, many villagers own printed versions of her myth, which are widely available in thin pamphlets. We bought one such pamphlet titled "Santoshi Mata: The Story of Friday's Fast," for Rs. 0.75 (Radheshyam, n.d.). Despite the inexpensive paper, the printing is clear, and the 32-page pamphlet has a multicolored cover showing the goddess, much like the drawing of Santoshi Mata in Channa (1984: 112). In both depictions, she has four arms and holds a trident, emblem of Shiva. The film version provided a connection between Santoshi Mata and Shiva, for Ganesh, Shiva's son, created her out of flames drawn from the breasts of his two wives (Kurtz, 1992: 113).

Like the myths of Hoi and Karva Chauth, two other popular festivals for goddesses, the myth for Santoshi Mata unfolds around the tense relationships that are of special concern to women. The story of Santoshi Mata highlights the relationships between mother-in-law and daughter-in-law and between sisters-in-law. As is standard in such scenarios, a young, innocent wife suffers at the hands of her older female in-laws. This happens to the young wife, the heroine of the myth of Santoshi Mata, after her heretofore indolent husband leaves home to seek his fortune. She worships Santoshi Mata for the return of her husband, thus introducing the theme of fertility, for without a husband a woman is infertile. Everything goes well until a taboo is violated and punishment follows. However, devotion to the goddess leads to a happy ending for everyone.

Villagers who observe Friday's fast read from a printed version of the myth of Santoshi Mata. The ritual to be followed is described in the story. The summary of the myth given below follows Radheshyam (n.d.) and the translations in Kurtz (1992: 111–113) and Channa (1984: 109–113). The three versions are very similar.

> There once was an old lady with seven sons. Six were earning but the youngest was idle. The mother fed her six working sons good food. After they had eaten, she fed the leftovers [polluted by saliva] to her youngest son and his wife. He was too innocent to suspect betrayal and believed that his mother treated him well. One day he said to his wife, "See how much my mother loves me." His wife replied, "Why not? She gives you only leftovers" He said, "How can this happen? Unless I see it myself, I won't believe it." She laughed and said, "When you see it, you will admit it."
>
> Some days later there was a festival. The mother cooked seven special dishes. The youngest son, pretending to have a headache, lay down in the kitchen covered by a fine cloth through which he could peep. He saw his six brothers come and eat the fine food. His mother collected the leftovers, woke her youngest son, and told him to eat. He refused to eat and told his mother that he was leaving home. She encouraged him to leave at once.
>
> After walking for days, he reached a city and found work with a

merchant. He learned the trade quickly, worked hard, and soon became his employer's partner. In twelve years, he had his own business and was rich.

In the meantime, his wife was treated badly by her in-laws. She was forced to do all the hard work and given only bread made from wheat husks and water of coconuts.

One day, she saw some women who were worshipping Santoshi Mata. She asked them, "What god are you worshipping and what good comes of it"? One woman answered, "It is a fast for Santoshi Mata. The fast removes poverty and misery. Lakshmi visits the home. Worries are banished and one has peace of mind. The childless are blessed with a son, an absent husband returns home, the virgin female gains the husband of her dreams, long-pending court cases are settled, money is earned and family property returns a profit. Santoshi Mata fulfills all desires."

The young wife asked, "How does one perform the worship"? The women replied, "Take gur and gram, fast every Friday, and tell the story of Santoshi Mata. If there is no one present, light a lamp, put a pot of water in front of it, and recite the *katha* [story]. This puja must be done without interruption until your desire is achieved. Then discontinue the fasts. To do this, you must feed eight boys, preferably sons of your husband's brothers or other relatives, otherwise, boys of the neighborhood. Nothing sour may be eaten inside the house."

The young woman worshipped Santoshi Mata, asking that her husband return home. The wish was granted. When her husband arrived home and saw her misery, he separated his household from that of his mother. The couple lived in great wealth and soon had a son.

She wanted to break her fast, so she summoned the sons of her sisters-in-law for a meal. These malicious women conspired to have the boys eat sour food, thus breaking the taboo. Santoshi Mata was greatly displeased and visited troubles on the couple. The young wife begged Santoshi Mata for permission again to perform the ceremony for breaking the fast. When the sons of her sisters-in-law again wanted to eat sour food, she sent them away and invited Brahman children instead.

Santoshi Mata was pleased. She decided to visit the young wife in her terrifying aspect. The mother-in-law was panic-stricken, but the young wife immediately recognized the goddess. On learning her identity, all members of the household threw themselves at her feet, asked forgiveness, and worshipped her. Anyone who reads and preaches the story of Santoshi Mata is blessed by her.

The film is similar to the printed version though elaborated with a more intricate plot, redefinitions of important roles and additional deities (Lakshmi, Parvati, Brahmani, and their husbands). It is especially noteworthy that the personalities of the seventh and youngest son, named Birju in the film, and his mother are recast to make them more appealing. In the printed version, Birju is an idler who is resented by his mother. In the film, he is endowed with artistic talent and spends his time singing devotional songs for Santoshi Mata. His kindly eldest brother nurtures his talent, and his mother takes good care of him. She does not feed him polluted food. The evil sisters-in-law of the film are the ones who resent Birju's idleness and give him polluted food (Kurtz, 1992: 113–115).

A seemingly minor change in the plot allows for a redefinition of personalities. In the pamphlet, the seventh son is already married as the story begins. Hence, readers may interpret the conflict of mother and son, which is ideally not characteristic of Hindu families, as a conflict of mother-in-law and daughter-in-law. In the film, Birju saves Satyavati, the heroine, from rape and marries her. Birju's mother is pleased by the beauty of Satyavati, and believes that marriage will settle her son down. The relationships between mother and son and mother-in-law and daughter-in-law are much happier in the film than in the pamphlet.

The happiness is shattered by the resentful eldest sister-in-law. She feeds leftovers to Birju, who, feeling betrayed and angry, leaves home to make his fortune, abandoning his beloved wife to the tortures of her in-laws. Santoshi Mata intervenes, Birju returns home, the taboo of sour food is broken, Santoshi Mata is angry and kills the sons of the evil sisters-in-law, Satyavati is blamed, Santoshi Mata again intervenes, the sons return to life, and the film has a happy ending with everyone reconciled.

Many elements of the story of Santoshi Mata find their analogues in the myths of Hoi and Karva Chauth. In the Hoi myth, there are seven married sons, as in the myth of Santoshi Mata. A taboo is broken, fertility (husband) is lost and regained, the unfortunate heroine is exiled for 12 years, she lives on miserable food, she serves a cow, she becomes rich, dead children are returned to life, and there is a happy ending with everyone reconciled. The highlighted relationships are the usual ones in women's festivals: between mother-in-law and daughter-in-law and between sisters-in-law.

In the myth of Karva Chauth, there are again seven married sons. A taboo is broken, the husband dies (lost fertility), the wife lives in exile for seven years, her devotion and service to a cow, and/or to a deity, or to the dead husband restores him to life (regained fertility), so all ends well. The relationship of wife and husband is basic in this myth, since the festival is for the welfare of husbands. The affectionate relationship of brothers and sisters also plays an important role. In the Shanti Nagar versions, brothers' wives do not play their customary malevolent roles. However, in versions collected in other villages, sisters-in-law are up to their usual nasty tricks.

Several villagers spoke of worshipping Santoshi Mata, usually taking up the practice after having seen the film or because other people were doing it. As practiced in Shanti Nagar, the ritual is much as described in the myth. Devotees fast, that is, eat only one meal during the day, tell the story, and light a lamp before a picture of the goddess. Some people distribute *prasad*, gur and gram. Sour food (*khatai*) is avoided. Once the blessing has been granted, devotees discontinue the weekly fast. They summon some children for a feast, as the myth stipulates.

A group of Brahman and Watercarrier women went into greater detail about the feast that ends the fast. Eight boys are invited for a feast of vegetables, puris and *khir*.

No sour food is served, and the boys are cautioned not to eat anything that is sour before coming to the feast. Afterwards, the boys are given cash and fruit.

The fast for Santoshi Mata has not remained exclusively a woman's festival. One informant, a Leatherworker woman, told us that one of her sons fasted in order to pass an examination in school. He was successful after completing 16 fasts. His mother then cooked a special meal and called five boys for the feast (see note 23). His mother explained that the women of the household began to observe the fast, so the boys also adopted it.

Despite their Arya-Samaj proclivities, Jat women expressed no reservations about observing the fast. Women of one Jat family described their ritual. On Friday, they prepare an altar with sand and dung, light a lamp, offer gur and gram as *prasad*, and read the story from a booklet. The senior woman of the household had seen the movie.

The blossoming of Santoshi Mata may be due not only to the popular film depicting her myth but also to her ability to fulfill all wishes. One can appeal to her for specific practical benefits, such as finding a job or passing an examination. Other goddesses featured in welfare festivals have specific limited domains. The Smallpox Goddess, for example, offers protection from contagious pustular diseases but is of no help in commonplace matters. The traditional goddesses basically exercise a protective function. They preserve the lives of husbands and children, a consuming worry for women in the rural India of not too long ago that featured a short life span and a high rate of infant mortality. These concerns may be fading as plagues such as smallpox are conquered, and life expectancy increases. Santoshi Mata may be a goddess well adapted to modern life.

4   FESTIVALS HONORING THE DEITIES

THE FUNDAMENTAL THEME of the festivals treated in this chapter is to honor the deities and to recall great events from Hindu sacred literature. The festivals of the preceding chapter, whose basic themes are welfare, fertility, and protection, involve chiefly the mother goddesses, forms of Devi (Shakti), who is one of the three great deities of modern Hinduism. The other two are Shiva and Vishnu. Vishnu and Krishna—Vishnu's most popular avatar—dominate the honorific festivals in Shanti Nagar, as can be seen in the list of these festivals presented in table 7. Shiva is honored only on his birthday, Shiva Ratri.

The distinction of the two categories, welfare and glorification, is clear but flexible. Thoughts of welfare are not excluded when honoring the gods, and in the back of their minds, people hope that the deity will grant them a good life. However, villagers regard the festivals and rituals held mainly to honor the gods as religious acts (*pun*) that are inherently meritorious. Performing *pun* (or punya) enhances karma and is rewarded in a future rebirth. Villagers do not routinely mention the aspect of personal or familial welfare when performing punya in glorification festivals, as they almost always do when speaking of such festivals as Karva Chauth (for husbands).

In the honorific festivals, welfare may sometimes assume an exalted, great-traditional form, as when a villager told us that the worship on the night of the full moon is "So Lord Krishna can be born again to reform the world." The reference here is to the tenth, and as yet unrealized, avatar of Vishnu. He will arrive mounted on a white horse, blazing like a comet, to destroy the present evil age, the Kaliyuga, and inaugurate an age of purity (Garrett, 1990: 718). In contrast, people are specific and down to earth about what they want to achieve when observing the welfare festivals. Sili Sat is observed to avoid dreaded epidemics. Hoi Mata is supplicated specifically for the welfare of children.

Villagers are more involved with Sanskritic Hinduism in the glorification festivals than in the welfare festivals. This difference is blurred somewhat by the placement of Choti Diwali and Diwali in the welfare category. Nonetheless, the difference is noteworthy. The distinction is most clearly seen in the *kathas* (stories) that are part of the ritual of some festivals of both categories. In the honorific festivals, *katha*s may be a feature of Purinmashi and Janamashtami. Among the welfare festivals, stories are always told for Karva Chauth and Hoi.

145

TABLE 7.

ANNUAL AND MONTHLY FESTIVALS FOR HONORING PRINCIPALLY
VISHNU, SHIVA, AND VEDIC DEITIES

FESTIVAL	GOD/GODDESS	THEME	RITUAL GROUP
Ekadashi (Eleventh)	Vishnu	Honor deity	Individual, Brahmans
Purinmashi (Full moon)	Chandra (Moon)	Honor deity	Individual, Brahman women
Amavas (New moon)	None	Inauspicious day	Individual, men
Amavas with solar eclipse	Sun, Agni	Honor deity, purification	All villagers, especially Brahmans
Nirjala Ekadashi	Vishnu	Honor deity, welfare	Individual
Dev Shayani Ekadashi [a]	Gods, Vishnu	Gods go to sleep	Individual
Janamashtami	Krishna, Moon	Honor Krishna	All villagers
Dassehra	Ram Chandra, Sita	Honor deity	All villagers
Dev Uthani Gyas	Gods, Vishnu	Gods awaken, honor Vishnu, gods, fertility	All villagers
Shivaratri	Shiva	Honor Shiva	Individual
Amla Sinchan Gyas	Vishnu, Krishna Sita, Mirabai	Bhakti, welfare	Women
Holi (Little Holi)	Prahlad, Vishnu, Holika	Welfare, pleasure	All villagers

FESTIVAL	GIFT EXCHANGE	IMAGE/PLACE	RITUAL
Ekadashi	None	Household	Fast
Purinmashi	None	Household	Fast, offer water, *katha*
Amavas	None	Household	Rest, men and bullocks
Amavas with solar eclipse	*Prasad* to Brahmans of Vasishtha *gotra*	Altar in center of village	Havan, fast, bathe
Nirjala Ekadashi	*Sidha* to Brahmans; fans, melon, sweet water to others	Household	Fast, no water or bathing until noon
Dev Shayani Ekadashi [a]	None	Household	Fast
Janamashtami	None	Performance, center of village	Fast, drama, offer water
Dassehra	None	Ten dung cakes, 10 pots of *khil*, barley, household	Worship

TABLE 7. *(Continued)*

FESTIVAL	GIFT EXCHANGE	IMAGE/PLACE	RITUAL
Dev Uthani Gyas	If a son born, family gives food money to girls, children	Drawing, household	Fast, sing, light lamps
Shivaratri	None	Household	Fast, offer water to Lingam
Amla Sinchan Gyas	None	Amla plant	Bathe, fast, procession, offer food, water, singing
Holi (Little Holi)	Family members exchange gifts	Bonfire	Women fast, bathe, procession, offer dung cakes, grain, water, games, fireworks

[a] This festival is not observed but is the known pendant of Dev Uthani Gyas.

For Purinmashi, a villager may sometimes hold an elaborate *katha*, inviting guests and summoning a Brahman to read the story of Sat Narayan from a book. Or the story may be told less formally and at no cost in the home. On Janamashtami (Krishna's Birthday) in 1958, the story of Krishna was told through the medium of a three-and-a-half hour drama enacted entirely by the villagers. The story of Krishna's birth is a highlight of the Bhagavata Purana and known so well in Shanti Nagar that actors could be recruited who were capable of staging the drama, as far as we know, without rehearsals. Krishna's history is also detailed in a well-known Hindi work, the Prem Sagar. The actors had absorbed the dialogue from childhood. Literacy is now common, but in pre-Independence India, *katha*s and dramas were of great importance in the transmission of the Sanskritic tradition to villagers.

The stories told at Hoi and Karva Chauth, while well known, lack such great-traditional sanction. They are told by women, all of whom were nonliterate not long ago, who had learned them from senior women. They did not learn the tales from books nor, in 1978, did they read them aloud from books during the ritual, although popular printed versions may then have been available. The principal characters in these tales are not deities from the Sanskritic tradition but rather everyday people: wives, sisters, mothers, and mothers-in-law. On these points—literary versus oral tradition and deities from the great tradition versus commonplace personages—the *katha*s of the honorific festivals stand in sharp contrast to the legends of the welfare festivals.

Just as the personages of the tales of the welfare festivals more closely resemble ordinary people than do the deities of the *katha*s, so too the welfare festivals present the moral and philosophical aspects of Hinduism in a way that reflects village behavior more intimately than do the *katha*s of the glorification festivals. The Krishna legend is replete with his amorous and martial exploits and the fascinating intrigues surrounding his birth. *Katha*s and dramas of Krishna's life easily hold the attention of a rapt audience. The basic Hindu moral concept of dharma takes second place to his exciting adventures except in the Bhagavad Gita where Krishna expounds sophisticated Hindu philosophy to Arjuna. The Gita touches on many issues, particularly the precedence of dharma (duty) over sentiment (the love of one's kin, in this case). Villagers easily draw moral lessons from the Gita that are applicable in their own lives, even though the context, a great war, is remote from village life. However, the tales told at Hoi and Karva Chauth translate dharma directly into specific daily behavior. The basic themes of selfless service, devotion to the husband, respect for the mother-in-law, and the sanctity of the cow are constantly enacted in the life of every family.

Another difference between the honorific and welfare festivals may be mentioned. Of the 18 welfare festivals, 13 are annual events. The exceptions are Akhta, held as needed, and the four weekly festivals. Only 6 of the 12 festivals of the honorific category are observed annually. Three festivals are monthly or fortnightly, namely, Amavas (New Moon), Purinmashi (Full Moon), and the Elevenths of each fortnight. Hanuman is venerated on Tuesdays, Mirabai on Wednesdays, and Brihaspat on Thursdays.

Finally, women are featured more prominently than men in the welfare festivals, three of which are observed only by women (Karva Chauth, Hoi, and Sili Sat) and another, chiefly by women (Devi ki Karahi). Among the honorific festivals, only Dev Uthani Gyas and Amla Sinchan Gyas are the exclusive province of women. On the other hand, the worship of Hanuman on Tuesdays is practiced mainly by men.

All festivals taken together, the participation of women is much greater than that of men. Wadley (1994a: 126) commented, "Women alone perform a large number of the yearly calendrical rituals in both rural and urban India and are essential to most others." Jacobson correlated differential participation in ceremonies with the relative social status of women and men: "The women of Senapur, who seem to be of significantly lower status than their menfolk, are responsible for nearly all religious ceremonies" (Jacobson, 1994: 95).

PURINMASHI

Villagers, mainly women, observe the fast of Sat Narayan on Purinmashi, the full moon. Narayan is one of the names of Vishnu. Sat Narayan (or Satya Narayan) is equivalent to Narayan. Satya Narayan means God of Truth (sat, *satya*). Rose (1919: 366, fn. 1) said that the Sat Narayans are orthodox Hindus who observe the fast of Sat Narayan on Purinmashi. However, both Banerjea and Bhattacharyya said that Satya Narayan was originally a Muslim saint who metamorphosed into a deity combining Hindu and Muslim ideas.

> One of the comparatively new entrants into the Hindu pantheon is Satya-Narayana, or Satyapir. *Pir* ordinarily means a Muslim saint, but in this context the word designates the one God (Allah or Rahim) of Islam. An

attempt was undoubtedly made some centuries ago to absorb him into the Hindu fold and it was laid down that there is no real difference between Rama and Rahim . . . [Banerjea, 1953: 75].

Bhattacharyya (1953: 200) said:

> A peculiar and popular folk deity is Satya-Narayana, who is worshipped once every month at dusk with elaborate offerings . . . . He has been metamorphosed from his medieval form of Satyapir, the combination Muslim and Hindu deity, and is now considered to be the great Narayana.

This interpretation of Sat Narayan, if valid, provides another instance of Muslim saints (pirs) being absorbed into Hinduism, as was the case with the Panch Pir.

The basic elements of the festival are a fast until moonrise and an offering of water (argha) to the moon. Villagers who knew a mantra, usually the Gayatri, would recite it. Devotees would ordinarily bathe sometime during the day before making the offering and break their fast with a festive meal. Before eating, they usually would give a piece of bread to a cow. Sometimes the ritual is performed to fulfill a vow. A few people light lamps, perform *arati*, and distribute *prasad*. The most elaborate and costly observance of the fast of Sat Narayan involves a *katha*.

In 1959, a young Potter man described a *katha* that he had arranged the previous year:

> I call Pandit Om Prakash [pseudonym] for a religious act like Satya Narayan's *katha*. It may be held on any full-moon day. One may fast for Purinmashi every month and invite a Brahman at the end of the year to do *havan*. On such an occasion, you invite guests, 15 to 20 Brahman men. This is a religious act. During a *katha*, the Brahman reads from a religious book like the Gita and people listen to him with devotion. This is thinking of God and is religious. The Pandit reads from a religious book, but I don't know which one. I arranged a *katha* last year. I fed Pandit Om Prakash and paid him Rs. 1.25. The guests also gave him a coin or two. I fed halva, puri, and vegetables to about 300 people from here and neighboring villages. Most were Potters but also other castes came. I spent about Rs. 150 to Rs. 175. I arranged another *katha* a few years before this one. It is good to do religious acts. One hopes that God will give one a good time in this life.

We were not at this *katha* but have attended others. They are much livelier than the Potter's description would suggest. In 1958, a young Brahman teacher of Sanskrit was in the habit of holding regular *katha*s. He read from the Bhagavad Gita and the Ramayana, explaining the text while the attentive audience commented on his explanations, asked questions, and agreed or disagreed with him. These *katha*s were not for Sat Narayan; there was no *havan* or feast. The young Brahman held these sessions because he took seriously his role of Sanskrit teacher.

Sat Narayan's *katha* may be held because it is a religious act, right behavior (dharma) by its very nature. The *katha* arranged by the Potter described above is an example. But sometimes, people sponsor a Sat Narayan's *katha* to fulfill a vow made when faced with a crisis. We attended one such *katha* in February 1978. When the son of a Brahman woman was very ill, she had vowed to hold the ceremony if her son recovered. We describe in some detail not only the ceremony but also the way the day unfolded to give an idea of what a day's fieldwork is like.

In the morning, the boy's grandmother came to invite us to attend a Sat Narayan's *katha* for her grandson. There was to be a puja and then a feast. The puja was scheduled to start at 9:30 A.M. We were still waiting at 11:00. In the meantime, some children came to tell us that there would be an oil bath, a ritual that precedes a wedding, for a Brahman girl. We wanted to attend, if possible. Later still, a Brahman man came to tell us the date of his daughter's wedding. It would be late in the marriage season because, at the moment, the sun, moon, and Saturn were in the fourth, eighth, and twelfth houses, a very bad conjunction. The Chhipi Dyer then sent word that he wanted us to come and take a photo of his father.

At 11:15, we decided to visit the Brahman family to check the preparations for the ceremony for Sat Narayan. If there was time, we would run to the Chhipi's, take the photo, and return for the puja. At the Brahman's house, we were told that a priest from another village, who had been asked to come to conduct the ceremony, would not be coming, so a local Brahman would perform the *havan*, assisted by another local priest, if he was asked. This day and the preceding day were civil holidays, so many people were at home. We then hurried from the Brahman's house to the Chhipi's, but his father had left. We promised to return another day.

Back at the Brahman's house, the puja had not yet started, so we waited in the men's sitting room (*baithak*) with a few other men, among them a schoolteacher and a priest, both from another village. The priest had come to visit us. After a few minutes, we were called into another room where the ceremony was to be held. The visiting priest accompanied us, but when it became apparent that we planned to stay for the entire ceremony, he became bored and left. We tried to avoid the other visitor because all he wanted to discuss was how evil Americans were. He also said that we were not seeing the real India in Shanti Nagar, a familiar charge. We replied that we understood that the local villages were similar to those in Haryana and Punjab. He said that Haryana and Punjab were not the real India either. The real India was in Bihar where people are very poor.

Figures 46–52 depict various moments in the course of the ceremony. As shown in figure 46, the altar for the fire ceremony was in front of the local priest who conducted the ritual. The couple who sponsored the *katha* sat left of the priest, and the child who had been ill was to his right. We sat directly opposite the priest. In the course of the ceremony, the priest from another village who was not going to come in fact arrived and sat near the altar. There were about 15 to 20 spectators.

We could not see the drawing on the altar clearly, for when we arrived wood had already been piled on it surmounted by a piece of a dung cake. Such drawings, which represent the nine *graha*s or planetary deities, are usually artistically drawn, but this one appeared to be no more than a few lines of wheat flour and turmeric. The common ceremonial paraphernalia were near the altar: pitchers of water and ghee, a stone tied with a red thread that represents Ganesh, a dish of incense, and a

FIG. 46. Sat Narayan's Katha, 1978. Arrangement of the principal participants at the start of the ceremony.

brass tray with wheat flour, turmeric, rice, gur or white sugar, and some rupee notes and coins.

The local priest conducted the ceremony rapidly, muttering what we assumed to be mantras, sprinkling water, and adding ghee and incense to the fire. He did not use a book of mantras. He tied red string on the right wrists of the participants and the children among the spectators. He put a tilak of turmeric on the Ganesh stone and on the forehead of the father.

When the out-of-town priest arrived, someone offered a coin that was placed on the tray. The Ganesh stone also was put on the tray. The local priest sent for more ghee, which he poured on the fire. The visiting priest and the local priest tied red strings on each other's wrists and exchanged tilaks. The local priest prepared a second tray to be used for arati[24] at the end of the ceremony. He called for cotton, which he twisted into a wick. He lit the lamp and placed it on the tray with some rice and wheat flour.

Someone asked that the story of Sat Narayan be recited. At this point, the visiting priest took charge. He told several stories about Sat Narayan (fig. 49). The local priest listened to the first story and then disappeared for a while. Our notes for the first story are sketchy, perhaps because the storyteller was just warming up. We have a more complete account of a later, different story, which we present below.

The first story concerned a natural calamity. People were suffering, and Narada (see below) wanted to help them. He meditated and concentrated on God, reciting the attributes of God. Worship leads to happiness, and one's soul is purified. Then God comes. (The priest used God and Sat Narayan interchangeably.) Then the priest began to sing, "Don't forget God if you want a life. At death no family members will save you." God came and asked Narada why he was upset. Narada said peo-

FIG. 47. *(left)* Sat Narayan's Katha, 1978. Priest and the boy who had been ill.
FIG. 48. *(right)* Sat Narayan's Katha, 1978. Fire ceremony.

ple were suffering because of the calamity. God said, "Pray to Sat Narayan and you will have a good life."

A point of interest in this cryptic myth is the appearance of Narada, one of the rishis. He is mentioned in the Rig-veda and appears in later Sanskritic literature. He is identified with the Krishna legend. Garrett (1990: 416) characterized the Narada Purana "as a sectarial and modern compilation intended to support the doctrine of Bhakti, or faith in Vishnu." Internal evidence suggests that this Purana was compiled during medieval times when much of India was ruled by Muslims.

A woman entered the room bearing a plate of sliced bananas, which she placed

FIG. 49. Sat Narayan's Katha, 1978. Visiting priest tells a story.

to the left of the storyteller. Sat Narayan is said to like bananas. This offering launched the priest into a discussion of offerings. He made the point that one-quarter should be added to an offering of flour, for example, one-and-a-quarter seers of wheat flour. There was no need for this lecture, as such offerings were standard in the village.

After the ceremony had lasted an hour, the storyteller began to tell this elaborate myth concerning a childless king and a merchant:

The king was worshipping Sat Narayan to grant him a child. A merchant, also childless, came to the city and saw the king. He asked the king what he was doing, and the king told him. The merchant promised to worship Sat Narayan if he had a child. A daughter was born to him. The merchant's wife reminded him that he had promised to fast and to worship Sat Narayan, but the merchant made some excuse not to do so. He said that he would worship Sat Narayan at his daughter's marriage.

The girl came of age and the merchant's servants found a husband for her. Again the merchant made an excuse and did not fast for Sat Narayan. He and his new son-in-law went on a business trip.

Sat Narayan became angry. He arranged for thieves to rob the king. When pursued, the thieves abandoned the stolen things near the merchant, where they were found. The king put the two men in prison. The king did not listen to their weeping because it was God's will. The king seized all their money and merchandise.

The women in the merchant's house were also robbed. The merchant's daughter went to a Brahman's house where they were worshipping Sat Narayan. She prayed to God and asked for relief. Sat Narayan listened. He appeared in a dream and told the king to release the two merchants and return their money and merchandise or he would be destroyed.

The king set them free, saying that he had made a mistake. He arranged for them to have a haircut, bath, new clothes, and double their money and merchandise. He told the merchant that his failure to fulfill the vow was the cause of his trouble.

[People were offering money to the storyteller. They put it on the tray. We counted Rs. 4 and change.]

The merchant departed on a boat. Sat Narayan came disguised as a beggar. To avoid giving alms, the merchant told the beggar that the boat was full of nothing but leaves. Sat Narayan went to a cave in the guise of a holy man. When the merchant looked into the boat, he found to his horror that it was indeed full of leaves. He fell unconscious. His son-in-law told him that this trouble came from a holy man in a cave. The merchant searched out the holy man and wept before him. God told him not to weep and reminded him of the unfulfilled vow. The merchant worshipped God.

The two men returned home with their wealth. The merchant's wife and daughter were worshipping Sat Narayan. The merchant's daughter ran

FIG. 50. Sat Narayan's Katha, 1978. Holding a tray with a lighted lamp and other paraphernalia, the boy for whom the ceremony was held prepares to perform *arati*.

to meet them, but she forgot to eat the *prasad*. The merchant alighted from the boat, but God was angry and made the boat and the son-in-law vanish. Then the merchant began to worship and asked his daughter which god she had offended. God spoke from the sky and said that she had forgotten to eat the *prasad*. If she ate it, her husband and the boat would reappear. She ate the *prasad*, and her husband and the boat returned.

God gives wealth in life and after death one gets release. One goes to Vaikuntha [the paradise of Vishnu].

After the storytelling, *arati* took place. The boy for whom the ceremony was performed held the tray and slowly rotated it (fig. 50). Everyone stood and sang. Then people held their hands over the flame and rubbed their faces and heads.

The final ritual faintly suggests a fertility motif, the dominant theme in the myth recounted just above. There were two pots, one with milk, curd, and other milk products. The other pot contained cooked wheat flour, known as *panjiri*. Pathak (1976: 630) defined *panjiri* as a sweetmeat given to puerperal females. The pieces of banana mentioned above were dipped in the flour. Then the milk products and the banana slices coated with *panjiri* were distributed to the participants and spectators. The boy's father told the visiting priest to take Rs. 1.25 from the offerings that he had received and give the money to one of the daughters of the household.

The local priest had returned by this time, and he showed us a book containing Sat Narayan's *katha*. He said that he was prepared to read the story if the visiting priest had not arrived. The visitor knew the stories by heart. Just before we left, we glanced around the room. The visiting priest had pocketed the money and was busy tying up the flour and other food in cloths that he had brought with him (fig. 51).

Sat Narayan's *katha*s, like the one described above, are special, adding a long, rather costly ceremony to what is otherwise a simple ritual in honor of Sat Narayan. In July 1958, we watched two Brahman women perform the usual ritual. They had fasted during the day. In the evening at moonrise, they went to the roof of their house carrying a pitcher of water with rice in it. There may be a connection between rice and the moon, for some rice is often put in the water offered to the full moon (Underhill, 1991: 67). However, a Chhipi Dyer woman used gram (chick peas). The Brahman women recited the Gayatri mantra and poured the water onto the roof. One woman touched the pitcher to her forehead after the offering but before reciting the mantra. The ceremony took only a minute or so. They told us that when a *katha* is held, it takes place during the day and involves a *havan*. Although we did not see

FIG. 51. Sat Narayan's Katha, 1978. Visiting priest packs the food that was given to him as part of his payment.

them feed a piece of bread to a cow after the ritual and before breaking their fast, they had done so on other Purinmashis, because, said one, "A cow is just like our mother and must be fed before breaking a fast."

Three other women who were with the Brahmans at the July Purinmashi did not perform any ritual. A Bairagi woman told us that she was too old to fast; a Brahman woman said that she just forgot to fast. A Sweeper woman said, "I have observed this worship once in my life. I have to work hard so how can I fast?" After the women finished worshipping, a Brahman man came to the roof to perform the ritual.

In 1978 people more frequently mentioned lighting a lamp than did our informants in 1958. Otherwise, there was little difference in how the ritual was observed at the two points in time. One Barber woman said that she lit a lamp in honor of both Sat Narayan and Shiva. She was the only person to mention Shiva of the many whom we interviewed, a fact that would be of little importance except that the connection of the moon with Vishnu is a bit curious. The moon, a relatively minor deity in modern Hinduism, is an emblem of Shiva (Underhill, 1991: 70). He is commonly depicted with the moon in his hair. However, on the night of the full moon in Shanti Nagar, Shiva is displaced by Vishnu by way of Krishna and Sat Narayan.

The Leatherworkers and Sweepers (Dalits)[25] do not observe the fast for Sat Narayan. However, observance is up to each individual, so some members of these castes may practice the ritual occasionally. We surveyed a sample of villagers concerning their festival observances. Four Dalits were in the sample. None observed the festival. Moreover, a Sweeper woman who was present at the Purinmashi of the

FIG. 52. Sat Narayan's Katha, 1978. Cooking puris for the feast after the ceremony.

Brahman women, described above, said that she had observed the festival only once in her lifetime. A Brahman woman told us that all castes except the Dalits observed the festival.

An eclipse of the moon (Chandra-grahan) may occur on the day of the full moon. All eclipses are inauspicious, both solar and lunar. In Hindu mythology, eclipses are caused by the demon Rahu, the ascending node of the moon. At the churning of the Sea of Milk, the demon assumed a disguise and, insinuating himself among the gods, drank of the Amrita, the beverage of immortality. The Sun and the Moon observed the theft and told Vishnu, who beheaded the demon as punishment. Having partaken of the Amrita, the demon was immortal and was placed in the heavens. The head of the demon is Rahu, and the tail, Ketu, the descending node. Because the Sun and the Moon betrayed Rahu, he pursues them with implacable hatred and periodically swallows them to cause eclipses. But having no tail, he cannot retain them and they pass through him in a short time.

Although Underhill (1991: 36) said that eclipses, whether of the sun or the moon, are very auspicious, the villagers of Shanti Nagar considered them to be dangerous, especially for a pregnant woman. If she worked during an eclipse, she might bear a deformed infant. For example, a pregnant woman should not grind grain during an eclipse. If she did, her child would be born clubfooted. An eclipse and clubfootedness were thought to be related because a woman sat cross-legged and bent over while grinding grain. This position during an eclipse was believed to cause the legs of the fetus to be similarly shaped, resulting in a clubfooted child. A number of people said that a Potter woman with a clubfooted son had been grinding grain during an eclipse. Lapoint (1981: 337; 343–344) cited a few examples of the link between a pregnant woman's (or animal's) position during an eclipse and the subsequent deformity of her infant. A pregnant woman could avoid trouble by distributing *prasad* during an eclipse. If she failed to do so her child might have peculiar features. The villagers said that the misshapen lips of a Leatherworker girl were caused by her pregnant mother's failure to distribute some food during an eclipse. Rose (1919, 1: 127) reported, "The husband of a wife pregnant for the first time should not look on any eclipse or his child will be deformed in some way and is peculiarly liable to hare-lip."

Villagers take account of eclipses when scheduling ceremonial activity. On Holi, which takes place on the day of the full moon, the villagers scheduled the lighting of the Holi bonfire to avoid a partial eclipse. Villagers know when an eclipse will take place, for they consult almanacs that note the exact time.

Villagers mark an eclipse with ceremonial activity and may give alms to beggars. A solar eclipse occasions a *havan*, a major ritual. Less is done for a lunar eclipse. One may chant a mantra, and some Brahman women told us that they put *dub* grass (see note 17) in all the household's cooking pots and water jars. Lapoint (1981: 334) reported that "*dabh*" (kusha) grass protects foodstuffs from contamination during eclipses. The less intense ceremonial attention paid to the moon reflects the fact that the sun is a more important deity. Also, lunar eclipses are more commonplace than solar eclipses in Shanti Nagar and may, therefore, receive less attention. Although on average more solar than lunar eclipses take place worldwide, lunar eclipses are viewed more often, that is, by everyone who can see the moon. The path of a solar eclipse is typically only 100 miles wide.

An eclipse is an occasion when Sweepers receive presents from their patrons (jajmans), usually grain and possibly a headcloth. These gifts are in fact payments that are part of the compensation that Sweepers receive under the traditional jajmani system. A young boy told a brief story to explain the reason for gifts to Sweepers. He said that in olden times, the sun and the moon borrowed salt from Sweepers and could not repay them. So whenever there is an eclipse, the villagers have to repay the Sweepers. When a lunar eclipse begins, Sweeper women call at the house of each patron to receive their due, no matter what the hour. People do not go to bed until the Sweeper has made her visit.

Lapoint (1981: 342) confirmed our young informant's story of the sun's debt to the Sweepers that is discharged by the villagers. Lapoint does not mention lunar eclipses in this context but in all likelihood the explanation of indebtedness applies to both lunar and solar eclipses. Another explanation is that because Sweepers have affinities with the demons who cause eclipses, they are therefore entitled to receive gifts on such occasions. However, the most popular reason that Lapoint's informants gave for the gifts to Sweepers at the time of a solar eclipse is based on the concept of ritual pollution. Sweepers clear polluting wastes from the village and thus lift contamination from people. Gifts to Sweepers are ritual acts that banish the contamination that comes from eclipses, both lunar and solar.

AMAVAS

Surya, the sun, is the deity honored on Amavas, but the villagers mainly observe the appropriate rituals in Delhi at the Yamuna River. In Shanti Nagar itself, the festival has little ritual, except when a solar eclipse takes place. Villagers may cook festive food (khir and halva), but as an appropriate symbol to mark a festival rather than as a feast to break a fast for a deity. Since the revolution of the moon is the basic element in both Amavas and Purinmashi, we expected to see many ritual similarities between the two festivals. However, there are almost none. As practiced within the village, Amavas lacks offerings, fasting, vows, havans (fire worship), and kathas, all of which are features of Purinmashi and many other festivals. As on Purinmashi, Brahmans may sometimes be fed on Amavas. One woman said that she always fed khir to a Brahman; a Watercarrier said that he sometimes did so. However, on Purinmashi, Brahmans are fed as guests invited for a katha. One of them may receive additional payment for performing the ritual. If a Brahman is fed on Amavas, it is done as a routine religious act. He performs no ritual.

Because ritual observances are a matter of individual choice (if a villager can shrug off critical gossip that may attend nonobservance), one can never say with complete confidence that a particular practice was not observed. Some rituals, such as an offering of water, are over in less than a minute and might escape observation. Fasting and vows cannot be observed at all. However, no villager told us about any specific rituals practiced in the village on an Amavas without an eclipse, which contrasts sharply with their specific accounts of fasting and offerings on Purinmashi. Of course, there are rituals that take place on Amavas that are daily events and are not specifically tied to the festival, for example, feeding bread to a cow.

The connection of the moon and Sat Narayan enhances the importance of Pur-inmashi. The linkage of Sat Narayan, Narayan, Vishnu, and Krishna brings into play popular sacred books, which in turn opens the door to *katha*s. Moreover, Sat Narayan is honored by a fast, an offering, a feast, and perhaps a vow, the normal rit-ual panoply.

In contrast, the two practices that are characteristic of Amavas are not a part of Purinmashi. First, the new moon is observed as a day of rest for bullocks and, to a lesser extent, for men. Bullocks are not yoked, even during the most active agri-cultural seasons. In 1958, the sugarcane harvest was a busy season, and the bullock-powered cane crushers ran continuously. But on Amavas the bullocks rested, which meant that men could rest also unless they found something to do that did not require bullocks. For example, on Amavas in March, many men went to the fields to cut sugarcane into small lengths. They buried the pieces in preparation for later planting. A Potter woman told us that on both the new and full moons, the Potters do not work with their horses and mules at the brick kilns. Such work is one of the chief occupations of the Potters.

The second basic feature of Amavas is a pilgrimage to the Yamuna for a bath. Individuals from any caste may make this pilgrimage. A dip in the sacred Yamuna is a ritual of purification, and might also be undertaken to fulfill a vow. Widowed per-sons especially tend to go regularly to the Yamuna on Amavas. In addition, villagers make offerings to the sun and other deities, distribute *prasad* and alms to beggars, and feed monkeys. If ritual is divided into two categories, activity and abstention from activity, on Amavas the village itself is the site of abstention and the Yamuna, the scene of activity.

We made one trip to the Yamuna with the villagers from Shanti Nagar, in March 1959. We noted people from seven castes, but Brahmans predominated. The road leading to the bathing place and temples was swarming with villagers from miles around. On their way to the river, they fed monkeys and gave food and alms to beggars lining the road. The river frontage has many temples and dharmsalas. In March the river is low and we crossed a bridge over a stagnant stream and then crossed a wide expanse of sand to reach the river. The sand was planted with veg-etables that were protected by screens of reeds. The pilgrims bathe by village groups, separated by sex, except that the children stay with the women. The villagers from Shanti Nagar have a customary spot for bathing, so even if people travel in separate small groups to the river, everyone arrives at the same place. People wear clothing while bathing. Old women stripped to the waist, but not the young women. Some people chant while bathing. After bathing, people may wash their soiled clothes. They put on clean clothes, and most of the women distributed *batasha*s. When we gave some *batasha*s to a begging child, we were admonished. You do not distribute *prasad* unless you bathe.

We went with a group of women to a small temple with images of many gods, among them Ganesh and Hanuman. The women made offerings of water and prayed. Some women made their offerings to the pipal tree, which has a connection with the sun. In fact many deities are said to assemble at the pipal tree. Other women faced the sun and worshipped it. The bathing and the ritual at the temple are religious acts, not undertaken for any specific benefit other than general well-being. Channa (1984: 103) wrote, "The sun-god is not asked any particular kind of favor. It is a generalised god and is prayed to independently or in association with the peepal tree. After the ritual of the peepal tree, water from a lota is poured. The votary sees the sun through the stream of water."

Villagers, especially the men, liked to have some fun in Delhi after the ritual, which took place in the morning. One possibility was the fair that was held near the bathing site on Amavas. Fairs usually accompany events that attract many pilgrims. However, on this particular Amavas, there was an added attraction: a circus was in town, and some of the villagers planned to attend it. In the afternoon, a Brahman man from our village came to fetch us, and we accompanied him to the circus. We saw several men from Shanti Nagar, but none of the women who were at the river in the morning. However, some women from other villages were there, queuing up separately from the men to buy tickets. Inside the tent, some village women were sitting with their husbands and children.

The one-ring circus looked like a typical Euro-American circus. Most of the performers were Indians except for a few men who looked European. The oldest European appeared to be the head of the circus; he merely directed and watched. The circus was mediocre at best. The audience was quiet, no applause to speak of, but everyone seemed to enjoy the acts, and all the low-priced seats were filled. Both Europeans and Brahmans were mocked in the comic skits, especially a memsahib for her walk, independent attitude, and her refusal to be intimidated or humiliated. The Brahman, who played a minor role, was satirized for his pretentious piety. A young woman who accompanied us thought that the memsahib was funny but not the pandit. The villagers laughed at the memsahib. The band played chiefly American popular tunes ("Chattanooga Choo-Choo," "Sheik of Araby"). Most of the spectators appeared to be villagers, who were probably in town because the day was Amavas.

An eclipse transforms Amavas into a dangerous celestial event, for both solar and lunar eclipses are inauspicious (R. Freed and S. Freed, 1964: 74, 84). Our assistant, a Delhi resident, said that during an eclipse the sun showers the earth with dirty gases. Lapoint (1981: 331) said that a solar eclipse is much more serious than a lunar eclipse. The occulted sun emits noxious rays (kiran) that endanger living beings and also contaminate comestibles. A partial solar eclipse took place in April, 1958. People fasted before the eclipse and bathed afterwards to rid themselves of the pollution emitted by the sun. Villagers poured out any water stored in their houses, for it was polluted, and drew fresh water. This remedy is more drastic than the one practiced on Purinmashi, when women put dub grass in the water, apparently to purify it, instead of replacing it. As on Purinmashi, Sweeper women visited their patrons after the eclipse and received food and sometimes a headcloth.

The ritual high point of the day of the eclipse was a havan performed by Brahman men in an open space near the center of the village. Women of many Brahman families brought offerings of food. During the eclipse, the Brahmans recited mantras, which they read from a book, and offered ghee and samagri (a mixture of aromatic substances) to the fire. Ordinarily, only men perform the *havan*, but on this occasion the Brahmans invited our female assistant, who had a university degree in Sanskrit, to take part. A young Brahman man, a teacher of Sanskrit, said that she was invited as a special favor. It seemed obvious that her learning overrode any reservations that the men might have had because of her gender. After the *havan*, the food and offerings were gathered and given to Brahmans of the Vasishtha *gotra* (clan), who lived in a neighboring village and were said to be descendants of the Rishi Vyasa, the alleged compiler of the Mahabharata. Lapoint (1981: 340–341) recorded a *havan* during a solar eclipse in a village in western Uttar Pradesh. The officiating priest recited the Gayatri Mantra, an invocation of the solar deity, 108 times. The villagers explained that the ritual removes pollution from the self, air, and place caused by the eclipse.

The young Brahman teacher of Sanskrit who participated in the *havan* told us that it is important to take a bath at Kurukshetra on Amavas. There is a connection between the Mahabharata, Kurukshetra, and a solar eclipse. Kurukshetra is a holy tract and place of pilgrimage centered around the town of Thanesar about 155 km north of Delhi. The ancient city of Kurukshetra is now united with Thanesar. The Mahabharata describes a war between the Pandavas and their cousins, the Kauravas, for control of the kingdom of the Kurus, ruled by Dhristarashtra. The ruins of his capital, Hastinapura, have been found about 57 mi northeast of Delhi on an old bed of the Ganga. The issue was settled in favor of the Pandavas by a great 18-day battle on the plain of Kurukshetra near Thanesar, said to have been fought about 1367 B.C.E. (Balfour, 1885, 2: 636). A solar eclipse was among the many terrifying omens portending victory for the Pandavas that preceded the battle (van Buitenen, 1973–78, 3: 449).

The combination of sun worship, an eclipse, and the epic battle fought at Kurukshetra have made Thanesar the site of a great pilgrimage. The fair held in conjunction with the ritual bathing is an added attraction. Bonner's (1986) account of the huge solar *mela* (fair) held at Kurukshetra in February 1980 caught the excitement. More than 1.5 million pilgrims arrived from all over India. Preparations for the eclipse on February 16 had begun years earlier with the renovation of the great bathing tanks, tantamount to small lakes. Two months before the eclipse, 80 acres of land were cleared for a tent city, and intense campaigns were mounted to rid the area of stray dogs, rats, snakes and mosquitoes. Thousands of water taps were installed, and latrine trenches were dug along the roads. About 10 days before the event, the pilgrims began to flood the area. Extra buses and trains were added and every hour thousands of people arrived.

The pilgrims see an eclipse as a struggle between Rahu and Surya. It is their duty to help the sun to break free from the clutches of the demon. On the day of the eclipse, 1000 holy men led a parade around the tanks, sounding horns and conch shells to frighten the demon. Pilgrims gave alms to beggars to relieve the sun's pain from being swallowed. As the eclipse began, vast crowds moved toward the tanks, descended into the water on the great stone ghats (steps), and muttered prayers while immersing themselves. Bathing and prayers were believed to help free the sun.

Pilgrimages to Kurukshetra were rare for the villagers of Shanti Nagar. The Yamuna at nearby Delhi was much more practical than the bathing tanks at distant

Kurukshetra. However, one Brahman man said that he had gone to Kurukshetra four or five times when there was a solar eclipse, and an elderly Jat woman claimed to have gone there once for an eclipse.

Both the villagers of Sikh Pura, one of the two villages studied by Bonner in Kurukshetra District, Haryana, and those of Shanti Nagar believe that eclipses are dangerous, but they point to different causes of the danger. The people of Sikh Pura, a predominately Sikh community, see danger in the conflict of a deity versus a demon. Their rituals are intended to avoid danger by insuring the triumph of the deity. Even bathing, usually considered to be a ritual of purification, is interpreted as a measure to aid the sun in his struggle with Rahu.

In Shanti Nagar, pollution appears to be the basic consideration during a solar eclipse, as it is in Garvpur in western Uttar Pradesh (Lapoint, 1981: 331–332). The villagers practice rituals for personal and household purification. Bathing, changing drinking water, and the postponement of cooking until after the eclipse are all measures taken to remove, or to avoid, pollution. The *havan*, the principal ritual performed during an eclipse, is best understood as a religious act, comparable to the *havan* at a *katha* held on Purinmashi. Offering water to the sun honors the deity.

EKADASHI

Ekadashis (Elevenths) are sacred to Vishnu. Gyas also means eleventh, and the two words serve equally in the titles of important festivals, for example, Dev Uthani Gyas (Gods' Awakening Eleventh) and Nirjala Ekadashi (Waterless Eleventh). Devotees observe an 11th with a fast and prayer. Mukerji (1916: 167) wrote, "So meritorious is the Ekadashi fast believed to be, that there is no difference between an Ekadashi of the bright fortnight and one of the dark fortnight . . . ." The merits of the fast are said to be extraordinary. It is described as the equivalent of feeding millions of starving beggars or of performing a penance of 60,000 years. Krishna transformed himself into Ekadashi to save humanity from the torments of hell. Krishna said, "It is the day that I have chosen in my mercy to save men and deliver them from their sins. . . . I expressly forbid them to eat rice on this day. I ordain that Sin shall dwell in the rice" (Imperial Record Department, 1914: 29–30). Widows are said to observe the fast strictly.

The people of Shanti Nagar claim that by fasting on every 11th, one does not suffer at death. Death is easy, and one attains release (moksha) from the round of rebirths. Nautiyal (1961: 164) reported a similar belief from the village of Mandi, with the qualification that 52 consecutive fasts are enough for positively attaining moksha. In Shanti Nagar, villagers also say that if a cow or any other cattle are suffering, the devotee may pray to God either to restore the animal to health or release it from life. Either way, the animal finds release from suffering. The villagers explain the prohibition from eating rice not in terms of sin but because rice consumed in violation of the taboo turns to worms after death.

Each of the 24 Ekadashis has its own name and story. The stories have been collected in popular texts (Babb, 1975: 126). The 11th days of the bright fortnights of Asharh and Karttik, known as the Mahaekadashi (great elevenths) are especially important. On the first of these days, Dev Shayani Ekadashi (Gods' Sleeping Eleventh), Vishnu and all the other gods go to sleep. No marriages can be celebrated while they sleep.

In 1958, a villager gave us the traditional explanation of the sleep of the gods, that is, they go to sleep on the 11th. We saw no reason to pursue the matter further. However, in a 1978 survey of village festivals, several people told us that the gods go to sleep the day after Asharh *sudi* 9, a day known as Bhadaliya Naumi. That day is good for marriages, but from the following day, the 10th, marriages do not take place because the gods are sleeping. Bhadaliya Naumi (various spellings) has been noted by several investigators who have worked in Delhi villages (Bhatia, 1961: 65; Ratta, 1961: 165; Srivastava, 1961: 68; Lewis, 1958: 224–225). In practical terms, it makes little difference whether marriages end on the ninth or one or two days later. However, it is well to note what may be regional variation.

On the bright 11th of Karttik, Dev Uthani Gyas (Gods' Awakening Eleventh), the gods awaken, and the marriage season begins. The two 11ths mark approximately the beginning and end of the four-month rainy season (Babb, 1975: 144–146). The 11th of the bright fortnight of Jyesth, Nirjala Ekadashi (Waterless Eleventh), is a third important 11th. By keeping this single fast, one gains as much merit as by observing all 24 (Underhill, 1991: 85–86).

Only three 11ths are observed by more than a handful of the villagers of Shanti Nagar. They are Waterless Eleventh, Gods' Awakening Eleventh, and Amla Sinchan Gyas (The Eleventh for Watering the Amla Plant). Gods' Sleeping Eleventh is recognized but not celebrated. Occasionally, someone in time of trouble will make a vow to observe the Ekadashi fast for a specific time until the vow is fulfilled. Bright 11ths seem to be slightly favored. For example, a Brahman woman told us that recently she had a stomachache and promised to fast once a month on five bright 11ths. She said that one fasts only after the new moon (i.e., during the bright fortnight) and not during the dark fortnight. Another Brahman woman, an elderly widow, said that she fasted on most bright 11ths. On the other hand, a married Chhipi man kept a fast on all 11ths. He said, "There is no difference between the dark and bright fortnights. As Krishna-Bhagwan has said, 'This is kept for God. God is supreme'." An elderly married Brahman woman also specifically mentioned fasting on both 11ths. The government nurse, a nonresident who regularly visited Shanti Nagar, claimed to fast on 11ths, making no distinction between the fortnights. An elderly Brahman widow, in mourning for her husband, kept the fast for a year after his death, apparently on both fortnights.

Despite the alleged extraordinary merit that one obtains from fasting on 11ths, we found only the above five villagers who did so. There were undoubtedly other devotees. However, we took a survey concerning the observance of festivals, and none of the 10 respondents in the sample fasted on any 11th other than the major ones. The sample included one respondent from each of the following castes: Jat Farmer, Gardener, Blacksmith, Potter, Merchant, Watercarrier, Bairagi, Leatherworker, Barber, and Sweeper. Brahman women predominated among the devotees. We believe that the apparent disproportional representation of Brahmans is not due principally to the small sample but because 11ths are observed chiefly by Brahman women.

Nirjala Ekadashi

Nirjala Ekadashi (Waterless Eleventh) falls on Jyesth *sudi* 11. The story of the festival centers on Bhima (Bhimasena), the second of the five Pandava brothers, heroes of the great epic, the Mahabharata. A man of great strength, courage, and possessed of a gluttonous appetite, Bhima found it impossible to fast on Ekadashi. The sage Vyasa told him that if he kept this single fast just once, neither drinking water nor bathing, he would obtain as much merit as if he kept the 24 fasts. To defeat the Kauravas in battle, he managed to observe the fast once in his life (Underhill, 1991: 86).

No villager ever told us this story. Only once did villagers tell us any story associated with Nirjala Ekadashi. A Potter man outlined in a few sentences a myth identifying Ekadashi as a goddess. He said, "Somewhere there is a temple for her. She did something wrong and is hanging upside down. If enough people fast for her, she will be set upright." We do not know the source of this myth. The punishment of hanging upside down recalls the myth of Karva Chauth reported by Marriott (1955: 204), where a scheming wife is hung by her heels as punishment.

Nirjala Ekadashi takes place at the height of the hot season when temperatures often exceed 40°C (104°F). A Brahman man commented that to fast and abstain from water in such heat is part of the Hatha Yoga, the way of self-denial. It teaches one to control the senses. Although the prohibition against drinking lasts only until noon, it is nonetheless an exercise in rigorous self-denial.

The ritual of the festival consists of a fast until noon, after which melons or other fruit may be eaten. Hence the villagers sometimes call the festival Kachare Khan Gyas (Muskmelon Eating Eleventh). Devotees can drink freely after noonday. Bathing is also prohibited, presumably until noon. At midday, melons, fans, and sweet water may be distributed without any further ritual, or the presents to be distributed may serve as the focus of a brief puja before being given away. A piece of bread may be given to a cow, but in all probability this is a daily act and not specific to Nirjala Ekadashi. Two Brahman women reported giving *sidha*, a gift of raw food, to an elderly Brahman woman the morning after the festival. A Barber family also gave *sidha* to Brahmans. The ritual core of the festival consists of fasting, abstaining from water, the distribution of melons, fans, and sweet water to various recipients, and a gift of *sidha* to Brahmans.

In 1958 we recorded three descriptions of the ritual of Nirjala Ekadashi. Two Brahman women, married to brothers, fasted and neither drank nor bathed until noon. Then they drank water and ate a few slices of muskmelon and a mango. Although they could drink freely after noonday, they ate only twice, once at noon and once later in the day. They consumed nothing but fruit. Each woman spent two rupees for 4 kg of muskmelon, four fans, and 1 kg of sugar for preparing sweet water, which they distributed as follows. At the time, two carpenters and three laborers were working on their house. The Brahmans gave a slice of melon and sweet water to each workman. They gave a melon, fan, and sweet water to their mother-in-law, to a cousin of their husbands, and to two Brahman women. The presents were distributed at midday. There was no other ritual throughout the day. These women did not observe the fast in 1978.

A married Chhipi Dyer woman observed a sparse ritual. She fasted, drank water only after midday, and in the evening ate what she described as a white granular powder that is cooked in milk. The result is a dish like rice pudding, but it contains no grain. Grains are not eaten on Nirjala Ekadashi. She distributed no gifts although she knew of the custom. In 1978, her husband told us that the family observed the day with a fast and the distribution of melons and fans. He said that they took only three drops of water, presumably just until noon when the prohibition of water ended. A Brahman woman also described the custom of taking only three drops of water. She said that the drops were licked from the side of the thumb.

A married Brahman woman fasted and then at midday performed the following ritual. Inside her house, she arranged a glass of sweet water, a fan, two slices of muskmelon, and a small coin (pice). She bowed to this offering, sprinkled some water, and then gave the *prasad* to an elderly Brahman woman. The next morning, she gave *sidha* to the same woman. She also gave bread to a cow.

In 1978, an elderly Barber woman said that her family observed the fast. In the morning, they gave *sidha* to Brahmans. Then they broke the fast with fruit. She remarked that people who could afford the cost sometimes served melons and sweet water to passersby. She implied that her family could not afford it.

It is clear from our surveys both in 1958 and 1978 that Nirjala Ekadashi is mainly for Brahmans, but not all of them observe it. Informants from all castes except the Brahmans, Chhipis, and Barbers specifically denied observing the festival. Our informant from the Merchant caste, a young woman, said that her husband's family did nothing, but that a younger sister, who did not live in Shanti Nagar, fasts on the festival. The Merchant family in Shanti Nagar follows the Arya Samaj, which tends to repress the observance of some traditional festivals.

Nirjala Ekadashi honors Vishnu. As in all festivals, devotees hope to acquire merit that will somehow be rewarded, but this is a minor theme. There is also an element of interaction in the festival. Presents are distributed, chiefly to Brahmans and relatives. However, specific relationships are not pinpointed, and there is a random element in the distribution. Devotees might give melons and sweet water to workers who happen to be present on the festival day or even to passersby. The relatively few people who observe the festival do it as a traditional religious act, whose essential element seems to be an exercise in self-discipline.

Dev Uthani Gyas

Dev Uthani Gyas (Gods' Awakening Eleventh) is celebrated on Karttik *sudi* 11, after the kharif harvest. Only women take part in the festival. In contrast to Nirjala Ekadashi, which few people observe, women of all castes celebrate Dev Uthani Gyas. Only the strictest Arya Samajis, or families that have suffered a death on that day, ignore the festival. The purpose of the festival is to awaken the gods after their sleep of four months so that weddings may again take place. Villagers commented that although marriages could be celebrated immediately after Dev Uthani Gyas in the cool season, the best time was during the warm days late in the marriage season when guests can wear light clothing and sleep in the fields. One Brahman man firmly stated, "Winter marriages are for the rich," indicating that only rich families could put up guests in comfortable quarters.

Har Narayan (Vishnu) is the chief deity of Gods' Awakening Eleventh. Four months earlier, Vishnu descends into the nether world where Sesha, the serpent-king, rules. The coils of this immense snake are the bed on which Vishnu sleeps, and the serpent's one thousand erect heads form a protective canopy over Vishnu's head. Vaishnavas maintain that Vishnu himself represents all the gods, so when Vishnu sleeps, all of the 330 million Hindu deities also sleep (Mukerji, 1916: 166–167).

Gods' Awakening Eleventh has links with Dassehra and hence with Rama, an avatar of Vishnu. On Dassehra, which celebrates the victory of Rama over Ravana, village women prepare 10 small dung cakes that are saved until Dev Uthani Gyas a month later and then burned as part of the ritual.

The second tie with Dassehra is the custom of women and girls running through the village in the evening of Dev Uthani Gyas, waving burning rags attached to poles. This custom commemorates the burning of Lanka, Ravana's capital city, in the course of the war between Rama and Ravana as described in the Ramayana. Hanuman, the Monkey God and an associate of Rama, was causing havoc. Ravana had Hanuman captured and brought into his court where, to mock Hanuman, he ordered that a cloth be tied to Hanuman's tail and set on fire, for a monkey is proud of his tail. Hanuman's tail grew to a huge size, and Ravana's demons had to use every rag and all the oil in the city to wrap it and prepare it for burning. As the citizens jeered him, Hanuman escaped and dashed about the city, setting it on fire by waving his burning tail. In an instant, the city was consumed (Growse, 1989: 502–508).

A Leatherworker man suggested a third link to Dassehra. He said that all the gods were imprisoned by Ravana. When Rama won his victory over Ravana, all 330

FIG. 53. Murals of Har Narayan drawn by a Jat woman for Dev Uthani Gyas, 1958. The figure (left) is drawn on the side of the stove; footprints of people and cattle on the ground.
     Sketches like the one on right are drawn on walls near doorways; a big sketch near the main doorway, smaller ones near the side entrance.

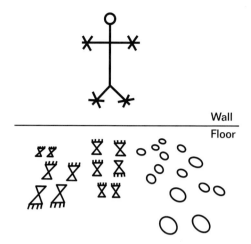

Wall

Floor

FIG. 54. Mural of Har Narayan for Dev Uthani Gyas at a Jat's house, 1958. The mural is drawn on the side of a stove; human footprints, left, and cattle prints, right, on the floor. There are also sketches of footprints and peacocks on walls near doors, and a large drawing near the family masonry well.

million gods were released. They were free then to roam about for a month until Dev Uthani Gyas when their vacation was over and they had to attend to their duties in weddings. The problem with this unique story is that between Dassehra and Dev Uthani Gyas, several important festivals take place. It would be no time for the gods to be on vacation. We do not know the source of the Leatherworker's story.

The essential ritual of the day, the worship and awakening of the gods, takes place in the evening. In preparation for the awakening ritual, women draw sketches of Har Narayan with a solution of red chalk on walls or cookstoves. The deity is surrounded by footprints representing family members and their livestock. The sketches usually show Har Narayan on the wall and at least some of the footprints on the ground. Sometimes Har Narayan is shown with a long foot that extends from the wall onto the ground. Food cooked the preceding evening and early on the morning of the 11th is placed as an offering in the center of the part of the design that is on the ground and then covered by a brass tray. Some people fast during the day, but observance is capricious. Although rice is forbidden on Dev Uthani Gyas, as for the observance of all 11ths, some people cook it as part of the festive meal after the ritual is over.

We visited several families on Dev Uthani Gyas. A Jat family, strong devotees of the Arya Samaj, had not yet prepared the drawing but said that they would make footprints of all family members and, added a young man, many more besides. The senior woman said that she was not fasting, which probably meant that no one in the family was fasting. She said that the women would cook rice pudding in the evening. Family members explained that the festival ushers in the marriage season and also insures good marriages.

At the house of another Jat, an elderly woman was drawing Har Narayan on the side of the stove (fig. 53). She identified him as a Brahman of olden times. He was depicted wearing a long braid that extended to the floor where footprints of people and cattle were outlined. In this case, there were fewer human footprints than family members. Other images of Har Narayan were on walls near doorframes. The woman told us that Har Narayan's braid was burnt on Dev Uthani Gyas. This comment refers to the custom of carrying burning rags through the village. The more likely interpretation is that the rags represent Hanuman's burning tail, as described above.

The mural drawn near the cookstove by women of another Jat family resembled that of the above household, except that the sketch of Har Narayan lacked a braid (fig. 54). The human footprints were fewer than the number of family members. There were sketches of feet and peacocks near doors, and a large drawing near the family well. The men of this Jat family were strong followers of the Arya Samaj. The women did not know which deity their drawing represented.

A Brahman woman in 1958 drew Grandfather (*dada*) Har Narayan on the wall, yet could not identify the deity (fig. 55) He had a long foot that extended onto the floor where there was a circular design with a heap of pearl millet (bajra) in the center (fig. 55, left). A brass tray (*parat*) covered the millet. A circular design in red was sketched on the bottom of the tray (fig. 55, right). Some of the food to be prepared later in the day would be added to the millet. The seven human footprints on the wall represented the five members of the family. We were told that it is good to have a few extra footprints, presumably as a symbol of fertility and family increase. Seven is an auspicious number in Hinduism. The woman sent her daughter to the Baniya's shop to buy either some sweet flour or water chestnuts (*singhara*) that would be put with the other food under the brass tray.

An elderly Brahman woman drew a sketch of Har Narayan that was different from the other drawings we saw in 1958. Her sketch resembled the square depictions of mother goddesses drawn on other festivals rather than the sticklike figures of Har Narayan on Dev Uthani Gyas (fig. 56, left). She drew additional designs near the door.

The Leatherworkers, Sweepers, Potters, and Barbers all celebrated Dev Uthani Gyas, 1958. We saw sketches almost everywhere, or we were told that they would soon be drawn. They were much like those seen at the houses of Brahmans and Jats. The sketch at a Potter's house was a bit different in that the footprints, drawn near the door, were separated from the drawing of Har Narayan on the stove (fig. 57).

Ritual activity was simple, starting at dusk and continuing well into the evening. The senior woman of each household tapped the tray covering the offering of food, and the gods awoke. Or a group of girls beat the tray and sang to awaken the gods. A lamp might be lit, and the dung cakes saved from Dassehra were burned. Groups of girls went from family to family singing and begging for food, principally grain. A little grain might be scattered as an offering on the footprints. The rest was taken to the Baniya's shop and exchanged for *khil* and *batasha*s, which the girls ate. The girls might eat the food that had been offered to the gods earlier in the day, or it could be given to cattle. Having rested under the brass tray most of the day, it was stale by the time the girls received it. The festive meal in the evening consisted variously of *malpura*s, puris, halva, noodles, and rice pudding. In 1977, people mentioned cooking *churma*. Rice was not supposed to be cooked on Dev Uthani Gyas, and the few people who fasted abstained from eating it. People who did not fast were willing to eat it on this day.

FIG. 55. Mural of Dada Har Narayan *(left)* for Dev Uthani Gyas drawn by a Brahman woman, 1958. The sketch is partly on the wall, partly on the floor, freshly plastered with cow dung. Seven pairs of human footprints are on the wall. Seven pairs of footprints of cats and dogs and cattle are in concentric circles around the principal design, the cattle prints forming the outer circle. A heap of bajra is in the center of the design.

Sketch *(right)* on the bottom of a brass tray *(parat)* used to cover the design.

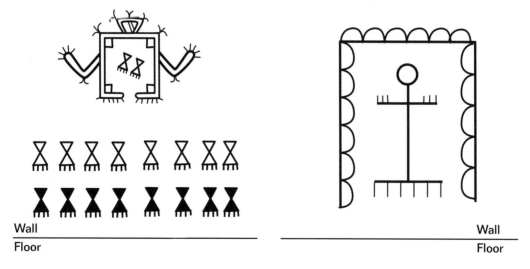

FIG. 56. Murals of Har Narayan for Dev Uthani Gyas at two Brahman houses, 1958. Human footprints *(left)* are inside and under the depiction of the deity. Additional footprints of humans and cattle are on the floor.

We followed one group of girls around the village at about 8:30 P.M. They called at a Jat house; a girl rapped the tray to awaken the gods, lifted it, and took the food from under it, which she put in a tray carried by another member of the group. The girls sang good wishes to all members of the family—to girls for the welfare of their brothers and to men for the welfare of their friends. The same couplet, "may your brother be blessed," or "may your friend be blessed," was repeated with the names of the blessed inserted. The girls' usual booty was a dish of wheat, but if a son had been born in the family during the preceding year, the group received Rs. 1.25 in addition. Women and girls had fun waving burning pieces of cloth, and we saw groups of women sitting and singing in front of houses. People take the soot from the lamps used in Dev Uthani Gyas and apply it around the eyes to protect them from soreness during the year.

We collected only one song sung at Dev Uthani Gyas. It is similar to a song sung by the Sweepers of Delhi that is published in Lewis (1958: 226). Our informant was a young Brahman woman. At first, she did not want to sing it, thinking it crude. When she sang it, she laughed.

> Look, this is the sleep that starts from Asharh and ends in Karttik.
> The gods and goddesses start sleeping in the month of Asharh and wake
>   in the month of Karttik.
> Now I myself will wake up, then awake everyone, and then touch my
>   hand to the *chhika.**
> There are four puris in the *chhika.*
> First of all, I will eat them, then give to the Brahmans and then to the
>   old cow.**
> They defecate in the center, urinate outside.
> There are many bricks, sand, and stones in the house.
> There are a great many bullocks left outside the house.
> A great many bottles [liquor?] are brought and these are being taken
>   by all.
> See, oh daughter-in-law, Dhanno, these are your sons.

---

*A wire basket like a rat cage in which vegetables and fruit may be kept and hung up anywhere.
**The expected order would be cow, Brahman, and then self.

Crooke (1968, 2: 300) described Dev Uthani Gyas chiefly as a festival that marks the beginning of the sugarcane harvest. He devoted only one sentence to the resumption of weddings, the aspect of the festival that is of the highest importance in Shanti Nagar. Mukerji (1916: 175), closely following Crooke, wrote: "Like the Gobardhan, [Dev Uthani Gyas] has degenerated into a bucolic ceremony inaugurating the cutting of the sugarcane crop." Wadley (1975: 171) also mentioned the worship of sugarcane on Dev Uthani Gyas. In the sketches drawn in Karimpur (Wadley's village) for the festival, two figures were in the center of the design. Wadley did not name the figures, but Crooke identified similar figures as Vishnu and his wife, Lakshmi. In Nimkhera, 45 miles from Bhopal City in central India, the festival cele-

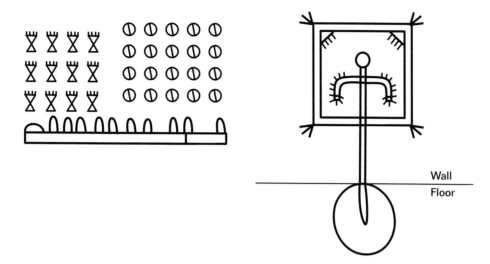

FIG. 57. Murals for Dev Uthani Gyas at a Potter's house, 1958. Sketch *(left)* on an inside wall near a door. Six pairs of human footprints are on the left, four rows of cattle prints on the right.

Har Narayan *(right)* drawn on the side of a stove. Cooked food covered with a brass tray will be placed on the ground near the drawing. Usually, the portrait of Har Narayan and the footprints form a single composition, but here they are separated.

brates both the awakening of the gods and the harvest. The designs are unlike those of Shanti Nagar. Women draw squares (*chauks*) on their porches and courtyard floors. The family head performs a ritual for "certain first fruits" on the designs (Jacobson, 1970: 396–397, pl. XXX). There was no evidence in Shanti Nagar of any connection whatsoever between the festival and the sugarcane harvest. Vishnu appeared only as Har Narayan, and Lakshmi played no role.

Amla Sinchan Gyas

Celebrated only by women, Amla Sinchan Gyas (Amla Watering Eleventh) is observed on Phalgun *sudi* 11 at the beginning of the hot season. The amla is a fruit tree, *Emblica myrobalan* (Pathak, 1976: 105; Underhill, 1991: 91) or *Emblica officinalis* (Maheshwari, 1976: 320–321), which is sacred to Vishnu. It is a moderate-to-large deciduous tree with yellow flowers and fleshy yellow fruit for which it is cultivated in orchards. The flowers bloom in March to May; the fruit ripens in the cold season. Interested in heat stress, Planalp reported that the amla was often an ingredient of summer beverages. A mixture of salt and dried amla, known as "black salt" (*kala namak*), may be added to hot-weather drinks. Hindus may consume this salt during fasts and ritual occasions when other forms of salt are prohibited. Amla is one of the fruits used to make *sharbat*, a beverage with a fruit or syrup base. Dried amla could also be steeped in water to make a summer beverage (Planalp, 1971: 156, 222, 244).

Underhill (1991: 89, 91) wrote that the amla tree is worshipped on Dev Uthani

FIG. 58. *(above)* Amla Sinchan Gyas, 1959. Multicaste group of women and children on their way to the garden of the Mali Gardener to make offerings to the amla plant.

FIG. 59. *(right)* Amla Sinchan Gyas, 1959. Women water the recently planted amla sapling and place their offerings of gur and *ber* in a basket that the Gardener had left beside it.

Gyas as well as on Amla Sinchan Gyas. This worship is a feature only of the latter festival in Shanti Nagar. According to Underhill, Vishnu is worshipped as Parasurama, his sixth avatar. However, in Shanti Nagar, the festival honors Krishna and Ram, Vishnu's most popular avatars, and secondarily, Mirabai, wife of a Rajput ruler and a famous devotee of Krishna. She is now a quasi deity and has her own fast day on Wednesday. She will be discussed in greater detail later.

Amla Sinchan Gyas is an important 11th in Shanti Nagar, observed by all castes except the Sweepers, Leatherworkers, and possibly most of the Potters. However, the only mention of it in other Delhi villages is in Nautiyal (1961: 156). Even Lewis

(1958), whose chapter on festivals was comprehensive and detailed, failed to note it, and his village was close to Shanti Nagar. The festival is hard to miss since it features processions of women singing on their way through the village to an amla tree. It is possible that the distribution of the festival is sporadic.

In 1959, we went with a procession of women, accompanied by children, to the Mali's garden where a small amla tree would be the focus of the ritual early in the afternoon (fig. 58). Shortly before noon, women began to prepare the offerings and practice the songs that they would sing on the way to the garden. An elderly Brahman woman said that only the women who fasted (did not eat grain) would perform the ritual. However, everyone, including children, who went to the amla tree bathed beforehand. We watched three Brahmans getting ready. One young woman filled a small vessel (lota) with water and put on it a metal dish with five bers (a small fruit) and two pieces of gur. Two girls had similar materials. The three Brahmans then began to practice their song.

We waited with them in front of the house for the arrival of other women. Not far up the street, a big crowd of women and children had gathered in front of a Brahman's house. We noticed Brahmans, Barbers, Bairagis, and Jats. They sang for about five minutes. Some of the women were not carrying offerings, which presumably meant that they would not worship, but had joined the procession for companionship and the pleasure of singing. The group moved toward us and together we all headed for the garden. The women began to sing again.

The Mali Gardener had recently planted an amla tree at the entrance to his garden. He had placed a basket near it, inviting the women to perform the ritual at this sapling rather than at a tree deeper in the garden. He told us later that he did not want the women to go into the garden because on the way the children would pick the flowers. The Gardener sold flowers in Delhi and naturally did not want people to help themselves.

When the women saw the basket, they stopped to make their offerings. They put bers and gur in the basket and poured water on the amla plant, letting it run over their right hands as they did so (fig. 59). One woman added flowers to the water. A little gur and one ber landed in the pool of water that was forming around the sapling. The women folded their hands in worship, and daughters-in-law pressed the legs of their older in-laws, probably in most cases mothers-in-law. Then the women walked away.

After the ritual, the Gardener gathered the offerings. He planned to grind the gur and mix it in his hookah tobacco. He gave the bers either to Brahman children, who ranked higher in the caste hierarchy than the Mali Gardeners, or to Potter children, who ranked lower and were poor. He did not use the bers because his garden produces them in plenty. If the offering was something that his garden did not produce, he would keep it. We asked whether there were reasons for selecting the Potter children as recipients of prasad other than for their low-caste rank and poverty. He said that there were none. In reply to our question about why the amla tree is worshipped, he said that on the 11th the amla tree is worshipped all over India.

An interview with a Brahman man in 1959 brought out a few details that we did not observe during the ritual in either 1958 or 1959. He told us that worshippers tied a yellow holy thread around the plant and put a tilak of turmeric on it. He carefully noted that Brahman women used a holy thread but that Jat and Merchant women used any type of thread. In 1978, several informants told us that they lit a lamp at the amla tree and put a tilak on it, in addition to making the offerings of water, *ber*, and gur. We did not observe lamp lighting during the rituals in the 1950s and we missed the festival in 1978. Although tilaks, lamps, and tying threads would be expected on occasions like Amla Sinchan Gyas, we did not note them in the course of the two rituals that we attended.

In the afternoon of Amla Sinchan Gyas, many villagers attended a fair in a nearby village. It had nothing to do with the festival. It was held in honor of an old man, still alive in 1959, who was said to have performed miracles involving water. An elderly Brahman woman told us two slightly different versions of the miracle. The old man either caused water to flow uphill or else he made water come from the ground. He was so holy that if he asked for rain, it would come. He sat in his own hut with a well, did nothing, and people fed him. Our elderly informant said that he had performed his miracles while she was yet a child.

This holy man was on his way to becoming a minor deity. The festival of Budh ki Duj represents a later stage in this process, so common in Hinduism. However, the fair on Amla Sinchan Gyas did not as yet have a religious aspect. People went for entertainment. The fair had a small Ferris wheel, toys and sweets were sold, and wrestling matches were held. Women and children attended the fair, but we saw principally men. They seemed to be attracted chiefly by the wrestling matches, which the women did not attend.

Songs for Amla Sinchan Gyas

This song was sung by a middle-aged Brahman woman:

I like going to see the icon of Shri Krishna.
See little Mira is going to sing holy songs [*bhajan*] for Ram.
At midnight and at early dawn we will go to water the vegetables.
We will go with you, even my mother, when you explain this
      to your Guru.
Give us the draught of knowledge to drink.
We will also become pure like you.
See little Mira is going to sing songs for Ram.
I like going to see the icon of Shri Krishna.
God is very kind.
He is the protector of his devotees.
Oh God, help us in crossing.
Do not let us remain in between.
This is not our destination.

Mira in the song is Mirabai, a 16th-century Rajput princess and devotee of Krishna. The principal theme of this song is devotion to God, in the form of Vishnu's avatars, Ram and Krishna. The devotees ask their guru for knowledge of the religious life to achieve purity and moksha (release). The last three lines of the *bhajan* refer to the fate of the soul after death releases it from the body. After lingering in the cremation grounds for 13 days, it journeys for a year to the Kingdom of Yama, Lord of the Dead. Yama decides the fate of a soul. It may obtain release (moksha), be reborn on earth, or become a restless, wandering ghost. A ghost is a soul between life and release or rebirth, a fate to be avoided. Hence, the appeal to God for help in the crossing.[26]

The following song was sung by the same Brahman woman who sang the preceding one:

> Oh Ram! There is a *chameli** tree in my courtyard and, oh Ram, there
>   are even rose flowers.
> Oh Ram! When it will rain, all the flowers will start to bloom.
> Oh Ram! When the winds and storms will blow, then all the flowers
>   will fade and fall down.
> Oh Ram! See the skill of my gardener. He picked up all the flowers.
> Oh Ram! See the skill of my gardener. He made a garland of those
>   flowers.
> Oh Ram! Now the gardener's wife puts it on her head and goes about
>   saying, "Buy garlands if you want."
> Oh Ram! My Shri Bhagwan will take the garlands for his Radha. Shri
>   Bhagwan will take the garlands.

---

*Chameli (*Jasminum grandiflorum*) is a shrub with fragrant white star-shaped flowers.

Basically devotional, the song calls attention to the gardener, an important personage in the festival of Amla Sinchan Gyas. In this song, Shri Bhagwan is Krishna. Radha, wife of a cowherd, became Krishna's favorite mistress.

The following song was sung by a young Brahman woman, the daughter of the woman who sang the first two songs:

> I saw two persons, oh Ram, talking on the earth. One was mother and
>   the other, father. They resembled Ram.
> I saw two persons, oh Ram, talking on the earth. One was brother
>   and the other, his wife. They were lying together and both looked
>   like Ram.
> I saw two persons, oh Ram, talking on the earth. One was father-in-law
>   and the other, mother-in-law. They looked like Ram.
> Father-in-law said that he had spent a lot of money, oh Ram.
> Mother-in-law said that she carried the burden for the full ten months,
>   oh Ram.
> I saw two persons talking on the earth, oh Ram. One was husband and
>   the other, wife.
> Husband said, oh Ram! I married and brought her a few days back.
> Now he will like her. They look like Ram.

Although this song was collected as one that was sung on Amla Sinchan Gyas, it probably could be sung on other occasions as well, for it deals with relationships that are important to everyone rather than with the features of a particular festival. The refrain highlights the idea that everyday people may have a divine aspect. In Hinduism, the distinction between humans and deities is by no means sharply drawn. Important historical figures gradually become deities and are worshipped. Mirabai is a case in point. Villagers clearly recognize the process. As for deities, many are very human in their behavior, emotions, and personalities. An individual may find a particular deity quite appealing. The idea of a personal deity is based largely on this attraction.

WEEKLY FESTIVALS

Weekly festivals are less prominent in the honorific than in the welfare category. Of the three honorific weekly festivals, only the worship of Hanuman on Tuesdays is widely celebrated in Shanti Nagar. The other two festivals, for Mirabai on Wednesdays and Brihaspati on Thursdays, are each observed only in a single household. Only one man, whose grandfather came to Shanti Nagar from Rajasthan, the region where Mirabai gained her fame, fasted for her. Only two Brahman women, sisters-in-law, worshipped Brihaspati. Brihaspati is a Vedic deity, not a regional one, which suggests that more people may light a lamp in his honor than we had occasion to observe. Both Mirabai and Brihaspati are worshipped in contexts other than their weekdays. Mirabai receives attention on Amla Sinchan Gyas, and Brihaspati is one of the seven *graha*s whose symbols are sketched for *havan*s. Saturday is the only day without a welfare or an honorific festival in Shanti Nagar. Elsewhere in India, Hanuman is honored on Saturdays as well as Tuesdays.

Tuesday's Fast for Hanuman

Hanuman is one of the most popular deities in Hinduism. He is honored as the devoted servant of Ram and worshipped as the remover of all obstacles and as a protector from ghosts and demons. Hanuman is often a familiar of bhagats and other exorcists, who summon his aid in rituals of exorcism. Every Hindu from childhood learns of his marvelous deeds, as recounted in the Ramayana. In Shanti Nagar, some villagers light a lamp for him every day, but mainly he is honored on Tuesdays. His birthday, Hanuman Jayanti, is not observed in Shanti Nagar.

The veneration of Hanuman on Tuesdays is widespread in Shanti Nagar. We found devotees in eight castes spread throughout the caste hierarchy from Brahmans to Leatherworkers. There is little reason to doubt that he is worshipped by people of all castes. About twice as many men as women observed Tuesday's fast for Hanuman. Channa (1984: 101) wrote, "Men fast on Tuesday in his honour but women are not supposed to fast for him, if they want to do so, they can do so after their menopause." Our interviews give some support to Channa, particularly that of an elderly Bairagi woman who said that she sometimes observed the fast but that her 13-year-old daughter did not "because she's too young." However, a Chhipi woman in her thirties sometimes observed the fast. Some informants said that they worshipped Hanuman daily, others observed the traditional fast on Tuesdays, while a few said that they honored him only once or twice a year without naming the specific occasions.

The chief features of the festival are a fast that is generally broken in the early afternoon, the feeding of monkeys, and special food, usually *churma*, for breaking the fast. A lamp might be lit, sometimes before a picture of Hanuman, and a devotional song might be sung. A Brahman woman mentioned feeding other Brahmans. A Leatherworker woman said that she invited Brahmans on Tuesdays, then quickly substituted "people" for Brahmans. Brahmans in the 1950s would not take food from Leatherworkers. She added that unmarried girls might be invited. In this context, unmarried girls would be ritually pure and thus more or less equivalent to Brahmans. A Brahman woman mentioned feeding *prasad* to a cow and distributing *batasha*s to children. Although the worship of the Monkey God, Hanuman, suggests that the feeding of monkeys would be an essential element of the ritual, it often cannot be done for practical reasons. People do not always have the time to visit places where monkeys congregate.

We found more devotees of Hanuman among Brahmans than in other castes. Although this disproportion may be due to the chance that is inherent in semi-opportunistic interviewing, there may be more to it than that. One Brahman woman pointed out that Brahmans favor Hanuman because he is seen as their protector. He is the deity who helped Ram recover Sita from the clutches of Ravana. At this point in the interview, her husband's brother commented that the family formerly worshipped Lakshman, Ram's brother, but it was Hanuman who saved Lakshman's life, which means that Hanuman is the more powerful of the two. Therefore the family worships Hanuman. His sister-in-law immediately contested the idea that the family ever worshipped Lakshman, saying that there never was any reason to worship him. In any case, she said that every Tuesday, the family made a large piece of bread that was fed to monkeys and then invited Brahmans for a festive meal. The festive meal suggests that at least some members of this large joint family observed a fast, but we neglected to ask which ones. That the festival has a strong hold on Brahmans is suggested by the comments of a young, well-educated Brahman man. He said, "I am not a religious man but a man of the 20th century." Nonetheless, he fasted on Tuesdays and sometimes fed gram to monkeys.

A 16-year-old Bairagi boy always fasted for Hanuman on Tuesdays. His father did not observe the day, but his postmenopausal mother said that she sometimes fasted. His sister was too young to fast. It is common to find that not all family members participate in a particular ritual. Individual choice is dominant. This Bairagi case was the only one that we encountered where welfare played a role. The boy's mother had injured her arm, and he was keeping the fast for her recovery. However, he would have fasted in any case.

The ritual of a young Brahman man, a college student, was more elaborate than those of most devotees. He fasted until he had fed some monkeys. He had a picture of Hanuman, lit a lamp before it, and sang a devotional song. He did not fast every Tuesday, only when he felt like it. He pointed out that Hanuman can remove difficulties. The young man was under considerable pressure in his studies, and a deity whose principal feature was the ability to overcome difficulties would be worth honoring.

Finding monkeys to feed became a problem in the late 1970s. In 1958, the village fields had many more trees than 20 years later, and there were monkeys within easy reach. Two Potter boys said that there was an army of monkeys in a nearby orchard. They fed gram and gur to these monkeys and folded their hands in prayer. In those days, we occasionally saw monkeys even on village houses. In the 1970s, we did not see a single monkey in the village. Some monkeys lived near a canal about a mile or so distant, and there were plenty of them in Delhi along the routes of pilgrimage. But devotees with limited time could no longer feed monkeys every Tuesday.

The only significant difference between the ritual as practiced in the 1950s and in the 1970s, the use of a printed prayer, was a consequence of the spread of literacy, especially to women. In the 1950s, few women were literate. Twenty years later, most young and middle-aged women in Shanti Nagar could read. These women, and men as well, often had a collection of inexpensive popular religious books, among them the Hanuman Chalisa (Hanuman's Forty Lines). The best way to pray to Hanuman is to read the Hanuman Chalisa and the Ramayana (Channa, 1984: 101).

In the 1970s, we interviewed members of a Brahman family whom we had previously interviewed in the 1950s on the subject of Tuesday's fast for Hanuman. In those days, the two adult women of the family were nonliterate, as were their husbands. In the 1970s, a 30-year-old wife in the succeeding generation of the family had gone to school. On Tuesdays, in addition to the usual family ritual, she read the Hanuman Chalisa to the family. She showed us her collection of books of religious stories and of devotional songs, among them the Bhagavata Gita, Mahabharata, Ramayana, and Prem Sagar.

The Hanuman Chalisa, which is much longer than 40 lines, names the parents of Hanuman, enumerates his attributes, describes his activities on behalf of Ram in Lanka, and notes the benefits that he bestows on his worshippers. He banishes disease and pain and saves from all troubles. The devotee attains peace and well-being. Channa (1984: 101–103) translated the prayer into English. Channa (1984: 103) commented "Tuesday is the day of offering [Hanuman] *prasad* and Saturday for praying to him, as Tuesday is the day of his victory and Saturday his birthday." Only one villager told us that he worshipped Hanuman on both Tuesdays and Saturdays. The rest of the villagers offered *prasad* and prayed on Tuesdays.

Wednesday's Fast for Mirabai

Only one man, whose grandfather came to Shanti Nagar from Rajasthan by way of Delhi at the time of the Mutiny, kept the fast for Mirabai. He observed it once a month, on one of the Wednesdays of the bright fortnight. He consumed only rice and tea and lit a lamp for her. She is also one of the deities worshipped on Amla Sinchan Gyas. Although Wednesday's fast for Mirabai is of little consequence in Shanti Nagar, it deserves notice as an illustration of the deification of a saintly person and the spread of her worship beyond the area where she came to fame.

Mirabai (c. 1500–1550) was the wife of a Rajput ruler of Mewar. After a disagreement with her mother-in-law on some religious matters, she left her husband to live as a wandering mendicant. Celebrated for her beauty and romantic piety, she became a famous poetess and bhakti (devotional) singer who wrote odes expressing her love for Krishna. Her lovely songs are still popular in western India and Rajasthan.

She dedicated her life to devotion to Krishna. According to legend, once her husband heard her talking to a man in another room. He rushed in with his sword to kill her for being unfaithful, but found no one. She believed that Krishna was with her and she was talking to him. Krishna transformed her into a multitude of forms so that her husband could not distinguish his real wife. Granting her devout wish, Krishna finally revealed himself to her and absorbed her soul into his (Balfour, 1885, 2: 956; Embree, 1972: 247, 252–253; Thapar, 1976: 188, 305).

Thursday's Fast for Brihaspati

One Thursday morning (Brihaspativar), we watched two Brahman women performing a puja for Brihaspati. Pictures and statues of deities were arranged on the family altar. A lamp or candle was burning before the largest picture. The women were seated before the altar reading to each other from a book (fig. 60). They kept a fast for the day.

The Brahmans of Shanti Nagar are members of the Bhardwaj *gotra* (clan), whose mythological ancestor (rishi) is Bhardwaj, the son of Brihaspati, the regent of

FIG. 60. Brihaspati worship, 1978. Brahman women light a lamp before images on the family altar.

Jupiter and the namesake of Thursday. Brihaspati is "the suppliant, the sacrificer, the priest, who intercedes with gods on behalf of men and protects mankind against the wicked. Hence he appears as the prototype of the priests and priestly order; and is also designated as the Purohita (family priest) of the divine community" (Dowson, 1891: 63).

This mythology is the context of the Brahman women's worship of Brihaspati. He is the father of their clan rishi and fills the role model of family priest. The chief ceremonial role of the Bhardwaj Brahmans in Shanti Nagar is to serve as family priests. We do not know the extent of Brihaspati worship in Shanti Nagar. The mythological context would apply equally to all the Brahman families, but whether the fast is kept depends always on individual choice. Even in the observed family, an adult woman was bathing her baby in the courtyard while the puja was being conducted inside the house.

JANAMASHTAMI

Janamashtami (Birth Eighth), also known as Adhi Rat Ka Brat (Midnight's Fast), the festival that celebrates the birth of Krishna, is observed on Bhadrapad *badi* 8. Krishna, the eighth avatar of Vishnu, is the most popular of all the Hindu deities. He is featured in a host of fascinating legends, among them his rescue of the people and cattle of Gokul from Indra's wrath when he held the mountain of Gobardhan over them as a giant umbrella. This tale is associated with the festival of Gobardhan. Krishna plays an important role in the Mahabharata where, as Arjuna's charioteer, he pronounces the famous religious-philosophical song, the Bhagavad Gita. The life of Krishna is related in detail in the Bhagavata Purana. It is widely available in a Hindi translation, the Prem Sagar.

Krishna was the eighth child of Devaki and her husband, Vasudeva. Devaki's cousin Kansa was king of Mathura. A prophet told Kansa that a son of his cousin, Devaki, would kill him and overthrow his kingdom. To avoid this danger, Kansa kept Devaki and her husband confined to the palace under close guard, and Kansa had Devaki's first six children put to death. The life of her seventh child, who was Balarama, the playmate of Krishna and like him an avatar of Vishnu, was saved by a miracle. By divine agency, Balarama was transferred before birth to the womb of Rohini, Vasudeva's other wife, and so was spared.

Krishna was born at midnight. While the prison guards fell into a magical sleep, Vasudeva carried the infant across the Yamuna River to a village called Gokul, where he placed him in the care of a cowherd, Nanda, and his wife, Yasoda. Yasoda had, that very night, given birth to a daughter. Vasudeva took the infant daughter back to the prison to replace Krishna. Kansa tried to kill her, but she soared triumphantly high in the air, declaiming that his future destroyer was safe in Gokul.

Kansa schemed to kill Krishna. He sent a demoness with poisoned breasts to suckle him, but Krishna was unaffected by her poison and sucked away her life. This episode in the Krishna legend probably heightens the anxiety of mothers in Shanti Nagar who have problems with lactation. If an infant does not thrive on its mother's milk, villagers blame the mother. The myth fosters the belief that milk from an evil woman is deadly or, conversely, that problems with milk reflect on a mother's character. Thus, lactational difficulties carry moral undertones that may enhance a mother's psychological problems and further impede her nursing ability (R. Freed and S. Freed, 1985: 136–137).

Krishna had a happy childhood and adolescence, playing pranks and consorting with milkmaids by moonlight. He married several of them. His favorite was Radha, already married and much older than he. Finally, the day came when he returned to Kansa's court to end the reign of the tyrannical king. Challenging Kansa to a fight, Krishna cut off his head with one sweep of his bare hand (Channa, 1984: 70–74; Dowson, 1891: 160–166; Garrett, 1990: 342–343; Imperial Record Department, 1914: 41–42; Mukerji, 1916: 88–94).

The fast of Janamashtami as observed in Shanti Nagar has both individual and communal components. The individual component is chiefly a fast, an offering of water to the moon at about midnight, and a festive meal. Devotional singing and a drama were the two communal activities. During the day and evening, small groups of women gathered here and there to sing devotional songs. However, the main communal activity, in 1958, was an amateur theatrical drama enacting the legend of Krishna's birth. The drama was staged and directed by the Brahman teacher of Sanskrit who held the *katha* sessions on Purinmashi. We were not in the village for Janamashtami during our second visit in the 1970s. However, we conducted interviews about festivals. No one mentioned that a drama had been presented. If the custom has been abandoned, we do not know what, if anything, has taken its place.

Many people fast from the evening (midnight) of the seventh until midnight on the eighth when Krishna was born. People from all castes may fast. However, as is true of all festivals, observance is up to the individual. People who do not observe a fast or festival usually offer reasons: a family death may have occurred on the day, a person works too hard to fast, or a mother is nursing children and needs her nourishment. The fast is the usual partial fast: grains are avoided but light refreshment is permitted. A few devout people are said to keep a full fast. At midnight, after offering water to the moon, family members break the fast with a special beverage and festive food. Some families prefer to wait until the next morning to eat. The festive food most often mentioned was *gond* (gum) described as the gum of the kikar (gum arabic) tree cooked in ghee with sugar, flour, and coconut.

A young Brahman man, a college student, described his routine on Janamashtami. He began to observe the day when he was 10 years old. He fasted from early morning until midnight. After taking his bath, he could drink sugar water once. He consumed nothing else. He spent the day reading sacred books. In the evening, he watched the drama of Krishna's birth enacted in the village. When he was younger, he had participated in the play. After the play and at about midnight, he offered water, with pieces of sugar and some rice in it, to the moon. He then broke his fast with a nectar called *charanamrit* (foot [*charan*] nectar [*amrit*]). His family, the only one we found that did so, called this ambrosia *charanabrat* (fast or vow, *brat* or *vrat*). It is a mixture of water, milk, curd, sugar, and holy basil (tulsi) leaves. Basil is sacred to Vishnu. The young man added a few drops of Ganga water. He said that both the tulsi leaves and the Ganga water had medicinal qualities. They destroy all germs.

An elderly Jat woman did not fast because she was a widow. She had kept the fast when her husband was alive, but stopped after his death. However, some family members were fasting, and she mentioned specifically a 14-year-old boy and a 10-year-old girl. She would cook a festive meal. At midnight, the family offered *charanamrit* to an icon, probably of Krishna, and then broke their fast with it. Food offered to a icon is called *bhog* and is sacred. After drinking the beverage, the Jat family ate some fruit. They delayed cooking a full meal until the next morning.

Charanamrit, foot nectar, is used to wash the feet of a living holy person or an image and is then drunk by devotees. This Jat family made the traditional use of the nectar. The Brahman college student made no mention of offering *charanamrit* to an icon before drinking it, but nonetheless it was a sacred drink because of the basil leaves and the Ganga water.

One might expect that adherents of the Arya Samaj would show little interest in Janamashtami, for it honors Krishna. However, some members of most Arya Samaji families kept the fast and prepared festive food. An elderly Merchant man, one of the strongest devotees of the Arya Samaj in the village, said, "I'm Arya Samaj and don't generally believe in any festival, but I like to do what the other villagers do. So my family sings devotional songs and takes part in the drama on Janamashtami. Or we just watch it." We do not know if anyone in his family kept the fast.

Singing devotional songs is often a social activity. A group of women get together and sing. The drama involves the entire village. Participation in a song session or a community drama is visible to everyone, whereas fasting is private. People doing business in a village would be inclined to participate in visible community activities to maintain good relations with everyone, especially on major festivals like Janamashtami.

During the day, children ran through the village announcing that a play would be performed in the evening. The drama, enacted at the midpoint of the main lane through the high-caste side of the village, began after sundown and lasted until nearly midnight. An attentive crowd of chiefly high-caste people watched from the street or from their houses. People from the low-caste side of the village gathered on roofs to watch. One of the young Brahmans involved in organizing the drama complained that it was difficult to find costumes, but the main problem was to persuade men to play the female roles. In the 1950s it would have been unthinkable for women to have performed. A middle-aged Jat man played his harmonium to accompany the drama. We were surprised to see him perform, both because he was one of the most important men in the village and also we never suspected that he had musical interests. We congratulated him the next day on his performance, and he was clearly pleased while disclaiming any particular musical talent.

The actors performed with surprising skill and enthusiasm, a bit too much so in the case of the young man who played Kansa. A rather combative person who clearly did not like to lose, he seemed for a few moments to be on the verge of defeating Krishna, who was supposed to slay him. Krishna became more and more discomfited. Finally, Kansa remembered the part he was playing and fell dead on his back, none too gracefully, we might add.

A Brahman man, employed in a factory in Delhi, was somewhat contemptuous of the village players. He stayed in Delhi for Janamashtami because the festival at the factory was "celebrated on a grand scale." The owner of the factory had formed a drama club, which staged a very good play depicting Lord Krishna's life. Drama clubs seemed to be popular in the 1950s.

The simplicity of the family ritual belies the importance of this great festival. The only generally practiced ritual act, aside from fasting, is the offering of water to the moon. Almost no one lights a lamp before an image of Krishna, sends gifts to relatives, or distributes *prasad*. There is no *havan*.

Other reports of the festival depict a more elaborate family ritual. Mukerji (1916: 94–95) said that orthodox families celebrate Krishna's birth by enacting a representation of the ritual that accompanies the actual birth of a son. Both Mukerji and Buck reported that images of the infant Krishna are placed in swinging cradles and worshipped. Buck (1917: 96) said that Brahmans place a salagrama, a particular black stone worshipped as an emblem of Vishnu, in a cucumber to represent the pregnant Devaki. At midnight, ghee and gur are offered to the image, the stone is removed, and birth ceremonies are performed. Channa (1984: 122) reported that children, especially girls, arrange dolls in a tableau representing the birth of Krishna.

Villagers in Uttar Pradesh practice more elaborate family rituals than those of Shanti Nagar. In Karimpur, east of Agra, the family ritual involves an offering of food to Krishna, which is then consumed to break the fast. Lower-caste women draw a brightly colored design of Krishna on a wall before which they perform their puja. Upper-caste women and most men worship before a picture of Krishna or at a specially constructed altar for Krishna. After breaking their fasts, both men and women in segregated groups sing devotional songs. However, Wadley does not mention a drama, tableaux, or enactments of rites of birth (Wadley, 1975: 158, 160).

The celebration of Janamashtami in Mohana, a village near Lucknow, centers on a communal puja conducted by a Brahman priest. The villagers place images of Krishna on a swing, gather before it, and sing devotional songs until midnight. Then the priest performs the puja. The image of Krishna is bathed with *panchamrit* ("five nectars," probably equivalent to *charanamrit*), dried, and offered *prasad*. After the ritual of *arati*, the *panchamrit* and *prasad* are distributed to all spectators, who use it to break their fasts. A few days later, the swing and its images are carried in a procession to every house in the village except those of the four lowest castes. The final event is an enactment of the youthful Krishna's prank of stealing butter and curds. There is no villagewide theatrical production, and the rites of birth are not enacted in individual households (Majumdar, 1958: 270–271).

We can only speculate as to why the element of a family puja for Krishna seems so attenuated in Shanti Nagar. Arya Samaj doctrine, with its opposition to the cult of Krishna, may be responsible. The two villages in Uttar Pradesh noted above are far to the southeast of Shanti Nagar. The influence of the Arya Samaj would not be so great there as it is farther to the west. On the other hand, the lengthy play depicting Krishna's life and the devotional singing highlight the importance of this most auspicious and joyous festival in the religious life of Shanti Nagar.

Dassehra

During the first 10 days of the bright fortnight of Ashvin, two major festivals are held simultaneously. They are Dassehra (Tenth), a day in the Ram Lila, and Sanjhi. For purposes of the following discussion, Sanjhi is considered to be equivalent to Durga although this identification had still not been established in Shanti Nagar in the 1970s (see below, Sanjhi). Because Dassehra and Sanjhi (Durga Puja) are celebrated during the same period, some writers, for example Lewis (1958: 215–216), treat them as a single festival. However, the festivals are distinct. Mukerji (1916: 119) wrote, "The two celebrations [Ram Lila and Durga Puja] are held independently of each other; and in some parts of India one or the other only holds the field."

The Ram Lila-Dassehra festival features an 11-day enactment of the Ramayana. The 10th day, Dassehra, marks the victory of Ram over Ravana,[27] which took place on Ashvin *sudi* 10. Hence, the day is known as Vijay Dashami (Victorious Tenth). Durga Worship, or Navratra (Nine Nights), is the worship of the goddess for nine nights. The two festivals share the scene, especially on the 10th day when a final ritual is performed for the goddess, known as Sanjhi in Shanti Nagar, and the Ram Lila reaches a climax. The rituals of the two festivals on the 10th day are separate. The only connection between the two is that Rama prayed to Durga for her aid in vanquishing the demon Ravana.

The Ram Lila drama is performed in the open air to accommodate huge crowds. It is staged in cities and towns all over India. A spectacular production is offered every year in Delhi before hundreds of thousands of people. Any interested villager could attend, but apparently few people from Shanti Nagar go to Delhi in any single year to view the spectacle. We interviewed a number of people about their observance of Dassehra. No one mentioned making a trip to Delhi in 1958 to see the Ram Lila. One man said that he would not go that year because he had seen it so many times in the past. A Jat farmer said, "I have never gone to Delhi for the Ram Lila. For a farmer, every minute is golden."

In fact, people have little time for ceremonial activity during the second fortnight of Ashvin (September–October). In 1958, the new moon was on October 12 and Dassehra, on October 22. On October 16, we wrote in our notes: "We went out this morning but were back in half an hour because the village was deserted. We noticed the same thing yesterday. Everyone is harvesting the kharif [summer] crop and plowing for the rabi [spring] crop. Also, the fodder problem seems acute, and women spend a great deal of time cutting up small clumps of grass for fodder."

Channa gave a detailed account of the history, staging, and day-by-day presentation of the Delhi Ram Lila (Channa, 1984: 45–58; 68–70). The story concerns the life of Rama, an avatar of Vishnu, who was born to the king of the city-state of Ayodhya. The heart of the story is the war between Rama and Ravana, king of the Rakshasas (demons), who lived in Lanka (modern Sri Lanka). Rama is exiled from his father's kingdom; Ravana kidnaps Rama's wife, Sita; Rama kills Ravana and rescues Sita with the help of a vast army of monkeys and bears commanded by Hanuman, the Monkey God, who is totally devoted to Rama; and Rama returns to his father's kingdom. His father had died, and Rama's younger brother relinquishes the kingdom to Rama, who becomes king. The tale continues with the trials of Sita. Although chaste, she had been in the power of the demon Ravana, which sowed the seeds of doubt. The versions of Valmiki and Tulsidas differ concerning the relations of Sita and Rama after he rescues her. In the Valmiki Ramayana, Rama and Sita are estranged over the issue of her chastity. The Tulsidas Ramayana defuses this issue and has a happier ending. (Dowson, 1891: 261–262, 264–265; Basham, 1954: 412–415).

The festival of Dassehra celebrates the victory of Rama over Ravana on the 10th day. During the preceding two days, Ravana had sent his relatives to fight Rama and his army. Rama beheaded the redoubtable Kumbhkaran, Ravana's brother. Ravana then sent his son, the indestructible Meghanada, into battle, but Lakshmana, Ram's brother, sliced off his head. Another of Ravana's sons, Ahi Ravana, lost his head at the hands of Hanuman. On the 10th day, Ravana himself came to the battlefield to fight Rama. Rama shot millions of arrows at Ravana, cutting off his heads and arms, but he regrew them as fast as he lost them. Rama could not kill him. One by one, Ravana defeated all of Rama's powerful warriors.

Ravana's younger brother, the saintly Vibhishan who unsuccessfully advised Ravana to follow the rules of morality and return Sita to her husband, had defected to Rama. He told Rama that Ravana had the elixir of life (amrit) in his navel. If he received an arrow in his navel, the amrit would dry up and he would die. When the two next met in battle, Rama shot Ravana in the navel, cut off his arms, beheaded him, and split his body lengthwise (Growse, 1989: 606–607). Thus, Ravana died. The next day, the 11th, Rama and Sita returned to Ayodhya.

Enactment of the destruction of the three demons, Ravana, Kumbhkaran, and Meghanada, is a high point of the 10th day of the Ram Lila. Three giant effigies of the demons, some 100 feet high, are erected, stuffed with firecrackers, and set on fire (Channa, 1984: 53–58, 123).

Many people in Shanti Nagar are quite familiar with the Ramayana. They know that Dassehra celebrates the victory of Rama over the demon Ravana. However, the ritual of Dassehra in the village is not what one might expect, given the accepted connection of the festival and the epic. Rama is the hero of the Ramayana, and so the worship of Rama would appear to be appropriate, perhaps by lighting a lamp before his image and making a food offering. Nothing like this happens. The ritual of Dassehra is much more appropriate for a harvest festival. In fact, Dassehra most likely was originally a harvest/sowing festival, for it comes at the end of one agricultural season and the beginning of another. In short, it was a fertility rite (cf., Crooke, 1915: 30). Although its origin has been to some extent obscured by Sanskritic accretions, it can be discerned in the ritual.

The villagers subscribe to the popular opinion that Dassehra is a festival for men. The Sanskritic mythology of the festival deals with war, basically a man's activity. However, in Shanti Nagar the ritual is performed mainly by women. On the other hand, Durga Puja, or Sanjhi, is a women's festival.

We observed the ritual for Dassehra as conducted in a Brahman household in 1958. In the morning, the women of the family made 10 small dung cakes, known as *thepari*, outlined them with wheat flour, and placed a sprig of barley (*nyorta*) on

FIG. 61. Dassehra, 1977. Brahman woman prays at the altar prepared for Dassehra.

each. They also filled 10 small pitchers with *khil*, each surmounted by one or two *batasha*s. They sprinkled a little wheat flour on the dung cakes. The 10 dung cakes, laid out in two rows of five, and the pitchers, similarly arranged, formed a kind of altar. The altar was situated in front of the representation of Sanjhi plastered on a wall (see front cover). The altar and the figure have no connection, but their juxtaposition recalls that the festivals of Dassehra and Sanjhi are celebrated simultaneously. Family members folded their hands before the altar and prayed (fig. 61). One of the women said that she prayed as follows, "Whatever I had I'm offering to you God, and you should accept it and give more to everyone." Her offering was dung and barley (grain), and the prayer asked for an increase of dung and grain. Festive dishes are prepared on Dassehra, such as halva, puris, *khir*, and noodles.

The dung cakes were saved and used in Dev Uthani Gyas, a month later. Some people said that Dassehra marked the beginning of the season when dung cakes could be made, for the rainy season was over. In fact, we saw dung cakes being made before Dassehra. The pitchers with *khil* and *batasha*s were distributed as *prasad* to relatives and friends.

The Brahmans interpret the 10 dung cakes as the 10 heads of the demon Ravana. The barley shoots are Ravana's crowns. On the other hand, a visiting Potter said that the dung cakes represent the 10 days of Dassehra. The Brahmans do not like the way that Ravana is portrayed in the Ram Lila: Ravana was a learned pandit, expert in the four Vedas and six Dharmashastras. Hence, he had 10 heads. He was a master of all the sciences in India. By village standards, he did nothing particularly bad. He kidnapped Sita, but she had voluntarily left the protective circle. Moreover, Lakshmana and Rama were at fault because they failed to protect her.

Lakshmana's mutilation of Ravana's sister, cutting off her nose and ears, was much worse than what Ravana did to Sita. A village Brahman explained to us that cutting off the nose implies an adulterous deed or a generally bad character. It was this insult rather than the mutilation that seemed to bother the Brahman.

The villagers mention a protective circle, line, or border (see the song below) as playing an important role in Ravana's abduction of Sita. Lakshmana drew the circle, and Sita was safe as long as she stayed inside it. Ravana lured her outside the circle and was thus able to seize her. The two versions of the Ramayana at our disposal, Lal (1992) for Valmiki's Ramayana and Growse (1989) for the Tulsidas Ramayana, do not mention a circle or line. The story of the kidnapping of Sita outlined below combines the versions of Lal and Growse.

The episode of the abduction begins with the demoness Shurpanakha, "foul-hearted and venomous as a serpent," sister of Ravana (Growse, 1989: 436). Smitten with the good looks of Rama and Lakshmana, she took the form of a beautiful woman and approached each brother in turn, but was rejected. Lakshmana turned her away scornfully, "The bridegroom for you must be a man lost to all sense of shame" (Growse, 1989: 437). Frustrated, she assumed her demonic form, menaced her rival, Sita, and attacked the brothers. Lakshmana quickly sliced off her ears and nose and drove her away, thus sending a challenge to Ravana. She rushed to her brother, who demanded to know who had disfigured her. Sobbing and trembling with anger, she named Rama and Lakshmana, vowing to drink their blood and that of Sita.

Ravana plotted revenge. He enlisted the aid of the demon Maricha who disguised himself as a beautiful deer. Sita lost her heart to the deer, and Rama left their hut in the forest to kill the deer and bring back its glistening golden hide. He slew the deer, who, as it expired, cried out in perfect imitation of Rama's voice. Sita heard the cry and implored Lakshmana to rush to save Rama. Lakshmana knew that the deer was in fact a demon in disguise and, remembering Rama's command to guard Sita, did not stir. Sita mocked Lakshmana:

> What is wrong, Lakshmana?
> Don't you love your brother? . . .
> Do you desire me so much
> That you'd have him dead?   [Lal, 1992: 71]

Lakshmana was convinced that nothing could harm Rama, and he said that he would obey Rama's orders to protect Sita. She flared up in anger and again accused Lakshmana of sinfully desiring her. Lakshmana then yielded, calling upon the gods of the forest to protect Sita. Thus, she was left unprotected, and when Ravana arrived disguised as a Brahman mendicant, she felt that she had to offer him hospitality. She invited him inside the hut for a meal, and he seized her, revealing himself as the Ten-Headed.

A Jat Farmer paid us a visit during the Dassehra ritual, and he and a visiting

Potter began a religious debate. Spontaneous discussions of religion took place rather often in Shanti Nagar, although in this case our presence may have been a stimulus. The Jat asked the Potter, "Who is the greater avatar, Rama or Krishna?" The Potter said that they are equal. The Jat then launched into a long discourse to prove that Rama was not so great: Lakshmana did everything, so the festival should be called Lakshmana Lila. For example, Lakshmana and Sita sustained Rama during his 14-year exile. The Jat also criticized Sita for unjustly impugning Lakshmana's motives in the episode of the golden deer, which, he complained, she did not have to do. The Potter argued that these events had to happen because they were all part of the larger plot that Rama should kill Ravana. He added that if you want to go into tiny details, then none of the gods is perfect. Swami Dayananda (the founder of the Arya Samaj) was perfect and yet he had his detractors. So it is with the gods. The worshippers of one run down the others.

This comment prompted the Jat to compare Rama and Ravana, arguing from the village context. Rama (actually Lakshmana) cut off the nose of Ravana's sister, thereby insulting her. All Ravana did in retaliation was to kidnap Sita. The Jat man said, "An insult to a sister is much more serious than one to a wife. If you insult my sister I will take action but you can say 20 things to my wife and I'll do nothing. The sister is more important than the wife and the mother is the most important of all." The Potter said that all this discussion was going nowhere and that he believed in the teachings of Swami Dayananda, which are like a clear light.

The barley shoots used on Dassehra were grown from seeds planted 10 days earlier on Amavas. The ritual seeding of barley provided sprigs for both Dassehra and Sanjhi. On the 10th day of Sanjhi, which is also the festival of Dassehra, sisters place barley shoots on their brothers' ears. On Dassehra, women put the sprigs on the 10 dung cakes used in the ritual. Because the ritual of each festival involves barley shoots grown from the same planting and takes place on the same day, it is possible to confuse the ritual between sisters and brothers as being part of Dassehra. It is best regarded as part of Sanjhi, although one informant, a young Brahman man who was a college student, said that women place the barley shoots from the dung cakes on their brothers' ears. We never saw the barley sprigs from the dung cakes used in this way, but some families may indeed do so. In 1978, one informant clearly connected Dassehra with the ritual in which sisters put barley shoots on their brothers' ears.

Both our Jat visitor and a Brahman man who arrived later in the day interpreted the Dassehra ritual as a fertility rite. The Jat said that to honor cow dung is important because dung is sacred and India lives on it. The Brahman said, "To put barley on the cow dung cakes is like putting barley on the ears of brothers. It is good and makes for good cow dung as well as for good crops." Good cow dung implies plentiful and healthy cows.

The comment of our Brahman informant suggests that an offering of barley sprigs is a fertility ritual in any context. When a sister gives barley to her brother and receives a present in return, the major theme of the ritual is to reinforce the already strong tie of brother and sister. The minor theme is fertility. Thus, Sanjhi, a festival of interaction, has an underlying theme of fertility, just as does Dassehra. Nautiyal (1961: 167) recorded a song sung during Sanjhi that makes both themes explicit:

After worshipping [Sanjhi] what reward would you get?
You would be blessed with brothers and [brothers' sons].

A brother aids and protects his sister and her children in many ways, even after her marriage. His son assumes this responsibility after his death.

Despite the undertones of a fertility ritual, Dassehra is best regarded as an honorific festival celebrating the victory of Rama over Ravana. Several villagers offered this interpretation of the festival. Concerning the 10 dung cakes, some villagers say that it is "just so," or that they are symbols of the 10 days of Dassehra, or that they represent the 10 heads of Ravana.

It may seem surprising that the ritual of a festival honoring Rama ignores Rama in favor of the demon Ravana. However, from the point of view of our Brahman informants, this interpretation makes sense. The Rama of the Ramayana is Ramachandra, the second Rama. Garrett described him as the first real Kshatriya hero of the post-Vedic age. He typifies the conquering Kshatriyas moving south, subjugating the barbarous aborigines represented by Ravana. Another interpretation held that Ravana, who reigned over Sri Lanka and South India, "was the head of a civilised and powerful state, a Hindu follower of Siva" (Balfour, 1885, 3: 665). In any case, the Ramayana seems to be founded on historical fact, namely the conquest of South India by Hindu Aryans from the north (Garrett, 1990: 501, 503–504). Although Ravana was chief of the Rakshasas (demons), he was a Brahman on his father's side, and his body was burned with Brahmanical rituals (Dowson, 1891: 265). Thus, the Brahmans of Shanti Nagar consider Ravana, a Brahman, to have been fighting a Kshatriya, a representative of the warrior and governing castes. The stuggle between Brahmans and Kshatriyas, that is, between religious hierarchy and temporal power, is ancient in India. It was definitely a feature of life in Shanti Nagar when we lived there. As for our Jat informant's denigration of Rama, it probably represents the influence of the Arya Samaj.

The festivals of Dassehra and Sanjhi run concurrently, becoming confounded only on the 10th day. Until then, the Ram Lila and the worship of the goddess are distinct. Confusion on the 10th day comes about because of the ritual with barley shoots. When barley shoots are placed on the 10 dung cakes, the ritual is part of Dassehra. But whether the ritual of the barley sprigs that involves sister and brother is part of Sanjhi or Dassehra is not clear. Part of the problem is that an informant will describe the ritual as taking place on Dassehra, but in the context, Dassehra might mean the 10th day of the Ram Lila (Vijay Dashami, Victorious Tenth) or the 10th day of Sanjhi. Moreover, Victorious Tenth refers not only to Rama's conquest of Ravana but also to Durga's victory over Mahishasura (Raktabij), the buffalo demon (Poster, 1994: 248, 250–251; Underhill, 1991: 54). We believe that the ritual is part of Sanjhi without being too insistent on the point. This interpretation fits our classification of the two rituals. Dassehra honors Sanskritic deities. Sanjhi is a festival of interaction.

Nautiyal (1961: 167) indicated that the distribution of barley shoots is part of Sanjhi. He wrote that on the 11th day of Sanjhi, a Brahman priest comes to the village and distributes barley shoots that had been planted on the first day of Nine

Nights (Ashvin *sudi* 1). Moreover, the word used for barley shoot, at least on the 10th, is *niorata*, the same (or very similar) word that is used as a variant of Navratra (Nine Nights). In the village where Marriott worked, the same, or similar, term has become the name of a goddess (Marriott, 1955: 201).

Most descriptions of Dassehra merge the festival with Sanjhi. Lewis gave pride of place to the worship of Sanjhi during Niortha-Dasahra, as he called the twin festival. He wrote that the story of Rama and Ravana is not well known in Rampur, the Ram Lila not having been enacted there for many years (Lewis, 1958: 215, 236). However, he noted several rituals practiced on Dassehra: the 10 dung cakes with barley sprigs that are retained and burned on Dev Uthani Gyas; a daughter's or sister's gift of *niortha*s to her father or brother, receiving a bit of cash in return; and a visiting Brahman who distributes *niortha*s (Lewis, 1958: 216–217).

Luthra noted the observance of Dassehra in his Delhi village but did not mention Sanjhi at all, probably an oversight. The villagers celebrate Dassehra by staging the Ram Lila a few days before the 10th and, on the day itself, by going to Najafgarh, a town about 6 miles distant, or to Delhi to watch the burning of the effigies (Luthra, 1961: 70). Bhatia (1961: 66) reported no special celebration of Dassehra in his Delhi village except that delicacies were cooked on the 10th and a few villagers went to Delhi to watch the burning of the effigies. The Ram Lila was enacted in nearby Najafgarh. Nautiyal (1961: 164–167) treated Dassehra as the 10th day of Sanjhi. He mentioned no ritual on the 10th that has anything to do with the Ram Lila. Farther east, near Lucknow, Majumdar (1958: 272–273) wrote that the villagers of Mohana offer food to village and family gods. Some people may go to Lucknow for the Ram Lila. He noted the connection of Dassehra and Durga Puja, namely that Rama was able to overcome Ravana by the grace of Durga.

Both Garrett (1990: 160–161) and Underhill (1991: 55–58) wrote that on Dassehra people worship the implements used in their daily work and that animal sacrifice is a prominent feature of the festival. There is no evidence of these practices in Shanti Nagar or in other Delhi villages. Underhill described various rituals associated with Dassehra, among them the worship of the mimosa tree and a ritual where men and boys cross the village boundary into neighboring territory and then return home with great rejoicing to be greeted by their women who wave lighted lamps around their heads. Such rituals were not practiced in the Delhi villages. Noting the apparently unconnected rituals of Dassehra, Underhill wrote that they occur together in one festival because of the festival's date between the two agricultural seasons and just after the monsoon. It is both a harvest festival and a day that in olden times marked the beginning of the postmonsoon raids by marauding chieftains. The theme of fertility in the Delhi region today receives less emphasis than the martial theme, which the Ramayana has transformed into the victory of good over evil.

In 1958 we recorded one song that women sang on Dassehra. It might also be sung on other ceremonial occasions. Rather than recounting the martial exploits of Rama, Lakshmana, and Hanuman, the song deals with the events of the Ramayana of special interest to women—namely, the trials of Sita in the hands of Ravana. Sita was the lovely daughter of King Janaka, who offered her to the man who could bend the wonderful bow of Shiva. Rama bent the bow until it broke, thus winning Sita for his wife, as told in the following song:

> When Ramchandra went to the jungles, he drew a line [*kor*] for Sita
> which she was not permitted to cross.
> Ravana disguised himself [as a religious mendicant] and came before
> Sita.
> [Ravana] Oh queen of palaces! Oh Ramchandra's wife! Give me some
> alms.
> [Sita] How can I give you something, because Lakshmana drew this line
> [which I am not allowed to cross].
> [Ravana] Put a wooden plank on these lines and then place your feet on
> the plank.
> Now Sita brought a plate full of pearls and on it were flowers and fruit.
> As Sita bent to give Ravana these things, he picked her up and took her
> away.
> [Sita] Oh fool! Go slowly, nobody is coming with us.*
> Ravana installed Sita in his golden [beautiful] garden where rows of
> flowers grew.
> Now Ravana's chief wife came with her friends to the garden.
> [Wife] Come friends! Let's go and see. Ravana has brought a wife.
> [Wife] Oh Sita! You are said to be very pure and powerful, but you have
> come with my husband.
> [Sita] Your husband picked me up and brought me. Now it seems as if
> you are being prepared to become a widow.
> [Ravana to Sita] I want to encourage you by saying, now you become
> my wife.
> [Sita to Ravana] I will break the bangles with a stone and throw away
> the necklace that you gave me into a river.
> Green bangles on brown arms will then be the good fortune of Ravana.
> Oh you cruel one! You kidnapped me but my husband is Rama.
> If you wanted to marry me, oh cruel one, why didn't you break the
> bow?
> Ramchandra picked up the bow and so Rama is my husband.

---

*At this point in the legend, Sita's rebuke, "Go slowly, nobody is coming with us," makes little sense. What happened here is that Ravana assumed his true 10-headed form and Sita was terrified when he declared his name. But she picked up her courage and challenged him, "Wretch, stay as you are; my lord is at hand. Like as a hare that would wed a lioness, so you have wooed your own destruction, O demon king" (Growse, 1989: 446). Thus Sita later taunts Ravana's wife with the fate of widowhood.

The lines following this taunt have to do with bangles as a symbol of a married woman. To break them indicates that a woman is no longer married. Thus, Sita would break any symbol that implied a marriage to Ravana. Finally, Sita mocks Ravana concerning his lack of strength. He could not bend Shiva's bow as Rama had done.

SHIVARATRI

On Phalgun *badi* 14, villagers observe a fast and worship in honor of Shiva. The festival is known as Shivaratri (Shiva's Night). It is also called Bhole ka Vrat (Shiva's Fast). Bholanath (Simple God) is an epithet of Shiva, which has been shortened to Bhola in village usage. Since a day is set aside for honoring Shiva in each fortnight of every month, the festival in Phalgun is often called Mahashivaratri (Great Shivaratri) to mark its special importance. Mondays are also days of fasting for Shiva. Few if any villagers observe the fortnightly days other than Shivaratri, but many women and some men fast on Mondays, and some people light a lamp for him daily in the evening.

Two aspects of the dating of the festival can cause confusion. Sometimes Shivaratri is said to take place in Magh, the month preceding Phalgun. One must remember that in North India the *purinmanta* system of dating is used. Where the *amanta* system holds sway, the new month begins a fortnight later than in the *purinmanta* system. Thus, Magh *badi* 14 (*amanta*) and Phalgun *badi* 14 (*purinmanta*) are the same astronomical day.

The other question about dating is whether the festival falls on the 13th or the 14th. Four of our sources (Channa, 1984: 136; Lewis, 1958: 228; Wadley, 1975: 161; and Underhill, 1991: 93) opted for the 13th, while six (Babb, 1975: 167; Buck, 1917: 83; Imperial Record Department, 1914: 75; Morgan, 1953: 97; Mukerji, 1916: 30; and Williams, 1883: 430) name the 14th. All but one of our informants in Shanti Nagar gave the 14th as the date. Marriott's (1955: 192) notation was 13–14, indicating that the festival is observed on both days. Boulanger (1987: 89) said that it occurs on either the 13th or the 14th in Kanchipuram, Tamil Nadu. Two of the Delhi village studies from the 1961 census (Ratta, 1961: 166; Luthra, 1961: 72) gave the 13th; Nautiyal (1961: 156) said that Shivaratri falls on Phalgun *badi* 4, but that date is obviously a misprint and should have been Phalgun *badi* 14. Wadley (personal commun.) wrote, "The actual name of the festival in Karimpur is Shiv Teras (Shiva's Thirteenth). There is no doubt there as to the date." The 13th should be the proper date, for 13ths are sacred to Shiva, just as 11ths are Vishnu's days.

The most likely explanation for the differences of opinion is that the fast and ritual of Shivaratri begin on the 13th, continue through the night with a final ritual and the breaking of the fast on the 14th. In Shanti Nagar, the 14th is the chief day, in fact the only day for most villagers. The worship takes place on that day, after which the fast is broken. People no doubt fast from the preceding evening, for they are sleeping at night, but no one mentioned any puja during the night.

Bahadur (1995: 30–39) explained that the 13th commemorates the marriage of Shiva and Parvati and is the day of Mahashivaratri.[28] Among Kashmiri Brahmans, the festival is observed during the entire dark fortnight of Phalgun. The four days beginning with the 13th celebrate the wedding. People fast on the 13th and the 14th is the occasion for a sumptuous meal. On the plains of North India, Shivaratri is celebrated with less pomp. "The real celebration of Shivaratri takes place in temples on the night of [the 14th] and lasts till the morning of Amavas . . . although the wedding starts from the [13th] . . ." (Bahadur, 1995: 37).

Shiva has the most complex, multifaceted personality of all the Hindu deities. He evolved from Rudra, a fierce, destructive Vedic deity, the god of storms. Shiva brings disease and death, but can also drive them away. Thus, he is known among many other epithets as The Destroyer; Death, The Remover; Lord of Ghosts; and the First Physician. The Vedic god Rudra merged with a non-Aryan fertility deity, so fertility and reproduction as well as destruction and death are seen in the modern Shiva. He is also a great ascetic who by perfect meditation achieved complete emancipation from the bondage of passion. Shiva controls life and death, the demonic forces of the universe, and the most powerful of human desires, the reproductive urge. Renowned for his short temper, he is prone to violent action at the slightest provocation. Perhaps less beloved than Krishna and Ram, he is held in awe and is the most worshipped of the Hindu deities. Stern but also beneficient, he is easy to please (Basham, 1954: 307–309; Channa, 1984: 11–15; Mukerji, 1916: 30–32).

Shiva is worshipped most often in the form of the Lingam (or Linga), a phallic symbol. The Lingam represents vital force and the power of procreation. In its simplest form, it can be a smooth, upright oval-shaped stone, or piece of wood, set up almost anywhere by a pious individual. The Lingams in temples are often carefully executed sculptures representing the upright male principle with the Yoni, the female principle, symbol of Shakti, embracing its base. In its full form, the Lingam combines the male and female principles, the necessary components for the creation of life.

Mukerji (1916: 33–37) said that Shivaratri is mentioned in the Mahabharata and recounted a legend from that epic associated with the festival. Underhill offered a shorter version of this popular myth, citing the Skanda Purana and the Shiva Purana as her sources. Although the legend is associated with Shivaratri, Underhill (1991: 93 –94) noted that it offers no solution ". . . of the origin of the fast and worship, which was already accepted as established, [but it] furnishes . . . reasons why it should be persisted in, and is always quoted to show the . . . benefits accruing to the man who keeps it." The myth below is based chiefly on Underhill (1991), but also on Buck (1917), Mukerji (1916), and Sivananda (1993: 142–144).

A man of bad character, setting out to hunt on Phalgun *badi* 14, passed a Shiva temple, saw people worshipping the Lingam, and heard them calling the name of Shiva. Mockingly, the hunter also cried out "Shiva, Shiva." Thus, by uttering the name of the deity on the sacred day, he unknowingly removed some of his sins. He shot a deer but, overtaken by darkness, had no time to sell it for food and so kept an involuntary fast. Fearing wild beasts, he climbed into a wood-apple tree (bel, *belpatra*, or *bilva*), sacred to Shiva, to sleep. Owing to the cold, he could not sleep, thus keeping an involuntary vigil. He wept bitterly because, having failed to return home with food, his wife and children would be hungry. Some of his tears fell onto a stone Lingam under the tree. Shivering from the cold, he shook bel leaves onto the Lingam. Thus, he accidently offered bel leaves and water to the deity. The next day he sold the deer and brought food to his family. Before they could begin their meal, a stranger appeared, who had to be served a meal before the family could eat. According to custom, a fast may not be broken until a Brahman has been fed. The stranger apparently served as a surrogate for a Brahman, and so the hunter inadvertently broke his fast as required by tradition. "The cumulative merit of all these involuntary acts not only released him from past sins, but caused his reception into Shiva's abode of Kailasa" (Underhill, 1991: 93).

Three men, a Baniya Merchant, a Brahman, and a Chamar Leatherworker gave us versions of the story associated with Shivaratri that is told in Shanti Nagar. The myth that they recounted has nothing to do with the legend of the hunter and his accidental worship of Shiva. Rather, it principally concerns Shiva in his procreative role and his volatile personality. A middle-aged Baniya Merchant gave the following version:

> Shiva was married to Parvati. In olden times, men and women had equal rights. Parvati said to her husband, "Though our sexual relations satisfy you, they fail to satisfy me." Shiva knew methods of inflating his body, and so he enlarged his male organ. Parvati also knew ways of dilating her body and so she expanded her female parts. However, she could not keep pace with her husband and started to feel uncomfortable. Then her disciples asked Shiva not to trouble her so much, but he would not listen. Whereupon, her disciples cut off his organ. Shiva was in great pain and started to run about. As he ran, drops of his blood fell to earth. They were round and so became round stones, or Lingams, to be worshipped. Parvati offered water to Shiva's Lingam to cool and calm him. Only the surplus Lingam had been cut off; Shiva retained his normal organ.

Our informant, who was a strong believer in the Arya Samaj, added some commentary about the worship of the Lingam. He said:

> They say that worship of the Lingam is improper. I know this and told my wife. Then she stopped fasting. My daughter fasts now, her husband and in-laws fast and she follows them blindly. I cannot explain this to my daughter because sex is involved. Most Vaishyas [Baniya Merchants are Vaishyas] are devoted to Shiva, and whenever one becomes wealthy, he thinks of building a temple to Shiva. The temples are, however, managed by Brahmans.

Our Brahman informant, a university student, recounted a version of this legend in which Vishnu played the role of Parvati:

> When Shiva was sleeping, a woman approached him. She was beautiful and dressed alluringly. This was Vishnu in disguise, who wanted to test Shiva's moral character. She tried to seduce Shiva. He became angry because she disturbed his prayers. He was so furious that he cut off his own penis. Enormous heat flowed from it, and the heat was destroying the world. When Vishnu saw that the world was being destroyed, he told mankind, "You must worship Shiva and his penis and throw water on it." So they made a stone Lingam and worshipped by bathing it.

This young Brahman, unmarried and a member of a traditional family, believed so strongly in this myth that, when he became sexually excited, he said that he poured water on his penis. If water were not available, he repeated Shiva's name. However, he was more a Vaishnava than a Shivaist. Sometimes he prayed to Shiva but usually to Vishnu. He explained his preference for Vishnu as following from the tripartite nature of God, of which Vishnu is the head, and Shiva, the arms. He said, "If you can reach the mind, why go to the arms."

A Chamar Leatherworker man told a third version of the myth. Vishnu is disguised as Parvati. Shiva appears in the myth as a kindly but excitable deity who easily grants boons. The role of a deity enduring punishment for lustful urges is assumed by a disciple. The Leatherworker said:

> Shiva is at the top of all the deities. He is kindhearted and can easily be pleased. He saved the Hindus who would otherwise have become Muslims. His worship is simple and, if pleased, he grants a boon. Once, Shiva was pleased with a disciple and granted him any boon that he wished. The disciple was smitten with Shiva's wife, Parvati, so when he received the boon, he made advances to the goddess. Shiva learned of it, came running, and chased his disciple. The chase went on for a long time, and Vishnu learned about it. Vishnu disguised himself as Parvati. When the disciple approached Parvati [Vishnu in disguise] to possess her, she said that she would become his wife if he danced as does Shiva. [Shiva is Nataraja (Lord of the Dance)]. He started to dance but did not hold his right hand, in which there was power, over his head. Parvati objected and asked him to put his right hand over his head. When he did, Vishnu caused him to be burned up by his own power. After this incident, Vishnu asked Shiva not to grant boons so easily.

Bahadur (1995: 31) wrote, "Shivji is easily pleased and grants boons and wishes to his [devotees] without going into the pros and cons of the situation . . . usually landing everyone in a mess!"

The Leatherworker's comment that Shiva rescued Hindus from Muslims is obscure. It may be adapted from the legend of the poison that arose from the churning of the Sea of Milk. After a deluge that submerged the earth, Vishnu appeared in his Kurma (Tortoise) avatar to recover valuable items lost in the deluge. He placed himself at the bottom of the Sea of Milk. His back was the pivot of a mountain, which served as the churning shaft. Gods and demons wound a great serpent around the mountain and churned the sea until all the desired objects were recovered. The last thing to emerge was Visha (poison), before which people and gods fled in terror. The poison would have destroyed the human race, but Shiva in his compassion swallowed it. The poison could not harm him, but it stained his throat blue. Hence, one of his epithets is Nila Kantha (Blue-throated) (Dowson, 1891: 35–36; Morgan, 1953: 366; Underhill, 1991: 91).

The ideal ritual, as described in Buck (1917: 85), Imperial Record Department (1914: 75–76), Mukerji (1916: 37–38), and Underhill (1991: 94), follows the legend of the hunter and takes place chiefly during the night. Its essential elements are a fast, a nightlong vigil, worship of the Lingam, reciting the names of Shiva and various mantras, and feeding Brahmans the next morning before breaking the fast. The story of the hunter is recited. To hear the story told on Shivaratri is fraught with blessing.

Various offerings are made to Shiva, principally flowers, bel leaves, water, and sometimes food, especially rice. Shiva is particularly pleased if worshippers coordinate the ritual with the four watches (*pahars*) of the night. At the end of the first watch, devotees bathe the Lingam with milk, then curds for the second watch, ghee for the third, and honey for the last watch of the night.

In its full-blown form, the ideal ritual is probably more often observed in temples than in homes. Shanti Nagar has no Shiva temple, though they are common in Delhi villages. The absence of a temple is probably due to the influence of the Arya Samaj. Shiva worship thus lacks a villagewide focus, which leads villagers to comment, "There is no Shiva in Shanti Nagar." A middle-aged traditional Brahman regarded the festival as unimportant. He said, "Owing to Arya-Samaj influence, Jats ignore the festival completely, and Brahmans give it only a little attention. The women, if they wish, may fast. Those who fast offer water to Shiva, who is the prime Indian god, in the evening. They eat special food." Another middle-aged traditional Brahman chimed in, "I have a shrine for Shiva in my house. My family worships at the shrine and any others who want to may also come."

The celebration of Shivaratri in Shanti Nagar by relatively few worshippers takes place in an ambience of indifference by most people. Most devotees are Brahman women, as explained above. Brahman men take little interest in the festival. Another Brahman man slightly lost patience with us in the course of an interview about religious observance. He dismissed Shivaratri with a sentence, and then commented, "You should not write about these little things but about the famous saints and others who stuck to their word or faith."

The ritual of Shivaratri is based on unobtrusive Lingams of stone in various households. Families with stone Lingams allow other people to worship them on Shivaratri. However, a stone Lingam is not necessary. People may make a temporary Lingam of mud for the festival, and even the third finger of the hand can serve as a Lingam. For want of a Lingam, people may worship the sun, which is also a great god. All worship takes place early in the afternoon, after which people break their fasts. Shivaratri is observed mainly by Brahman women. We saw many women worshipping the Lingam, but not one man, and only one Brahman man claimed to fast. We heard of only one Jat who celebrated the festival, a 10-year-old girl. Her mother said that she fasted and might offer water to a Lingam.

Informant testimony about Shivaratri offers various interpretations of the festival and some variation in ritual. The two constant ritual elements are a partial fast —that is, a fast limited to the avoidance of grains—and the worship of the Lingam with water and other offerings. A middle-aged Brahman man with little interest in ceremonies told us that he was fasting, but that he did not know why the fast was kept. At a large Brahman joint family, a young man told us that probably two women were fasting but none of the men. Another Brahman who was present added that only women fast. Two elderly traditional Brahman men said, "We are not fasting. Those who fast have to offer water to Shiva. There is no Shiva in the village, but there is one in [the next village]. Some people use their third finger as Shiva and offer water to it. All the gods are contained within our body. People may make a Shiva of mud and worship it."

People of the lower castes did not generally observe Shivaratri. Several Chuhra

Sweepers, both men and women, said that they did not celebrate Shivaratri because it is a Muslim festival. One woman said that she had never heard of Shivaratri. Three Chamar Leatherworker men said that they did not celebrate Shivaratri. One said that it is a Muslim festival, but another man said "No, it is Shiva's 14th." Another Chamar Leatherworker man and his wife said that they did not celebrate Shivaratri because they were working at the sugarcane crushers. In early March, the cane crushing season was nearing its end, but all the village crushers were still operating. All of the Chamars were working as usual.

We observed the ritual at the shrine in a Brahman household in 1959. The elder wife of the head of the household had brought four stones from Hardwar three years earlier. She gave one to her husband's sister and installed the other three as a Lingam in her rear courtyard close to a banana tree. The central stone was larger than the two on the sides. People came individually to offer water to the Lingam. Our informant named Brahmans, Baniyas, Barbers, and Watercarriers among the visitors. Chamars, Chuhras, and Potters did not come.

A Brahman woman came with a lota (pitcher) of water and five ber (a round fruit). The number five is associated with Shiva (Daniélou, 1964: 353; R. Freed and S. Freed, 1980: 344). The Brahman woman borrowed some gur from the host household for the ritual. She sat beside the Lingam, placed the fruit on one side, put a little gur on the large stone and on one of the small stones, emptied the lota of water over the stones, and watched as it flowed to the banana tree. She put the remaining lump of gur on a little brick wall to one side, folded her hands, and bowed her head. Then she arose and pressed the legs of the co-wives, first the senior wife. The old women blessed her in turn. After her departure, the unmarried daughter of the household retrieved the gur.

Another Brahman woman followed a similar routine, except that she brought a lamp with the other offerings. She washed the area around the Lingam, put five ber and a lump of gur near the stones, lit the lamp, and placed it between two stones with the wick facing east toward the Yamuna River.

The senior co-wife said that eight other women came to worship: five Brahmans, one Watercarrier, and two Barbers. She said that many others were fasting and would worship at home with a Lingam made of mud. The daughter of the Baniya Merchant came but did not worship. When we asked her why she did not worship, she did not reply. In 1978 the Baniya's son was married, and we interviewed his wife about Shivaratri. She said that her mother-in-law would not permit her to observe the festival. She said that she used to fast for all the festivals (in her natal village), but now she has forgotten everything. The junior co-wife said that in her village men fasted as well as women. In Shanti Nagar, men did not fast.

At another Brahman's house, there was a stone Lingam in the courtyard and, beside it, a lump of earth. The stone represented Shiva and the lump of earth, Parvati, his wife. A wife of the household put five ber, a lump of gur, and a lota of water near Shiva and Parvati. She folded her hands and bowed her head in worship. All the women of the family fasted and worshipped Shiva in this manner. The ber and gur were given to an unmarried daughter of the household as *prasad*, but could have been given to any unmarried girl.

A Brahman woman reported that she and a large group of women gathered in front of the house of the co-wives about 2 P.M. They sang and then all together entered the house to worship. However, both co-wives said that no women had come singing to their home. Though the woman who made the report was one of our best informants, it may be that our persistent questioning had made her overly conscious of ceremonies.

Except for an elaborate, unique ritual conducted by a Leatherworker devotee of Shiva, our information concerning the ritual in 1978 comes from 13 interviews, all but one with women. The informants ranged through the caste hierarchy from Brahman at the top to Sweeper at the bottom. As in 1959, the festival was observed chiefly by Brahman women. Leatherworkers and Sweepers did not observe it. However, our Potter informant claimed to fast and to offer water and a lighted lamp to a lithograph of Shiva late in the afternoon. Since there still was no Shiva temple in the village, people worshipped stone Lingams in various households with water, gur, and bers.

Some women made their offerings of water, ber, and gur at the shrine for Bhumiya, and there seems to have been some devotional singing on this occasion. Bhumiya was the founding male ancestor of the village, or ". . . the first old man to die in the village after its founding . . ." Lewis (1958: 201). In the region of Shanti Nagar, such a man becomes a godling. The Bhumiya shrine did not contain a Lingam in 1958–59 (fig. 38) The shrine seemed to have been slightly altered by 1977–78, and we do not know what was inside (fig. 39). In any case, the shrine possibly serves as a substitute for a Shiva temple, offering a villagewide focus for the ritual of Shivaratri. Bhumiya is worshipped on the 14th, the same day as Shivaratri, which could lead to the possibility of identifying, or confusing, Bhumiya with Shiva. Moreover, the personalities of the two deities are similar. Just as Shiva is easy to please and destructive in his anger, so too some Bhumiyas are easygoing and good-tempered while others are revengeful and malignant. The same Bhumiya may combine both qualities (Rose, 1919: 194).

A middle-aged married Brahman woman explained one of the reasons that women kept the partial fast for Shiva: "All unmarried girls keep this fast to get a good husband. Even the married women keep the fast. They don't eat any grains on this day." Sweet dishes were favored, such as "potato halva," made of potatoes mashed with gur. Finding a good husband, one like Krishna, is perhaps the dominant concern of unmarried women. This motive is also expressed in the festival of Ganga Nahan. Bahadur said that on Shivaratri all women pray to Parvati, Shiva's wife, for married bliss and a long and prosperous married life. "The unmarried girls pray [for] handsome husbands with wealth, knowledge, and talent" (Bahadur, 1995: 30).

One unusual Leatherworker man, whom we call Illusionist, had a special relationship with Shiva. Illusionist was a bhagat (exorcist). In his roles of Lord of Ghosts and First Physician, Shiva is usually the chosen deity of curers, especially bhagats, whose function is to exorcise the malevolent ghosts that cause illness. Moreover, villagers reported that they saw Shiva visit Illusionist's house. Illusionist said, "When [my wife] fell ill, Lord Shiva came to my house . . . . I did not see him, because I was on night duty, but some of my relatives told me that he came. . . . I had been praying to Shiva" (R. Freed and S. Freed, 1993: 194). After this theophany, his wife was completely cured, and Illusionist became a bhagat. The story of Illusionist and his life as a bhagat is described in R. Freed and S. Freed (1993: chap. 17).

The daylong *havan* (fire ceremony) that Illusionist carried out on Shivaratri far surpassed the customary brief ritual practiced in Shanti Nagar. He called the day Shiva Chaudas (Shiva's Fourteenth). To prepare for the worship, he purchased for 28 rupees a shell, bell, trident, and Lingam. The trident (*trishul*) and the Lingam are symbols of Shiva. The shell, probably a conch although we did not identify it, is usually a symbol of Vishnu, but it is also the trumpet of Ganesh, Shiva's son (Zimmer, 1946: 138, and fig. 34). Illusionist removed a few bricks from his veranda to make a *havan kund* (pit). Around the pit, in addition to these four items, he arranged a pitcher of water, a dish of ghee, a tray of *prasad*, a dish of *samagri*, a coconut wrapped in thread as a symbol of Ganesh, and a lithograph of Shiva. His *prasad* consisted of various sweets (sweetmeats are associated with Ganesh) and betel leaves, the latter an uncommon offering in Shanti Nagar. He placed his prayer rug near this altar, his attaché case containing various ritual paraphernalia beside it.

Illusionist arose early in the morning of the 14th and took his bath. He wore a yellow turban and a necklace of beads, representing the strings of *rudraksh* (a kind of berry) beads that Shiva wears around his wrists, upper arms, and neck. There was a yellow tilak on his forehead. He fasted, taking only two cups of tea during the day. He prepared the tea himself on the sacred fire, explaining that he could not accept tea from anyone else on this day. He arranged dhak wood in the fire pit but awaited the arrival of an elderly religious teacher from a neighboring village before lighting it. He said that the elderly teacher was an expert on mantras. After his guest arrived, the two men began the puja.

Illusionist first did *arati* for Shiva using *samagri* and the small bell. Then the two men began to chant mantras. The first mantra was to the sun, after which they offered *prasad* to the fire. Then they both chanted the Shiva mantra, *Om Namah Shivaya* (Om! To Shiva I bow). This is one of the chief Hindu mantras. After a few mantras, *prasad*, ghee, and *samagri* were offered to the fire. The elderly teacher left after some time, and Illusionist continued to chant the Shiva mantra throughout the day. His wife supplied ghee to help him maintain the fire. He said that he left his prayer rug only once during the day. A few visitors came, and Illusionist gave some *prasad* to each one. In addition, he might add a blessing. He blessed one Jat woman, telling her that she would have a son. He said that he spent five rupees on *samagri* and burned 10 kilos of wood.

5 HOLI AND DULHENDI

HOLI AND DULHENDI are not easily classified with other festivals. Celebration of Holi begins with Phalgun *sudi* 1 and reaches a climax 15 days later on Phalgun Purinmashi. The festival of Dulhendi, closely linked to Holi, follows on the next day, Chaitra *badi* 1. The festivals are popularly known as Little Holi (on the full moon day) and Big Holi. Little Holi features a ritual, but Big Holi is strictly a day of interaction with no visible religious aspect. The twin festival is often called a Saturnalia, principally because of the merriment and license displayed on Dulhendi. The two days are so different that it is tempting to classify Holi as an honorific festival and Dulhendi, a festival of interaction. However, the two days are best viewed as different phases of a single festival. It is a festival of thanks for the spring harvest, a fertility rite, and a ritual of purification and renewal.

Similar festivals have a worldwide distribution, which indicates that the origin of the basic elements of the festival may well be pre-Vedic. The most characteristic features of Holi are a bonfire, the roasting of ears of grain from the new harvest, licentiousness, red color splashed on participants, and painful abuse, both physical and mental. These features are in all likelihood ancient rituals. Referring to a documentary and distributional study by N. Bose, Marriott (1966: 210) wrote, "[S]pring festivals featuring bonfires, a degree of sexual license, and generally saturnalian carousing had probably existed in villages in many parts of India for at least the better part of the past two thousand years." Basham (1954: 207) said, "The most popular festival in early times was the Festival of Spring, in honour of Kama, the love-god . . . ." It was a bloody fertility rite. Holi is the modern form of this festival, where red powder and physical pain symbolize the blood and sacrifices of the ancient fertility rituals.

Holi is the last festival of the year. The new year dawns a fortnight later. The sacred bonfire (called *holi*), by far the most spectacular symbol of Holi, represents the beginning of the new year, purification, and the lighting of new fire (cf., Mukerji, 1916: 43-44). Crooke recounted a tale that ties the Holi bonfire to the Hindu year:

> Lastly, a tale told at Hardwâr brings us probably nearer the real origin of the rite. Holikâ or Holî was, they say, sister of Sambat or Sanvat, the Hindu year. Once, at the beginning of all things, Sambat died, and

Holî . . . insisted on being burnt on his pyre, and by her devotion he was restored to life. The Holî fire is now burnt every year to commemorate this tragedy [Crooke, 1968, 2: 314].

Sivananda, Channa, and Mukerji noted the purificatory aspect of Holi. After cleaning their houses and burning dirty articles, wrote Sivananda (1993: 39), "[People] believe that their houses are rendered pure and free from disease." Channa (1984: 137) said that people throw unusable items from home into the bonfire. Mukerji (1916: 44) said that the bonfire served the interests of public health by consuming the year's accumulated rubbish, and the resulting smoke effectively purified the atmosphere. Marriott (1966: 201) reported that Holi is a time for lighting new fire: "Household fires throughout the village had been extinguished, and [worshippers] carried coals from the collective fire to rekindle their domestic hearths."

Authors with a knowledge of European folk customs compared Holi rituals with similar observances in Europe (e.g., Balfour, 1885, 2: 93; Crooke, 1968, 2: 314, 317; Growse, 1883: 101–102). However, much closer parallels can be identified between Holi and a harvest ceremony of the American Indians of the southeastern United States known as the Busk, or Green Corn Dance. The Busk marked the beginning of the new year and was a time of amnesty and forgiveness. Continuing for eight days, the rituals included cleaning the town, fasting, extinguishing all fires, lighting new fire, offering newly harvested maize to the sacred fire, a special beverage of purification, competition between men and women, physical pain, dances, and a ceremonial lacrosse game (Swanton, 1928: 546–614). All of these features, *mutatis mutandis*, are part of Holi. The beverage in the Southeast was an emetic. In Kishan Garhi, the "festival drink" was a delicious mixture of sugar, milk products, nuts, and spices generously laced with marijuana (Marriott, 1966: 203–204). The Indian game played on Holi was the popular *kabaddi*.[29] It is a rough game but not violent as was lacrosse, the game played during the Busk, which, before modern rules and equipment took some of the danger from the sport, was known as "the little brother of war." The diffusion of a ceremonial complex cannot be considered in the case of Holi and the Busk. Rather, it may be that spring harvest festivals independently tend to generate similar beliefs and activities.

The ancient festival has been overlaid with Sanskritic legends. The story told in Shanti Nagar to explain Holi is the Puranic legend of Prahlad and Holika, the sister of Prahlad's father. Prahlad was a devotee of God (Vishnu, Ram). His father, Hirnakush (Hiranyakashipu), was king of the demons and had sovereignty over the three worlds. Inflated with pride, the king wanted his son to pronounce the name Hirnakush in devotion rather than the name of God. The pious Prahlad did not oblige, and his father tried in vain to kill him in various ways. Finally, the demoness Holika, Prahlad's aunt, said that she would kill him. She was made of stone (that is, she was a strong woman) and believed that fire could not harm her. She took her nephew in her lap and sat in a fire. But because Prahlad believed in God, he survived, while his aunt died. This happy event is celebrated in Holi when everyone makes merry.

Buck (1917: 86) and the Imperial Record Department (1914: 38) recounted another version of the Holika myth, which was never heard in Shanti Nagar. The demoness Holika used to devour children, and each family in the region where she held sway had to supply her in turn with a daily victim. A woman was bewailing the imminent loss of her grandson. A holy mendicant heard her wails and said that Holika could be killed if forced to hear vile and obscene language. The whole village assembled the next day and subjected Holika to such filthy abuse that she dropped dead and the boy was saved. The children made a huge bonfire of her remains. The bonfire and the vile language used on Holi are said to have come from this legend.

Mukerji (1916: 41–42) offered a version of the legend of Holika as a cannibal that replaces verbal abuse with death by fire. Her cannibalism was causing such havoc in the neighborhood that people formed a plot against her, caught her, and burned her to death. The Holi bonfire commemorates the immolation of this fiend.[30]

Of the two versions, the one featuring the piety of Prahlad is more appropriate for the modern festival, which has an association with Krishna, an avatar of Vishnu. The merriment and pranks of Holi are said to represent the frolicking of Krishna with the Gopis. Moreover, in an episode of the myth of Prahlad and Holika, Vishnu becomes enraged at Hiranyakashipu, assumes his man-lion avatar (Narasinha), and slays the demon.

Mukerji (1916: 40) said that Holi is the most important Vaishnava festival and, in its geographical extent, exceeds even the Durga Puja, the great fall festival. The deities connected with Holi are Radha, Balarama and especially Krishna. Mukerji reported that an image of Krishna as a baby is placed in a cradle and worshipped; hence Holi is sometimes known as Dolayatra (Swinging Festival) (cf., Imperial Record Department, 1914: 18–20). However, "the religious element has . . . disappeared . . . and Holi has now become a purely secular festival characterised by mere rout and revel, with not even the mention of Krishna's name, except in 'amorous ditties' also called Holi . . ." (Mukerji, 1916: 41). Growse pointed out that the connection of Holi with Krishna, Radha, and Balarama can only be of modern date, from the early 17th century. "But the [Holi] scenes that I have described [go back to] a far earlier period and are clearly relics . . . of the primitive worship of the powers of nature on the return of Spring" (Growse, 1883: 101).

The name of the festival is supposed to come from the fiend Holika. It is unlikely that the great all-India festival of Holi, centered on a bonfire, has its origin in the myth of Holika. Religious festivals are usually older than the interpretations given to them. In its original time and place, a festival is self-explanatory. With the passage of time, a need may arise for a new interpretation to bring the festival into accord with a changing culture. Mukerji's comment is relevant:

> The Holi bonfire is supposed to commemorate the fate of Prahlad's wicked aunt. This may be true; but it may also be true that some Vaishnava commentator of our religious books may have found an excellent origin for the Holi bonfire in this story of Prahlad, which is to this day a household tale in India [Mukerji, 1916: 43].

Buck offered another etymology of Holi. He said that Holi is a corruption of the Sanskrit word, Holaka, meaning "half-ripe corn." Holi seems originally to have been "the Spring festival when ceremonies were performed in honour of the crops and to ward off disease . . . . Even now there is a remnant of these in the eating of half-ripe wheat and barley and in the burning of cakes of cow dung. The main festival, however, has developed into something quite different and has become the Saturnalia of India" (Buck, 1917: 85–86).

Drawing on Growse's (1883) description of Holi in Mathura District, Crooke elaborated the idea that Holi is an aboriginal festival absorbed into Brahmanism. The bonfire is really intended to represent the passage from the old to the new year and to exorcise evil spirits that cause disease and famine (Crooke, 1968, 2: 320). Growse (1883: 93) described a ritual enacted by the local priest. After soaking his garments in a pond, he feigns jumping into the bonfire. Crooke interpreted this ritual as a survival of human sacrifice. The blood that is frequently drawn in sham battles between women and men "is regarded rather as an omen of good fortune . . ." (Growse, 1883: 92). Such bloodletting may also be a survival of an early sacrificial ritual.

HOLI (LITTLE HOLI)

The night of the full moon with its bonfire and ritual was the climax of Holi, but the preceding 15 days were part of the festival. This fortnight abounded in dramas, dancing, and singing throughout the village. It was a joyous time, filled with gentle, clever amusements. Every evening, groups of women gathered to "play Phalgun," to sing, dance, and watch skits enacted by the more talented among them. The "actresses" performed to amuse themselves and the other women gathered to watch. The fun also attracted the usual crowd of children, whom the women completely ignored. Ordinarily, men did not attend these entertainments. The groups of women were generally composed of neighbors, thus often multicaste. We observed groups mainly of Jats, Brahmans, and Bairagi Mendicants, for such a gathering formed nightly, close to our quarters in 1959. Several companies might be in action on any evening, scattered at various spots in the village. We also saw groups of young, unmarried girls and boys. The girls danced and sang; the boys watched.

The following skits were all presented in 1959. Four days before Holi we watched a drama group of about 15 high-caste boys who performed for their own amusement. One boy had blackened his face, wore some kind of pigtails, and sported a mustache made of twisted cotton. He was complaining about pigs that had entered his fields. Other actors advised him to go to the Sweepers (who were the only people who kept pigs) to find out why they had let pigs into his fields. Although the drama seemed to be composed on the spur of the moment, versions of it had probably been enacted previously. Some skits were performed more than once, so in all likelihood the more popular dramas are put on every year. In any case the boys laughed at every twist in the plot. Although we saw only this one drama performed by males for males, it bears notice that the plot involved caste conflict. There was to be an investigation, perhaps leading to a hearing before the village panchayat. Law, politics, and power were all suggested in the brief skit. These activities are the province of men. The skits of women focused on interpersonal relations within the family, especially the triangle of wife, husband, and mother-in-law.

After watching the boys, we moved on to a Brahman's house where some 15 Jat and Brahman women were singing, dancing, and playacting. One Jat woman took a lampstand and dressed it like a woman with a shirt, skirt, and headcloth. She put the lampstand doll on her head so that the skirt covered her own head and shoulders and danced to the singing of the women onlookers. After a while, the dancer went to a Jat's house, saying that the doll was hungry and had gone home to eat. Nothing much seemed to be happening, so we left. Returning to the same group about 45 minutes later, we found the women putting on a skit of a plowman, his wife, and his mother. We saw this same skit presented a few days later (described on p. 205).

On the low-caste side of the village, nothing was happening in the Sweepers' or Leatherworkers' compounds, but two groups were performing in the Potters' quarter. A woman, dressed in the uniform her husband wore as an employee of a school, was dancing and singing. She tried to persuade the women onlookers to sing also, but they were not too enthusiastic. A child was beating time on a rubber membrane stretched over a pot. (This instrument, called a *ghara*, is illustrated in Nautiyal, 1961: 162.) Three men were watching, which was unusual. One of them acted as if he were in a trance, making jerking movements with his hands, face, head, and shoulders while uttering incoherent words and noises. After a few minutes, he emerged from the trance and the men went home. Everyone enjoyed the trance.

Five women and some children sitting in a circle composed the second group of Potters. The women sang intermittently. Two of them danced during the singing. The song was about some of the male in-laws (father-in-law, husband's elder brother, and others) throwing sweets at one of the dancers, who threw them back.

We visited the Potters' quarter on Holi eve. Again there were two groups of women. One of them consisted of only four or five women. One woman was dancing vigorously, and the onlookers complained that she was being immodest. The other group was larger, but only two or three girls, 10 to 15 years of age, were trying to dance. They were not good dancers. The other women were doing nothing. Since it takes practice to learn to dance gracefully, not all women could do it, although some were skillful dancers. Soon the little girls suggested that everyone go to watch the Leatherworker women dance.

In the Leatherworker quarter a few dancers were performing before a crowd of about 30 upper-caste women sitting on stairs and roofs. A few young Jat men tried to enter the compound, but a woman told them that they had to leave. They reluctantly did so. The women began to dance again, but noticed that Jat men were watching from the roof. The dancers stopped, and a woman with a stick chased the men away. However, they soon returned. This scenario was repeated a few times.

Two nights before Holi, we watched one group of about 25 women, Brahmans and Jats, for about an hour. Activities began about 9 P.M. with some singing and dancing. From two to six women danced at one time, each starting and stopping as she wished. The women who were watching sang continuously. All the dancers, one of them a 10-year-old girl, wore long, full, colorful skirts (*ghaghris*), which twirled as they danced. A number of boys had gathered to watch. They played no roles in the skits, but some of them wore or carried clownish accoutrements. One boy held a stick with a shirt on it, something like a scarecrow, close to his body. The women took no notice of the boys.

The skits drew their inspiration from daily village life, particularly from familial relationships or from caste interaction. One skit involved a man, his wife, and his mother, a triangular relationship teeming with problems and drama. One of the performers pretended to be a plowman working in the fields. His wife brought him his meal. He complained that she was late and that the *roti*s (bread) were poorly prepared. She said that his mother had cooked the *roti*s and perhaps had put too much salt in them. She wanted to put ghee on his bread, but his mother would not permit it. He complained that there was no vegetable. His wife said that maybe his mother did not make any. Thus, the wife placed all the blame for the poor meal on her mother-in-law. The husband said that the two "widows" (an insult) must have been quarreling. His wife replied that she had quarreled with no one, but that his mother was threatening to send her to her parents and that she would have to go if his mother insisted. Generally, wives want to visit their parents, but their husbands are reluctant to let them go. In addition to shifting the blame for the poor meal to her mother-in-law, the wife raised the specter that her mother-in-law might force her to go to her parents. This was another way of trying to sow discord between mother and married son. After the suggestion that she might go to her parents, she asked her husband to buy a buffalo so that she would have some milk. The conversation continued in this vein and was repeated many times. The spectators laughed at every line.

Another skit featuring the delicate, complicated relationship of mother-in-law and daughter-in-law concerned a series of visits from the daughter-in-law to her mother-in-law to invite her to a feast at Holi. First, the daughter-in-law asked her husband's mother if she covered her face properly and wore her skirt correctly because her husband, implying immodesty, had criticized her on these points. Her mother-in-law assured her that she behaved correctly. The daughter-in-law then visited her mother-in-law repeatedly: first, to tell her to bring her own flour to the feast since she and her husband were short; then to report that her husband had said that she should also bring her own ghee and sugar; again to tell her that her husband wanted her to bring her own dishes; finally, to advise her that they had decided not to give a feast for her that year, but would do so the following year. All the onlookers enjoyed the skit immensely. In this skit the wife puts the blame on her husband when talking to her mother-in-law. In the previous piece, the wife was talking to her husband so she put the blame on his mother.

The same Brahman woman who organized the preceding skit put on another one about a demanding mother goddess who kept refusing to let a devotee worship her. She selected a woman to play the role of the goddess, outlined the plot, and told the woman that she should continue to refuse to give her devotee permission to worship. Then the woman playing the devotee picked up a pan used for collecting dirt and refuse, collected some fibers of sugarcane from the street to serve as an offering, put them in the pan, carried it on her head to the goddess, and asked if she might worship. The mother goddess refused. The devotee decided that she had forgotten to bring her sons. She picked up some more dirt, put it in the pan, and returned with her sons. Again, no permission. She thought that maybe she had forgotten her daughters. She returned with them, but again was unsuccessful. There were several of these trips. Finally she said, "Maybe I forgot to bring the children's father." Then she seized one of the men of our group and asked him to become the children's father for a day. The mother goddess said that now she could worship. Everyone enjoyed the little play.

What is striking in this and other skits is that someone is made the target of gentle, flattering joking rather than of physical abuse or verbal arrows aimed at a victim's vulnerable spot, as takes place on Dulhendi. We also were targeted in another skit (p. 222). We do not know, however, if village men would have been treated in the same way. They do not watch the games of women, and the women do not want them there. Some of the skits have sexual nuances and the dances can be suggestive, which may account for the absence of men. In any case women have their activities and men have theirs.

A skit involving caste relationships revolved around a daughter who went about the village to visit people of many castes, leaving younger siblings at home unattended. The spectators, who were singing, formed two rows leaving a narrow lane between them. Two girls took their positions at opposite ends of the lane and ran up and down, each one beating time with a pair of shoes (fig. 62). One played the "recalcitrant daughter"; the role of the other was not clear. She seemed to be singing with the mother and may have served as a counterpoise to the daughter.

The mother, annoyed, asked her daughter where she had been. Running down the lane and beating time with her shoes, she replied that she had gone to the Potters. The mother asked why she had gone there; the daughter answered that she had gone to get some pots. At approximately this time, the second girl ran in the lane beating her shoes together. Angered, the mother said, "I will set you right. I will break your pots. Why did you leave my children alone." Next, the mother repeated her initial question as to where her daughter had gone. The girl replied, "To the Waterman." Her mother asked why; the girl answered that she had gone to get some water, and so on. This basic episode was repeated for almost all the castes of the village. Even though this skit deals with relations between castes, the focus is within the family, the relationship of mother and daughter. When the boys dealt with caste relations, their skit emphasized caste conflict and power.

The next evening, Holi eve, a group of high-caste women formed before the same house where women had performed the previous evening. The skit of a daughter-in-law inviting her mother-in-law to a feast was repeated. Then another woman put on a piece that we had not seen before. It was an autobiography of the difficult life of a young woman. The onlookers sat in two parallel rows and sang a standard two- or three-line refrain sympathizing with the sufferings of the recently married young woman, a "daughter" or "sister" of the onlookers. The dancer moved down the lane between the rows of spectators, bowing low and twirling around as she decribed incidents in her life. She worked in the fields, harvested, wedded, went to her in-laws, became pregnant, her sister-in-law called a midwife (*dai*) for the childbirth, the traditional gift for a newborn arrived from her parents, and so on. This sequence was standard for village women in the 1950s. A few decades later, other possibilities would have opened, such as study at a college and salaried employment.

Although the unrehearsed performances by groups of women throughout the

village attracted spectators, the major attraction in the fortnight ending with Holi
was the Chamar Leatherworker quarter. Here, Chamar men, skilled singers, dancers
and actors, presented skits and songs before large crowds of villagers of all castes.
These men were semiprofessional performers. They studied, practiced, rehearsed,
and taught their accomplishments to youngsters. They used a number of musical
instruments, whereas the women had none. Leatherworkers were paid for their performances. No tickets were sold, but well-off individuals would contribute a rupee
or two. Leatherworkers claimed to have earned as much as Rs. 100 in an evening, but
in 1958 the return was Rs. 45. The men performed only on ceremonial occasions. In
addition to Holi, they might perform at marriages and childbirths. They sometimes
danced in other villages.

In 1959 the Leatherworkers began to practice for Holi a fortnight before the festival. Hearing the drumming the first night of practice, we went to see what was happening. Five young men were taking turns beating a kettledrum (*nakara*). At first,
there was only drumming, but then other men began to accompany the drumming
with various percussion instruments in time to the beat set by the drummer. The
Chamars owned only percussion instruments: the kettledrum, a small two-headed
drum suspended from the neck (*dholak*); cymbals (*jhanjh*); rattles in the form of
tongs with small jingling attachments (*chimba*); light and heavy metal gongs (*jhar*
and *gharnyal*) struck with a wooden hammer; and a tambourinelike instrument.
Most of these instruments are illustrated in Nautiyal (1961: 160, 162–163). The
Leatherworkers hoped eventually to buy a harmonium (a small hand-pumped organ);

FIG. 62. Holi, 1978.
Women playing
Phalgun: A scene
from the skit of the
"recalcitrant daughter."
She runs back and forth
between two rows of
women and children
beating time with
her shoes.

in the meantime, they borrowed one from a landowner when needed. The brass bands that played at weddings were recruited from outside the village.

After the drumming stopped, one man whom we call Leading Singer, began to sing a *holi* (a song sung at Holi) from a booklet. Soon it developed into a chorus. Leading Singer sang a line and the other men repeated it. At first there was only singing, but then the singers began to play their instruments in accompaniment. The practice attracted a crowd of about 25 Leatherworkers, mainly men and boys, but a few young girls were also there. Most of the older men present only watched, but one of them provided a little guidance, showing the singers how to stand and move their hands. The enthusiastic crowd stimulated the players to put a lot of life into their performance.

Three days before Holi, the Leatherworkers put on a big performance that drew a large, multicaste crowd. The stimulus was probably the arrival of three men from out of town who were going to play with the village artists. The evening would clearly be special, for the Leatherworkers had borrowed a harmonium from a wealthy Jat. In preparation for the performance, one of the visitors was practicing on it. Boys were making a racket beating the kettledrum and the gongs. A man asked the boys to move away and sit down, promising five sweets to those who stayed put, but only two sweets for the others.

A young, well-educated Brahman man arrived to say that one of the visitors who was playing the small drum (*dholak*) was wanted on the high-caste side of the village to accompany a visiting artist. The drummer said that he was committed to stay with the Chamars and could not leave. All the Chamars supported him. A quick-tempered Leatherworker who had just arrived contemptuously dismissed the Brahman, "You have studied 14 classes but all the learning seems to be wasted. We did not ask this man to come here to send him over to the other side [of the village]." The Brahman was very disturbed and said that one should not talk like that to a visitor, but he went away.

The spectators spanned the caste hierarchy from top to bottom. Early in the evening when the crowd was small, some upper-caste men sat on cots with Leatherworkers and Sweepers, but as the crowd grew, men tended to sit in caste groups. Jat landowners to whom several Leatherworkers owed debts were given cane easy chairs. The onlookers formed two circles around the kettledrum and the dancers. Men sat in the inner circle, and women, in the outer circle. All the daughters-in-law of the village kept their faces covered, revealing only their eyes. In addition, people watched from the roofs of houses that surrounded the open courtyard of the Leatherworker quarter.

The entertainment began with singing and dancing. The principal dancer was the best in the village, a man whom we call Illusionist (R. Freed and S. Freed, 1993: chap. 17). He had bells tied to his ankles and beat time with a *chimba*. Five or six men sang and moved their hands in accompaniment. At this point, the harmonium malfunctioned, and the Leatherworkers borrowed another one from a Jat. With the arrival of the important Jats, the dancers seemed to perform especially for them.

One popular piece, with visitors playing the small drum and harmonium and local Leatherworkers dancing and singing, was a tune from a film. A young wife in the song complained that her husband had learned bad habits, smoking, drinking, gambling, and using opium, and that he was ruining her. Then followed a series of impersonations. One man came dressed as a holy man with beard and braids. Another man wore a woman's outfit, carefully covering his face. A boy of seven or eight years portrayed a girl. Then three men and the boy danced together. Three of these four performers wore female costumes. All the dancers performed with great verve to loud drumming.

Leading Singer apparently did not judge the evening's performance to be satisfactory, for the next evening he and another man were still giving lessons to other Chamars on how to sing *holi*s, in anticipation of the major performance that would take place on Holi night. The students were told that their pronunciation had to be clear if spectators were to understand what they were singing. They were also instructed in the use of gestures for hands, arms, and bodies that would correspond to the flow of the recitation.

Leading Singer outlined the history of the Leatherworker performing artists. He said that the use of the kettledrum dated only to 1945, when the first one was purchased. He and a few other men used to watch performers in villages south of Delhi, became interested, and bought instruments to use during Phalgun. The original drum was sold to Chamars in a neighboring village, and the local men bought a new one.

Some villages had kettledrums, and some did not. Use of the kettledrum was not a monopoly of the Leatherworkers or of low-caste persons in general. Leading Singer said that the Tagas (a caste) of a large neighboring village had a drum. No Tagas lived in Shanti Nagar, so we have had no experience with them. However, they must be one of the higher castes, for they are said to have been Brahmans originally (India, 1912: 66). The fact that high-caste persons apparently can use drums explains a Leatherworker's comment that surprised us. He asked us why the upper castes were jealous of the Leatherworker's kettledrum. When we asked him what he meant, he became very vague.

Although Leading Singer did not mention him, Illusionist played a major role in the formation of the Leatherworker entertainers. When he was five years old, he was sent to live with relatives away from Shanti Nagar, among them a maternal uncle who lived in a village where the Leatherworkers danced and sang. His uncle's wife dressed him up nicely and told him to begin to dance. This was in 1940 when he was about 13 years old. He returned to Shanti Nagar in 1947, just when the Chamars were learning to perform, and he taught several men how to dance. Illusionist certainly would have been influential. He had charisma and was by far the star performer.

*Holi*s, the songs sung at Holi, range from short songs of a few lines to long, elaborate myths published in booklets. The short songs are heard in the skits performed by groups of women. The Chamars sing such *holi*s, but they also have recourse to booklets. Many booklets of *holi*s are readily available at low prices. The Chamars had about 15 of them priced from half a rupee to Rs. 1.50. New songs are constantly being composed; hence the performances of the Leatherworkers sometimes have a current, nontraditional flavor that was generally absent in the skits performed by women. Songs from films that are sung on Holi add to the modern aspect of holis. The holis offered below are intended only to give an idea of what holis are like. A full study would be tantamount to a long, independent research project.

A middle-aged Brahman woman sang two songs for us. One was a simple two-line ditty that expressed one of the basic ideas of Holi, or rather Dulhendi, namely that everyone was equal for a day. The ditty was repeated as often as the singers wished.

> We play Holi, beat drums, throw the red color on everyone.
> Go and ask that big proud woman to come and play Holi.

The other holi described a bitter, unresolved dispute between a wife and husband. Two women, representing husband and wife, sang the song, facing one another, their arms raised in a threatening manner. There was considerable ambiguity in the first few lines, and some interpretation was necessary. We interpreted the "man" and "friend" of the opening lines to refer to the woman's husband in order to conform to the logic of the basic theme. As for the "first drink," one takes a buffalo calf to its mother so that she will let down her milk. We believe that the idea here is not that the calf gets the first drink but that the husband drinks first. Also, "speak" may mean "to have sexual relations."

> One day I called in a man to milk my buffalo.
> He took the calf to the buffalo to drink some milk first.
> I will not speak to you.
> You are a very selfish friend.
> I will never talk to you.
> [Husband asks] Where is my hookah, where have you placed it?
> [Wife replies] Your hookah is on the shelf.
> I will give you a slap, you will die and then I will never talk to you.
> [Husband asks] Where is my bedding and where have you placed
>   my cot?
> [Wife replies] Your bedding is kept on the cot and your cot is in
>   the courtyard.
> I will give you a slap, you will die, and I will never talk to you.
> You come at midnight, you come when the moon is hiding, so I won't
>   talk to you.

A young Jat man of the village became greatly interested in holis and wanted to compose some. We saw him once with a Leatherworker man who was explaining to him how a holi is made. The Chamars told him that they would sing his compositions if they proved to be any good. On Holi night, we heard him sing one of his compositions. The melody was from a film; the text he had composed advised people to love one another and be good, because one could not take anything from this world. On the night of Dulhendi, we heard him sing an erotic song. We collected two bawdy songs from him. We do not think that he composed the two following songs, but our notes are ambiguous on this point.

What do you want to know about my in-laws, Chandna De.
The night used to slip by like a moment, Chandna De.
The first night when my lover came, I felt shy.
Sitting on the cot he tickled me, and I was dizzy.
It became all dark when he grasped my hand, Chandna De.
At first I was afraid but then I took heart.
He threw his arm over my neck and onto my breasts.
Unsatisfied yet, he lifted my leg, Chandna De.
He held me fast, put mouth to mouth.
In this I got all the pleasures of the world.
He bit me and pressed me hard, Chandna De.
Gulab Singh says he turned me round onto his knees.
I got stroke after stroke, sister, I was in ecstasy.
I was dead till the dawn came, Chandna De.

The foregoing song describes the relations of a wife and husband, especially on their first night together. The following song deals with the tender traditional relationship of an older brother's wife (*bhabhi*) and a husband's younger brother (*dewar*). A *bhabhi* can confide in her *dewar*. He is the one in-law with whom she can relax and have fun, and a discrete sexual relationship is permitted between them, especially when the husband is away from home for an extended period. The junior levirate, the custom of a younger brother marrying the widow of his older brother, is commonly practiced among some of the castes of north Indian villages.

Underneath was the petticoat, over it was tied the sari.
Eyes had barely closed, he said *bhabhi* let me lie on [the bed] too
Whatever is disturbing you, I will remove all your worries.
I want to kiss you, it is shivering cold outside.
I am young, my wife is tall, woman and man get entangled.
I want to hold your nipples, pick them like soft cotton.
Your youth is like a firefly, don't you make much noise.
I am nuder than you are, let me lie on a little.
Your youth is like a fairy's, says Lakhmi Chand of Janti.
Between your legs is my organ, one feels an ax there.

Simple informal *holi*s inspired by daily village life, such as conflicts of husbands and wives or the adventures of *bhabhi*s and *dewar*s, give no idea of the mythological complexity and high artistic merit of published *holi*s based on tales from the epics and Puranas. Leatherworkers used booklets of *holi*s but performed only excerpts from them. There would not be nearly enough time to present a *holi* of some 70 pages in the course of a few evenings, in addition to skits, impersonations, and informal *holi*s.

To give an idea of published *holi*s, we sketch the myth and cite a few lines, translated, from a booklet titled "Holi Raja Harischandra" (King Harischandra's *holi*) (Singh, 1955?). The *holi* is divided into 20 parts, each a stage in the development of the story. Each part in turn is divided into several units that are convenient for recitation in the sense that each one marks a more or less distinct advance in the story. Thus, the Leatherworkers had available for presentation short excerpts that made dramatic sense.

The myth, recounted in the Markandeya and other Puranas, tells of the sage Vishwamitra's implacable persecution of King Harischandra (Dowson, 1891: 118–119, 367). Harischandra manages to provoke Vishwamitra, who strips him of wealth and kingdom, leaving him only his garments, wife, and son. To escape his oppressor, the king goes to the holy city of Kashi, but the relentless sage is waiting for him and demands additional gifts. The king has no other property, so his wife and child are sold to a Brahman and he himself, to a hideous low-caste Bhangi (Sweeper) who is the god Brahma in disguise.

Vishwamitra, disguised as a Brahman, goes to the garden of the house where the queen lives, turns into a serpent, and fatally bites the prince. The queen bewails her misfortune. She is penniless and cannot buy even a shroud. She tears her sari in two, using half to wrap her son. She carries him to the cremation ground, makes a pyre, and sets fire to the corpse. The cremation ground belongs to the Bhangi to whom her husband was sold. He has become the Bhangi's tax collector. He sees the smoke, throws the corpse out, and demands the tax before he can permit the cremation. He tells the queen that his orders are strict and he has to be loyal to his master.

The queen reminds him that the child is his own son and implores, "How can you be so hard-hearted? Take mercy and light your son's pyre yourself." The king replies that the world is meaningless. "No relative survives death. The brave soldiers of the world have no attachment to anyone. They hold to truth and die for it. Forsake truth, and you fall. Kingdom, wealth, and fame are all mere dreams. The enlightened ones stick to true dharma [right action]. In view of these verities, even a son is a trifle." At the end of the myth and after many twists in the plot, it is these ideas, truth and dharma, that are the salvation of the the king and queen, who ultimately reach heaven.

The confrontation of king and queen in the cremation ground is the setting for "Payment of tax at the cremation ground," one of the 20 parts of the *holi*. This episode has four units. Units are separated by a *tor* line. The leader of the chorus begins by reciting the *tor* line. The six terms, namely, *tor, lavni, jhulana, thola, alha*,[31] and *lahar* indicate different meters. The manner of recitation is determined by the meter of a line. The instruments have their own rhythms, which may or may not support the meter of the recitation. The chorus leader may modify the written text during the recitation. The excerpt below (Singh, 1955?) gives an idea of the arrangement of meters. The king is reprimanding the queen for trying to burn the corpse of her son without paying the tax.

Lavni	Don't you know this, listen you visitor.
	Corpses are taxed here, you were ignorant of this yet.
Jhulana	Those who come to burn corpses,
	They pay the coffin tax here.
	Afterward they light the fire.
	After we have taken five *taka*s.[32]

	The Bhangi's orders are strict.
	No one can avoid this.
	Five *taka*s is our tax.
	We exact that first.
Thola	Woman, you were trying to be deliberately smart.
	Without paying the tax, you lit the fire.
	Listen, oh stupid visitor.
	You felt no fear of me.
	My heart is filled with anger.
Alha	That five *taka*s is our tax, the whole world knows.
	Whether it is a poor beggar or a very wealthy man.
	No one is burned here without paying the tax, man or woman.
	Kala Bhangi's orders are harsh, they can never be waived, dear.
Lahar	Whose salt I eat, his welfare I want.
	If the Bhangi gets the news that you escaped the tax,
	He will trouble me.
Tor	I will take five *taka*s first, it cannot be reduced one pie.[33]

Nothing in the story of Harischandra would seem to connect it to Holi other than its value as entertainment. But that is enough. Holi is the time to have some fun, and a story featuring the trials of a king and queen, armed only with an unshakable commitment to truth, as they try to escape the machinations of a powerful, clever, and implacable enemy has an irresistible allure. Vishwamitra's final scheme is to kill the son of a merchant and place the corpse on the sleeping queen, giving the impression that she is a demon who eats corpses. Harischandra was summoned and was deceived. He trembled, but resolved to stick to the truth and kill the queen. She cried, "Am I not your queen. Who made me a demon?" He replied, "For truth I gave up my kingdom, for truth I threw my son's corpse away, for truth I call you a demon and for truth I shall slay you." At this point, the great god Brahma appeared and took the king and queen to his heart for their devotion to truth.

In 1978, playing Phalgun was still a well-established traditional entertainment, but it seemed to have faded a bit. For some women, playing Phalgun may have come to mean just getting together and singing. For instance, six days before Holi in the evening, we were just finishing an interview with a Jat man when some children came to announce that the Sweepers wanted us to come to their quarter to watch them play Phalgun. We hurried to the Sweeper quarter. A few women were sitting and singing in front of a house. That was all. We were puzzled—they had made a point of calling us, after all. Disappointed, we stood around talking for a few minutes and then went home.

The skits that we did see in 1978 had themes similar to those of 1959 but were simpler and less clever. The performers were young women, but the ideas for the skits were suggested by old women. In 1959, the young performers knew all the skits and needed no guidance from older women. We were particularly impressed by the absence of the husband, wife, and mother-in-law triangle from the skits of 1978. The mother-in-law did not appear in any of the skits that we saw. Skits in which the

FIGS. 63–66. Holi, 1978. Women playing Phalgun. *Clockwise from upper left:* A woman with a cloth under her shirt to feign pregnancy approaches another woman to invite her to a feast (figs. 63–64). Suddenly she has to give birth. Figure 65 shows the woman (left, center) reclining on her back, her face completely veiled. After giving birth, she happily holds her "child" (fig. 66).

presence of a mother-in-law would have introduced a web of subtle interaction instead featured only a husband and wife. For example, the "Plowman" piece was not performed. In the "Plowman," a wife manipulates the three-way relationship so that she can demand a water buffalo from her husband. In a 1978 skit, there is no mother-in-law and a wife simply asks her husband for presents.

We watched some Brahman and Barber women playing Phalgun three days before Holi. The evening began with some singing and dancing. Then the women put on several short pieces. One featured a husband and wife. The main idea was that the wife made demands and the husband yielded. First, the wife asks her husband for a necklace, and he replies that he will sell his land. She repeats her demand, and he replies that he will have to go to a neighboring town to buy one. He asks her where she will wear it. She points to her bosom. Then she asks for earrings. He says, "These days are bad. Someone will steal them and cut your ears." She replies, "No, just get them this once." Then she wants a gold ring. He says, "Now I have no tomatoes. The one acre in which tomatoes were planted is spoiled." Unimpressed by his problem, she points to the finger where she will wear the ring. Then she wants a wristwatch and points to her wrist where she will wear it. The skit continues with various other demands. There is a song refrain that is repeated after each demand.

The skit involving caste relationships where two women played mother and daughter that we saw in 1959 was enacted in 1978. Two young girls played the roles. They ran back and forth in a lane between two rows of women. The dialogue was similar to what we had heard some 20 years earlier. The mother asked her daughter where she had gone. She replied, "To the Merchant to buy sweets." This basic line of dialogue was repeated for almost all of the castes of the village (fig. 62). This version was less clever than the earlier one, in which the mother criticized her daughter for having abandoned younger siblings.

Pregnancy and childbirth were the basic themes of two skits. In the first one, a performer dressed as a pregnant woman. She had stuffed a cloth underneath her clothing. Then she repeatedly approached another woman, asking her to do various tasks. The idea seemed to be that the pregnant woman could not do the work because of her condition. In the final scene, the woman gave birth. She lay on her back and other women pulled the cloth from under her clothing and threw it into the air.

The second skit with a pregnancy theme seemed intended to poke fun at a Watercarrier family. The skit was enacted in front of the family's house. A Brahman woman stuffed a cloth under her clothing to feign pregnancy. Playing a Watercarrier, she ran to a group of women and girls to invite people to come to tea at her house after she delivered her child. She made several trips back and forth to issue invitations. Finally, her child was born in the middle of this activity (figs. 63–66). The reason for thinking that the skit was aimed at the Watercarrier family is that a young wife of the household had a very sudden delivery while she was bathing. Also, the woman who played the role of the pregnant Watercarrier was the woman who came to cut the umbilical cord. The villagers immortalized the event by nicknaming the boy, "Came Out By Himself."

We were co-opted for a very brief skit. A peddler and her assistant tried to sell us various implements. We offered only a few paise. Apparently, our response was what a villager would have done, which seemed to please the women.

Another short skit mimicked a husband and wife having sexual relations. Two performers covered themselves with a sheet and were bent over back to back with their derrières touching.

One skit involved a play on rhyming words, *jaith* (husband's elder brother) and *pet* (stomach, also pregnancy or the womb). A woman who was hard of hearing was cooking some fine food, apparently anticipating the arrival of her *jaith*. A second woman played the role of the *chulha* (stove). She sat with her legs folded under her and her head bent down to the ground. A girl came to tell the deaf woman that her *jaith* had come. The woman misunderstood and asked who was the pregnant woman and why had she come.

FIG. 67. *(above)* Holi, 1978, the preceding day. Procession of women and children to the shrine of the Panch Pir.

FIG. 68. *(right)* Holi, 1978, the preceding day. Women offering water to the Panch Pir.

The themes of pregnancy, childbirth, and sexual relations were prominent in these skits. Several young men were watching and periodically the women would ask them to leave, but they stayed. An older Brahman man watched for a few minutes, but he was too senior to stay and the women chased him away.

The day before Holi in 1978, we saw Leatherworker women make offerings at the shrine of the Panch Pir (figs. 67–71). The women told us that they performed Sayyid (saint) worship (or mother goddess worship) before Holi and Diwali. A group of about a dozen women and some 20 girls and boys, singing steadily, paraded from

FIG. 69. *(above)* Holi, 1978, the preceding day. Woman offering a garland of marigolds to the Panch Pir. The woman to her right prepares to light a lamp.

FIG. 70. *(left)* Holi, 1978, the preceding day. Women lighting ceramic lamps fueled by ghee at the shrine of the Panch Pir.

the village to the shrine. On their heads, the women were carrying dishes and trays that contained the ceremonial offerings: *churma*, *batasha*s, gur, incense, burning dung cakes, marigolds, several small lamps, ghee, and a few small coins. A few women had cloths, but we failed to notice what they did with them. No cloths are seen in the photographs of the offerings that we took at the shrine. The women also carried pitchers of water; some contained what looked like a mixture of milk and water. Arriving at the shrine, the women first walked around it spilling water continuously from their pitchers. Then they lit their lamps and placed their offerings on top of the shrine and on the sloping sides where there were niches suitable for gur and dung cakes.

After the offering, the women distributed *prasad*: *batasha*s, *churma*, and small pieces of gur. Then they and the children sat at the edge of the path to eat the *prasad* and to chat. Two dogs that had been lurking nearby climbed the shrine and devoured all the edibles. After 10 or 15 minutes, everyone started back to the village. They returned singing just as they had come, only there was less singing on the way home. On the way they stopped at a ridge where two women made an offering of *churma* and gur to a deity that was probably Gurgaonwali Mata. When the women arrived at their houses, they splashed some water on either side of the doorway before entering.

A Brahman man who happened by told us that on Holi many people from all castes make offerings at the shrine. The worship takes place during the day, followed by the worship at the Holi bonfire in the evening. We never saw any other group worshipping at the shrine of the Panch Pir either on Holi or on the preceding day. However, we were busy with the activity in the village and at the bonfires and could have missed it.

Events on Holi itself, the day of the full moon, unfold in three phases. In the afternoon, women make offerings at the pyre. After dark, the pyre is lit and games for children and youngsters may be organized. Later in the evening, the Leatherworkers entertain villagers in their quarter with dancing and *holi*s. We begin with a description of the preparations for the day and then offer a general sketch of the worship at the pyre, combining our observations from the festivals of 1958, 1959, and 1978. We next describe each of the three festivals in turn. The general sketch highlights the salient features of the worship but fails to give a feeling for the day, which is recovered in the individual accounts. Moreover, the village had changed from the 1950s to the 1970s, and Holi had changed accordingly.

The principal change was that the single bonfire for the whole village in the 1950s had become two bonfires in the 1970s. The village was more populous. Many more villagers were well educated, and their interests reached outward from the village much more than was the case 20 years earlier. Village unity, still very strong, nonetheless suffered. The two bonfires of 1978 can be seen as a symbol of changing times.

Preparation for the offering to the *holi* or to Holi Mata (the bonfire is called *holi*, or sometimes Holi Mata) begins a few days before the event. Women make small dung cakes in the form of rings to use as part of the offering. The smaller ones (*barkaley*) have an outer diameter of about 2 in. and an inner diameter of about 1 in. The larger ones (*dhal*) have comparable dimensions of about 4 in. and 1 in.

The Holi pyre consists mainly of the branches of trees. Most of the combustibles are collected by adolescents and young men, but we have seen children of many castes stripping branches from nearby trees to add to the pyre. A Brahman woman told us that Brahmans begin to collect dung cakes for the Holi bonfire on Basant Panchami. Basant Panchami (Spring Fifth) on Magh *sudi* 5, more than a month before Holi, is a festival for the worship of Saraswati, the Goddess of Learning. It is her birthday. It is also considered a holiday marking the arrival of spring (Sivananda, 1993: 57). Although Basant Panchami is an important Hindu festival, we learned of no one in Shanti Nagar who observed it by worshipping Saraswati. The only notice taken of the day seems to be its connection to Holi (Wadley, 1975: 179, n. 18; 212). On this day villagers begin to collect fuel for the Holi pyre. Lewis (1958: 228) reported, "Starting on Basant Panchami wood is collected for Holi, particularly a pole or 'foundation stick' for the bonfire."

People plaster their houses as needed in the days before Holi. On the day itself women plaster their kitchens, bathe and wash their hair, dress in colorful new clothes, and stain their hands red with henna (*mehndi*). At least one man also stained his hands. As on every festival, observance varies from person to person. Some women do not stain their hands or make the small dung cakes customary for the festival. Some women fast. Holi occurs on the day of the full moon (Purinmashi). Thus, women have a choice of how to conduct their fast. Women who observe Holi and also fast because of Purinmashi do not break their fast until moonrise. Women who take the day only as Holi eat and drink after making their offering at the *holi*. Holi is the occasion for a festive meal with halva, *khir*, and puris. Some women ignore Holi altogether while fasting for Purinmashi.

In the afternoon, groups of women parade to the pyre to make their offerings. Each group represents a single caste, or most women of the group are of the same caste. The odd member from a different caste is a neighbor or friend of the other women. The ritual varies only slightly from group to group. The women carry a pitcher of water and, on their heads, a platter with the ceremonial offerings: wheat, wheat flour, gram, *batasha*s, a pice, turmeric, gur, and string. Their children who accompany them carry garlands of the special dung cakes prepared for Holi. The women tie a string on a branch of the *holi* or entirely around the pyre; throw their garlands of dung cakes on it; pour some water on the ground; mix turmeric with water and put a tilak on the ground, on the dung cakes, and on all the participants; make seven piles of wheat flour on the ground and pour water over them; place gur on the ground; fold their hands before the pyre; and circle it while emptying their pitchers of water. Sometimes women bring a little green gram and a few wheat stalks to place on the *holi*. After the offerings at the *holi*, daughters-in-law press the legs of mothers-in-law and receive the usual blessing, "Live long, have children."

In 1958, we had to split our attention between Holi rituals and an important multivillage panchayat meeting that was held in the afternoon (S. Freed and R. Freed, 1976: 198). Politics at that time was the province of men. Holi was a convenient day for the panchayat meeting. It is a two-day national holiday, which meant that men with urban jobs were on leave and could attend the panchayat. Besides, men were not involved in the afternoon ritual, which was entirely the affair of women and children. We attended the meeting, but also managed to see some of the activity at the pyre.

As we were watching the panchayat proceedings at the Jat men's meeting house, a group of Brahman women dressed in colorful skirts and headcloths came singing down the street accompanied by a crowd of children. We followed them. The women were fasting and had bathed and washed their hair before the ceremony. They carried a pitcher of water and a tray on their heads with wheat, wheat flour, turmeric, and gur. The children carried garlands of dung cakes to be thrown on the pyre. At the *holi*, located just outside the village, the women placed gur and wheat flour on the ground in a circle around the pyre. They folded their hands in worship. They then circled the pyre, outside the circle of gur and flour, pouring water on the ground. Circling is a ritual of protection that takes place in many ceremonies. Although it was not done by this particular group of women, another circling ritual on Holi is to tie a string around the pyre.

In the evening we returned to the pyre. By this time it was a big pile of brush decorated with garlands of dung cakes. A string was tied around it. In 1958 there was only one *holi* for the village, and we were told that "the whole village will be there" when the pyre was lit. In fact, perhaps 150 people were there, the great majority children. Everyone was quite joyous. The children played with skyrockets, firecrackers, and sparklers. After waiting a while, two of our companions, Jat men, went away, saying that nothing was happening. Indeed, everyone was just standing around. Finally, a Brahman lit the fire, but no one paid much attention. There was no ceremony. About this time one of our Jat friends returned and started to organize games with the children, which they played with considerable spirit. There was a game called "goat and lion," (described in Ratta, 1961: 168) and then some wrestling among the small boys. The games were well handled and little bad feeling developed. Activity at the fire ended with a game of *kabaddi*, and then everyone returned to the village.

In 1959 we watched six groups of women performing the ritual at the *holi*. One

FIG. 71. Holi, 1978, the preceding day. Dogs consuming the offerings at the Panch Pir shrine after the women had left.

group consisted of about half a dozen Brahman women and their children. Another group was composed of the women and children from six Brahman families and the daughters of the Baniya Merchant. Only one Merchant lived in the village in the 1950s, and women from that family usually joined Brahman women when engaged in public rituals. Likewise, the woman from the only Chhipi family came with two Potter women. Worshipping with friends and neighbors of other castes was a common practice for the women of small castes, especially those represented by a single family. The mixed group of Brahmans and Merchants performed the standard ritual, except that no one tied a string around a branch on the pyre. Instead of strings of dung cakes, the girls threw pieces of dung cake on the *holi*. They sang a song praising Ram, Mahatma Gandhi, and Nehru. The Potter and Chhipi group went through the standard ritual, adding some green gram and wheat to their offering.

A Barber woman and her daughter came alone. The Barbers' ritual was quite similar to that of the Brahmans except that they brought along neither dung cakes nor gur. The mother poured some water on the ground, made seven piles of wheat flour on the moist spot, mixed some turmeric with water and put a tilak on her daughter's forehead, then sprinkled water around the piles of wheat flour and around the pyre. She was fasting and would drink water after returning home. Later in the day, she planned to give flour and gur to any Brahman woman.

We were told that people offer water to the sun after returning from making their offerings at the pyre. Also, some people make offerings to various mother goddesses. Kanti Mata and Gurgaonwali Mata were mentioned specifically. Household gods and ancestors may be worshipped. The Chuhra Sweepers sacrifice a cock to the caste deity (fig. 31). We saw none of these offerings.

Most castes were represented at the pyre. We saw Brahmans, Jats, Merchants, Bairagis, Barbers, Chhipis, and Potters. We did not see any women of the two lowest castes, the Leatherworkers and the Sweepers. However, in the evening, some Sweeper women came for the lighting of the bonfire. They stood farther away from the *holi* than did members of the higher castes and kept very much to themselves.

At about 7 P.M. we made a round of the village. Children were playing and setting off firecrackers, but there was no organized activity. Some people were still cooking and eating. We went to the *holi*. The bonfires in two neighboring villages were lit and made an impressive sight. At about the same time, adults began to arrive. The children had started to gather earlier and were playing. The crowd grew steadily. Shortly after 8:00 P.M. a Brahman man touched off the bonfire without any warning or ceremony. The many groups of women who came to watch the fire brought stalks of wheat. They roasted the ears in the fire, ate some, and distributed the rest. They told us that it is a religious act. It is quite clearly an offering of first fruits. A Brahman woman pointed out that sparks and smoke from the fire rose high in the air, foretelling a good year for men and bullocks.

A Brahman woman ingeniously reinterpreted the first-fruits offerings of wheat and dung cakes to bring them into accord with the myth of Prahlad and Holika. When Prahlad and Holika entered the bonfire, King Hiranyakashipu stationed a guard of soldiers armed with swords and shields around the pyre. The Brahman woman said that the wheat stalks represent swords and the dung cakes stand for shields.

The boys were playing games. A man was refereeing a game of *kabaddi* played by Jat and Brahman boys. A prominent Jat man, whom we call Tippler, arrived and suggested some wrestling. He had been drinking, as had some other men. Two men wrestled to no decision. Then a Jat man said that he would wrestle anyone, with the exception of one man whom he named. Somehow, a man from another village entered the picture who was much too strong for the Jat who had issued the challenge. An argument erupted. Tippler took off his shirt and offered to wrestle the man from out of town. He said that he made his offer because the local Jat had issued an open challenge and now he had to step in to wrestle the stranger. Tippler protested that the way the situation had developed was not his fault. A Brahman retorted that his fault was to take off his shirt. Tippler exploded, shouting at the Brahman that the affair was none of his business. We left the pyre. We heard the next morning that the two men had not wrestled but only argued.

We walked back to our quarters. Women were getting ready to present their skits. There was a large crowd of Brahman, Jat, and Bairagi women in front of our house. It was about twice as big as the groups that had formed before Holi. The women from the house of an elderly Jat who was probably the most powerful man in the village had come to watch Phalgun playing for the first time, and the performers paid them considerable attention. A few pieces were put on again because these women had not seen them before.

Four skits were presented in front of our house on this occasion. The first one featured two Jat women playing husband and wife. Seated on the ground facing one another, they raised their right and left arms alternately, making threatening gestures. Occasionally they advanced toward each other in a menacing manner. The women spectators, gathered in a circle around the performers, were singing. We collected the song for this skit (see p. 210).

For the second skit, the women formed two groups. One group said that they had lost their sheet at the Washerman's and wanted to know what the second group would give to replace it. The second group replied that they would give their father-in-law. The first group declined because he was too old and worthless. Then the first group offered their mother-in-law. She was refused on the same grounds. Then they began to offer one caste after another, but each offer was rejected. Finally the second group offered the Americans. The first group accepted while making it quite clear that the Americans were not worth so much as the sheet.

The women formed two rows for the third skit. There was supposedly some kind of an animal sitting on the roof of the house of a prominent Jat, and two women, both Jats, were going to scare it away. They ran back and forth in the lane between the rows of women, beating shoes over and under their legs as they ran.

For their fourth skit, the women were arranged as in the third one, but this time the two performers sang alternate lines based on common household tasks, such as: "I am cooking the milk. I am making the curds. I am churning the butter. I am selling the ghee." As in the third skit, the two women ran back and forth between the lines of singing women clapping shoes as they sang. After this skit a Jat woman dressed up as a man and imitated a cloth merchant. We walked around the high-caste side of the village but saw no other groups playing Phalgun.

Two groups were active in the Potters' quarter. In the main lane about eight Potter women were playing. The Chhipi's wife and children, who lived nearby, were also there. Two women were dancing skillfully. Two teenagers just learning to dance were trying to imitate the older women. The other women watched the dancers and sang. At one point a black cloth was spread over two children, and this "elephant" just walked around.

The other group of Potters, about six women and girls, was performing in another lane. Three of them were sitting and singing. The others danced wildly and seemed completely oblivious to everyone except themselves. They were having a great time. There was no drama or plot, just uninhibited action.

We moved on to the Leatherworker quarter where the largest crowd had gathered. All castes were present. The Leatherworker performers were all men and quite professional. We made note of only one skit, a transaction between a Washerman and his client. The man playing the client counted the clothes that he was giving to the Washerman. In the process, he made frequent references to items connected to male and female private parts, such as, a woman's underwear, a cloth stained with feces, and clothes that were worn around the buttocks. These allusions invariably raised laughter. A Jat gave a rupee to the Leatherworkers for their fine performance.

A few men from other castes sang during the evening at the Leatherworkers' quarter. We have already mentioned the young Jat who sang a *holi* that he had composed. Then two Sweepers sang a song in praise of Nehru and Gandhi for abolishing caste disabilities and untouchability. The Leatherworkers followed this optimistic song with a pessimistic piece to the effect that times have changed but bad and dishonest people have not.

We left the Leatherworkers at about 11:00 P.M. At about 1:00 A.M., there was a lunar eclipse. The village dogs made an infernal racket. The Sweepers went through the village collecting grain. Several Sweepers came to our house, where the mother of our landlord was sitting on the doorstep ready with grain. No one got past her to reach our apartment. She said that we were sleeping.

In 1978 there were two pyres (*holi*s) for Holi. One *holi* was mainly for the Brahmans, but their neighbors, the Watercarriers, also used it. The other one, which was basically a Jat *holi*, served the other castes. The two *holi*s probably represented heightened tension between the Jats and Brahmans. If indeed this was the case, we can only speculate about the causes. A prominent Jat had murdered a Brahman, and the case could have left a general residue of ill will. Also the Jats and Brahmans competed in panchayat elections.

In the afternoon we visited both pyres to watch the ritual. At the Jat pyre, three groups of women arrived almost when we did, shortly after 2:00 P.M. The ritual was similar for each group and closely resembled the ritual practiced in the 1950s. The women had trays containing turmeric, ber, gur, wheat flour, string, and ears of wheat. They carried pitchers of water and garlands of dung cakes. The women threw the garlands on the pyre, circled the pyre while pouring water from their pitchers, presented their offerings, and made seven piles of wheat flour, six piles in a tight circle and one pile in the center (figs. 72–74). They put a tilak on the center pile. Then a woman tied a thread completely encircling the pyre. Finally, the younger women

FIG. 72. *(left)* Holi, 1978. Woman places dung cakes on the Holi pyre. The top of a woman's head that partially obscured the pyre to the lower right of the standing woman was removed from this photograph. The empty area was repaired with part of a similar photograph taken from the same angle a few seconds later.

FIG. 73. *(below)* Holi, 1978. Women and children circle the Holi pyre, sprinkling water from their pitchers.

pressed the legs of the older women. After we finished watching these three groups, we were surrounded by some young men with whom we got into an aimless discussion. As we saw no more women approaching, we went to the Brahman pyre.

We followed a large group of Brahman women and children from the village to the *holi*. They sang on the way. The song was not special for Holi; it was a song for Ram, Lakshman, and Sita, which was sung on other occasions. The women carried the usual wheat flour, gur, turmeric, pitchers of water, and garlands of dung cakes. They poured a little water on the ground and made seven piles of flour. They put tilaks on the children and the garlands. The children threw the garlands on the pyre. The women circled the pyre pouring water from their pitchers. Daughters-in-law pressed the feet of their mothers-in-law. The women distributed batashas and *khil* as *prasad* and then returned singing to their houses.

We saw another group of six women and children at the Brahman pyre. They represented several related families. The women were carrying neatly arranged trays with ears of wheat, turmeric, wheat flour, and sugar. A girl carried garlands of dung cakes, which she threw on the pyre. We concentrated on one woman as she made her offering. First she took off her shoes and then washed her hands. She made seven piles of wheat flour and put a tilak on each. Then she put a tilak on a child. All the women circled the pyre pouring water from their pitchers. The younger women pressed the legs of the older women. Before leaving, the women put tilaks on the foreheads of all the children.

While the women were in the middle of their ritual, a Brahman woman arrived complaining bitterly that someone had thrown a mango log belonging to her onto the pyre. The servant of her family was with her. She poked into the pyre and identified the mango log and two other large pieces of wood that were hers. She and her servant extracted all three. They rolled the large mango log to one side away from the pyre and carried the other two logs back to their house (fig. 75). Mean-

FIG. 74. Holi, 1978, at the pyre in the afternoon. Women offer seven piles of wheat flour.

while, the woman was complaining in a loud voice, as was her custom. After this woman and her servant left, another woman came and removed some branches from the pyre.

Two young Brahman men, 19 and 20 years old, watched what the women were doing. Declaring that people were going to remove all the wood from the pyre, they settled the matter by lighting the pyre on the spot in the middle of the afternoon. It all happened quickly in front of us. We couldn't believe that the two young men would start the fire, and we failed to take a photo until the blaze was well begun (fig. 76). The pyre was blazing fiercely in about 30 seconds.

A crowd began to gather, all of whom were Brahmans except for two Jat men and a Barber boy. A Brahman man arrived and berated the servant who had returned for not saving other pieces of wood that belonged to his employer. The Brahman accused the Barber boy of having taken the wood, which made the boy angry. Then people said that adults had stolen the wood. As the fire burned down, three other large logs that also belonged the the family of the Brahman woman became visible.

People believed that the early ignition of the *holi* was a bad omen, and the older people were angry. A few practical girls were roasting ears of wheat in the fire. We commented that 20 years earlier, it would have been next to impossible for youngsters to light the *holi* prematurely, to which a man replied, "No child is under the control of the parents. Why talk of 20 years? Even four or five years ago, such a thing would not have been possible." It was interesting that no one scolded the two young men who lit the fire. One man blamed the victim for not having stored his wood securely. Two men criticized children in general. The owner of the big mango log arrived and began to complain angrily that someone had stolen it and thrown it on the pyre. Trying to calm the man, someone broke in to say that children had done it. The victim replied that it was not the work of children.

The log was said to be easily worth Rs. 100. The owner said that he had willingly given six big pieces of wood for the *holi*. But he did not like the idea that someone took his mango log without his consent. A man said that such disputes over property could lead to factions and fights in the Brahman community. Another man endorsed this point of view and added that the guilty children should be badly beaten. To insist that children were the culprits had the effect of defusing the situation. However, the log was heavy and we think that the owner was correct. The theft was not the work of children.

We remarked that now everyone would go to the Jat pyre. A young man said that this would not be possible and another pyre would be made. Indeed, people were already gathering material for a pyre. Brahman and Watercarrier boys went to each Brahman house and asked for fodder and sticks. Every family contributed, and in an hour the *holi* was ready. The children gathered around the *holi* to protect it, fearing that someone might come and light the fire prematurely.

We asked why one fire would not be sufficient. People said that anyone can make offerings at a pyre, but that people from "this [Brahman] side" of the village used this pyre and that people from "that [mainly Jat] side" used the other pyre. They explained that it was too far for the people of that side to come to this pyre. Yet many Jats lived closer to the Brahman pyre than did many Brahmans. Without offering any explanation, one man said that it would not be possible for people from "this side" to go to the other pyre. One or two people commented that people no longer have faith in Holi. We had heard similar comments on other occasions. We are not sure what the comment means, but suspect that it refers to a weakening of the socially unifying aspect of Holi rather than to its ritual elements. In any case, the sentiment about the necessity of separate fires was rather intense.

In the evening we watched the firing of the *holi*s. At the Jat pyre there was a small crowd, principally children. A Bairagi lit the pyre without any ceremony. Two young Jats then wrestled for a few minutes. Although the afternoon worship by the groups of women and children was as well attended as it had been in the 1950s, the evening activities were an attenuated version of what we had seen 20 years earlier. Perhaps the lunar eclipse that began at 8:03 P.M. put an early end to the evening's activities. The pyres had to be lit before the eclipse began.

Knowing that the two pyres might be ignited at almost the same time because of the eclipse, one of us had gone to the Brahman pyre while the rest of us were at the Jat *holi*. As our contingent at the Jat pyre hurried toward the Brahman pyre, a red glow in the sky told us that we had just missed the lighting. A Brahman man said that he lit the fire after having recited the Gayatri mantra. There still was a crowd at the bonfire, composed mainly of young people and children. Periodically, the crowd would shout, "Hail to Holi" and "Hail to Prahlad." One man wanted to wrestle, but he chose a much smaller opponent, so the smaller man declined.

Stationing someone at the Brahman pyre turned out to be a wise move. Our assistant had accompanied a group of Brahman girls who went singing to the pyre. A few drunken Jat boys there tried to prevent the lighting of the pyre. The Jat and Brahman boys scuffled for about five minutes, and then the Jats went away. According to this account, it was not the Brahman man who lit the fire but some Brahman boys.

We returned from the Brahman *holi* and watched from our terrace as the eclipse developed. No women were playing Phalgun in the street, and there was no activity in the Leatherworker quarter. The eclipse apparently had put an end to the usual evening entertainment. We decided to call it a night when several men came to visit. The men had been drinking, and one of them, whom we have nicknamed Emotional (S. Freed and R. Freed, 1987: 62–63), became aggressive so we excused ourselves and went into our apartment.

The next morning we learned that Emotional had made a scene in the street. He claimed to have come only to receive some sweets but that we had barred the door. One of our assistants was upset by the scene. We tried to reassure him by pointing out that people like Emotional were to be found everywhere and were simply one of the hazards of fieldwork.

We decided to try to smooth things over by giving Emotional a gift of *batasha*s, but were strongly, and quite rightly, advised not to do it. People pointed out that he would be drunk, for it was Dulhendi. The warning proved to be prescient. Later in the morning when we were sitting with a Jat man and watching some people playing *holi*, a man was thrown, or staggered, out of a house. It was Emotional, drunk as predicted. Our companion commented that Emotional's lineage was the worst in the village.

On Holi, families send the gift known as *sidha* to married daughters and sisters, if they are currently living with their in-laws. Some people said that if married sisters and daughters are visiting their parents, they receive no gifts, but other villagers pointed out that gifts are given to them when they leave their parents' house to return to their husbands. *Sidha* is traditionally a gift of food or the money to buy food, but clothing is sometimes included. Lewis (1958: 355) defined *sidha* as a gift of rice, gur and ghee, and most of the *sidhas* recounted by our informants in the 1950s conformed to this definition. *Sidha* is sent chiefly on four festivals: Holi, Diwali, Tij, and Makar Sankranti. Some informants added other festivals, principally Salono, to the list.

The value of *sidha* varies depending not only on the wealth of a family but also on the generosity of the family head. A young woman married into a wealthy Jat family received a suit of clothes (*tirh*), a headcloth, five seers of sugar, one seer of rice, two rupees for more rice, one seer of ghee, and one rupee for glass bracelets. Women traditionally buy new glass bracelets on Holi. However, another Jat family in quite comfortable circumstances sent only two rupees to each married sister. A moderately well-off Brahman family sent a married daughter ten seers of rice, five seers of sugar, and one rupee for ghee. A poor Leatherworker gave his sister three rupees for Holi, one rupee each for rice, sugar, and ghee. A poor Sweeper family sent a married daughter two seers of rice, one and one-half seers of sugar, and one rupee for ghee. In proportion to family resources, the gifts of these two low-caste families probably exceeded the *sidhas* of more wealthy families.

The foregoing *sidhas* were all from the 1950s. The only *sidha* that we recorded in 1978 was not the traditional gift of rice, sugar, and ghee. A Brahman woman received sweets, oranges, bananas, and 10 rupees. However, the money could have been intended for the purchase of the three traditional foods, for in the 1950s money was often sent for this purpose, especially for the purchase of ghee. This Brahmani's

FIG. 75. *(left)* Holi, 1978. Brahman woman and her servant recover stolen log from the pyre.

FIG. 76. *(right)* Holi, 1978. Brahman pyre ablaze in the afternoon, as teenage boys protest the removal of the log.

parents had sent her a sari for the first Holi after her marriage, but not after the first one. Concerning this custom, Bahadur (1995: 42) wrote, "Holi is a festival when new clothes are made for a married daughter and her children. There is a special *sari* made for the daughter known as *dandia* . . . which is a must for a married girl."

Barbers and Sweepers receive gifts and payments from their patrons on Holi and Diwali. If a Barber carries his patron's gift to the recipient, he is given one rupee. This is a payment under the jajmani system and not a gift. Sweepers are given some of the festive food that their patrons cook for the festival and may also receive old clothing if they ask for it. Although Sweepers do not do any specific work for their patrons on Holi, as do the Barbers, their gifts are nonetheless payments under the jajmani system. In addition, if an eclipse takes place on Holi, Sweepers receive the customary gift of grain.

Two Holi rituals common in other villages either do not take place in Shanti Nagar or survive in an attenuated form. One ritual involves the planting of the main pole of the Holi bonfire. In the village of Indrapur, in eastern Uttar Pradesh far from Shanti Nagar, Henry (1988: 123) reported an elaborate ritual. A multicaste crowd of men and boys parades cheering and singing to the accompaniment of drums and cymbals to the site of the bonfire. Older men erect a tall branch and bury auspicious symbols at its base. Dung cakes are packed around the branch. Everyone circles the branch five times, singing *phagua*s, songs sung only at Holi, and clapping in time. The crowd then returns to the point from which it started and continues to sing.

In a village farther west near Lucknow, Majumdar (1958: 260) reported, "In the evening [of Basant Panchami] is the ceremony of the planting of a branch of the castor plant. . . . Once the branch is planted, firewood is heaped around it for burning on *Holi* day." Still farther west in Delhi Union Territory, Lewis noted that the main pole of the Holi pyre is selected on Basant Panchami and boys start to collect wood for the bonfire. He made no mention of a ritual. Ratta (1961: 166) mentioned that a "foundation pole" is selected on Basant Panchami, but described no associated ritual. Nautiyal (1961: 161) also noted the erection of the "Holi pole" (*danda*) on Basant Panchami but did not describe any ritual. The obvious phallic symbolism of an upright pole planted in the earth supports an interpretation of Holi as a fertility and first-fruits festival.

Although one of our informants told us that the collection of dung cakes and other combustibles for the pyre began on Basant Panchami, we learned of no ritual involving a foundation pole. We never peered into the interior of a pyre looking for details of its construction. However, when the Brahman pyre burned down during the afternoon of Holi, we saw no sign of any large foundation pole, although a thin pole would have been consumed. It is possible that the mango log recovered by its owner was intended to serve as a foundation pole, for it was large and impressive. However, it was not set upright in the pyre. In any case, it was not so sacred that its owner hesitated to retrieve it.

The second ritual, absent in Shanti Nagar but observed elsewhere, takes place at the lighting of the pyre. The only trace of such a ritual is the villagers' claim that the time for igniting the bonfire is set by a Brahman. A Brahman would consult an almanac for the time when an eclipse began so that a pyre would be touched off before that moment. But otherwise, the igniting of a pyre was a casual affair. If villagers observed a particular moment for lighting their pyres, the bonfires in all villages would blaze up more or less together. However, in 1959, bonfires in nearby villages were burning well before the pyre in Shanti Nagar was lit. As for a ritual, none took place in Shanti Nagar. Henry (1988: 124) spoke of a brief fire sacrifice in his village. Channa (1984: 137) described a rather elaborate ritual: a puja, offerings, and a circumambulation of the fire while the participants shout "Hail to Ganga Mother" and "Hail to Prahlad."

A third feature of Holi in Shanti Nagar, and in other Delhi villages, caught our attention as being a bit different from the festival as observed farther to the east. Holi in Shanti Nagar is chiefly a festival for women. Men play a lesser role there than in Indrapur (Henry, 1988) or in Mohana (Majumdar, 1958). Boys help to collect fuel, a man or boy touches off the pyre, and men or boys wrestle and play *kabaddi* in the evening. But except for the performances of the Leatherworker men, the activities of women dominate the fortnight preceding the full moon, and women perform all the pujas at the pyre in the afternoon. Women receive the gifts (*sidha*) and of course do all the cooking and household work for the day.

Dulhendi (Big Holi)

Dulhendi is celebrated the day after Holi, on Chaitra *badi* 1. The common names of the two festivals, Little Holi and Big Holi, suggest a close connection between them that goes beyond propinquity. However, if there is a link, it is weak and probably relatively recent. It could be argued that there is a tenuous connection of both Holi and Dulhendi with Krishna legends, and hence with each other. Although the Holi bonfire is usually associated with the cremation of the demoness, Holika, Marriott (1966:209) reported another mythology of Holi "from many other localities [than Kishan Garhi] . . . ." The bonfire is said to represent the cremation, not of Holika, but of another demoness, Putana, whom King Kansa sent to kill the infant Krishna with her poisonous mother's milk (see also Crooke, 1968, 2: 313–314; S. Gupta, 1991: 40–41; B. N. Sharma, 1978: 66). As for Dulhendi, its licentiousness recalls the cavorting of Krishna with the milkmaids (*gopis*), especially with Radha. The myth evokes devotion to God (bhakti) and love of a personal deity. "Radha's longing for Krishna . . . is thought to symbolize the soul's intense longing for union with God. Radha's willingness to commit adultery was thought to express the ultimate priority which must be accorded to love for God" (Henry, 1988: 119). However, the Sanskritic embellishments of Holi and Dulhendi no doubt took place well after the beginnings of those festivals.

The independence of Holi and Dulhendi, historically and ritually, is suggested both by their dissimilarity and by ritual details. Holi features considerable ritual activity ending with the bonfire as the conclusion of the festival. There are no loose ends to be taken care of the next day—no fast to be broken, no ritual remains that must be ceremonially discarded, and no symbol to be affixed to an empty ritual site. The meaning of Holi is clear. It is a ritual of purification, protection, fertility, renewal, and an offering of first fruits in thanksgiving.

What is the meaning of Dulhendi? There is no ritual at all. The day lacks any focus, such as the bonfire, processions, or the worship of village shrines or household deities. Instead, the day is devoted solely to personal interaction, much of it violent and seemingly chaotic.[34] Therefore, the study of Dulhendi requires an explanation of the structure and meaning of violent interaction.

Two principal interpretations have been proposed. First, Dulhendi is a festival of love. Second, the essence of the festival is social renewal. The established order is overturned for the day. Then the normal order reasserts itself. The day of licentiousness is thought to release accumulated tensions and make the constraints of everyday life bearable for another year.

An interpretation of the rowdiness that dominates Dulhendi as an expression of love may be viewed with considerable scepticism. A beating is not affectionate behavior. Yet the villagers of Kishan Garhi where Marriott worked offer just that explanation. After the uproar that began on Dulhendi eve and continued through the next morning, Marriott called attention to his aching shins and the bruises of his friends and increduously asked, "A festival of love?" "Yes!" replied his friends. "Just as the milkmaids loved Lord Krishna, so our wives show their love for us . . . [by beating us]" (Marriott, 1966: 204–205). This gentle judgment seemed at odds with the terror of Dulhendi eve and morning. The night was especially bad. (For a similar description, see Tandon [1968: 96–97].)

> [G]angs of young people were . . . pursuing each other down the lanes. . . . I felt the thud of large mud bricks thrown over my courtyard wall. . . . I was awakened . . . by the crash of the old year's pots breaking against my outer door. . . . Pandemonium now reigned: a shouting mob of boys called on me by name from the street and demanded that I come out. . . . [A]nyone who emerged was being pelted with bucketfuls of mud and cow-dung water. . . . Household walls were being scaled, loose doors broken open . . . . Relatively safe in a new building with strong doors and high walls, I escaped an immediate lynching. . . . I was summoned . . . to give first aid to an injured woman. A thrown water pot had [hit] her head . . . . [A]s I returned from attending to the lacerated scalp, there was an intermittent hail of trash and dust on my shoulders . . . [Marriott, 1966: 202–203].

Dulhendi clearly has a dark side. Growse reported a sham battle between men and women, the latter armed with long, heavy bamboo bludgeons. "Not unfrequently blood is drawn, but an accident of the kind is regarded rather as an omen of good fortune and has never been known to give rise to any ill-feeling" (Growse, 1883: 92). Lewis (1958: 232) reported that a man "was struck so severely across the legs that they ached a month later." Lewis noted that injuries received on Holi are not taken to the courts, which may lead people to take advantage of this immunity. A woman may with impunity beat a man at the instigation of her husband. Ratta (1961: 167) said that "cases of slight injury are quite common on that day, but none minds it. Everyone enjoys the fun."

Other descriptions condone as innocent merriment the horseplay, pranks, the general throwing about of colored water, or the beatings that women hand out to men. Channa (1984: 139) said "Nobody is supposed to mind any pranks played on him." Most participants may indeed see the day as an occasion for merrymaking. However, for some participants it is a day for settling specific scores, as Lewis suggested and as we have observed. A Leatherworker man said, "The people who are educated understand [Holi]. But the rowdies and bad characters will be rough. Drinking . . . is a risk. No five fingers are alike and there are deviants." Dulhendi is a festival for people with a taste for mayhem and a mean streak. However, the interaction is carefully structured and the limits of violence well understood. Rowdiness does not rage out of control.

The refrain that no one minds being "slightly injured" runs counter to common sense. In a game where all players are equally engaged, the participants, especially youngsters, can accept in fun a bucketful of water or a handful of mud or dung. But the surprise assault, even with water, is a psychological shock. An unexpected blow with a club is more than a psychological shock. It can result in serious injury. The line between slight and serious injury is a fine one and easily crossed in the excitement of Dulhendi. A lacerated scalp is not our idea of a slight injury. We have seen, and received, forceful blows on Dulhendi. They are no joke. There was a one-legged man in Shanti Nagar. Our informant explained, "Some years ago on Dulhendi he had color on his face and was run over by a jeep, thus the amputation." We did not pursue the inquiry. The man could have been drinking. But he lost his leg. Some fun.

However, Dulhendi is indeed a festival of love. The explanation is that the day has two phases. Until early afternoon, people play *holi*, that is, administer beatings, throw water, and to some extent run riot. In the afternoon, people visit each other to express affection, usually by putting a tilak on the forehead of a friend and by embracing. Marriott's hosts took him with them as they visited each house that was bereaved during the year to express condolence (see also Jacobson, 1970: 400). Majumdar (1958: 262–263) also described this custom of calling on friends and embracing. After the mayhem of Dulhendi morning, Marriott asked his neighbor, the barber, what was going to happen in the afternoon. His neighbor replied with a beatific sigh, "Holi is the Festival of Love."

The anomaly of love and violence is resolved when the Janus-faced nature of the festival is understood, riotous behavior in the morning, affection in the afternoon. The theme of love, evident during the afternoon, is not easily applied to the morning's mayhem, despite allusions to Krishna and the cowgirls. Indeed, the two phases of Dulhendi appear to be unconnected. We have only our impressions as a guide, but the afternoon ritual of exchanging tilaks and embraces with friends seemed at the time to be an afterthought, something added to the day to balance the morning's rowdiness.

Since "love" is unsatisfactory as an explanation of the licentiousness of Dulhendi, the second common interpretation, social renewal, must be considered. In this view, the annual disorder of Dulhendi represents social upheaval, the familiar world destroyed and then renewed (Henry, 1988: 133; Marriott, 1966: 212). If the social order is truly upset, then the normal definitions of status and role lose their authority. People deliberately assume roles denied to them in everyday life. Women beat men. Wives beat husbands. Low-caste people freely assault high-caste people, or at least mix with them on the basis of equality. Almost all women say that they like Dulhendi. During the year, their husbands can beat them but they cannot beat their husbands. On Dulhendi, they say, they can beat their husbands who cannot respond in kind. Although women do beat men on Dulhendi, we never saw a wife beating her husband.

We have seen Dulhendi in Shanti Nagar three different years. Activity there was similar to accounts from other villages but more restrained, especially as compared to what took place in Kishan Garhi. People began to play a little *holi* before Dulhendi, but most of the activity was reserved for Dulhendi. The ritual of Holi was not over until dark and then there might be an eclipse. Turbulent action would have disturbed the ritual at the pyre during the afternoon and evening, and so roughhouse could not really start until the next morning.

In Delhi, however, rowdy behavior did not wait until Dulhendi. On Holi in 1958, we were in Delhi in the morning but returned to Shanti Nagar on the noon bus to be on time for the afternoon's ritual. Our woman assistant asked us to call for her in a taxi, fearing to be on the streets. The taxi driver told us to keep the windows up, and we noticed that the body of the automobile was covered with grease, presumably to protect it from colored water. A few men from our village were on the bus, including a young Jat man. He was in fine fettle, dressed in very old clothes, and had some color on his face. He had obviously begun to celebrate. The bus driver was a Muslim and the conductor, a Sikh. We were told that Sikhs do not mind being sprayed with water, but Muslims do not like it. Therefore, the Sikh was kidded a little but the Muslim was teased unceasingly, especially by the young Jat, who probably had taken a few drinks. The bus windows were closed and the door latched. A number of passengers were carrying small bottles of colored water. As one of them was leaving the bus, he turned and doused the driver. The Muslim took it good-naturedly, but said he would now have to bathe and pray.

On Dulhendi morning, our landlord's wife, a Brahmani, came to our second-floor apartment to play *holi*. Stanley was her husband's younger brother (*dewar*) in the village fictive kinship system (S. Freed, 1963). She was his *bhabhi*. She beat him with a rope and he threw water on her. There were many threats but not much action. Although theoretically a woman can attack any man, *holi* is usually played by *bhabhi*s and *dewar*s. Jacobson (1970: 399, fn. 1) observed that the women and men who play *holi* are always affines. Women never beat the men of their natal villages.

So many people were arriving that we locked the door and went visiting. The first stop was the house of a distinguished elderly Jat. All was serene. After lunch we paid a visit to the house of a young Jat, in which a group of young Jat men were playing *holi*. The roughhouse and joking were relatively unrestrained. A man struck one of his close friends a blow with a stick that must have really hurt. Another physically powerful man played like a fiend, beating and rubbing color on everyone. When villagers set out to tease someone publicly, their intimate knowledge of everyone's foibles can make the victim squirm. On this occasion much of the joking was directed at two men who had recently lost their wives, one by suicide (rumored to have been murder) and the other through divorce. The two men, isolated on a cot, were teased by everyone, an ordeal that they bore as good-naturedly as possible.

After about an hour, we went outside. The Brahmani who had come to our apartment in the morning to play *holi* was playing in the street with a young Jat, a good friend and fictive *dewar* (younger brother of her husband). Spectators of many castes were watching the players. The Brahmani had a stick; the Jat, a bucket of water. They guardedly approached each other. Then suddenly, the woman rushed forward and tried to strike her opponent as he dodged and threw the water at her. When the woman threw her stick at him, he fled. A spectator returned her stick, someone gave the man another bucket of water, and so the game continued. It was not particularly rough. The Brahmani carefully threw the stick at the Jat's legs and not forcefully. This couple was the only one we saw playing *holi* on the high-caste side of the village. We do not know if their game arose spontaneously or if they had agreed in advance to play. They were both rather aggressive people. They probably had played in other years and enjoyed it. We saw no Brahman men in the street. They all seemed to have gone into hiding.

We next went to the low-caste side of the village in the company of a young Jat man. Activity was somewhat more vigorous. Two Sweeper wives and several men, two of whom were Leatherworkers, were playing. One of the women hit us and our companion twice. After that we watched unmolested. Although the women struck

with their sticks a good deal harder than had the Brahman woman, they were clearly getting the worst of it. The pattern of play was similar to that observed in the
high-caste quarter. The women tried to strike the men who dodged and threw water.
After about an hour of this activity, the Leatherworkers brought out their musical
instruments and there was singing and dancing.

The Holi of 1958 was our first. We expected much more action after having
read published descriptions. Villagers told us that they were unusually restrained
that year because of the recent death of the most prominent man of the village, a
lambardar.[35] Although at the time, there was no single village leader, or pradhan, as
there was in 1978, this lambardar had been, in effect, the unofficial village headman.
Despite this explanation, the following year the activity on Dulhendi was even more
subdued than in 1958, and there had been no comparable death.

However, the villagewide mourning for the lambardar did have a noteworthy
effect, for the pre-Holi skits enacted by women were not performed the year that he
died. The Leatherworker musicians did perform a little on Dulhendi, and a Leatherworker told us of one performance by this group before Holi. We did not see it. In
any case, the Leatherworker musicians were less active than in 1959. As is customary after a death, the family of the lambardar withdrew from observing festival customs. When a Brahman friend wanted to embrace one of the lambardar's sons and
put a tilak on his forehead, the son refused the gesture because he was in mourning.

On Dulhendi morning in 1959, the village was quiet. People were working in
the fields. In the late morning, we toured the village. At the house of a prominent
Jat, everyone was sleeping. As we left the house, we watched a senior Jat walking
down the lane. His daughter-in-law, who was sitting on a cot, respectfully arose as
he passed her. In the Brahman lane, a woman was placidly playing *holi*. Children
were throwing water on her, but she rarely caught any players to beat them. Children and a few young men were watching, but there really was nothing to watch. No
energetic *bhabhi*s appeared that year on either side of the village.

After lunch we went to the low-caste side of the village. On the way we spotted a Jat friend resting in the men's house of another Jat. He told everyone he was
sick in order to avoid playing *holi*. There was a little singing in the Sweeper quarter.
A few Leatherworkers were playing *holi* sporadically, and there was some half-
hearted singing. One of the principal singers was partially dressed up, but did not
look very happy. We had the impression that a dispute had been simmering all day
in the Leatherworker quarter. Nevertheless, many Brahmans, Jats, and Bairagis were
watching the action from rooftops.

Absolutely nothing was going on in the Potter quarter save for routine daily
activities. We searched for one of the wives whom we knew well, and she drenched
us with water. But we had to ask her to do it. At a Jat house adjacent to the Potter
quarter, men were playing *chaupar* (pachisi) as if Dulhendi did not exist. Seeing no
Dulhendi activity on the high-caste side, we returned to our apartment.

Some Brahman women arrived and tried to extort money by threatening to beat
Stanley. They had heard that we had given Rs. 10 to the wife of our landlord to avoid
a beating and hoped for a similar bribe. We denied having paid and asked how they
could beat their (fictive) brother. Women are always brought up short when this

emotionally powerful kinship tie is invoked. The women drifted out having done nothing. A woman who watched the scene was disgusted. "You came to beat him," she told the women, "but he said that he was your brother and you didn't do it."

The three strategies for avoiding a beating are to pay a bribe, to claim the fictive relationship of brother, and to submit to a blow or two, which theoretically provides immunity from further punishment. However, the third method is by no means infallible. A Jat man assured Stanley that, both of us having received a blow, we could watch the Dulhendi action unmolested. But one should never relax. A young girl in the household of a friend sneaked up behind Stanley and gave him so forceful a blow in the back with a stick that, had it struck a vulnerable spot, it could have resulted in serious injury.

We saw at least as much and perhaps more activity on Dulhendi in 1978 than in the 1950s. In the morning we were working with a middle-aged Brahman man. A Brahman schoolteacher, a gentle, friendly man, came to put a tilak on Ruth. For people like him, Dulhendi is really a festival of love. A few other men also came to exchange tilaks with us. Our interlocutor's younger brother's wife came with a stick and acted as though she would beat him, but he waved her away. This relationship was inappropriate for a beating. Women generally do not beat senior men. It is the older brother's wife who beats the husband's younger brother.

At about 11:30 A.M., we took a turn around the village. We were halfway through the high-caste quarter before anything happened. Then in the Brahman lane a few people threw water on us. As we continued down the main street, a Jat called us. He offered us milk and then we went out into the street to watch people play *holi*. There were two very active *bhabhi*s playing with several *dewar*s. We and our companion did not recognize any of the veiled women, but one of the men was a Barber, probably playing with women of higher caste. The women had heavy cloths twisted and doubled with which they tried to strike the men. They were rarely successful, whereas the men frequently drenched them. Again we wondered what the women got out of playing *holi*. They always had the worst of it because the young men ran faster.

In addition to the play of the *bhabhi*s and *dewar*s, there was much general throwing of water. There were many handpumps in the village so that water was available everywhere. Spectators, especially elderly men, could watch the play without being disturbed (cf., Wadley, 1994b: 230), but most people stayed at home on Dulhendi. After about an hour we moved on to watch another group playing *holi*. Some Jat *bhabhi*s were playing with a number of Jat *dewar*s. The women were soaked. We never saw them catch a single *dewar*.

After lunch, activity started in the Leatherworker quarter. Much of the action was on rooftops. A large crowd was watching and laughing. Somewhat later, the Jat *bhabhi*s we had seen earlier started playing again. We went home and changed our clothes, believing the activity finished for the day. Then at about 4:00 P.M. a group of boys arrived to throw water on us. We told them that we had just changed our clothes and had no more clean clothing. The boys settled for an exchange of tilaks. Dulhendi activity was finished by 4:30 P.M.

Despite what seemed to us to be a respectable amount of Dulhendi action, a few informants spoke as if the playing of *holi* was not as common as formerly. As the principal reason, they suggested that the rough play of Dulhendi could create bad feelings between families. Marriott (1966: 204) reported, "As an effect of the festivities in one nearby village, there had occurred an armed fight between factional groups." Toffin (1982: 10) observed, "Ethnologists working in South Asia know that violence is inherent in festivals and that it can cause serious problems. They know that factional struggles double in intensity during the festival period, often ending in general fighting. Moreover, it is not a phenomenon entirely new . . . ." Majumdar (1958: 262) noted that "people lose their temper if any coloured water is thrown on them because it spoils their clothes." A Sweeper woman said, "I don't play much because there could be fights between families. I give sweets to some families. Men drink on this day." Some women make *pakora*s for the men to have with their drinks. Drinking had probably become more common because the village was more prosperous and liquor was obtained easily.

A high-caste woman gave several reasons for what she saw as the relative absence of *holi* playing. "The Jats are very tired after coming from the fields and so they don't play *holi*. Everyone used to play *holi*, but now people are not on good terms with each other and so they don't play. Because of many deaths, they don't play." Fatigue and death are constants of village life and could hardly be invoked to explain a decrease in the playing of *holi*. It would be impossible to determine whether the incidence of feuds between families had increased since the 1950s. Feuds are always present, sometimes smoldering, sometimes erupting in violence.

Dulhendi in Shanti Nagar was not a day when the normal social order was temporarily overturned. It was a day of formalized interaction rather than one of general license. Low-caste people do not assault high-caste people (cf., Majumdar, 1958: 262; Ratta, 1961: 167). The apparent "role reversal" that was seen in the horseplay between *bhabhi*s and *dewar*s in fact only exaggerated the "teasing" aspect of their normal relationship, which was affectionate and informal. It is true that the opportunity to assault even a *dewar* might give women an emotional outlet for a year's frustration of being under the dominance of men, but we never saw a woman attack a senior member of her family (cf., Ratta, 1961: 167). Fathers-in-law, for example, were not targets. Our Brahman friend simply waved away his younger brother's wife when she approached him. Although any stray man was vulnerable to assault, we observed that if the most prestigious men of the village happened to walk through the streets, they were not assailed.

Women used a certain degree of discretion. Thus, we observed that a Brahman woman, approaching a group of Brahman men and an older Barber man, pelted the Barber with wet cow dung while the Brahmans watched and laughed. One would hesitate to characterize this behavior as an example of role reversal, for the Brahmani was of a much higher caste than the Barber. At first, the Barber was angry, but when everyone laughed, he calmed down a bit and smiled sheepishly.

This episode of the Brahman woman and the Barber man is one of several that led us to think that Dulhendi screens personalities much more than do other festivals. Anyone can light a lamp on Diwali, but not every middle-aged person finds it acceptable behavior to throw cow dung at an unsuspecting elderly friend and family retainer. The Brahmani was ordinarily combative, constantly fighting with her mother-in-law, her husband, and her sister-in-law who lived next door. Her alleged punitive and careless behavior with one of her sons contributed to his death. She suffered from ghost possession. In view of her circumstances, it would be unfair to say that she had a mean streak, but she certainly was aggressive. The Barber was a middle-aged man who served the woman's family under the terms of the jajmani system. The Brahmani was the wife of his fictive younger brother, hence not a *bhabhi*, the relative who might be expected to play *holi* with her *dewar*. The Barber had no reason to be on his guard. He did not expect such treatment and was understandably angry. The "can't-you-take-a-joke?" approach does not excuse everything. The behavior of the young Jat men provides further examples of aggression rather than playfulness or, at best, aggressive playfulness. The young Jats who beat and teased their friends were strong, assertive men.

Dulhendi is not a day when everyone is equal. The normal roles of caste, kinship, and age may be slightly infringed but are definitely not abandoned. What characterizes Dulhendi is that psychological quirks and individual personalities come into play more than at any other festival. But even the most enthusiastic player of *holi* in the morning becomes, in the afternoon, a dignified, respectful visitor come to exchange tilaks with friends. The young Jat who played *holi* so energetically on the bus in 1958 came to visit us on Dulhendi 1959 and complained about the lack of afternoon bus service. He explained, "I have to go back to Delhi this afternoon and distribute sweets to my city friends. There are six families that I must visit. I have to keep up my social relations."

The revelry of Dulhendi morning is not an expression of affection except in the case of some *bhabhi*s and *dewar*s, nor does it represent the destruction and renewal of the social order. On the contrary, it asserts the supremacy of the social order over individual impulses. Contesting the "catharsis" theory of festivals, Bouillier (1982: 113–114) commented, "The strengthening of values that festivals bring about does not operate through psychological release or through temporary inversion but through idealization, the identification of participants with divinities. Women express the essence of their daily relations in their festivals . . . ." We would be inclined to substitute "dharma" for "divinities" in this formula, but they are here perhaps tantamount to the same idea, for dharma "depends on the victory of gods over the demons" (Reiniche, 1979: 62). The dominant message of the day is, "One can go so far and no further." Women can beat their *dewar*s but not their fathers-in-law.

The riotous behavior may best be understood as the survival of an ancient sacrificial and fertility cult. It is a matter of interpretation rather than of concrete evidence. Thus, the red powder, representing blood, and the pain of beatings are taken as symbols of former sacrifices. The bloodletting reported by Growse also suggests an early sacrificial ritual, the more so that the blood is seen as an omen of good fortune.

Dulhendi may once have been a day of sexual license. In Shanti Nagar, the erotic songs, dancing, and some of the dramas support this view. Whether songs and dancing today lead to more illicit sexual activity on Dulhendi than on other days is another question. For people with such inclinations, any day may be a potential Dulhendi.

Sexual licentiousness is apparently more pronounced elsewhere than in Shanti Nagar. Marriott (1966: 204) reported that two housewives were detected in adultery. One assumes that the two cases were only the tip of the iceberg. Channa wrote that sexual license occurs in the days preceding Holi, but that it is no longer as common as in the 1950s "when nude women usually prostitutes, painted in multi-colours, danced at the head of processions, and some men, dancing in the procession, displayed their genital organs which were often specifically painted for the occasion" (Channa, 1984: 139). The mention of prostitutes suggests that the processions in question took place in the city. Prostitution is a city phenomenon.[36]

The license of Dulhendi is almost always described as merrymaking, but for many people it is an ordeal to be endured. People stay at home out of harm's way. If they participate at all in the day's rough activities, it is as spectators, safely watching the stylized play of *bhabhi*s and *dewar*s from rooftops.

Dulhendi will probably continue to be observed in this fashion for the foreseeable future. However, two features of current village life hold the seeds for mischief. The village population is increasing and becoming more anonymous. Thus, the kind of social control based on personal acquaintance is being diluted. Second, the festival beverage is liquor, either commercial or country. The combination of drinking and licensed violence is a recipe for trouble. The brief fight of Brahman and Jat youths at the Brahman Holi pyre is a case in point. On the other hand, people drink at home, usually out of sight, so such confrontations are unlikely.

Dulhendi in Shanti Nagar and in Kishan Garhi, Marriott's village, are strikingly dissimilar. In Kishan Garhi, interaction breaks out of traditional channels. In Shanti Nagar, behavior is much more restrained. The normal social structure is barely infringed. It is not a question of changing customs, for both villages were observed in the 1950s. It is tempting to point to the restraining influence of the Arya Samaj for the relatively controlled behavior in Shanti Nagar. In any case, uniform conduct from village to village is not to be expected. Unwritten folk customs can easily drift in somewhat different directions.

6 FESTIVALS OF INTERACTION AND HONORING THE DEAD

HINDUISM IS REMARKABLE in the number of festivals devoted chiefly to strengthening kinship ties. In Shanti Nagar, five festivals basically are occasions for interaction among relatives (table 8). They serve to reinforce the bonds of kinship, principally through the exchange of gifts. The sixth festival of the "interaction" category, Shraddha, honors ancestors, but it also renews social relations by virtue of a ceremonial meal for selected guests. Dulhendi, seventh on the list and a festival of pure interaction, has a close connection to Holi and is described in chapter 5.

Welfare is a feature of some of these interactional festivals but not in the same form as in the festivals included in the "welfare" category. The latter festivals enlist supernatural aid for the benefit of the family, especially for the protection of husbands and children. On the other hand, the interaction festivals have little to do with deities. Their purpose is to strengthen social bonds among kin, castemates, and friends, people who selectively might be available for support in time of trouble or who would be expected to send gifts at festivals, births, and marriages.

Ideally, the relationship of sister and brother is perhaps the closest tie among relatives, with the exception of mother and child. Villagers emphasized the love of brothers and sisters, pointing out that a sister is more important than a wife. Although a woman moves to her husband's village when she marries, her brother continues to play a leading role in her welfare and security. He will be available to her most of her life and is expected to assume the familial obligations to his sister after the death of their father. The sister-brother relationship is central to two festivals, Raksha Bandhan and Bhai Duj, and is recognized on Sakat. On these occasions, brothers vow to protect their sisters.

Friendly relations between families related by marriage are important for the welfare of married women, and the required gift exchanges are carefully maintained. Prudent individuals do not allow their bonds of kinship, either consanguineal or affinal, or their friendships to lapse, for such relationships often prove to be quite useful in such vital activities as obtaining employment or finding a husband for a daughter. Affinal relations are emphasized in the festivals of Makar Sankranti, Sanjhi, and Tijo.

TABLE 8.

ANNUAL FESTIVALS OF INTERACTION AND HONORING THE DEAD

FESTIVAL	GODDESS/GOD	THEME	RITUAL GROUP
Tijo	None	Swinging, pleasure	Women
Raksha Bandhan	None	Strengthen tie of sister and brother	Sisters and brothers
Shraddha	None	Remembrance, worship of ancestors	Bereaved family
Sanjhi	None (1958), Sanjhi (1977), (Durga)	Kin ties of married women	Family, caste
Bhai Duj	Yama, Yami	Kin tie of sister and brother	Sisters and brothers
Makar Sankranti	Sun	Kin ties, settle quarrels	Family
Dulhendi	None	Saturnalia	Village

FESTIVAL	GIFT EXCHANGE	IMAGE/PLACE	RITUAL
Tijo	Gift exchange between in-law families, money, clothes, sweets	Trees in village	None
Raksha Bandhan	Sisters tie charm on brothers, who give money, clothes to sister	Household	None
Shraddha	Feed guests, gifts to guests, Brahmans	Household	Offer *kusa* grass, water, mantras
Sanjhi	Households give raw food to young women	Sculpture	Offer *prasad*, singing, procession
Bhai Duj	Sisters and brothers exchange food, money	Household	Fast, story
Makar Sankranti	Wives give clothes to in-laws	Household, family, *kolhu*	None
Dulhendi	None	Village	None

TIJO

Tijo (Third), or Tij, is celebrated on Shrawan *sudi* 3, a day that falls early in the monsoon season when the weather cools and greenery appears in the fields. Tijo has no religious significance in Shanti Nagar. It is a festival of happiness, celebrating the good weather and the rain. There is a saying in the village that "Tij has come and spread the seeds," which means that many festivals will take place after Tijo. There is a complementary saying, "Holi has come and taken away everything in her sack," which means that after Holi there will be no festivals until Tij, seven months later (cf., Lewis, 1958: 205). In effect, Tij ushers in a five-month festival season that ends with Holi.

Although Tijo has a practical side, the cementing of good relations between families united by marriage, an observer sees chiefly its joyous aspect. It is an occasion for women and children to have some fun. Swings are suspended from every suitable tree, and children and young women enjoy swinging and singing. Older women sit placidly on cots gossiping and watching the youngsters at play. Like many festivals, Tijo is principally for women. Men may help the women tie swings to trees, but they rarely swing or spend much time watching the swinging.

Although the festival takes place on the third day of the bright fortnight, the swinging begins on the first day of Shrawan, that is, the first day of the dark fortnight and lasts for a fortnight plus three days. We saw the festival in 1958, a year in which there was an added month of Shrawan. The festival was observed on the first of the two possible days, that is, during the added month. The dates for the entire festival were therefore from true (*nija*) Shrawan *badi* 1 to added (*adhika*) Shrawan *sudi* 3. One Jat woman claimed that Tijo would also be celebrated on the second possible day, that is, during the bright fortnight of the true month. In fact, the second day was not observed.

In Shanti Nagar and elsewhere in the Union Territory of Delhi, no deities are worshipped on Tijo nor is there a ritual of any kind. The day features swinging and singing, festive food, and gifts (Lewis, 1958: 205–207; Bhatia, 1961: 65; Luthra, 1961: 70; Nautiyal, 1961: 164; Ratta, 1961: 163; and Srivastava, 1961: 67). In Karimpur, Uttar Pradesh, on the other hand, the worship of Parvati and Shiva dominates the festival (Wadley, 1975: 158). Women make tiny clay figures of Parvati or of Parvati and Shiva. Married women perform a ritual (puja) for them so that their brothers (and sometimes their husbands) will be healthy and have a long life. Some women fast until after the puja. Wadley pointed out that a woman's brother is her only refuge and protection if something goes wrong in her husband's family. Wadley mentioned neither swinging, the most noteworthy feature of the festival in Shanti Nagar, nor the exchange of gifts. Tijo in Karimpur is clearly a "welfare" festival. Although the sister-brother relationship and those between families related by marriage are prominent in the interactional festivals of Shanti Nagar, pujas play no role.

Like Wadley, Bahadur (1995: 81–82) described a puja for Parvati as a feature of Tijo. Bahadur's account apparently is based on Tijo as celebrated in Rajasthan and Gujarat. An image of Gaur Mata (Parvati), an idol or a picture, is placed on a ceremonial square that is drawn on the ground or floor. Bahadur (1995: 81) advised, "If you want to go completely traditional, make a figurine of mud, and place it instead of a picture." Clay figurines are used in Karimpur. Women offer water, rice, and flowers among other items to the goddess, and an elderly lady of the household chants a short verse asking for Parvati's blessing. The day is meant for fun, and there is feasting, singing, and dancing.

Bahadur (1995: 79–82) described a festival known as Sindhara that takes place on the second day of the bright fortnight, the day before Tijo. Sindhara and Tijo are related. The pujas for the two festivals are almost identical, and there is swinging and exchanging of gifts. The only difference is that Sindhara is for daughters-in-law and Tijo is for daughters. During an interview with a Brahmani the day before Tijo, one of our assistants, a Delhi resident, remarked that the day was Duj (second) and was for daughters. The Brahmani immediately responded, "We don't do that here. Everything is on Tijo, for both married and unmarried girls."[37]

Several informants explained that *sindhara* is the present sent on Tijo by in-laws to a new bride who is still living with her parents. The parents reciprocate with a gift of double the value, also known as *sindhara*. In the years after the first Tijo following the wedding, the *sindhara* is no longer exchanged, for the bride, now a wife, would be living with her husband's family. Craven (1893: 532) defined the term as a "sweetmeat sent by a bridegroom to his bride."

Some swings were hanging in Shanti Nagar the day before the full moon, and others would soon appear, for swinging and singing in the evening begin on the first day of the month, more than a fortnight before Tijo. Most of the swings were hung from trees in the habitation site, not from trees on village common land. On these points, Tijo in Shanti Nagar differs from the festival in other Delhi villages. In Rampur, swings are not hung until Tijo eve, when young men go to the village common land in search of suitable trees. There is competition for the trees, even for separate branches, and sometimes fighting breaks out. The swings are in place by early morning, but swinging does not begin until later in the day (Lewis, 1958: 205–206). In the 1961 census, village studies report practices similar to those of Rampur—namely, the swings are set up on village common land either on Tijo eve or the day itself. The only swing located slightly away from the village habitation site in Shanti Nagar was near the Gardener's garden where the Bairagis had suspended one on a tree that they owned. The Gardeners also swung there but probably put up their own rather than using the Bairagis' swing.

The large swings have two boards and are hung from big trees in the lanes or in caste compounds where they can be used by many women. At least two women sit on a swing, one on each board facing each other and holding the seats apart with their feet (fig. 77). Sometimes women swing with children in their arms. Women on the ground pull on ropes tied to a swing to set it in motion and keep it moving. Sometimes more than two women sit on a swing, giving the effect of a suspended human mass. Spectators, mainly women but also a few boys and young men, stand around or sit on cots to watch the action. The women sing.

The swings for children were smaller than those for women. There were several small swings in the Leatherworker compound and one at the Jat meeting house. One family hung a private swing for a child in its courtyard. Another year this same family installed a swing inside the house for an adolescent daughter. She did not go out to swing with the other girls. A young wife of this family, 26 years old, had not swung since she left her parent's house. The family head, a strong believer in the Arya Samaj, tended to exercise considerable control over the ceremonial activities of the women of the household.

Two days before Tijo, women were buying bangles for themselves and for all the girls of their families, even the youngest. We noticed that one 2-year-old girl was

FIG. 77. Tijo, 1958. Women swinging.

quite conscious of her bangles. On Tijo eve, women put henna on the palms of their hands so that it would dry overnight. In the morning, they put on their fine clothing and jewelry, especially anklets that would be visible while they swung.

The women assembled at swings close to their homes. The groups of women at most swings were based chiefly on caste affiliation but also on proximity to a swing and, presumably, on friendship. When we made a tour of the village on Tijo, 1958, we saw several multicaste groups of women in action. The members of one group who were using a swing in front of a Watercarrier's house represented Brahmans, Jats, Blacksmiths, and a Potter who was only watching. In the Potter quarter where there was a swing, both Potters and Jats from neighboring houses were swinging. However, we saw only Leatherworkers using the swing that was set up in their compound, and only Sweepers used the swing in their quarter. While the higher castes could easily participate together on ceremonial occasions such as Tijo, the Leatherworkers and Sweepers were more ritually and socially isolated in the 1950s. They were at the bottom of the caste hierarchy with the Sweepers well below the Leatherworkers. The village wells told the story. The Leatherworkers and Sweepers each had their own well. The other village wells could be used by all the other castes (S. Freed and R. Freed, 1976: 144–146).

There are several names for the gifts that are exchanged on Tijo by families related by marriage. The use of one or another of these terms depends on whether the married woman linking the families is living with her parents or with her husband's family. On the first Tijo after her wedding, she will in all likelihood still be living in her parental home, in which case her in-laws will send to her the gift known as *sindhara*. In return, her parents send a *sindhara* of considerably greater value to her in-laws.

After the first Tijo, a married daughter will probably be living with her husband's family. Her parents, or brother if her father is dead, then send her a gift called *kothli*. A *kothli* is literally a small bag, but the term also means the gift sent on Tijo. In this sense it is extended to include all the items that comprise the gift. Tijo is also one of the festivals on which a family sends the gift of *sidha* (rice or flour, sugar or gur, and ghee) to a married daughter living with her husband's family. A *sidha* is presumably part of a *kothli* on Tijo, for a *kothli* is a larger gift including clothing and possibly money as well as food. The gifts that compose a *kothli* are distributed in the husband's family. For example, a young Jat wife who had been living with her husband for three years received a *tirh* (woman's outfit) and Rs. 20 for Tijo. She retained the clothing but her mother-in-law took the money.

Expensive gifts are sent for the first Tijo after marriage; the value of the gifts in subsequent years diminishes sharply. Especially after a woman has a few children, gifts for Tijo are greatly reduced, perhaps to as little as five rupees and no clothing. An informant explained that at this stage of life, a woman loves her husband's family more than her natal family. A very old woman may receive nothing at all. A family in mourning does not send gifts on Tijo.

A *sindhara* includes the seat of a swing. A well-to-do Jat family whose married daughter was still at her parents' home received sweets, clothes for the daughter, fruit, and the seat of a swing. The return gift was 14 sheets, 7 sets of women's clothing, and Rs. 100. The gift from the groom's family to the bride's family was less costly than the return gift. In general, a married daughter's family regularly sends gifts to in-laws. In the case of reciprocal gifts, the married woman's natal family should send the more expensive gift.

*Sindhara*s can be elaborate and costly for the first Tijo after a wedding. A Brahman family, which took delight in sending handsome presents, sent a *sindhara* to the family of their son's bride, which included a decorated seat and a beautiful colored rope for a swing, a generous selection of clothing for women and children, sheets, toys, cosmetics, sweets, and various household items. Although most of the gifts were purchased, the women of the household made the rope and also hemstitched the sheets.

The most expensive Tijo gifts are sent by well-off families to their daughter's bridegroom on the first Tijo after the wedding. A Jat farmer and schoolteacher, who kept careful monthly accounts, spent Rs. 623 for a *sindhara* after a wedding that took place in 1976. He said, "This was the first Tijo after the wedding and so I sent expensive gifts. Otherwise, I would have spent only five or ten rupees. I consider this Tijo gift as a wedding expense." He spent about Rs. 20,000 for the wedding, the usual expenditure for a man in his circumstances.

Women prepare a special meal for Tijo, cooking some of the usual festive foods such as puris, halva, *gulgulas* (sweet cakes of flour and gur fried in oil), and *khir*. People give some of this food to the Sweeper woman and to the wife of the Barber who serve their family. Patrons make such payments to clients as part of the jajmani system.

Songs For Tijo

The songs that women sing on Tijo display all the essential elements of the festival. It is a joyous time for women, especially young wives who do much of the hard daily household and agricultural work. It is an occasion for sending gifts to married daughters and to daughters-in-law, thereby maintaining cordial relationships between families united by marriage. The usual relatives so important to women are emphasized in the songs. The dominant mother-in-law receives considerable critical attention. Husbands who are indifferent to the emotional frustration of their wives or who try to thwart their desire to visit their parents are depicted unsympathetically. The allies of a young wife, especially her husband's younger sister and her *dewar*, are celebrated. The fine qualities of the gifts are mentioned. These themes permeate the lives of village women. We collected four songs from a middle-aged Brahman woman and her married daughter.

In the song below, a young wife seeks a bit of pleasure and freedom on Tijo. Her husband's mother tries to impose limits, invoking as justification the basic attributes of the role of daughter-in-law, namely, hard work and chaste behavior. First, the mother-in-law raises the question of suitable companions. The wife counters by naming her husband's sister and his younger brother, perfectly proper companions for a young married woman. The mother-in-law's next gambit is to remind her son's wife of her household chores. The wife flatly refuses to be distracted. Finally, the mother-in-law brings up the matter of the chaste behavior that is appropriate for a young wife. On Tijo, she will dress in fine clothes and wear jewelry. Her husband is not at home. The mother-in-law asks, "My son has gone to another country, now why do you decorate yourself?" From the bottom of her heart, the young wife defiantly cries out, "If your son has gone, then let him go. I will decorate myself for my own heart."

> [Mother-in-law] Oh daughter-in-law, I will get a silk rope made for you.
> But going to swing in a garden is forbidden for you.
> I will get a silk rope made for you, and will fix a swing in the middle of
>   the palace, oh daughter-in-law.
> Going to swing in a garden is forbidden for you.
> [Daughter-in-law] I will burn your palace, break the silk rope into
>   eleven pieces.
> Otherwise let me go out to swing in the garden.
> [Mother-in-law] Who will go with you, who will help you in swinging?
> Going to swing in the garden is forbidden for you.
> [Daughter-in-law] My husband's sister will go with me, my husband's
>   younger brother will help me swing.
> Let me go into the garden to swing.

> [Mother-in-law] There is something kept on the grinding wheel which is
>   to be ground.
> Get up in time in the morning and grind that.
> Going out in the garden to swing is forbidden for you.
> [Daughter-in-law] I will spread all the things to be ground
>   on the floor, break the grinding wheel into eighteen pieces.
> I will go out into the garden to swing.
> [Mother-in-law] Oh daughter-in-law! My son has gone to another
>   country, now why do you decorate yourself?
> You are forbidden to swing in the garden.
> [Daughter-in-law] If your son has gone, let him go.
> I will decorate myself for my own heart.
> Let me go out to swing in the garden.

The main theme of the next song is a husband's indifference to his wife's unhappiness. A comparable theme, the emotional frustration of a wife due to her husband's absence, her unhappiness aggravated by a dominant mother-in-law, is clearly portrayed in the song above. In the current song, the husband's younger sister comes to the rescue.

The wife complains that her husband is too young to understand her yearning for love. Ideally husbands are a few years older than wives, presumably not too young to develop an emotionally fulfilling marital relationship. Sometimes, wives are a few years older than their husbands, in which case they might take the leading marital role, at least initially. Commenting on his bride's sexual expertise, a young Jat man once told us, "I was 15 years old when I married and my wife was two or three years older. I did not realize it at the time, but she was quite expert in this work."

In the song, the husband's rejection of his wife is overcome by the good offices of his sister. His wife thanks her extravagantly and promises her the traditional Tijo gifts, a *tirh* and *sidha*, in the "sixth month." Tijo takes place in the fifth month. Our informant may have made a mistake or the reference may not be to Tijo but to another occasion. However, there is no festival in the sixth month that requires gifts for in-laws.[38]

> There is a banana tree in the courtyard of my home.
> Oh you banana tree, why are you standing so sad?
> Oh banana tree, I will feed you with milk and curd.
> My husband's younger sister asks me of my heart and says,
> Oh brother's wife, why are you standing so sad and still?
> [Wife] Your brother is too young and a babe.
> He does not know the longings of my heart.
> [Sister to brother's wife] Take your bath, adorn yourself, and comb your
>   hair nicely.
> Oh brother's wife, come with me, I will make you meet my brother.
> [Sister] Oh brother! Open these locked doors, your dearest is standing
>   outside.
> [Brother] Oh sister! This door cannot be opened.

These are made of iron.

[Sister] It is drizzling outside and your dearest is getting wet.

Locked doors have been opened, iron bolts have also fallen.

[Wife to sister] May your brother live long!

You have made me meet your brother.

Oh husband's sister! I will give you a beautiful *tirh*.

Because we were angry with each other, and you made us meet again.

Oh husband's sister! May your brother live long, and your brother's wife
    may live forever with her husband alive.

Oh husband's sister! I will give you a beautiful *tirh* and a dish of *sidha*
    in the sixth month.

The following ditty describes a brother bringing gifts on Tijo to his newly married sister. We were puzzled by an apparent conflict of kinship terms, which seem to
indicate that the woman is in her parental home, with the arrival of her brother
bringing the *sindhara*. A woman's brother takes the *sindhara* to his sister when she
is at the house of her in-laws. In fact the woman is at her in-laws house (*susral*),
where she uses the correct terms of address for her mother-in-law (mother), sister-
in-law (sister), and refers to herself as the wife, or daughter-in-law, of the house.[39] In
any case, the essential idea is that families related by marriage send gifts on Tijo. Barbers as well as brothers might carry gifts between families. Barbers are paid two
rupees for this service. The singing bird portends a visitor. There is an Indian saying,
"Even when a crow calls, someone is coming."

The *papiha* [sparrow-hawk or whistle bird] sings in the garden.

I know someone will come.

Someone will come, my brother will come.

He will bring a *tirh* for my mother, one for my sister,

And bring anklets for the daughter-in-law of the house.

The *papiha* sings in the garden.

I know someone will come.

Someone will come, my brother will come.

The frequency and duration of a young wife's visits to her parental home are
often a bone of contention between wife and husband. The wife feels entitled to frequent long visits. Her husband finds reasons to keep her at home. Families that allow
liberal visiting privileges have a reputation for kindness and decency. As women
grow older, they visit the homes of their parents less frequently than in their youth.

The next song, the *Barahmasi* (Song of the Twelve Months),[40] develops at length
the theme of an importunate wife and a resistant husband. The lyrics run month by
month through a year, noting in passing some of the festivals, agricultural activities,
and changes in climate. Having exhausted his excuses, the husband finally yields.
However, he cannot resist a final barb. He urges his wife to sleep with a relative as,
presumably, a guarantee of her virtue. His spirited wife replies in kind. The husband
then complains of the sauciness of women in general and his wife in particular.

The last six lines are tantamount to reciprocal taunting. One informant said that when a husband and wife want to fight they may sing this song back and forth. The last few lines trigger the dispute.

> Oh my king! The month of Asharh has come so send me to my
>   parents' house.
> Oh my queen! Listen, who has come to fetch you, with whom will
>   you go there?
> Oh my king! Listen, my younger brother has come to fetch me. I shall
>   go with him.
> Oh my queen! Listen, we have to get the house built in Asharh, so you
>   should go to your father's house in the month of Shrawan.
> Oh my king! The month of Shrawan has come so now send me to my
>   father's house.
> Oh my queen! We have to swing on the swings in Shrawan, so you
>   should go to your father's house in Bhadon.
> Oh my king! The month of Bhadon has come so now send me to my
>   father's house.
> Oh my queen! The nights of Bhadon are dark, so you should go to your
>   father's house in Asauj.
> Oh my king! The month of Asauj has come, so send me to my father's
>   house.
> Oh my queen! You have to feed the Brahmans in the month of Asauj,
>   so you should go to your father's house in Karttik.
> Oh my king! The month of Karttik has come, so you should send me
>   to my father's house.
> Oh my queen! You have to go to bathe in Ganga this month, so you
>   should go to your father's house in Mangshar.
> Oh my king! The month of Mangshar has come, so send me to my
>   father's house.
> Oh my queen! You have to work even in the month of Mangshar, so
>   you should go to your father's house in Poh.
> Oh my king! The month of Poh has come, so you should send me to
>   my father's house.
> Oh my queen! It is very cold in Poh, so you should go to your father's
>   house in Magh.
> Oh my king! The month of Magh has come, so you should send me to
>   my father's house.
> Oh my queen! You have to get your ornaments made in the month of
>   Magh, so you should go to your father's house in Phalgun.
> Oh my king! The month of Phalgun has come, so you should send me
>   to my father's house.
> Oh my queen! You have to play *holi* in the month of Phalgun, so you
>   should go to your father's house in Chaitra.
> Oh my king! The month of Chaitra has come, so you should send me
>   to my father's house.

Oh my queen! You have to reap the crops in the month of Chaitra, so
you should go to your father's house in Baisakh.

Oh my king! The month of Baisakh has come, so you should send me
to my father's house.

Oh my queen! You have to gather the crops that are cut in Baisakh, so
you should go to your father's house in Jyesth.

Oh my king! The month of Jyesth has come, so you should send me to
my father's house.

Oh my queen! It is too hot in the month of Jyesth, so you should go to
your father's house in Asharh.

Oh my king! The month of Asharh has come, so you should send me to
my father's house.

Oh my queen! We have to do a ceremony for our new house in the
month of Asharh, so you should go to your father's house in
Shrawan.

Oh my king! Twelve months have passed so send me to my parents'
house.

Oh my queen! Listen, the nights in the month of Bhadon are dark so
you should not sleep alone.

Oh my queen! Take your younger brother and make him sleep with
you. Sleep together. Do not sleep alone.

Oh my king! The nights of Bhadon are too dark. Do not sleep alone.

Oh my king! Take your younger sister and make her sleep with you.
Sleep together. Do not sleep alone.

Oh my queen! It is the habit among women that if one tells them
anything they always reply in a taunting way.

Oh my queen! It is a habit among women that they always work in
a tit-for-tat manner.

RAKSHA BANDHAN (SALONO)

Raksha Bandhan (Protection Tie or Charm Tying), celebrated on the full moon of Shrawan, is a festival with three distinct facets (Wadley, 1975: 166). Each facet may once have been a separate festival, but in the course of time they have tended to merge. The dominant theme of the day is interaction, the exchange of presents—protective charms (rakhi) and money—between particular relatives. The festival is therefore termed Raksha Bandhan, the name by which it is most commonly designated throughout much of India. However, in the 1950s in Shanti Nagar, the day was almost always known as Salono (various spellings), the name of a deity described as the nymph of Shrawan. Salono is honored on Shrawan sudi 15. In 1978, Salono seemed to be losing ground to Raksha Bandhan as the name of the festival, in all likelihood the result of influences from Delhi and from the schools. The third aspect of the day is an agricultural festival "known as the barley feast, the Jâyî or Jawâra of Upper India, and the Bhujariya of the Central Provinces" (Crooke, 1968, 2: 293).

The exchange of protective string-charms (ponchi, pohonchi, or rakhi) and money between a sister and brother is the chief activity of Raksha Bandhan in Shanti Nagar. A Leatherworker man described the custom.

> On Salono, sisters tie *ponchi*s on their brothers' [right] wrists. They can also tie them on the wrists of their cousin-brothers. In return, a brother gives his sister a rupee or whatever he can afford, even a cow or a buffalo. I will go to fetch my [married] sister before Tijo. Sisters want to come to their parents' house during Shrawan. Old women might not want to come [then], but they will want to come for Salono. But some do not come. I will have sweet puris made as a gift [for my sister's in-laws]. This is *sindhara*, which the Jats call *kothli*. Among Harijans, brothers-in-law [that is, husbands] also come to the home of their wife's parents and tie *ponchi*s on the wrists of their wife's brothers. Then the wife's brother gives his brother-in-law one rupee or what he can afford.

A ceremony that seems so simple, the tying of the *rakhi* and the return gift, represents the powerful emotional and practical ties that bind a sister and brother and also the complicated relationships that join families united by marriage. Bahadur glorified the bond of brother and sister as the most sacred relationship that nature has bestowed on mankind. A sister depends on the unstinting support of her brother. He accepts the obligation with love (Bahadur, 1995: 86–87). Nautiyal (1961: 164) quoted a saying, "One is widowed if her brothers are dead." Both unmarried and married girls and women tie the *rakhi* on their brothers' right wrists. Although a brother's support of his sister does not really come into play until after her marriage, and especially not until after the death of their father, a sister is concerned with the well-being of her brother from her early childhood. Among other considerations, parents are handicapped in the search for a husband for their daughter if she has no brother.

In the case of a married woman, tying the protective charm on her brother's wrist has implications for the families united by marriage. The parents and brothers of a married woman cannot accept a present from a married daughter or her in-laws without returning something of greater value. A woman's husband who comes to his in-laws house to reclaim his wife after her fortnight with her parents, from about Tijo until Raksha Bandhan, as in the Leatherworker's account above, also receives a gift from his brother-in-law in return for a *ponchi*.

In 1978, several women said that some girls tie *rakhi*s on the wrists of their older brothers' wives (see also Lewis, 1958: 208). In return, they receive either money or a woman's suit of clothes (*tirh*). Even though a married woman's gift of a *tirh* to her husband's younger sister takes place in the context of charm tying, it is part of a *sindhara* or *sidha* that a married woman receives from her parents on specific festivals (Nautiyal, 1961: 164). Some of the items received as *sidha* are distributed in the husband's family. This particular gift shifts the focus of Raksha Bandhan from the brother-sister bond to the tie between families united by marriage.

A daughter is supposed to return to her parents' home to tie the *rakhi* and to receive *sidha*. However, a visit is not always possible, in which case the *rakhi* and the money may be exchanged through the mail. The rest of the *sidha*, the food and clothing, could be sent by messenger if the parents so wished. A Sweeper family said that because their daughter had not come for a visit on Salono, they gave her nothing. Otherwise, they would have given puris and clothing. In comparable circumstances, a Brahman family sent gifts to a married sister. What is done in such situations is always a matter of individual choice. Families that are ordinarily conscientious about sending gifts to married sisters and daughters on appropriate festivals abandon the practice if a death occurs on that date. A Brahman family whose eldest son died on Salono did not celebrate the festival for 20 years. Then a grandson was born on that day, and the family resumed observance of the festival (see also, Opler, 1959b: 275).

Charm tying was not limited to relatives. Brahman family priests formerly tied charms on their patrons (jajmans). The custom has largely been abandoned although it survives in a few families. In 1958 we asked a Brahman man about the custom. He emphatically denied that the custom existed. He said:

> We gave it up a long time ago. Feelings have changed. The Jats stopped giving grain on Salono and so we Brahmans stopped tying the charms. The change came about 30 years ago. Jats and Brahmans stopped regarding each other as jajman and family priest [purohit]. The relationship is now one of equality. The old relationship exists in many villages but not here.

However, a Jat farmer who kept a meticulous written record of expenses noted the gift of one rupee to his family priest on Salono, 1958. He said, "Purohits usually do this to their jajmans." His budget for 1977 noted only that his expenses for Raksha Bandhan were Rs. 15. There was no separate line for a gift to his purohit. In 1958, our purohit tied a rakhi on us, as did the woman who cleaned our rooms and also the driver of the Delhi-Shanti Nagar bus.

In our survey of festivals in 1978, none of our informants mentioned giving money to the family priest. One Brahman woman said that her family had once tied charms on the wrists of three jajmans but had discontinued the practice. She added that a guru came from a neighboring village to tie a charm on the wrist of her husband. They gave him money in return. In any case, the jajmani system was growing weaker. The custom of purohits tying rakhis on their jajmans may have all but disappeared.

In Karimpur and Kishan Garhi, the ritual of tying a protective charm is mingled with Jawara, the Barley Feast. In Karimpur, wheat takes the place of barley in this agricultural festival. Wadley wrote:

> [On] Snake's Fifth (Savan sudi 5) . . . broken clay pots are filled with earth in which wheat seeds are planted. The wheat is allowed to grow for ten days and the quality of the "crop" is believed to represent the quality of that household's next wheat harvest. After ten days, on raksha bandan, these pots of wheat are worshipped and rakhi are tied on the seedlings, with the obvious implication of "tying on protection." In this instance, the protection is that of a food supply . . . [Wadley, 1975: 166].

FIG. 78. Drawings for Raksha Bandhan (Salono) on the wall of a Potter's house, 1958. The sunflower in a pot (center) is to the right of a door; the other large drawing (left), probably some kind of a tree, is to the left of the door. The small sketch (right) is on the doorjamb.

Barley plays no role on Raksha Bandhan in Shanti Nagar. However, one woman drew a mural of a flowerpot with a flower on Salono (fig. 78). We never saw a similar mural on any other festival, but for one of the rites of childbirth known as "Sixth," among the protective and auspicious symbols drawn on walls are creepers and flowers. They symbolize fertility and increase (R. Freed and S. Freed, 1980: 376). Thus, the flower and flowerpot in Shanti Nagar might be analogous to the barley shoots in Karimpur, both representing fertility and increase.

Barley is used differently in Kishan Garhi than wheat in Karimpur. Marriott identified two festivals on Shrawan *sudi* 15, Salono and Raksha Bandhan. Salono is the festival on which sisters exchange gifts with brothers, but barley shoots rather than string-*rakhi*s are a sister's offering. Marriott wrote:

> On *Saluno* day, many husbands arrive at their wives' villages, ready to carry them off again to their villages of marriage. But, before going off with their husbands, the wives as well as their unmarried village sisters express their concern for and devotion to their brothers by placing young shoots of barley, the locally sacred grain, on the heads and ears of their brothers. Since brothers should accept nothing from their sisters as a free gift, they reciprocate with small coins [Marriott, 1955: 198].

Barley shoots are used on two festivals in Shanti Nagar, Dassehra and Sanjhi. They symbolize fertility in each case. On Sanjhi in Shanti Nagar, sisters place barley shoots on their brothers' ears and receive a small return gift, a ritual which takes place on Salono in Kishan Garhi. It is helpful to think of rituals of this nature as ceremonial elements that may be observed on different festivals in different places. The village of Mohana furnishes another example. There women swing on Raksha Bandhan as well as on Tijo (Majumdar, 1958: 268, 272).

Raksha Bandhan in Kishan Garhi is the festival when *purohits* tie *rakhi*s on the wrists of their patrons, utter a blessing, and receive a return gift. Marriott analyzed the relationship of Salono and Raksha Bandhan in terms of the Sanskritic (great) tradition and the little tradition. He wrote:

Parallels between the familial festival of *Saluno* and the specialized Brahmanical festival of Charm Tying—between the role of sister and priest—are obvious. The likelihood that Charm Tying has its roots in some such little-traditional festival as *Saluno* tempts speculation. The ceremonies of both now exist side by side, as if they were two ends of a process of primary transformation [Marriott, 1955: 198].

In Kishan Garhi, the separation of Raksha Bandhan from Salono—that is, the *purohit*-patron tie from the sister-brother tie, symbolized by a *rakhi* in the former case and barley shoots in the latter—is being eroded. Some sisters have begun to tie charms of the priestly type on the wrists of their brothers. *Rakhis* are especially convenient for sending through the mail. Thus, Raksha Bandhan in Kishan Garhi is becoming increasingly similar to the festival in Shanti Nagar in that *rakhis* are used by both sisters and *purohits*. On the other hand, the festivals are increasingly dissimilar, for the ritual of protection tying by the family priest has almost disappeared in Shanti Nagar.

The third component of the festival on the full moon of Shrawan is the worship of a deity known as Salono. Mukerji (1916: 79) explained, "'Salono' is a corruption of the Persian term *Sal-i-Nau*, 'the new year'; and it is a name given to the full moon of *Sravan*, because it marks the point of transition between the old and the new Fasli or agricultural year." Whatever the origin of the word, it now identifies a minor deity. Balfour said that "Salone" is the spirit or nymph of the month of Shrawan. "The Rakhi festival was instituted in honor of the good genii when Durvasa the sage instructed Salone . . . to bind on rakhi, or bracelets, as charms to avert evil" (Balfour, 1885, 3: 356).

Salono and Raksha Bandhan thus have a mythological connection through the sage Durvasas. "He was wandering over the earth when he beheld in the hands of a nymph of the air [Salono?], a garland of flowers, with whose fragrance he was enraptured. The graceful nymph presented it to the sage" (Garrett, 1990: 193). Soon after, Durvasas encountered Indra and gave him the garland. Indra treated the garland in a contemptuous manner, so enraging Durvasas that he cursed the "ruler of the three worlds." Because of the curse, Indra was defeated by a race of demons known as the Daityas, or Danavas. The three worlds then fell into decay. The gods, oppressed by the Danavas, turned to Vishnu for salvation.

The connection of the Danavas with Raksha Bandhan brings Bali, king of the Danavas, into the picture. The legend of King Bali is recounted earlier in association with the festival of Hell Fourteenth. An episode of the legend involves the protective power of the *rakhi*. Underhill (1991: 134) related, "[W]hile men and gods were still under Bali's tyranny, Indrani, wife of Indra, procured [a *rakhi*] from Vishnu, and tied it round Indra's wrist, whereby he became protected from Bali." The mantra that a *purohit* is supposed to recite while tying the *rakhi* derives from this myth. Mukerji (1916: 83) translated the mantra as follows, "Thus I tie the 'Raksha' round your wrist,—the same which bound the arms of the mighty Bali, king of the Danavas. May the protection afforded by it be eternal!" *Purohits* no longer tie the *rakhi* in Shanti Nagar, and so this mantra, if it was formerly used, has fallen into disuse.

Bahadur (1995: 86–91) wrote that after the worship of the household deities on Raksha Bandhan, the eldest lady of the family recites the following story. It has nothing to do with Salono, Durvasas, Bali, or Indrani. Rather, it is the popular story of the pious Shravan Kumar and Dasaratha, father of Ram and his brothers.

The dutiful Shravan was an only child. When his parents were old, blind, and feeble, they wanted to make a pilgrimage to the Ganga to take a dip and wash away their sins. Their son took a long pole with a basket at each end and, placing his mother in one basket and his father in the other, he set out to carry them to the Ganga. They stopped to rest, and Shravan Kumar went to a nearby stream to fetch water for his parents. Raja Dasaratha was hunting nearby. He heard some rustling in the bushes and, thinking that it was a deer, shot an arrow into the thicket. Hearing a cry, the king rushed to the mortally wounded young man. He offered to take the water to the elderly couple, but Shravan feared that his parents would not take water from a stranger. The king tried unsuccessfully to deceive them. They refused the water and cursed the king for killing their son. The king was childless. The curse referred to a son of the king, "May your death be due to agony of the heart while waiting for your son . . ." (Bahadur, 1995: 90).

The royal astrologers were delighted by the curse, for it would surely bring children to the king. Ram and his brothers were born. Ram and Lakshman later went into exile for 14 years, and Dasaratha died of a broken heart, thus fulfilling the curse. What does this story have to do with Raksha Bandhan? Bahadur (1995: 91) explained that Shravan Kumar died because he did not have a sister and no one ever tied the protective *rakhi* on his wrist.

Lewis (1958: 208) recorded several mythological explanations of Salono. The village Brahmans trace the festival's origins back to Paras Ram who, after fighting 21 battles against the Rakshasas (demons), called in his allies and tied *ponchi*s on their wrists to remind them of their duty. The Jats interpret the story in less heroic terms. Paras Ram tied *ponchi*s on the wrists of his subjects who did not pay their taxes and forced them to pay. Paras Ram is no doubt Parasu-Rama (Rama of the Ax), the sixth avatar of Vishnu. He fought 21 battles with Kshatriyas, not with demons, although the Brahmans may have regarded the Kshatriyas in some sense as demons (Daniélou, 1964: 171). In any case, the story evidently indicates an ancient struggle for supremacy between Kshatriyas and Brahmans, a conflict that today in Shanti Nagar takes the form of tension between Jats and Brahmans. Yet another legend traces the protective power of the *rakhi* back to Abhimanyu, a warrior in the great battles described in the Mahabharata. He was invulnerable when wearing the *rakhi*, but was slain when it broke in battle.

None of the villagers of Shanti Nagar spontaneously told us a story connected with Salono, and we never asked if there was one. In view of the many different tales that villagers may recite on Salono, we suspect that had we asked villagers for a story, we might have heard one or even several.

On Salono, some women draw murals with ochre (*geru*) on each side of their doorway, or near it (figs. 78, 79, and 11) (see also Wadley, 1975: fig. 13a). The images are called Salono. Literate women write *Om* or various names of God (Ram, Isvara, Paramatma) on the wall near the drawings, or names may be written without any

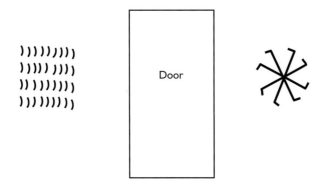

FIG. 79. Drawing for Raksha Bandhan (Salono) on the wall of a Brahman's house, 1958. The four rows of vertical marks, of unknown significance, are to the left of a door. The wheellike figure, which could be two superimposed swastikas, symbols of good fortune, is to the right of the door.

drawing. Women prepare a festive meal, which may include sweet puris, halva, *khir*, and, especially, sweet noodles (*seviya*) that seem to be a specialty of the day. They then perform a brief ritual. Taking a bit of the festive food, they stick it on the pictures. Some women may stick a garland on the wall. The family then has its meal, and afterwards the *ponchi*s are tied. No mantras are recited. We asked only one villager, a teenaged Potter boy, whether this brief ritual was a worship (puja). He did not consider it to be a puja. In reply to the question about why the women made the offering of food, he replied, "You just do it." However, the ritual could be regarded as a puja. In any case, this ritual practiced in Shanti Nagar is much simpler than the rather elaborate worship of household gods described by Bahadur (1995: 87–88).

The historical connections of the rituals of barley, *rakhi*, and Salono, the three facets of the festival of the full moon of Shrawan, are obscure. As Marriott suggested, some ancient festival of the little tradition may be at the root of the threefold nature of the modern festival. On the other hand, three originally unrelated festivals observed on Shrawan *sudi* 15 may in the passage of time have come to be considered aspects of a single festival. In any case, the elements of the festival can be combined in rather different ways in different places, as can be seen in the villages of Karimpur, Kishan Garhi, and Shanti Nagar. In Shanti Nagar, the principal theme of the day is interaction, both between sister and brother and between families related by marriage. A sister does not appeal to a deity for protection on Salono. Rather, she reminds her brother of his duty. She invokes dharma, perhaps the most powerful moral concept of Hinduism.

SHRADDHA (KANAGAT)

Kanagat, or Shraddha (homage), is a 16-day festival when families commemorate their ancestors. The villagers use both terms, but primarily Kanagat. The bettereducated people tend to use Shraddha, the more common term in northern India. The festival begins on Bhadrapad Purinmashi and ends on Ashvin Amavas; thus it lasts a fortnight plus one day. Except for the full-moon day, the festival falls in the dark fortnight of Ashvin. In South India, the festival is observed simultaneously with the northern version but in the dark fortnight of Bhadrapad instead of Ashvin. The month begins a fortnight earlier in the north than in the south, which means that the last (dark) fortnight of an *amanta* month is the first (dark) fortnight of the following *purinmanta* month.

Shraddha has the general meaning of a funeral ritual. Hindu literature cites a host of occasions for holding a *shraddha* for an ancestor. Garrett (1990: 596–604) and Balfour (1885, 3: 728–729) refer to many festivals and other times for honoring family ancestors; Underhill (1991: 112) noted precisely 96 such occasions. Williams (1883: 305) listed 12 classes of *shraddhas*, among them a daily ritual of offering water to ancestors with the morning and evening prayers.

In Shanti Nagar, matters have been simplified. Villagers observe various funeral rites for twelve months following a death (R. Freed and S. Freed, 1980: 508–542). After the initial year, an important ancestor may be commemorated on the anniversary of his/her death. All ancestors are honored during the fortnight of Kanagat. The Sweepers have a community memorial for their caste ancestor and make sacrifices and offerings there on Diwali and Holi (fig. 31). Some Brahman, Jat, and Bairagi families have small memorial shrines (*thans*) for a dead male ancestor (always one who was very important to the family), which are a focus of worship on various festivals and other occasions. They are usually simple structures made of a few bricks or just an arrangement of several stones. For recently dead ancestors, worship takes place every day. In due time, the observance of these daily rituals is reduced to such occasions as a wedding, the day a cow begins to give milk, the appropriate day during Kanagat, days of fasting, and periods of illness in the family when there is need to supplicate the ancestor. Followers of Sanatan Dharma used the word "puja," worship, to describe the ritual at a memorial. People who followed the principles of the Arya Samaj denied worshipping the ancestor, claiming only to fold their hands at the *than* and to remember the ancestor. No matter what their guiding principles were, all families who had a *than* lit a lamp at the memorial, poured water on it, and left offerings of brown sugarcakes, milk, or cooked food on the appropriate occasions.

To the extent that Kanagat partakes of a funeral rite, it involves Hindu theories of the soul and its fate after death. In brief, the body is considered to be ephemeral as compared to the soul, which goes on forever. Although the body can be seen and touched, it and the mundane world it inhabits are maya, illusion. The world of the soul is nonillusionary and eternal. When a person dies, the soul leaves the body to begin a journey that leads usually to rebirth or, in the case of a person of great piety, to release from the round of rebirths (moksha). The soul's passage to the land of the dead for judgment by Yama, the God of Death, and its subsequent rebirth take a year. One purpose of funeral rites is to help the soul on its way. The necessities of life on earth—water, food, and fire—are projected into the afterlife and provided to the deceased in the form of ritual offerings.

An individual is not honored during Kanagat until a year after death. Because the cycle of death and rebirth is completed in one year—except in the case of an untimely death, which condemns a soul to become a wandering ghost until its allotted time on earth has expired—a soul presumably would have no further need of sustenance in the form of offerings on Kanagat or at any other time. This apparent anomaly does not trouble the villagers, who explain Kanagat in terms of provisioning the soul. Two elderly men, a Brahman and a Jat, recited the following myth as the reason for Kanagat. They attributed the story to the Mahabharata. The Jat gave the following slightly more detailed version than did the Brahman. (See also, Crooke, 1968, 1: 181.)

> A bastard brother of the Pandavas [Raja Karana] was in the habit of giving one and a quarter maunds [roughly 50 kg] of gold as charity every day. When he died, he found only gold waiting for him in heaven. Then he returned to earth for fifteen days and gave away a lot of food so that he would have food in the afterlife. This is the origin of the fifteen days of Kanagat when people distribute food for their dead relatives.

This elderly Jat, who was a respected village leader firmly committed to the principles of the Arya Samaj, took a jaundiced view of Kanagat. Commenting on the fairly elaborate ritual of a prominent Brahman, he said that the Brahman's Kanagats were mainly for show.

Oblations to ancestors during the first year after death sustain the soul on its journey either to rebirth or to moksha. The annual festival of Kanagat is also interpreted in this light. However, offerings to ancestors gradually assume a different role. After a time, revered ancestors come to be regarded as semidivine beings. Such ancestors are usually called pitris in the case of men and *devatas* (*devtas*) for women, but both men and women may be referred to as *devatas*. Oblations are made at *thans* to enlist the protection and aid of ancestors. A similar view can be taken of Kanagat. Offerings are still intended to honor ancestors, to provision them in the afterlife, but also to have their aid available in time of need and, conversely, to avoid their enmity if not propitiated.[41] Thus, the apparent anomaly of provisioning souls after their posthumous journey has been finished is resolved. The reason is that ancestors become semidivine beings. The transformation of Bhumiya, the founding male ancestor of the village, into a godling is an example of this general process.

Despite the honorific side of Kanagat, we consider it to be chiefly a festival of interaction. The festival focuses attention on relationships within the patrilineal joint family, the basic unit of Indian social organization. The two most important sets of relationships in Indian society are, on the one hand, those within the joint family, generally patrilineal, and, on the other, those between families united by marriage. The linchpin of the joint family is the father-son relationship. The relationship of a married sister and her brother is the basis of the affinal tie. Marriage connects two families just as strongly as it binds two individuals.

Organizing the festivals by basic theme brings Kanagat and Salono into juxtaposition for easy comparison. In a strictly chronological scheme they are separated by several intervening festivals. The sister-brother relationship is basic to Salono. The exchange of gifts between sister and brother and between families of in-laws strengthens this important nexus of relationships. Kanagat does not have quite the same effect, for the main relationship is between a family head and his dead father and other ancestors. However, grandsons are usually present at the ritual. The ceremony impresses them with the continuity and importance of the family, which transcends the life of any individual.

Basham strongly expressed the interactional interpretation of Shraddha:

> The family, rather than the individual, was looked on as the unit of the social system . . . . The group was bound together by *shraddha*, the rite of commemorating the ancestors . . . . Thus, the dead and the living were linked together by this rite, which . . . was a most potent force in consolidating the family. Shraddha defined the family . . . [Basham, 1954: 155–156].

In her detailed description and convincing analysis of the important festival of Pitra Paksha (Ancestors' Fortnight) in two villages in Karnataka, Hanchett also viewed commemorative rituals as consolidating and strengthening the family, bringing together ancestors and descendants. Pitra Paksha, observed in the dark fortnight of Bhadrapad (*amanta* system), is the south Indian equivalent of Shraddha. Hanchett called attention to the semidivine nature of ancestors and to their protective function. "[Ancestors] . . . are thought to remain involved with the family as protective spirits after death. To remain on good terms with their descendants, they are said to require only this annual offering" (Hanchett, 1988: 226). The ritual connects the generations of a family, thereby promoting its future.

The 16 days of Kanagat mean that all *tithi*s (lunar days) are represented, the full moon and new moon bracketing the other 14 days. A remembered ancestor is commemorated during Kanagat on the lunar day that corresponds to the *tithi* on which he died. For example, the father of our Brahman landlord died on Magh *sudi* 3. Thus he was honored on *tij* (third) during Kanagat. Our landlord also commemorated his death on Magh *sudi* 3. Prominent people could be remembered both on their anniversary of death and also during Kanagat. The people honored during Kanagat were almost always members of three ascending generations, that is, deceased parents, grandparents, and great-grandparents. However, children who lived into adolescence might also be honored. A beloved promising son of our landlord's family who died at the age of 16 years was commemorated on Kanagat. The 16th day served not only for persons who died on Amavas but also as the day to honor relatives whose lunar days of death had been forgotten. In addition, ancestors whose names were no longer remembered were considered to have been commemorated on the 16th day.

We attended Kanagat observances held by our landlord's family in both 1958 and 1977. The ritual was similar in all observances. To judge from interviewing members of other families in various castes, this particular Brahman family practiced a more elaborate ritual than did most other families. The denigrating comment of the elderly Jat noted above referred to this family. The family honored five of its deceased members during Kanagat: the family head's father, father's father and mother, father's father's father, and its promising deceased eldest son.

The family was a household of three generations: the family head and his wife, two sons, five daughters, and the head's mother and her brother. The head's father, who had much to do with the family's currently favorable circumstances, died on *tij* (third). The head's son also died on *tij*, and so the Kanagat on the third theoretically took care of both grandfather and grandson. Five Brahman men were invited to observe the ritual and to share the feast on Kanagat *tij*. We were also invited both as a courtesy and as honorary family members. The family head and his mother's brother completed the list of participants, but all family members shared in the festive food.

The ritual was conducted in the house by an elderly man, one of the guests. He and the family head sat facing each other, a brass dish between them. Some unidentified leaves were on the dish. The family head held some grass (probably kusha grass, see n. 17) and some four-anna coins. The guest poured water over the head's hands while both recited mantras, among them the Gayatri. This act of catching water in the palm of the hand is called *chullu*. The grass was allowed to drop into the dish. The idea was that the head's father would have grass to walk on in the afterlife. The chanting ended with the name of the head's father. The head then gave a four-anna coin to each guest. The feast was sumptuous: first halva and *khir*, then lentils, vegetables, and puris.

One of the guests told us that the family head performed a fire ceremony (*havan*) before the ritual of *chullu*. The guest said that we had arrived too late to see it. We later interviewed the family head about his observance of Kanagat *tij* and he did not mention a fire ceremony, although he did offer water to the sun. In 1977, we attended the Kanagat for the head's grandfather and saw no *havan*. Although they may take place from time to time, they are certainly uncommon. However, Babb (1975: 35) described a *shraddha* whose chief ritual was a *havan*.

In our extensive interviewing about observances on Kanagat, only a recently widowed Jat ever mentioned fire ceremonies. She was the widow of a wealthy man who was a lambardar and in all likelihood the most important village leader before his death in 1958. Speculating that she might have a fire ceremony for him after the initial year of mourning, she explained:

> On Kanagat, we'll feed five to ten people and may give away five to ten rupees. We might have a fire ceremony. Not everyone does this, only one or two families. It happens only when a good man dies. We'll call Ram Krishan [an expert pandit from a neighboring village] for the *havan*. And we'll give clothes to our family *purohit*.

Any clothing given to a *purohit* would have to be brand new. Old clothes would not be acceptable, for they might have belonged to the dead man and, in any case, worn clothing was given traditionally to people of the lower castes. However, they were beginning to resist this practice. The Leatherworkers no longer would accept old clothes. Only the Sweepers, who were at the bottom of the hierarchy, would take them (R. Freed and S. Freed, 1980: 521–522). On the other hand, the deceased's good clothes, usually worn only on festive and important occasions, were given to relatives. A man's clothing would be given to a young male affine. Clothing frequently formed part of the gift sent on funerary occasions.

The death and cremation of this Jat lambardar is described in detail in R. Freed and S. Freed, 1980 (pp. 511–514). His family planned to have an elaborate monument constructed in his honor. It was called a *samadhi* because of its projected size and because the family hoped that holy men would use it as a place of meditation. The lambardar's bones and ashes were collected three days after his cremation and divided into two parts. One part was taken to the Ganga for disposal, the other was buried at the place where his memorial would be constructed. The widow said that a *havan* conducted by five Brahmans was held at the site. The spot was marked by a few bricks until the building could be built. Family members lit a lamp there daily, poured water over the bricks while facing the sun, left food offerings, and bowed to the ancestor.

The *samadhi* was contrary to all Arya Samaj principles and to the usual thriftiness of the Jats. "There are sixteen samskaras [ceremonies of purification] . . . ending in the cremation of the dead body. It is everybody's duty to perform these samskaras. But nothing should be done for the dead after cremation" (Saraswati, 1956: 853–854). Some of the members of this family's lineage were strict followers of the Arya Samaj, and they expressed subtle disapproval of the memorial's construction as well as of the funeral and mourning ceremonies followed by the family. Nonetheless, the *samadhi* as it was planned in 1958 had been built by 1977. There were two structures. The one covering the lambardar's remains was an impressive monument with four columns and a cupola. The other building was a guest house that the family hoped would attract holy men. The guest house had an unfinished look, and no one was living there while we were in the village. The *samadhi* was far grander than the small, simple *than*s of other families. It had attracted no imitators. It was a unique monument to a remarkable man.

Although we were sometimes told that Kanagat was principally a Brahman festival, it seemed to be widely observed. But no one described a ritual with grass, mantras, the distribution of coins, and offerings of water to the sun as was done in the Brahman family's Kanagat. Rather, most families observed Kanagat with a minimum of ritual. By far the most common practice was to feed a piece of bread to a cow every day during Kanagat. However, for some families, the custom is a daily observance and perhaps not specifically for Kanagat. For most people, the special feature of Kanagat was at least one festive meal. A family may prepare a meal for each relative honored during the festival. A simpler practice is to prepare one meal on the 16th day, which is the day reserved for honoring all ancestors.

Festive food is offered to Brahmans and, of course, to cows. It is also given to the family Sweeper, dogs, and crows. Two four-eyed dogs are associated with Yama, God of Death (Dowson, 1891: 373–374). Babb (1975: 153) noted that crows "personify the dead"; Lewis (1958: 214) said that they "are believed to be the descendants of a Hindu sage." Sometimes a gift of raw food (*sidha*) is sent to a Brahman. The Dalits do not give food to Brahmans, for Brahmans judge them to be ritually too impure to provide acceptable food for Brahmans (S. Freed, 1970: 10, table 1). If a family of middle-caste rank was concerned about such a problem, it could be skirted by inviting a Brahman woman to cook the festive meal, as did one Watercarrier family in 1958. Anyone could accept food cooked by a Brahman. This Watercarrier family was preparing a feast to honor the father of the current family head and planned to feed an elderly Brahman man. The other Watercarrier family was holding a Kanagat service to honor the father's mother of the family head. The Watercarrier woman would do the cooking, and no Brahman would be fed.

In 1978, a 35-year-old Watercarrier woman described the use of leaves in her family's Kanagat Amavas ritual. She said:

> We feed Brahmans during Kanagat. We remember the day when an ancestor died and feed Brahmans the same day. We offer bread to cows. We don't use our grinding stone for the 16 days of Kanagat. When Kanagat ends on Amavas, we make *khir* and get 16 dhak or *tori* leaves. We put some *khir* and one piece of bread on each leaf and pour water around it. We offer the *khir* and bread to cows and crows. The leaves are stored in the house for one year. We do this for all dead persons whom we might have forgotten.

The leaves of the dhak tree (*Butea frondosa*) are used for serving food and wrapping edibles. *Tori* leaves (*Cucumis acutangulus*) probably serve the same functions. We did not identify the leaves used in the Brahman family's ritual of Kanagat *tij*, but they may have been from the same plants. Only this Watercarrier mentioned preserving leaves for a year. She offered no explanation, and we did not ask for one.

A Barber woman described a ritual on Kanagat Amavas similar to the one practiced by the Watercarriers. She said, "We give bread to cows and dogs for 15 days. On the 16th day, Amavas, we make *khir* and put it in 16 plates. Then we give it to cows, dogs, and crows. We do this for the ancestors whom we forgot to celebrate during the first 15 days." The Brahman family whose Kanagat *tij* we attended also made 16 portions of food on Amavas, in this case thin bread (*manda*) instead of *khir*, to take care of all the forgotten relatives. The essential feature of the ritual on Amavas is the 16 servings of food, which means that there is a particular serving that represents each day of Kanagat. Whether the food is served on plates or leaves is inconsequential.

Three women said that hand mills for grinding wheat should not be used during Kanagat. This prohibition would be difficult to observe, for wheat is ground daily to make the day's bread. A Watercarrier woman claimed not to use her hand mill for the 16 days of Kanagat. On the other hand, a Blacksmith woman said, "In olden days, women didn't use the grinding stone for 16 days, but now they don't follow these rules much." In view of the modern diet, which is based on wheat bread, we suspect that few women avoid using their hand mills. However, it could be done if a family were willing to use wheat flour ground in commercial mills.[42]

The distribution of food on Kanagat is affected by the principles of the Arya Samaj, the withering of the jajmani system, and the insistence that Brahmans and Jats are now equal. In 1978, a Jat woman explained:

> The Jats don't do all that much on Kanagat. Its more the Brahmans. I do it for my husband's mother on the third and for his father on Amavas. We make *khir* and give it to our Sweeper and to dogs. We also give our Sweeper four pieces of bread. In the old days, we used to feed a Brahman, but not now. In this village, Jats and Brahmans are equal. So we don't feed them.

The different opinions of Jats and Brahmans regarding Kanagat were expressed in a brief exchange of views that took place just after our Brahman family celebrated Kanagat *tij*. A Jat man, a strong believer in the Arya Samaj, ridiculed the explanation advanced by a Brahman concerning the use of grass in the ritual, that is, the deceased would have grass upon which to walk. Laughing, joking, and seemingly ill at ease, he dismissed Kanagat as "just a belief in ritual." Although he laughed, it was clear that he believed his point of view to be the only one. The Brahman's reply would appear to be unsophisticated, but in fact it underlined an important component of the ritual, the feast for guests. He told the Jat that if he did not believe, then he would not get nice food. The Jat became quite excited, replying that everyone should die so that people could have nice food. In fact, if the feast is so important, then there should also be a feast on the day of death. The Brahman explained that a feast is not eaten on the day of death because everyone is sad. But as time goes on, the day of death is observed as a memorial and festive food is given to Brahmans and nice persons. Although Brahmans are the chief guests at a feast, a family might invite castemates as well. Another debate about death rituals by these two men is reported in R. Freed and S. Freed (1980: 524–525).

Children learn about festivals by watching adults, and they have the essential elements of a festival well in hand at an early age. Their familiarity with ritual is easily seen in their play. After having noticed children playing with rag dolls, we decided to set up a modest program of doll-play sessions (R. Freed and S. Freed, 1981: 85–96). We reserved a room for doll play, furnishing it with dolls representing men, women, and children, a set of tin doll dishes, and a large blunt knife. We did not impress children into playing. When they entered our quarters, they saw the dolls themselves or we pointed to them. The children then did as they liked. Their play enacted skits based usually on common village activities, such as the rites of marriage and festivals, Kanagat among them.

We watched four boys playing Kanagat: a Brahman (B), 12 years old; a Merchant (M), 11 years of age; a Potter (P), 13 years old; and a Barber, 9 years old, who did not talk, perhaps because he was much younger than the other boys.

> (B) Today is Aunt Chameli's Kanagat. What shall we make? (P) Dal, *pera*, *balushi* [both sweetmeats], *khir*. Let us cook. [They all begin to cook.] (M) Everything is ready. Let us invite. Let us invite Sweepers and Brahmans. (P) Let us invite the Freeds and their assistants. Quick. Call the watchman too. We could not find Ruth. Now all have come. (B) Here is a wrestler and a strong man. Let us start eating. [He enjoys his imaginary food. They distribute the food among themselves.] (M) Eat vegetables, potato, onion, and something spicy. Today Akhta is over. (P) No it is Kanagat. (M) [addressing the Brahman] How have you liked the *khir*, panditji, and the dal too? (B) Fine. [He distributes everything for the aunt's Kanagat.] (P) Let us play another game. (B) A thief came in the village . . . [and so on].

For these boys, Kanagat meant special food. They made no mention of any ritual. In 1958, Akhta was observed during Kanagat. The Merchant boy's confusion about Kanagat and Akhta in the doll-play session probably accounts for his invitation to the Sweepers. Sweepers and Brahmans are given a feast on Akhta, although the two castes do not sit together; but only Brahmans and special friends are invited to a family's feast during Kanagat. However, Sweepers are given some of the festive food as part of their compensation in the jajmani system. Wrestling was a popular feature of rural fairs and also a sport for village boys. The invitation to the watchman was a surprise. The watchman's only compensation was Rs. 90 collected semiannually. He did not participate in the jajmani system.

SANJHI

Sanjhi is an 11-day festival celebrated from Ashvin Amavas (also Kanagat Amavas) to Ashvin *sudi* 10. Sanjhi is the name of a woman, also a minor deity. Sanjhi is sometimes translated as "evening," because worship takes place in the evening (Bhatia: 1958). Dassehra is observed during the same period as Sanjhi. The two festivals are distinct. Dassehra commemorates the story of Rama as told in the Ramayana, with its grand climax, Rama's victory over Ravana taking place on the 10th day, Ashvin *sudi* 10. Villagers emphasize that Dassehra is a man's festival. On the other hand, Sanjhi is basically a *laukik* (popular) festival, the tale of a woman, named Sanjhi, moving back and forth between the homes of her parents and in-laws. It is a woman's festival, theoretically observed only by families with daughters, but in fact some families paid no heed to this restriction. Although the two festivals are contemporary and involve similar rituals with barley shoots on the 10th day of the bright fortnight, they can be distinguished with no particular difficulty. Dassehra is a Sanskritic festival of interest to men. Sanjhi is a non-Sankritic festival, important to women but largely ignored by men.

Sanjhi as a female has two personas. She is a young wife trying to balance complicated relationships that involve two families, her husband's and her parents'. This persona dominates the folksongs of Sanjhi (Bhatia, 1958). She thus represents an important theme in the lives of women. She is also a minor goddess, a devi, with only a nebulous connection to any of the great goddesses. During the festival, she is honored with offerings and devotional singing. Because of this feature of the festival, it could be classified as an honorific festival. However, the dominant theme is clearly interaction between a woman's natal and marital homes and between sisters and brothers. We therefore classify it as a festival of interaction.

The focus of the festival is a realistic depiction of Sanjhi in low relief attached to a wall with wet cow dung. The body is made of many small, star-shaped flat disks of dried mud colored white with a touch of vermillion in the center. A single oval plaque forms the face, its features clearly represented. Sometimes, only the skirt is formed from disks, the body from the waist up represented by a plaque (fig. 80). Sanjhi's braid is shown, as are all her ornaments: anklets, bracelets, hand ornaments, and a star to be worn over the heart. Her hands, feet, breasts, and nipples are usually realistically displayed. She is veiled, for she is living at the time in her husband's household where wives observe a form of purdah. Children begin to prepare the earthenware forms well in advance of Amavas so that everything will be ready for creating the image.

FIG. 80. Sanjhi, 1977. A well-ornamented Sanjhi at the house of a Brahman, her torso formed from a single plaque.

On Amavas 1958, we watched the women and children of a Brahman family prepare their Sanjhi. The senior woman of the household used cow dung to outline a figure on the wall that would serve as a guide for pasting the clay disks. Girls of about 8 to 11 years of age were doing the work. As an additional touch, they put kohl around the eyes of the image. Little boys watched. Everyone was having a good time. After Sanjhi was on the wall, a small figure representing her daughter was added. Some people say that this figure is Sanjhi's sister. In 1977, the small figure was said to be Sanjhi's younger sister, but we have only one identification from that year. Nautiyal (1961: 164) identified this figure as a Sweeper woman, Sanjhi's servant. In any case, her name is Bambo. Members of the Brahman family we watched in 1958 covered the faces of the two figures with red veils. One of the women explained that Sanjhi had to cover her face before men, but for the little girl "it was just a custom." That is, it was a custom for the festival image, but not for everyday life. Unmarried

FIG. 81. Sanjhi, 1958. Image of Sanjhi and her daughter or younger sister at a Brahman's house.

girls do not observe purdah. We saw two other images where the little girls did not wear a veil, and one where Sanjhi herself was without a veil. In general, however, the figures were veiled (fig. 81 and front cover).

One of the wives of this family said that the clay ornaments could be used as gifts. If a married daughter was at her in-laws' house, her parents would send the presents there. If she was with her parents, her in-laws would send the gifts. Only this woman described this use of the clay ornaments, and we think that in all probability it is uncommon. Our notes are ambiguous and she may have been talking about Sanjhi rather than a daughter. Nonetheless, such an exchange would fit well with an interpretation of Sanjhi as a festival of interaction.

The image is worshipped with offerings of food and devotional singing for nine days. On the ninth day, two figures may be added to the wall, one representing a Barber and the other, her brother. The idea is that the Barber and brother have come to fetch Sanjhi and take her back. There is ambiguity in our notes about where Sanjhi is to be taken. We originally assumed that Sanjhi was visiting her parents and at the end of the festival, she went back to her husband. This is the traditional version (Bhatia, 1958; Kinsley, 1988: 113–114). However, the villagers were generally clear that Sanjhi was visiting her husband, and at the end of the festival returned to her parents. This point will be discussed in greater detail below. In any case, Sanjhi leaves on the 10th day, and the image is removed from the wall.

After having watched the Brahman children put Sanjhi on the wall, we visited several other families. A small Brahman nuclear family had assembled the material but had not yet started to paste the disks on the wall. The wife would have to do all the work, for the family's only daughter was just three years old. We wondered why this family had not joined with a related family to celebrate Sanjhi. Several families often joined forces to make an image that served all of them.

One of the three Barber families had Sanjhi and her daughter on the wall, their faces covered by a red veil. Although a young woman and a 12-year-old daughter were in the family, an elderly widow had done all the work. They used their own daughter's name as the name of Sanjhi's daughter. Another Barber family had not put up an image but said they would do so later. The third Barber family would make no image because it had no daughters.

Although the Merchant family had three daughters, they did not make an image. The Merchant was a strong follower of the Arya Samaj and discouraged the women of his household from such activity. The housewife said that her mother used to make Sanjhis, but she had to respect her husband's wishes.

Seven Brahman families assembled at a Watercarrier's house for Sanjhi. The houses were close together, and the families were good friends. Several of these Brahman families did not observe Sanjhi in their own homes, citing as a reason a family death that occurred on Sanjhi. However, it was apparently proper to join another family for the festival, that is, to participate in devotional singing before that family's image. The Watercarrier family had prepared the faces, with lips painted red, for both mother and daughter and said that the images would be glued to the wall that evening. Three other Brahman families planned to form another group to observe the festival. A common practice was for several families, usually related, to join forces for Sanjhi. The work of making the image was shared, and devotional singing was more pleasant when women from several families formed a group.

In the low-caste Sweeper quarter, two images would be set up for the enjoyment of all 17 families. Bambo was identified as Sanjhi's sister—not her daughter. Informants said that she was named Bambo, a nickname, because she was plump.

On the wall of a men's sitting house in the Leatherworkers' compound, we saw a big Sanjhi with a small Bambo and also a third figure, a Sweeper to beat a drum. Sanjhi was veiled. When we asked the men about Sanjhi, we were told to ask the women. However, one Leatherworker man with an intellectual bent offered to explain the festival. He took as his point of departure the fact that Sanjhi wore a veil. He said:

> There were 32 [the usual figure is 33] crores [320 million] of devis captured by Ravana. Rama Chandra promised to free them. Sanjhi covered her face since she was a devi and went to Rama Chandra to remind him of his promise. On the tenth day [Dassehra] Ravana was killed and the devis were set free.
>
> Nowadays two to four houses get together and make a devi; formerly there was just one for the whole village. I don't remember exactly if there was just one, but everything is changing. Everybody wants to have their own devi or just skip it.
>
> When I was a little child [he was 40 years old in 1958] one or two Sanjhis were made in the village. Then gradually there was less and less getting together and some families even make individual devis.

This Leatherworker recounted the same story when speaking of Dev Uthani Gyas. He modified the tale to fit the festival of Sanjhi simply by adding the participation of the goddess in the conflict between Rama and Ravana. A particular legend can be cited on more than one festival just as the same devotional song can be sung on several occasions.

A Jat man, a strict follower of the Arya Samaj, told the following historical tale to account for the origin of the festival of Sanjhi. This historical origin of the festival would better fit Arya Samaj doctrine than the one told by the Leatherworker, for it avoids the question of multiple deities.

> Sanjhi was the name of Prithvi Raja's daughter. Prithvi Raja was a Rajput king around the end of the first millennium. Prithvi Raja and Jai Chand were cousin-brothers. Prithvi Raja kidnapped Jai Chand's daughter, Sanyukta [Sanjogata or Samyogita]. Sanyukta and Prithvi Raja wanted to marry but Jai Chand would not let them. Sanjhi was Prithvi Raja's daughter and used to go to the River Yamuna daily to bathe. Her father was afraid that, because he had kidnapped Jai Chand's daughter, Jai Chand would in turn kidnap Sanjhi. Prithvi Raja built the Qutb Minar so Sanjhi could climb the tower and see the Yamuna. Water was brought from the river to the Qutb so that she could bathe there privately. As a celibate, she was very powerful and was seen bathing in the Yamuna and at the Qutb

Minar at one and the same time. She was a very great Sati because she meditated a great deal and became one with god so that she had god's powers at her command. Because of her, Prithvi Raja lost no battles. However, he came to know that she continued secretly to go daily to the Yamuna for a bath. He learned this on the tenth day and asked her if she wanted to disgrace him. The girl said, "If you are so concerned about your prestige, don't worry. Here I go." So she drowned herself in the river. The festival of Sanjhi celebrates this event. From that day Prithvi Raja went downhill. To remember her, we have Sanjhi. This festival is for females, not men. The women sing a song about angels [apsarases, Indra's heavenly nymphs who emerged from the ocean] coming to take her. "Since the end of Kanagat these things have started happening to you. And through you, we will have a view of the angels."

Our Jat friend's account of the origin of Sanjhi conforms closely to the history of the great Rajput prince, Prithvi Raja III, the last of the Delhi kings. Born in 1154, Prithvi Raja became a ruler at the age of 16. The Rajputs held Delhi at that time. The Muslims first attacked Prithvi Raja in 1191, and were hurled back. They tried again in 1192 and this time routed Prithvi Raja's enormous army. Prithvi Raja was captured and executed.

Samyogita (Sanjogata) was the daughter of Jai Chand (Jayachandra), king of Kanauj and Prithvi Raja's cousin-brother. Jai Chand was mortified by the preference shown to his cousin. He arranged a major ceremony in his capital in the course of which his daughter was to select her husband from assembled suitors. Prithvi Raja was not invited, or perhaps refused to attend. Jai Chand placed a mocking ill-shapen image of him as doorkeeper. To the consternation of everyone, the princess placed her garland around the neck of the statue. Before anyone realized what was happening, Prithvi Raja, hiding nearby with his attendants, seized her and carried her away in broad daylight. This act, in defiance of a father's will, at the time was judged to be an abduction and rape, and Prithvi Raja lost important followers as a consequence. Bitter internecine conflict ensued with much loss of life, which contributed to the later Muslim conquest of North India. However, the abduction is also considered a heroic act, and Prithvi Raja, the daring lover, has become a popular hero. Bereaved by his daughter's death, Jai Chand ended his career by drowning himself in the Ganges at Chandawar (Ferozabad), or else lost his life there in a battle with Muhammad Ghori in 1193. Sanjogata, sometimes said to be an incarnation of Rambha, an apsaras, was remarkably charming and considered in her day to be the perfect model of a Rajput woman (Balfour, 1885, 2: 401, 3: 296; Beames, 1869; Majumdar, 1966: 54, 105; Nehru, 1946: 233; Sharma, 1959: 77–80, 96–99; Thapar, 1976: 235–236).

It would serve no purpose here to attempt to reconcile details of the story recorded in Shanti Nagar and the accounts of the life of Prithvi Raja. Suffice to say that Sanjogata is probably the village Sanjhi, or if not she, then an unidentified daughter of Prithvi Raja. The glorification of this Rajput princess resembles that of Mirabai, wife of a Rajput ruler and a famous devotee of Krishna who is now a quasi deity. The deification of a saintly person is a common process in India.

We next visited the adjacent quarter of mingled Potter, Dyer, and Jat houses. The senior woman of the only Dyer family had made a very attractive Sanjhi with lifelike hands and hand ornaments. The Dyer was a skilled artisan, and her talent was visible in her image. We saw images at several Jat houses. As Arya Samajis, the Jats would be expected to ignore the festival. However, Sanjhi is a festival for women, and they are much less influenced by Arya Samaj doctrine than men.

Each of the 12 Potter families, some without daughters, had made its own image of Sanjhi. Similarly, the three Barber families each had its own image. One of the Barber families had no daughters, and when we visited on Amavas, the wife said that she would not make a Sanjhi for that reason. We visited her again the next day, and she had put an image on the wall. A neighboring Jat family had some surplus stars and gave them to her. That she had not prepared the materials for an image shows that what she told us on Amavas was true. However, she simply changed her mind when a neighbor offered her some stars. It is well to keep in mind that generalizations about customary behavior have exceptions.

There is a good reason for each family to have an image. Offerings are made to the image every day for nine days, so it would be more convenient to have one at home than to go to another household. Separate images do not necessarily indicate social fragmentation. Women from several families could still assemble at one household for devotional singing before the goddess.

Continuing our survey on Amavas, we visited seven Jat families at the opposite end of the village from the Jat-Dyer-Potter quarter. One family would make no Sanjhi because there was no daughter in the house. Another family also would not have an image because, according to a young man, "My family does not accept Sanjhi, although the rest of the village does." We asked if it was because of Arya Samaj beliefs. He said that he did not know.

Five of these Jat families planned to observe the festival. One family already had a Sanjhi on the wall, but there was no image of the daughter. The senior woman did not know why they made an image, only that they would offer her ghee, sugar, and the skim from milk in the evening. They planned to plant barley to have shoots ready for the 10th day. Two other families would make a Sanjhi. One family planned to mount the image in the evening. At the other household, which was a strong proponent of the Arya Samaj, a small girl was making a very nice Sanjhi. An adult man of the household, observing the work, said "It is all the play of children." Two families said "We are not making a Sanjhi because they are making one at [so-and-so's] house and it is all one lineage." Thus, five of these seven families and also the Jat families in the combined Jat-Dyer-Potter quarter observed the festival, which indicated that most Jat families accepted Sanjhi despite counter influences from the Arya Samaj.

The 9th day sets the stage for the departure of Sanjhi on the 10th. Two figures are added to the tableau, a Barber and Sanjhi's brother, who came to fetch Sanjhi. We visited two Brahman families on the ninth. One family had added the figures, saying that they would offer them sugar and ghee as a feast in the evening. The brother was carrying a *kothari*, or *kothli*, a gift sent by parents to their daughter's in-laws. When a brother calls for his sister at her husband's house, he brings this gift.

At the second Brahman's house, the Barber was carrying two bundles (*kothlis*), one with food, the other with clothing. The Barber was lame; one of his legs was shorter than the other. A woman explained:

> The Barber is carrying the sack. The brother gave it to him. It is called *kothari*. You get *kothari* in [the month of] Shrawan [at the festivals of Tijo and Raksha Bandhan]. *Kothari* contains food. They have two *kotharis*, both carried by the Barber. The other one has clothing. Sanjhi comes to her in-laws once a year and will be going tomorrow evening. So the *kothari* is brought. In Sanjhi's village the custom is to have only lame Barbers. When a wife's brother comes, the custom is to laugh and cut jokes with him, and also with the Barber.

The departure of Sanjhi on the 10th day is the climax of the festival. She comes to every house the evening of Amavas and leaves the evening of the 10th. During the 10th day, her image is scraped off the wall. We observed the process in a Brahman family. Sanjhi's face and necklace were carefully taken off the wall; the rest of the image was just allowed to fall down. A woman swept the wall with a broom and washed it. She then drew a swastika, an auspicious symbol, where the image had been and stuck three or four barley shoots to the top of the swastika, or on its "ear" as they phrased it, just as sisters put barley shoots on the ears of their brothers earlier in the day (see below). The swastika would remain there for a year when the next image of Sanjhi would be mounted. Some women replaced the image with a drawing or with a bas-relief in dung of a peacock or peahen rather than a swastika (fig. 82). Three families replaced Sanjhi with a drawing of a *teran*, a wooden implement used to wind thread, which has two long parallel bars and one or two shorter connecting

FIG. 82. Sanjhi, 1977. Bas-relief of dung depicting a peacock that replaced the image of Sanjhi shown in figure 80.

bars. The idea behind replacing an image with a drawing is to fill a void and prevent the entry of an evil spirit. The pieces of her body are put in a basket, carried to a village pond, and dumped unceremoniously into it. Her face and necklace are saved for an evening ritual of departure.

For the evening ritual, women took a large pot and made holes around the side near the rim like portholes in a ship. The pot was called "Sanjhi's ship." Sand was put in the bottom of the pot so that the pitcher would not crack from the heat. Sanjhi's face and perhaps an ornament or two and a lighted lamp were put in the pot.

After dark, groups of girls and children paraded singing to a village pond where they launched the glowing ships, pushing them away from the shore so that they floated near the middle of the pond. Leatherworkers and Sweepers used one pond; the other castes usually used another. The lighted pots floating on a pond make a lovely sight. In 1958, we accompanied a Brahman family to the pond. Young girls, children, and a few trailing teenage boys formed the procession. There were no adult men. The children carried small pitchers that earlier were used in the distribution of *khil* and *batasha*s for Dassehra. They had made holes in them and put a light inside. On the way to the pond, they swung them around their heads. After Sanjhi's ships floated for a while, children waded into the pond and broke them with sticks. At about the same time, they swung their small pitchers out into the pond. A young man offered a charming explanation of the ritual: "Sanjhi leaves for home in the late afternoon, but after dark, she needs a light to find her way." That Sanjhi's home turns out to be water fits the interpretation of Sanjhi as an apotheosis of Sanjogata who in turn is an incarnation of an *apsaras*. The *apsaras*es emerged from water. However, Sanjhi needs no connection to the *apsaras*es to end her days in the village pond, for gods and goddesses are sometimes sunk in water to cool them.[43] For example, at the end of the Durga Puja in Bengal, the icon of Durga is cast into the waters (Balfour, 1885, 1: 993).

After sinking Sanjhi's ships, the girls prepared to go begging. Women and girls from a lineage are the core of a mendicant group. A few friends and neighbors might be included. The Brahmans whose ritual we observed went begging with Watercarriers and Merchants who lived in the neighborhood. They paraded singing to all the houses of the lineage begging for grain to take to the Merchant's shop and exchange for *khil* and *batasha*s. One woman said that the girls collect Rs. 1.25 from families where the birth of a son or a marriage had taken place. The sweets are then distributed among the girls and in the lineage. We estimated that they collected about 20 kg of grain that night.

Food, both as an offering and for distribution, is important on Sanjhi. Some food is offered to Sanjhi every day of the festival. On Amavas and the 10th, the first and last days of the festival, the usual festive dishes, halva, *khir*, puri, and noodles are prepared. On Amavas, the festive food is first offered to Sanjhi after she has been mounted on the wall. The family then enjoys their holiday meal. The special food celebrates more than just the festival of Sanjhi, for that particular new moon is Kanagat Amavas, and moreover, Amavas is a festival in its own right. The 10th day is also Dassehra as well as the last day of Sanjhi.

In addition to the distribution of *khil* and *batasha*s on the 10th day, *bakli* is distributed daily to lineage members and friends during the festival. *Bakli* is seasoned boiled gram (chickpea) or wheat. We became aware of this tradition when members of two friendly Brahman families brought us *bakli* (made with maize on one occasion) on the seventh, eighth, and ninth days. Distributions of food highlight the interactional aspect of the festival.

The ritual of Sanjhi as described to this point seems unconnected to the story represented in the tableau. Sanjhi is a young married women moving back and forth between her natal and marital families. Other personages are her daughter (or younger sister), who plays no role, and her brother and a Barber who are her escorts and carry gifts. Village women worship Sanjhi with oblations of food and with singing. Goddesses are usually worshipped in the expectation of specific benefits or the avoidance of misfortune, as are Santoshi Mata and Shitala, for example. But there is nothing in Sanjhi's scenario indicating that she grants boons. The interaction enacted in the tableau is between married sister and brother, that is between natal and marital houses. But the distribution of food in the village and the processions of females emphasize lineage unity and not a woman's dual roles of daughter and wife.

However, there is a ritual with barley shoots that is closely tied to the theme illustrated in the tableau. Barley seeds are planted on Amavas and the shoots are harvested on the 10th day. A sister then places them on the ears or heads of her brothers the morning of the 10th day and receives a small payment in return, usually one rupee. This ritual is equivalent to charm tying on Salono (Raksha Bandhan). A sister ties the *rakhi* on her brother's wrist and receives a return present. The ritual symbolizes the close tie of a brother and sister and, therefore, of her parental and marital families. Also, parents send gifts (*kothli*) to in-laws on Salono. Similar gifts are sometimes sent on Sanjhi. Sisters not only put barley shoots on the ears of their brothers, for which they receive money, but also on the ears of their older brother's wives, for which they receive a gift of clothing (*kothli*).

The reasons for considering the village festival of Sanjhi predominantly one of interaction derive from the story represented in the tableau, the ritual with barley shoots, and the distribution of food as a symbol of lineage unity. Fertility is a subordinate theme. The ritual with barley symbolizes fertility as well as the powerful tie of sister and brother. Nautiyal (1961: 167) recorded a song for Sanjhi that speaks of fertility as the reward for worshipping her.

In 1958 women had different views as to whether Sanjhi was in her natal or marital family during the festival. A Brahman woman said, "Sanjhi is a goddess who comes to her parents' house and stays 10 days. Then she goes to her in-laws' house [the pond]." But another Brahman said, "Sanjhi's brother is carrying a *kothari* [gift of food]. The brother brings this *kothari* for Sanjhi. Sanjhi has come to her in-laws. Now the brother has come with a *kothari* for Sanjhi. It is customary that when a brother is sent for a girl, he usually brings a gift for his sister because she is at her in-laws." In 1977, we recorded four statements on this point, all of them declaring that Sanjhi was in her husband's house during the festival. On the 10th day she returned to her natal home.

Although Sanjhi could theoretically be in either place, only the interpretation that she is at her in-laws during the festival fits the story represented in the tableau. Her brother calls for her with a gift, which would happen only if she were in her marital household. Were she in her natal household, her husband or one of his brothers would be her escort, and he would give nothing to her parents. Moreover, she wears a veil from the day that her image is put on the wall, proper behavior in her husband's village. Married women do not wear veils in their parents' house or in their natal village.

One of the songs sung on Sanjhi supports the interpretation of the tableau that places Sanjhi in her husband's house during the festival, after which she returns to her natal household.

> Look, Sanjhi is going to her father's house,
> Get 900 bullocks for her
> Our Rameshwar is too slim,
> Send away our Sanjhi, oh Ram
> Our Dayananda is too slim,
> Send away our Sanjhi, oh Ram.

Rameshwar and Dayananda are the names of the brothers of the singers. As many names are mentioned as there are brothers in the family. The significance of these lines is unclear.

We recorded a synopsis of only one other song sung on Sanjhi. After floating the face of Sanjhi on the village pond on the 10th day, the girls sang this song as they went through the streets begging for grain and money. The song is based on an episode in the Ramayana. When Ram was off hunting the golden deer, Sita was left alone. Ravana arrived and tricked Sita into leaving the magical protective circle. Then he kidnapped her. This song is appropriate for Dassehra and we collected a similar one in the context of that festival. Sanjhi and Dassehra are observed concurrently, a conjuncture that would naturally be reflected in the choice of songs. In any case, women sing such devotional songs their whole lives, and many songs may be sung whenever the women please.

The festival of Sanjhi takes place during the Nava Ratra (Nine Nights), the great festival for the worship of Durga (Durga Puja). This correspondence of dates strongly suggests that Sanjhi is equivalent to Durga, and that her festival is Durga Puja in local guise. Durga is a mighty warrior goddess, slayer of demons, whom Rama worships for success in his mortal conflict with Ravana. She is worshipped with animal sacrifice, especially a buffalo, perhaps recalling her triumph over Mahishasura, the dreaded buffalo demon. It is difficult to see Durga, the fierce battle queen, in the persona of Sanjhi, a young married woman quietly enacting the roles of daughter and wife, nor do the sweets offered daily to Sanjhi resemble the blood that nourishes Durga. (Concise descriptions of Durga and Durga Puja can be found in Kinsley, 1988, chap. 7; Mukerji, 1916, 115–125; and Underhill, 1991: 54–58.)

However, Durga has a benign side. She is identified with Parvati, wife of Shiva and mother of four divine children. During the nine days of Durga Puja, she visits her parental home where she can relax in the affection showered on her by her parents and family. On the 10th day, she returns to a more stressful life with her husband's family. At the end of the festival, her image is carried to a river or pond and immersed, symbolizing her departure from her natal village. From this point of view, Durga Puja and Sanjhi are similar.

In the 1950s, the villagers did not see it that way. They did not equate Sanjhi and Durga. Several people said that they observed the festival only because it was a custom. They claimed to know nothing more about it. Only three of the many people with whom we discussed the festival said spontaneously that Sanjhi was a goddess, and one woman denied it.

An elderly Brahman pandit, probably the villager most versed in Sanskritic literature, was the only person who connected Sanjhi with the great tradition. He had studied in Kashi (Varanasi), the great center of Hindu learning, and served as a family priest in Shanti Nagar. A brief account of his life is given in R. Freed and S. Freed (1993: 86–89). He said:

> Sanjhi is the nine goddesses. She is worshipped for nine days until Dassehra. During the time of the Mahabharata, the Pandavas worshipped a girl who said that they should worship a goddess if they wanted their desires to be fulfilled. So they established nine goddesses in this area: Mansa Devi in Narela, Kalka Devi in Chirag Delhi, a devi near Beri [he did not list all nine]. Each goddess has her own worship. The kings were repressive and did not permit people to worship openly. So they put up a little goddess in their homes for nine days. If a person had his wish fulfilled, a Brahman might advise him to read the Durgaji. It took nine days to read. All the goddesses are from the Mahabharata. Navaratra Devi is another name for Sanjhi. Sanjhis will be kept on the wall for nine days, then taken off, and immersed in the pond. The place will be plastered. All castes accept this.

Four identifications of Sanjhi seem possible from this account. In perhaps her initial form, Sanjhi is a girl on her way to becoming a goddess. Not yet having achieved that status, she invites the Pandavas to worship a goddess. Durga is the goddess whom the Pandavas worship in the Mahabharata (Kinsley, 1988: 107–108), but instead of Durga, the Pandavas substitute nine local goddesses according to our pandit. Finally, Sanjhi (Evening) is equated with Navaratra Devi (the Goddess of the Nine Nights). Despite these possible identifications, the best interpretation of the pandit's account is that Sanjhi is a deity who represents nine different local goddesses. In the 1950s, no villager equated Sanjhi and Durga.

Marriott's experiences were comparable to ours. Sanjhi in Kishan Garhi is known as Naurtha (Ninenights) or Nau Durga (Nine Durgas) (Marriott, 1955: 192). When Marriott asked the villagers what Naurtha represented, most people said that Naurtha is one of the Nine Durgas and an aspect of the Big Goddess. No one "was able to tell me what seems obvious . . . that the word 'Naurtha,' considered to be the name of an indigenous goddess, is nothing more than an old dialectic variant of *nava ratra*, which means 'nine nights'. . . . [B]y sheer linguistic confusion . . . in the contact between great and little traditions, a new minor goddess has been created. But no sooner has [she] been born . . . than she is reabsorbed . . . as a new manifestation of the great Goddess principle" (Marriott, 1955: 201). In Marriott's terms, Naurtha is an example of parochialization.

Marriott (1955: fig. 3) published a photograph of an image of Naurtha. Near her right hand is a drawing of a goddess on a tiger, a common representation of Durga. Over Naurtha's head is a semicircular element that recalls the crenellated roundels that surround depictions of Durga (Daniélou, 1964: pl. 26; Poster, 1994: 300–301).

One may find vague traces of the great goddess Durga in the images of Sanjhi in Shanti Nagar only by stretching imagination to its limits. Such "traces" may be of little significance. We mention them only for the sake of taking everything into account. The most intriguing clue, because it is specific and not a feature of any other festival, is the personage of the Barber with one leg shorter than the other. Ganesh, the son of Shiva and Parvati, who is identified with Durga, has a broken tusk that is shorter than the other one. This shared defect, a shortened appendage, could mean that the Barber represents Ganesh in the tableau. The other son of Durga, Karttikeya, has a peacock as his vehicle, and a peacock is sometimes drawn on the wall where the image of Sanjhi rested during the festival (fig. 82). However, this kind of speculation can easily be pushed too far.

A clear indication that Sanjhi is not Durga comes from Karimpur where Wadley worked. In Karimpur, there are several festivals in the bright fortnight of Ashvin that concern goddesses. One of them is Nau Durga, which Wadley gave as Durga Ninth because it is observed on the ninth day of the fortnight. Marriott called this festival Nine Durgas. In any case, it is equivalent to Navaratra or Durga Puja.

The festival in Karimpur that corresponds to Sanjhi in Shanti Nagar is called Simara-Simariya or Neothar, which Wadley translated either as Nine Days or Nine Nights. It begins on Ashvin *sudi* 1 and lasts until Ashvin *sudi* 9. The festival is basically a form of play for girls. It features the wedding of two mythical personages.[44]

> A large figure of a woman called *neutariya*, the Ninth One, is made on the wall of the house, and below her are two clay figures, Simara and Simari (Simariya). Before dawn, the girls from various houses or joint family clusters gather together to "play" with and worship the goddess with songs and games. In addition, each day the girls make tiny clay figures called *gauri* (Parvati) and do *puja* to them, using flowers as offerings. All the *gauri* are kept, and on the last (ninth) day they are immersed in a pond along with the other images. On the last day . . . smaller representative images of Simara and Simariya are "married" to each other, with accompanying songs, fireworks, and hoopla [Wadley, 1975: 168].

The large figure (Ninth One) corresponds to Sanjhi; the two smaller ones (Simara and Simari), to the Barber and Sanjhi's brother, despite the fact that Simari is a female name. In Sanjhi, the scenario concerns the passage of a young married woman between her marital and natal families. In Neothar, the distinctive action is a wedding, realistically enacted. Both festivals are chiefly for girls. Although in each case offerings are made to the goddess, the basic theme is the interaction of husband and wife, sister and brother, and natal and marital families.

In Karimpur, Nau Durga (Navaratra or Durga Puja) is a separate festival that takes place during the same nine days as does Simara-Simariya. While girls are making offerings to the Ninth One and playing with Simara and Simariya, their mothers are honoring Durga during Nine Durgas. This separation of Durga and the Ninth One, Sanjhi's alter ego, would support the contention that Sanjhi and Durga in Shanti Nagar are not the same.

There is yet a third goddess in Karimpur who is called Teshu-Sanjhi (Wadley, 1975: 211).[45] She is honored from Ashvin *sudi* 10 to 15. The ritual is described as "children's play" without further details. Although the name of this goddess contains the element "Sanjhi," her connection, if any, to the Sanjhi of Shanti Nagar cannot be determined.

In 1977, the identification of Sanjhi and Durga seemed to be coming about haltingly as a consequence of modern influences: schools, films, and increased literacy. Three women said that they think of Sanjhi as Durga. After fixing Sanjhi's image on the wall, an elderly Brahman woman said, "Sanjhi is a goddess and she is now in the house. She is Durga. I know that Sanjhi is Durga because the pandits say so. Rama worshipped Sanjhi [Durga] for 10 days to conquer Ravana. In the Ramayana, it is Durga worship and not called Sanjhi. They say that the Jats put Sanjhi on the wall but don't worship her." One of her grown daughters chimed in to explain that Arya Samajis think that Sanjhi is a horrible lady and do not want her in the house. While a few very strict Arya Samajis may ban her image, most Jat families mounted an image. And women from houses that made no image could participate in the festival by going to other houses.

Opinion about whether Sanjhi is Durga is by no means unanimous. One woman said, "Navaratra and Sanjhi are not the same. We worship Sanjhi every evening. She is a girl, maybe a Leatherworker girl. No one knows the true story. We celebrate but we don't know why. For one year Sanjhi lives in her natal village and for 10 days she stays with her in-laws. Then she goes back to her parents' house and that's the end of the festival."

The reference to the Leatherworker girl recalls the story of Sanjhi recounted in Lewis (1958: 215–216). She was the wife of a Leatherworker who worked as a weaver. He collected thread in a village to weave some cloth, but the villagers were afraid that he would run away with it, as other weavers had done. Indeed he did. First, he sent his wife, Sanjhi, to another village, and then decamped with the thread. A year later, some boys tending cattle unexpectedly come upon Sanjhi, beat her to death, and threw her body in a pond. The sketch of a weaver's implement (*teran*), instead of the usual swastika or peacock, that sometimes is drawn to replace the image of Sanjhi may symbolize the myth of Sanjhi as the wife of a weaver. We never saw a sketch of such an implement in any other ceremonial context.

Somehow, Sanjhi began to be worshipped. This is not surprising. The process by which an unusual person becomes an object of worship occurs frequently. Women have about 10 or 20 songs that they sing on Sanjhi, and we once asked a group of women where the songs came from. Of course, we knew without asking that some are based on tales from the sacred literature. But the women explained that there was another source. "If an incident occurs we'll put it into a song and relate it to something else." One woman gave an example. "In my father's sister's village, a girl killed a policeman by hitting him with a heavy pestle. That incident became a song. Women sit together and compose songs. I have composed a song." In any event, the incident of the girl and the policeman is now celebrated in song. She has become a rural heroine. It is quite possible that in the course of time, a cult will form around the killer and she will become a minor goddess. Phoolan Devi, the "Bandit Queen" who is now the subject of a film, book, and many newspaper and magazine articles, seems to be following a similar path (University Seminar, 1995)

In all likelihood something like this happened in the case of Sanjhi, the weaver's wife. She was a girl who met a sad end because of what her husband did. The theme of husband and wife is again played out in ritual. Or perhaps Sanjhi represents the celebrated daughter of a Rajput king. The basic theme in this scenario is a daughter's virtue as the keystone of family honor. In either case, the process is the same: the evolution of an individual with unusual qualities or a distinctive history into a deity. Pandits see Sanjhi as an anomaly, displacing the great goddess Durga during her festival. For if Sanjhi is not Durga, then Durga Puja is not observed in Shanti Nagar. So pandits tell village women that Sanjhi is Durga. As of 1977, the idea was still difficult to sell to the women of Shanti Nagar.

Bhai Duj

Bhai Duj, or Bhaiya Duj (Brother Second), is observed on Karttik *sudi* 2. It is the last of five consecutive festivals in mid-Karttik. Diwali, on Amavas, is the highlight of the first three days. The two preceding days, Dhan Teras and Giri, are essentially preliminaries to Diwali. Gobardhan, the day after Diwali, is a separate festival having only a weak link to Diwali. Bhai Duj has no connection at all to the preceding four festivals.

The ritual of Bhai Duj is an exchange of gifts between sister and brother. Its purpose is to recognize and reinforce this relationship, so vital to family life in India. The ritual takes place within the family. In its fullest form, perhaps observed by only the Merchant family in Shanti Nagar, a woman fasts until midday. Then her mother-in-law recites the tale of Bhai Duj. If the woman is unmarried, presumably her mother or another senior woman tells the story. The sister then places a sheaf of barley on her brother's ear and a tilak on his forehead. He in turn gives her money. She then serves him a festive meal that she had prepared. One Brahman woman said that a married woman also receives the gift of a costume (*tirh*) from her *bhabhi*, the wife of her older brother.

In terms of ritual and theme, Bhai Duj resembles Salono and Sanjhi. On Salono, a sister ties a charm on her brother's wrist for his protection and as a symbol of their close tie. He in turn accepts the obligation to protect his sister. The charm is equivalent to the barley shoots of Bhai Duj. The ritual of barley shoots is also enacted on Sanjhi. The importance of the sister-brother tie is shown by the fact that it is symbolized on three of the five festivals that we classify as festivals of interaction.

Bhai Duj is observed by a minority, perhaps by only a few, of the families of Shanti Nagar. In the festival survey that we took in 1978, only 5 of 13 respondents (all but two were women) said that they observed Bhai Duj. A married Merchant woman said, "I fast until noon and then my mother-in-law relates the story. If my brother comes, I put barley sheaves behind his ears and a tilak on his forehead. Then I eat." A married Brahman woman said, "A sister goes to her parents village, taking coconuts and sweets for her brother. Then her brother gives her money and her *bhabhi* gives a *tirh*." A married Gardener woman said that sugar pitchers, presumably like those used on Karva Chauth, and coconuts were the gifts.

The eight respondents who did not observe Bhai Duj represented eight castes. Two of the eight made the general point that Bhai Duj was not celebrated in villages. One speculated that it was a city festival. Another said that only the Merchants observed it.

Bhai Duj does indeed seem to be uncommon in Delhi villages. None of the five village studies of the 1961 census include Bhai Duj in their lists of festivals, which means either that the festival was not practiced or that it was too unimportant to include in the list. Even Lewis (1958: 199), who most likely tried to compile a complete list of festivals, did not mention Bhai Duj.

All our information about Bhai Duj comes from interviews. We never saw anyone enact the ritual. The festival would be easy to overlook. There are no images, processions, bonfires, lamps, communal singing, and dramas that would attract attention. Rather, the brief ritual takes place in the home. We depended on our host family to call our attention to such rituals. For example, we were called to witness the puja for Brihaspati. Without this assistance, we would probably never have spotted the ritual, which was enacted in an interior room. We think the reason that we were not called for Bhai Duj, although our host's mother warned us a day in advance, was that at the time of the festival in 1958 an important and sensitive dispute was claiming much of our host's time. He and his family had other things on their mind that day. The dispute was described in S. Freed and R. Freed (1976: 173–175).

Wadley gave a brief account of Bhai Duj in Karimpur with a fine photograph of a young girl feeding her brother (Wadley, 1975: 170, 175; see also photograph 19 in Bouillier, 1982). Wadley's photograph showed a puja in session. She did not describe the action but it can easily be deduced. The brother, about 20 years old, squats on a ceremonial sitting board (*patra*), a wooden plank raised a few inches off the ground. His sister, a girl about eight years old, puts sweets in his mouth. There is a tilak on his forehead. Between the brother and sister are the paraphernalia of a puja: a drawing on the ground probably made of wheat flour, a brass tray, and a pitcher probably containing water. No barley sheaf is visible.

Raheja (1988: 176) described a similar scene: "Each sister prepares a tray containing a bit of turmeric [for the tilak] and rice and some sweets. The brother is asked to stand on a wooden stool, and the sister places another *tilak* on his forehead and feeds him some of the sweets. He then puts the [gift of cash or cloth and raw food] he has brought on the tray for her to accept." Earlier in the day, the story of Bhai Duj was recited, and there was a ritual involving small lamp-shaped objects made of dough that a woman swallowed at the end of the story.

Bouillier (1982: 97–100) recounted at some length the ritual of Bhai Duj, called Bhai Tika among the high Hindu castes of Nepal. Sisters and brothers assemble in a freshly plastered room. The brothers sit in a row. The eldest sister performs a puja, and then the sisters walk around their brothers three times, tracing a magical protective circle. One sister pours oil on the floor, the second pours water, and the third carries a lamp. The sisters give their brothers tilaks, scatter flower petals on them, put necklaces of flowers around their necks, and feed them auspicious food. The brothers reciprocate with a tilak and gifts, clothing, or money. Then each brother places his forehead on the foot of each of his sisters as a gesture of respect. A coconut is placed on the doorsill and shattered with a pestle, a gesture interpreted as smashing the skull of Yama, God of Death. Finally, there is a feast.

This ritual closely follows the mythological charter of the festival. Bouillier collected two versions of the myth. In one version, a demon wants to eat a small boy. Yami, his sister, draws a protective circle of oil and water around him, places a necklace of flowers around his neck, and begs the demon to spare her brother until the circle dries and the flowers wither. When the circle stays moist and the flowers remain fresh, the demon is vanquished and the boy is saved. In the second version, Yami plays no role and the demon is replaced by Yama, come to carry off a boy whose time has come. The boy's sister pays homage to Yama and saves her brother. Satisfied, Yama asks the woman to compose a wish. She pronounces a long protective formula involving, among other practices, a protective circle and a necklace of flowers. While the circle stays moist and the flowers fresh, Yama will not come for the boy. The puja of Bhai Duj prolongs the life of brothers.

Karttik *sudi* 2 is sacred to Yama, God of Death, and his twin sister, Yami (or Yamuna). A middle-aged Brahman man explained, "On this day, a sister places a barley sheaf behind her brother's ear and cooks food for him. He gives her money. The day formerly commemorated the relationship between Yama and his sister, Yamuna." Yama and Yami are considered to have been the first human pair. Yami urged Yama to mate with her to perpetuate the species, but he is sometimes said to have resisted physical union. Yami loved him passionately. When he died, she mourned him and later became the river Yamuna (Daniélou, 1964: 132–134; Dowson, 1891: 373–375).

The festival on the second honors the occasion when Yami invited her brother to dine with her, thereby securing for him immunity from death (Imperial Record Department, 1914: 10). This immortality is somewhat puzzling, for Yama was the first mortal to die. Perhaps it is a question of his immortality as the God of Death. Be that as it may, any ritual offering by a sister to her brother not only emphasizes his obligations to her but also has a supernatural protective aspect, as for example the charm that a sister ties on her brother's wrist on Raksha Bandhan.

Although Bhai Duj honors Yami and Yama, the story of the festival recited in Shanti Nagar concerns a nameless brother and sister. Nevertheless, the protagonists in all likelihood represent the divine siblings. A Jat woman told the following version:

A son asked his mother, "Do I have a sister? If so, I should visit her on Bhai Duj." The mother replied, "Your sister is very bad and abusive. But you have a sister." The son said, "I shall go to visit her no matter what type of person she is." He went to visit her and as soon as he arrived, she started abusing him. So the son knew that his mother was right. However, the sister cooked for her brother and fed him. When he was getting ready to leave, she cooked *churma* which she gave to her brother to eat on the way. However, when she ground the wheat to make the *churma*, she also inadvertently ground up a scorpion and mixed the ground scorpion with the flour. After her brother had gone, she saw that there was some blood on the grinding stone. She realized what had happened and ran after her brother. She found him sitting under a tree. She started abusing him, calling him a eunuch. Again the brother decided his mother was right, that she was abusive. She asked him whether he had eaten what she gave him. He had hung the food on a tree. She threw it away.

She accompanied her brother because he was to be married and she wanted to go to the wedding with the *barat* [wedding procession]. Villagers told her that girls cannot accompany a *barat*, but she wanted to and did. She followed her brother, the groom, when he went into the bride's house. She made a new door with flowers and would not let her brother pass through the other door. The door of flowers collapsed, at which point she said, "It is good that my brother did not pass under the other door because he would have died."

Then she said, "I will go to the fire ceremony with my brother." In that ceremony a snake came to bite the brother. The sister caught hold of the snake, killed it, and saved her brother's life. The sister put a tilak on her brother's forehead and gave him a coconut and sweets. Then all was well. She saw to it that her brother was married and brought him home.

The principal elements of this tale are the desire of a brother to find his sister, the perils that the brother faces, and a sister who is abusive but nonetheless saves her brother's life. A sister does not normally abuse her brother. But this sister both subjects him to savage verbal abuse and also saves his life. This apparent role conflict is at the heart of the story.

Bahadur (1995: 54–61) published a similar but more fully developed version of this story that suggests the answer to the apparent role conflict. Again, a man sets off to find a sister, whom he has never known, to celebrate Bhai Duj. He faces mortal danger on the way: a swollen river, a snake, a landslide, and a hungry tiger. He told each danger that he was on his way to visit his sister for Bhai Duj but that each one could kill him on the return journey. His sister was not at all abusive, and her brother had a pleasant visit. At his departure, she prepared lentils for him but accidently mixed in the skin of a snake. After he left, a dog ate some of the lentils and died. The sister was terrified, pursued her brother, and threw away the poisoned food. She decided to accompany him and managed to parry all four dangers.

She planned to attend his wedding. On the way, she met some gypsies who foretold the death of her brother. She begged the gypsies for a remedy. An old woman said, "If his sister goes on cursing him, right from now on and continues to curse him all through the wedding . . . this boy can be saved." The sister returned to her brother and began to abuse him. She was unpleasant to everyone and continued to abuse her brother all through the wedding. The perils of the snake and the collapsing building were narrowly avoided. The *pheras* (the seven rounds of the fire) that are the climax of the wedding ceremony, arrived. After the first round, "the boy fell down in a dead faint, because of the evil spirits who had come to take him away. The sister woke up on hearing the noise and came cursing into the courtyard. Hearing the abuses and seeing her blazing eyes, the evil spirits fled." The wedding guests then let the sister do as she wished, and she saved her brother from yet another danger. In the denouement, the sister explained everything about the gypsies and why she had to act as she did. The story ends with the declaration that the power of a sister's love for her brother should never be underestimated.

Verbal abuse and physical pain are common methods for exorcising ghosts. Abuse is not directed at the victim of ghost possession. Rather, the intruding spirit is the target. Villagers hope that insults and threats in conjunction with mildly painful or unpleasant measures, such as wafting the smoke of burning pig's excreta in the victim's face, will persuade the ghost to leave. Thus, the anomaly of the abusive sister is explained. She is not abusing him. On the contrary, she is trying to save his life by exorcising malevolent spirits.

Channa (1984: 131–136) recounted a similar story. There are four dangers: poisoned food because of a snake, the collapsing door, a falling tree, and a snakebite. Potters instead of gypsies tell the sister that her brother will die unless he is cursed. She begins to curse her brother, surprising everyone. In the end, everything is explained, and the sister is sent home with great affection. Channa gave no reason for the abuse, but exorcism appears to be the best explanation. Channa concluded that the ritual of Bhai Duj is so important that, for individuals who lack a brother or a sister, a cousin or someone else will play the appropriate role. No man's forehead should be without a tilak on Bhai Duj. If this is so, the apparently sporadic observance of Bhai Duj in Shanti Nagar is puzzling.

Beck et al. (1987: 121–123, 305) reported a version of the tale with a different theme. The storyteller was an elderly woman who lived in Delhi. Our version and those of Bahadur and Channa have a theme of sister-brother aid that is both unconditional and of two kinds: she renders him supernatural aid; he responds with mundane assistance. She puts a barley sheaf on his ear as a symbol of supernatural protection. He gives her money. The aid is unconditional but of a different nature. In Beck's version, the relationship is both conditional and equal: blessing for blessing, curse for curse.

A poor brother decided to visit his rich sister on Bhai Duj. When he arrived, his sister asked her servants, "How has he come?" When told that his clothes were in tatters, she lodged him at the potter's kiln and went about her activities. At bedtime, she remembered having sent no food to her brother. She ran to the kitchen but found nothing except stale greens and a dry piece of bread, which she sent to her brother. He pocketed the dry bread and left without a word. Long afterwards, he came for a second visit on Bhai Duj. He had become rich and arrived with a procession of servants, elephants, horses, and musicians. The sister received her brother with affection and fed him well. He gave her some lovely anklets that tinkled. She asked what the jingling meant. He replied, "The jingle goes: 'Here comes darling little brother! Bring out the stale greens and dry bread'." The sister was ashamed and apologized.

Beck's tale suggests that a sister's devotion to her brother depends on his ability to aid her. If he is rich, she is affectionate. But if he is poor, she is selfish and inconsiderate. In turn, he seethes with anger and is vindictive. He shames her, extracting an apology. However, there is no genuine reconciliation based on love and understanding. Their hostility ends in a cautious truce. This story does not represent the spirit of Bhai Duj.

The theme of the other three tales is the ideal relationship of sister and brother. They love each other even in the face of bizarre, unpleasant behavior. The reaction to abuse is not vengeance but acceptance. In the end, of course, abnormal behavior is explained. Men with many sisters sometimes complain that they are burdens. Expensive gifts must be sent, especially when their sisters' children marry. But with rare exceptions men meet their obligations. It is Hindu dharma.

Makar Sankranti

Makar Sankranti is the festival that marks the passage of the sun into the zodiacal sign of Makar (Capricorn). A sankranti is the moment when the sun leaves one zodiacal sign and enters another. Makar is a sea monster, the name of a sankranti, and also the name of a solar month. A sankranti takes its name from the zodiacal sign-name of the month it introduces. There are twelve sankrantis in a year, each a festival, but only Makar Sankranti and Mesha Sankranti (Baisakhi) are observed in Shanti Nagar.

Makar Sankranti is also the Hindu winter solstice. The year is divided into halves: *uttarayana*, the period after the winter solstice when the sun appears to move northward, and *dakshinayana*, the six-month period after the summer solstice when the sun's apparent path is southward. Thus, Makar Sankranti is also known as Uttarayana Sankranti, but we never heard that designation in Shanti Nagar.

Makar Sankranti is one of only two Hindu festivals observed in Shanti Nagar whose dates are set by the solar year.[46] The rest of the dates of Hindu festivals are determined by the lunisolar calendar. On the other hand, the civil festivals and Christmas, which from the point of Hindus is a civil holiday, follow the solar calendar. In terms of lunar months, Makar Sankranti may fall either in Paush or Magh. The solar date of the festival, which from year to year varied slightly from about January 12 to January 14, is now fixed everywhere in India on January 14 (Bahadur, 1995: 19; Hanchett, 1988: 40).

The astronomical winter solstice takes place about December 22. Makar Sankranti, the Hindu winter solstice, occurs somewhat more than three weeks later. The reason is that the Indian solar year has been sidereal for the last 2000 years (Sewell and Dikshit, 1896: 7). The sidereal year is 20.4 minutes longer than the tropical year because of the precession of the equinoxes. Events determined by the Indian sidereal year move slowly forward through the seasons at the rate of appoximately two weeks every 1000 years.

Makar Sankranti is a joyous festival. It marks the passage from the unlucky half of the year (*dakshinayana*) when the sun is traveling southward toward the abode of Yama, God of Death, to the lucky six-month period (*uttarayana*) when the sun is moving northward. The southward course of the sun is known as "god's night", the movement to the north as "god's day" (Underhill, 1991: 31). The festival traditionally features bathing, charity, presents, prayers to the sun, general rejoicing, and feasting. Brahmans offer oblations to ancestors. In North India, the characteristic festive dish is said to be *khichri*, a mixture of rice and a pulse. According to Mukerji (1916: 1), "Khichri" became a popular name for the festival (see also Gnanambal, 1969: 18).

Sesame seeds, either alone or mixed into a sweetmeat with other condiments, are a signal gift (Imperial Record Department, 1914: 56). Gnanambal (1969: 19) said, "The use of sesamum (*til*) forms an essential item of the ritual complex of the festival. In parts of North India the festival itself is known as 'sesamum Sankranti' (*Til Sankranti*)." Balfour (1885, 2: 800) noted that sesame seeds are the favorite grain of the sun. Underhill (1991: 40) speculated that the use of sesame may be due to the belief that it can ward off evil spirits. She noted that sesame seeds are mentioned in the Mahabharata as a superior gift that produces everlasting merit. The sugared seeds are given to all family members with the admonition, "Eat sweet sesamum and speak to me sweetly" (Underhill, 1991: 39). This sentiment is in accord with a theme of Makar Sankranti in Shanti Nagar, namely, the strengthening of kindly feelings among relatives.

Both Mukerji (1916: 6) and Underhill (1991: 31) connected Makar Sankranti to the story of Bhishma as told in the Mahabharata. Bhishma was regent for Pandu and Dhritarashtra, ancestors of the Pandavas and Kauravas, respectively. When war between the families erupted, he took the side of the Kauravas and became commander of their army. He was mortally wounded by Arjuna during the *dakshinayana*. However, he had obtained the power of fixing the time of his death. He was determined to live until the sun turned northward, and so survived another 58 days until the *uttarayana* Sankranti, all the while delivering several long didactic discourses (Dowson, 1891: 53–54).

Makar Sankranti in Shanti Nagar has effectively lost all the religious traces mentioned above. No particular deities are worshipped, not even the sun. There are no pujas, and Brahmans do not worship their ancestors on this day. *Khichri* is not the principal festive dish. In fact, it may be rare, although we did visit a home where a pulse was being prepared. The festive meal features the usual treats: halva, *khir*, and puris. Sesame seeds were not mentioned. The day is still thought to be auspicious. A young Brahman schoolteacher commented that good times for the whole year begin on Makar Sankranti. If it rains, then it will rain the rest of the year. We asked him to tell the story of Makar Sankranti, but he did not know any. No one told any story connected with Makar Sankranti.

The day is devoted entirely to interaction. Newly married women give gifts, provided by their parents, to their fathers-in-law, mothers-in-law, husband's sisters, and husband's older brothers and their wives. The husband and his younger brothers might also receive gifts. If a woman's parents cannot afford to give presents to everyone all at once, the distribution will be spread out over the years. The idea is that a young wife wants to please her husband's relatives, to reestablish friendly relations if there had been some quarreling, and to win their good will for the year to come. The festival features parades of women singing through the streets carrying their gifts. The recipients are rarely at home. Feigning anger, they are at the sugarcane crushers (in 1959) or at the cattle shed. The gifts symbolically lure them back home. Wives offer expensive gifts for the first two or three years after their wedding. Then, the value of the gifts declines, and some years none may be given.

An elderly Brahman man explained the significance of Makar Sankranti:

> After getting up in the morning, you bathe in warm water so that you can cool your head, particularly if there is a devil in your head that makes you quarrel. You drench your head with water to cool it for the whole year so that you won't get into any fights with anybody. Then people try to make up with anybody with whom they've fought in the previous year. They say "Maybe I've made a mistake so I apologize. Well, here is a gift for you. Look at me with a clean heart from now on and I shall always be obedient to you. Forget about the mistakes I've made in the past lest someone come into your mind again and you think of me as a bad person." All people get into arguments. Then it depends on you whether you forget about it or not. It is said here that if you don't mend what is torn and make up with people annoyed with you, then the world cannot go on. Good people are those who make up after five minutes. Everyone is going to die so why do we get into fights.

Twice in this discourse, the pandit speaks of spirit (ghost) possession as the cause of quarrelsome behavior. The intrusive spirit is exorcised by mild physical shock (dousing the head with water) or by offerings. These references to exorcism recall Underhill's statement that sesame seeds are used on Makar Sankranti because they are believed to banish evil spirits.

Women clean their houses for Makar Sankranti. Early in the morning, they cook the festive meal. In 1959, two families invited us to share their meal. First, we ate with our Brahman landlord's family. Somewhat later, at 8:30 A.M., we called on our second host where we were fed the traditional feast of halva, *khir*, puris, and vegetables. We might add that many village housewives are excellent cooks. The meals for special occasions served in well-to-do families are usually a treat, and the best professional cooks who serve at rural weddings are masters of the culinary art. In our experience, the best village cookery surpasses by far the cuisine of fashionable city restaurants.

We left the home of the second family in midmorning after the festive meal. We returned about 4:00 P.M. for the presentation of gifts, which always takes place late in the afternoon. The family was headed by a middle-aged celibate man. His brother's widow had three sons and two daughters, all married. Thus, there were three potential donors (the son's wives) and four recipients (uncle, mother, and her two daughters). A donor could also be a recipient. An older brother's wife could receive a gift from the wife of her husband's younger brother and, in turn, give gifts to her husband's sisters. A fictive mother's sister, a member of another family, was an additional recipient. The basic exchange is from a woman's natal to her conjugal family. A married woman receives clothing and money from her parents or brothers, which she then distributes to her husband's relatives.

On this occasion, the major donor was the wife of the youngest son. She would distribute nine gifts during the afternoon ceremony. She gave a woman's costume (*tirh*) made of satin and two rupees to each of her husband's sisters. They received the best gifts. The next best gift, also a woman's costume, went to her husband's mother. The two wives of her husband's older brothers received the poorest gifts. Gifts within ranks must be equal; otherwise, people will quarrel. As it happened, the headcloths for the two husband's brothers' wives were not equal, and a small quarrel broke out, which was settled by some shifting around of gifts. The best skirt cost Rs. 60 and the best headcloth, Rs. 16. We looked through the piles of clothing and could find only skirts and headcloths. Shirts, the third component of a woman's costume, were absent. These gifts were expensive. At the time, an agricultural laborer earned only Rs. 1.50 per day.

Men also were among the recipients. The youngest son's wife gave her husband's uncle a shawl that cost Rs. 35 and 5 rupees. She gave two shawls to her husband's elder brothers, each worth Rs. 5. She gave her husband a bush shirt (sport shirt). Finally, she gave a costume to a Brahmani who came from a village close to that of her husband's mother and was therefore called "mother's sister." An extensive discussion of fictive kinship in North India, of which this relationship is an example, was provided in S. Freed (1963). The young wife had brought the gifts for the women from her natal family when she came to visit her husband for the first time after the wedding. Her brother brought the presents for the men when he paid his sister a visit a few weeks before Makar Sankranti.

The day before the festival, mother and uncle said that only the younger son's wife would give presents to her father-in-law (the uncle), mother-in-law, and older sisters-in-law. She had not yet met this customary obligation. The other two wives previously had given the required gifts and did not have to do it again. We asked if a daughter-in-law had to give only once or every year. They replied that it had to be done at least once and more often if the girl's parents could afford it. These gifts (*sidha*) come from a girl's natal family to her conjugal family. They are considered to be gifts to a daughter, but they are passed along to her in-laws. On this occasion, the wife of the oldest son gave gifts that were not really required to her husband's two sisters, a sari and cloth for a blouse. The wife of the middle son gave no gifts at all. Finally, the mother gave a costume to each of her daughters.

The gifts distributed in a wealthy Jat household were comparable to those of this Brahman family. A 20-year-old wife, married for seven years and living with her husband for three years, gave a woolen shawl and 10 rupees to both her father-in-law and his brother, and a woolen shawl and 5 rupees to two of her husband's three younger brothers. The youngest, only four years old, received no gift. She gave women's costumes to her mother-in-law and to three senior women residing either in her household or in that of her father-in-law's brother. In addition, she gave a costume to her husband's married sister (but not to an unmarried sister), to her father-in-law's sister, and to the senior woman of a distantly related family. The gifts came from her parent's house.

At 4:50 P.M., the Brahman women loaded their gifts on low baskets or brass trays, which they would carry on their heads to sugarcane crushers where men would be waiting to receive them. Instead of following this procession of women, we allowed the youngest son to take us directly to the crusher for the presentation. He assured us that nothing of interest would happen until the women arrived there. This was one of the few times when we were given bad advice, for we missed an interesting ceremony that took place at the main village well. The women later described the ceremony.

At the well (fig. 83) the mother mounted to the top step. Her youngest son's wife put Rs. 1.25 in her lap. Then she helped her husband's mother down one step and gave her one rupee. On the next lower step, the gift was 12 annas, then 8 annas, and finally 4 annas. The total amounted to Rs. 3.75. In 1978, we asked a well-informed pandit if the ceremony of descending steps was still performed. He said it was, but pointed out that any staircase would do. However, his own family had performed the ritual of descending the stairs at the well in 1958. Thus, the only examples of this ceremony that came to our attention were at the village well. The mother-in-law pretends to be angry as she descends the steps. The idea is to please the mother-in-law by showing respect.

That the ceremony took place at the main village well invites speculation. The well has both an auspicious and an inauspicious aspect. The well is a mother goddess. Forty days after a woman gives birth, she worships the well (R. Freed and S. Freed, 1980: 389–395). The rite marks the end of the 40-day period of birth pollution during which a mother's activities are restricted.

The well is also allied with sorrow, pain, and death. Drowning in the main village well is a prime means of suicide, especially for high-caste women. Family problems are almost always the chief cause of such suicides. Villagers named 10 married women who committed suicide in the well (R. Freed and S. Freed, 1993: 168). Women who commit suicide become malevolent ghosts.

FIG. 83. Makar Sankranti. Village well used by the higher castes, site of the ceremony when a daughter-in-law pleases her mother-in-law with small gifts of cash as the latter descends the steps.

As a mother goddess, the well has no connection with the ritual of Makar Sankranti, for it is not worshipped. However, the well's association with unhappiness, tragedy, and suicide makes it an appropriate place for a ritual manifesting the opposite qualities of happiness and reconciliation. The ritual is designed to make peace in a family, to please the mother-in-law, to appease her anger, chiefly directed toward her daughter-in-law, and step by step to draw her away from the fateful premises toward a home now rid of tension and hard feelings. If the mother-in-law is pleased, then the daughter-in-law will be happy. Daughters-in-law are the most likely suicides. Thus, daily life is improved by the ritual, and the potential problem of a malevolent ghost troubling the family is lessened.

We saw four processions of women, two of Brahmans and two of Jats, circulating through the eastern half of the high-caste side of the village. Processions numbered about 20 women, augmented with the usual crowd of children. Most of the women wore their daily costume, but a few of the young wives were specially dressed. On the western side of the village, there was almost certainly one Jat group, perhaps two, for we later recorded some of the gifts that were presented there. We followed as many groups as we could, at least through part of their trajectories. Each group represented chiefly a single large lineage or allied lineages.

There are two groups of Brahman families in Shanti Nagar known as the Inside Brahmans and the Outside Brahmans (S. Freed and R. Freed, 1987: 27). The two groups have no genealogical connection. Their origin goes back to the founding of the village. Events from that distant time are obscure, and our informants were understandably vague about details. Nonetheless, the two groups are clearly marked, and a fair amount of hostility, usually latent, exists between them.

The women of the two Brahman processions came from one or the other of these two groups, to judge from their points of departure and from the individuals whose presence we noted. One group started from the house of an Inside Brahman. These were the women who practiced the ritual at the well. The other Brahman group was organized in front of the house of an Outside Brahman.

We joined the procession of Inside Brahmans just before it arrived at the sugarcane crusher. Women recipients were given their gifts in a lane near the crusher. Daughters-in-law pressed the legs of their mothers-in-law. The recipients put their gifts in a basket and went home. The procession continued onward to the crusher where the men were given gifts. Each donor put her presents in the lap of the recipient, joined her hands in the traditional gesture of respect and greeting, and bowed deeply. Then the procession moved on to other sugarcane crushers. We trailed the procession and noted that the recipients were both Inside and Outside Brahmans, which suggests that the two processions of women may at some point have partially merged.

The Jat processions represented lineages. Two groups, organized at different houses, began the day. One of these processions was later joined by women representing a third lineage. We followed one of the Jat processions (fig. 84). At the point of departure, the women took their time assembling, singing all the while. Then they began a leisurely parade to one of the sugarcane crushers, singing and stopping occasionally. The donors were young wives of the family where the procession assembled. Each of two daughters of the house carried a big brass tray with the pre-

FIG. 84. Makar
Sankranti, 1959.
A woman carries
a brass tray piled high
with gifts of blankets
and clothing.

sents. When they reached the crusher, there was a lot of singing before the wives
gave their gifts to their father-in-law seated inside the small temporary hut that is
constructed at a sugarcane crusher. On the way back from the sugarcane crusher, the
elderly grandmother also received gifts from the two wives of her grandsons.

Partially retracing their steps, the singing women paraded to the house of a large,
important Jat family that belonged to another related lineage. Two wives were scheduled to present gifts to their father-in-law. The procession had to wait for the young
women to emerge. Finally they appeared, both beautifully dressed. One wore a traditional skirt (*ghaghri*) with a well-ornamented, green headcloth. The other wore a styl-
ish blue *salwar* suit (*salwar*, *kurta*, and headcloth) with attractive decoration at the
waist and hem of the *kurta*. At the sugarcane crusher where their father-in-law was
seated on a cot, they each gave him one blanket, one white woolen shawl, and 10
rupees. He blessed them. Afterwards, an older wife, who had not dressed up for the
occasion, gave him a small white cloth and either 5 or 10 rupees. He blessed her. Ordinarily a reserved and dignified man, he seemed very happy and pleased. This sequence
of gifts illustrates the principle that younger wives give more valuable gifts than do
older wives, which is generally the case with other festivals. The parading was over
by 6:00 P.M. After the celebrants returned home, they displayed their gifts on cots.

All processions were in the streets at about the same time. Since we chose to
watch the high castes, we missed whatever took place on the low-caste side of the village. We were later told that nothing happened in the Leatherworker quarter, but that
the Potters observed the festival. A feature of this festival that made surveying difficult is that the processions went to different destinations, for in the 1958–59 season,
there were eight sugarcane crushers in operation. In contrast, different destinations

were not a fieldwork problem on Holi. All the processions ended up at the single pyre. An observer could remain at the pyre and watch the ritual of each group as it arrived.

Food is a traditional part of the gift of *sidha* that is sent to a daughter, but people said little about it, preferring apparently to concentrate on the gifts of clothing and money. However, a Brahman woman reported that her family sent a gift mainly of food to her married daughter: one seer of ghee, one seer of *rawa* (flour for making halva), five seers of rice, five seers of sugar, a suit of women's clothing, and one rupee. She commented that nothing had been received from her recently married son's wife's parents, but the bride was still living with her natal family, in which case the *sidha* is not sent. The wealthy Jat family whose Sankranti gifts are listed above also called this rule to our attention. The family did not send a gift to a married daughter because at the time she was with her parents. When next she was with her conjugal family, she would be given four blankets and Rs. 40. These gifts would presumably be for men. She already had enough women's costumes to take care of her obligations to women. The costumes were part of her dowry.

Two men reported sending gifts of flour, ghee, pulses, and other foodstuff to Brahmans. A Dyer man gave such a gift to his family priest. A Merchant man mentioned a long-standing relationship with a Brahman who lived nearby. "He used to come to eat during the old days, but he hasn't come for many years now. I used to send raw materials for [cooked] food, flour, ghee, etc. to Brahmans. However, with the increasing influence of the Arya Samaj, all this has tended to decrease."

FIG. 85. Makar Sankranti, 1978. Brahman woman pressing the legs of a cow that a daughter-in-law gave to her husband's sister.

FIG. 86. Makar Sankranti, 1978. Jat man displays clothing and cash that he received from his daughter-in-law.

With so much activity going on, observers sometimes forget that they are also participants. It did not occur to us until late in the day that our host's mother expected a gift. Our host was the fictive older brother of Stanley, which meant that his mother was the mother-in-law of Ruth. She was really hurt by our oversight, and we were even more disturbed. She was a marvelous friend, helping us with all our inquiries. Fortunately, before the day was over we were able to set things right, giving her a gift of Rs. 10 and a bag of oranges. We also gave one rupee to our sweeper and a rupee each to a mother and her daughter who did our housework.

In 1978, we visited the same two Brahman families where we had been given a feast in 1959 and followed one procession of Jats. Four days before the festival, our host, an Outside Brahman, showed us the *sidha* that he would give to his youngest married daughter, 23 years old. There were two saris, one for his daughter and the other for her mother-in-law, a blanket for her father-in-law, and two shawls, one for each of her husband's two brothers. He spent Rs. 154. The blanket for the father-in-law was the most expensive gift, the shawls for the brothers, the least expensive. Our host explained:

> My daughter's father-in-law pretends to be angry. Then she touches his feet and gives him presents and he is pleased. I have to give presents to my daughters' husbands' families once or twice on Makar Sankranti. My daughter-in-law brought a pair of dhotis [a man's long loincloth], a shawl, and a sari, which she will give to her husband's sisters. When I give presents to my daughters, my wife tries to add something. I give enough, but still she adds something. I love my daughters. They do a lot of work. I have to give presents to my daughters on Diwali, Raksha Bandhan, Makar Sankranti, Holi, Tijo, and Karva Chauth, the first time [after marriage].

On Makar Sankranti, we spent the afternoon until about 4:45 P.M. interviewing in the fields. Then a man came to tell us that the daughter-in-law in our host's family wanted to please both her father-in-law and Stanley. He was the fictive younger brother of his host and eligible for a gift. We went to sit in the family cattle shed. In 1978, sugarcane crushers were no longer in use, and men received their gifts in their cattle sheds. Carrying the gifts on brass trays, the women arrived with a great crowd of children. Stanley received sweets, two rupees, a necktie, and a shawl. He was hugely pleased.

We left the family cattle shed at about 5:15 P.M. for a survey of the village. We went first to the family of Inside Brahmans who had given us a feast in 1959. There was a cow on the veranda. The wife of the youngest son, who had given handsome presents in 1959, was as generous as ever. The cow was her gift to one of her husband's sisters. She also gave her a headcloth and a sari. She gave a shirt to her husband's mother and a blanket worth Rs. 85 to her own husband. He commented that formerly gifts were given only to women but that now men also receive them. There was no singing because of a death in a family of Outside Brahmans. The headcloth was draped over the cow because a naked cow should not be used as a gift. When we arrived, her mother-in-law and one of her sisters-in-law were putting coins at the cow's feet and pressing the cow's legs as one presses the legs of older relatives to show respect (fig. 85). One of the older brother's wives gave a headcloth to her mother-in-law. Despite the constantly repeated assertion that gifts on Makar Sankranti had to be given just once or only a few times, the younger son's wife was still at it 19 years after an earlier generous distribution of gifts.

We headed toward the village well and turned the corner. At the end of the street, we saw a group of Jat women and children carrying gifts. First, they went to the house of a Brahman, said to be the oldest man in the village, and pleased him with a gift. They said that he was honored because of his age, but we suspect that his caste status also played a role.

The women then moved along to a Jat's house where the family head's son's wife, all dressed up, was holding a tray with two nice blankets. She joined the procession, and the group continued on to the family's men's sitting house-cattle shed where the family head was waiting with the husband of either his sister or daughter. Each man was given a blanket (fig. 86).

BAISAKHI

Baisakhi is observed on April 13. It is one of only two religious festivals—Makar Sankranti is the other—whose dates are fixed by the solar year. Baisakhi eludes classification in terms of our three categories of festivals: welfare, honor, and interaction. However, there is a connection between Makar Sankranti and Baisakhi because both of them are dated by a sankranti, the entry of the sun into a zodiacal sign. We therefore describe Baisakhi just after Makar Sankranti, but it is not a festival of interaction, as it is celebrated in Shanti Nagar. Another connection between the two festivals is that each represents a prominent zodiacal point. Makar Sankranti is the winter solstice, and Baisakhi is the vernal equinox.

There are two systems of sankrantis, one of which takes precession into account (*sayana sankranti*, or sankranti with movement) and one which does not (*nirayana sankranti*, or sankranti without movement). When we speak of sankranti, the reference is always to "sankranti without movement," and the sun's entrance into a zodiacal sign is calculated in sidereal longitude from a fixed point in Aries. With precession taken into account, longitude is measured from the vernal equinox. The coincidence of the sidereal and the tropical zodiacal signs is lost. The Gregorian calendar adjusts for precession. Thus, the Hindu zodiac, which is fixed, moves forward against Gregorian dates and advances through the seasons. Celebration of Makar Sankranti, the winter solstice, takes place in mid-January. Mesha Sankranti, the vernal equinox has moved into mid-April. Moreover, because Baisakhi is dated by the solar year, its date shifts with reference to lunisolar dates (Sewell and Dikshit, 1896: 9–10; Shil-Ponde, 1993: 38–44).

Although Baisakhi is an official Indian holiday, descriptions of it seem to be rare and sparse. The festival is chiefly a pleasant occasion with a minimum of ritual. Buck and Bahadur gave concise accounts of the holiday. Buck wrote:

> Bathing in the Ganges and other sacred rivers is propitious. . . . Parched gram and a water-pitcher should be given to Brahmans for the benefit of *pitra* or *manes* (deceased ancestors); shoes and umbrellas may likewise be bestowed. In order to divert any evil which the New Year may bring, it is necessary to take a bath . . . just at the time when the sun is entering Aries . . . . The day is not sacred to any special deity, but nevertheless pious Hindus visit the temples of their favourite gods . . . . Gala dress is worn and the day is passed in merriment . . . [Buck, 1917: 89–90].

Bahadur noted that the festival is prominent in North India, particularly in Punjab where it is an important day for the Sikhs. On this day in 1699, the 10th Sikh Guru, Gobind Singh, initiated the Five Beloved Ones and founded a new Sikh organization, the Khalsa (the pure). Bahadur (1995: 72–74) described Baisakhi as it is observed by Sikhs. After bathing in rivers or tanks, people go to temples where they give thanks and pray for good fortune. After that, the day is devoted to enjoyment at fairs and to visiting friends. No ritual is performed in the home.

In Shanti Nagar, people who observe the day go to Delhi to bathe in the Yamuna. A few people may go to Hardwar to bathe in the Ganga. Nothing else is done. We were in Delhi on Baisakhi 1959, and a number of people from Shanti Nagar came to visit us after bathing. Brahman visitors predominated, but that was because we lived in a Brahman's house in the village. People who came to Delhi to bathe could be of any caste. Villagers from miles around streamed into the city, making for an impressive throng near the river.

In our survey of religious practices taken in 1978, more than half of the respondents said that Baisakhi was not observed in the village. While remarking that nothing was done in Shanti Nagar, a Potter woman said that in her parents' village, sweet cakes made of new wheat were offered to the deities. Such a ritual would mark Baisakhi as a harvest festival. Bahadur (1995: 72) commented, "This festival is also agriculture based, celebrated . . . by the . . . hardworking farmers of Punjab after the [rabi] harvest." In Shanti Nagar in the 1950s, the rabi harvest began in mid-March. Harvesting, threshing, and winnowing were generally completed by the first week of May.

Conclusion

FESTIVALS TREAT THE emotional and social needs of individuals. Fear of disease and death, the maintenance of important relationships, the enhancement of character and karma through pious acts, and the desire occasionally to break the daily routine, eat some special food, and have a little fun, all play a role in the yearly round of festivals.

Festivals, especially those of the welfare and interaction categories, serve the needs of women more than men. The status of women can change overnight from respected wife to lowly widow. The security and prestige that an only son provides are tenuous. Even two sons may not be enough. The anxiety of women is apparent in many festivals. Women can enhance their peace of mind with observance of the welfare festivals and, through the interaction festivals, maintain their security by reminding critical relatives of their obligations.

Women more than men need the variety of regular festive activity. Their lives traditionally are restricted to the home. Economics, politics, village government, and the arbitration of disputes concern men much more than women. Thus, there are "women's festivals," where men have little or no part. Even in festivals where men are the principal devotees, women play important roles. In Gobardhan, for example, agnates worship the image, but women create it and cook the festive meal.

Festivals have social functions. They integrate the society in several ways. Gift exchange maintains ties between families related by marriage. The distribution of *prasad* focuses attention on lineage membership and, to a lesser extent, on caste-mates and friends in other castes. The parades and communal worship at several festivals emphasize village unity. Pilgrimages at such times expand village unity to encompass a larger region. The honorific festivals remind villagers of the great literary Hindu tradition that they all share. Intensified commitment to this tradition, where moral principles are presented in the context of spellbinding drama, enhances social cohesion. Though the personages of Hindu myths are deities, their problems, motives, and behavior closely resemble the human condition and serve as guides for individual daily behavior.

Since Independence, India has undergone two transitions with profound consequences. One passage has been from an autocratic hierarchical society to one that extols equality and practices democracy. Traditional India, with its caste system in full flower, was the epitome of a hierarchical society. Hinduism developed in that context. The important religious concepts of purity and pollution are integrated with the caste system; ritual purity declines from Brahman to Sweeper. The basic moral concept of dharma also is linked with caste. Dharma is defined as right or proper conduct, but what is proper conduct differs among castes. The dharma of the Kshatriya differs somewhat from that of the Brahman. But the Brahman, Kshatriya, and Sweeper were all integrated into a cohesive whole. Although those at the bottom of the scale no doubt disliked the system, it was accepted by all participants, for there was no competing alternative. Now there is one. Equality is in conflict with hierarchy.

Thus, Hinduism now functions in a different social context. What repercussions on village festivals are to be expected from equality and democracy? In his classic work, "Democracy in America," Tocqueville wrote:

> [E]quality, which brings great benefits into the world, nevertheless suggests to men . . . some very dangerous propensities. It tends to isolate them from each other, to concentrate every man's attention upon himself; and it lays open the soul to an inordinate love of material gratification. The greatest advantage of religion is to inspire diametrically contrary principles [Tocqueville, 1947: 258].

Tocqueville was concerned with the interaction of religion and society. Equality affects both society and religion, leading to a general lack of cohesion. Because equality has its greatest effects in secular life, the impetus in the more conservative realm of religion is to retard social disunity. Tocqueville (1947: 258) wrote, "Religious nations are therefore naturally strong on the very point on which democratic nations are weak; which shows of what importance it is for men to preserve their religion as their conditions become more equal."

The two decades that cover our fieldwork in India are obviously too short a period to make any pronouncements concerning a tendency toward individual isolation and a lack of social cohesion. We are disinclined to make too much of the two Holi bonfires in place of one, or the alleged multiplication of the images of Sanjhi. They probably represent expectable minor variations within a basic stability.

The other noteworthy transition in India involves developments subsumed under the term modernization. They include urbanization, industrialization, and a large rise in literacy. Under such circumstances, one might expect less interest in local festivals or at least an increase in their identification with great traditional festivals and deities. There are pressures in this direction from the media and schools. But in Shanti Nagar, Sanjhi has not yet become Durga and Gobardhan is still clearly distinct from Krishna. Modern communication might also be expected to lessen the great variety of ritual practices from village to village. There is little evidence that this development is taking place, although with the passage of a few more decades, the tendency may be clearly marked, especially in the *shastrik* festivals. Finally, the cynicism toward religion that sometimes characterizes modern educated people might become increasingly manifest. Such a trend has not yet been discerned in Shanti Nagar, even among those who take pride in being modern. The

Brahman who declared, "I'm not a village man but a man of the 20th century" nonetheless observed selected rituals. The Jat man who regarded Sanjhi as the play of children said, in another context, "If you had read the Bhagavad Gita, you would become a Hindu." Villagers have Hinduism deep in their hearts.[47]

Internal reform movements do have an effect on village Hinduism. In Shanti Nagar, the doctrines of the Arya Samaj are an important influence, as has been pointed out throughout these pages. The Arya Samaj is best seen as an effort to reform current Hinduism and also to defend it from other faiths. Whereas Ram Mohan Roy, founder of the Brahma Samaj, was strongly influenced by Christianity and Islam, Swami Dayananda Saraswati preached a return to the Vedas, to traditional Hinduism. In so doing, he condemned much ritual and belief that characterizes village Hinduism, such as the doctrine of avatars, idolatry, and ancestor worship (*shraddha*) (Farquhar, 1915: 32, 36–37, 110–111, 121). Although the Arya Samaj has a place in the village Hinduism of northwestern India, Sanatan Dharma, the "eternal religion," goes comfortably on its way.

Notes

Introduction

1. Doniger O'Flaherty (1980) wrote with great erudition and insight about the problems of evil and theodicy in Hinduism.
2. The blessing that one receives from seeing a divine being.

1: Dating the Festivals

3. It is sometimes claimed that the Hindu and Nazi swastikas are different, the former with arms bent to the left and the latter with arms bent to the right. The idea is to draw a distinction between "good" and "bad" swastikas. However, a swastika is a swastika. In India, both styles of swastikas are impartially drawn. We have photos of both styles from Shanti Nagar (figs. 4 and 39). Marriott (1955: 205) reproduced a rural mural drawn for the festival of Pitcher Fourth that has both left-handed and right-handed swastikas in the same design. The swastika was used in India millennia before the rise of Nazism. As a religious symbol, it has diffused widely. Its connection with Nazism is recent (S. Freed and R. Freed, 1980a: 68).

2: Classification of the Festivals

4. *Prasad* (blessing, kindness, grace) often means food that has been offered to a deity, hence, sanctified food. However, the term includes many other substances offered to a deity and thus sanctified, such as ash, flowers, and water. These substances are endowed with the deity's power and grace, which are transferred to devotees when swallowed or placed on their bodies. *Prasad* is usually distributed at the conclusion of festivals. The auspicious connection of a deity and devotee through the act of taking *prasad* does not last long (Fuller, 1992: 74–75).

3: Festivals of Welfare, Protection, and Fertility

5. Guru Gorakhnath, a famous medieval saint of North India, founded the Kanphata Yogi sect. Members of the sect are mendicants. They slit their ears, hence the name of the sect, and wear a small cylindrical object in the incision. They are associated with Bhairava, a terrible manifestation of Shiva.
6. Chambard (1961: 72) noted self-flagellation with an iron chain studded with iron points as a means of inducing possession by the Goddess (Durga).
7. Wadley wrote that such a pot used to collect the disease represents a womb. Shitala carries a pot full of poxes, for example. "I think it is interesting to note here that Hinduism can't just get rid of 'evil,' but must redistribute it. It can't be destroyed, only shifted" (letter to authors, July 2, 1996).
8. This comment probably alludes to the relationship of "hot" and "cold" food to the humors (*tridosa*s) and to the gunas (qualities, associated with personality types) in Ayurveda. The theory is complicated and cannot be summarized here. See R. Freed and S. Freed (1993: 46–49) for an extended discussion. In brief, certain foods are contra-indicated in specific circumstances. Rice, even when cooked, is thought to be "cold as ice" and should not be consumed in cold weather. Wheat, the staple food in the Shanti Nagar region, is neutral and can be eaten at any time.

9.   We could have saved Drs. Nicholson and Tyson the effort of calculating the begin-
      ning of *tithi*s had we consulted an Indian almanac (*jantri* or *panchang*). Indian
      almanacs contain astronomical information as well as astrological predictions.
      They provide the local time for the beginning of each *tithi*. However, the calcula-
      tions presented here have the advantage of showing the astronomical basis of *tithi*s.
      An ethnographer working in India should buy a good almanac as soon as possible
      and learn to use it. Probably some Brahmans in every village own almanacs, and
      when villagers need precise calendric information, they consult one of these local
      authorities who, in turn, looks up the information is his almanac.

10.   This elderly Brahman man was one of three informants who said that a woman
      worships her husband on Karva Chauth. In his view, when a woman distributes
      *karva*s, she is worshipping her husband. "He's a god for a woman," he said. A week
      before Karva Chauth, two Brahman sisters, married to brothers, said that on Karva
      Chauth, women worship their husbands. "They get a pitcher from the Potter, fill it
      with grain, and worship around it." However, we attended the ritual in their house
      a week later, described on pp. 71–72 (see also fig. 16), and when one of them wor-
      shipped a pot, she denied, in response to our direct question, that it represented her
      husband. Karva Chauth, for the welfare of husbands, underlines their great impor-
      tance for their wives, but husband-worship, as such, was inconspicuous. The Brah-
      man woman worshipped the pot as an icon of Ram and not as a representation of
      her husband. Concerning this point, Wadley wrote to us (letter, July 2, 1996), "I sus-
      pect that there may be a heavy Arya Samaj influence here that is submerging the
      husband worship that is so dominant elsewhere."

11.   The gesture of pressing the legs expresses deference and respect to the recipient.
      Both hands are used, one for each leg. One bends from the waist, strokes and occa-
      sionally squeezes the back of the legs from the knee to the ankle once or a few
      times, and finishes with a touch on top of the feet. The gesture can be used with
      cows as well as people (see fig. 85).

12.   Temple (1884–1900, 1: xvii) noted that the healing and revivifying powers of blood,
      the blood of the little finger by choice, runs throught the whole of Indian folklore.

13.   Hanchett (1988: 57) regarded a pot of water used in a ritual as a condensed symbol,
      a complex element that "is used to represent a temporary embodiment of a deity . . .
      receiving offerings." Babb (1975: 42) said that the pot of liquid (*kalash*) is even more
      important than other symbols, such as pictorial images, that may be present during
      a ritual. It is the tangible form of the deity.
            In Shanti Nagar pots are used in ceremonies both with and without pictorial
      images of a deity, Hoi and Karva Chauth, respectively. At Karva Chauth, the pot is
      the object of worship. It may itself be a deity, or represent a god (Ram), or perhaps
      be a form of a mother goddess. We did not pursue the point because people might
      suggest deities just to please us, as did the young man who fed the response, Sat
      Narayan, to his mother.
            At Hoi, the combination of a mural of Hoi Mata and pots as offerings
      impressed us as a unified whole of elements with different functions: an image of
      the goddess and offerings to her. Nothing in the ritual suggested that the pot repre-
      sented the principal image of the deity and the mural was secondary.

14.   The "a" in both words is pronounced the same, as in "father."

15.   Although it might seem that standardization would necessarily follow the wide dis-
      tribution of printed texts, that development has not yet taken place. After analyz-
      ing nine texts on festivals written for Hindi-speaking Hindus, Wadley concluded:

            [T]he variety of ritual behavior presented in these guides far outweighs
            any apparent concern for standardization, or we must assume, any con-

census on "correct" ritual behavior. . . . The resulting conclusion must be that literacy and mass literature will have minimal effect in eroding the variety of North Indian religious practice [Wadley, 1983: 100–101].

16. Gayatri mantra, the most sacred verse of the Rig-Veda, is the best-known mantra in Shanti Nagar. It is an invocation to the Sun as Savitri, the supreme generative force, to be kind to worshippers and to bless their undertakings. Translations and interpretations vary, but the Gayatri basically is an appeal to the Sun to shed a benign influence.

17. The relation of this grass to kusa or kusha grass (*Eragrostis cynosuroides*), the grass commonly used in ritual, is not clear. In Delhi, both *dub* (*Panicum dactylon*) and *dab* (*Eragrostis cynosuroides*) are found (Maheshwari, 1976: 390, 395–396).

18. Krishna was represented by a printed image and not by the cow-dung figure itself. A photograph in Gupta (1991: 145) showed a cow-dung figure that represents Krishna holding Mount Gobardhan aloft in his right hand. Women are shown worshipping the figure. In Shanti Nagar, chiefly men worship Gobardhan. When the figure is taken as a representation of Krishna, it is possible that women are more prominent in the worship, whereas men play the leading role in the worship of Gobardhan. In the village of Senapur, north-central India, Gobardhan is entirely a women's festival (Opler, 1959b: 282–283).

19. Babb described the concluding ritual of Gobardhan in a village in Chhattisgarh (central India) in terms of purity and pollution and as a symbol of friendship between participants.

> A large hexap of cowdung is placed in an open field, and a herd of cattle is driven over it at full speed. The cowdung, having been touched by the feet (a relatively polluted part of the body) of bovine divinity, is now taken in handfuls by the men . . . and applied to each others' foreheads (relatively, the purest part of the body). This reciprocal application of cowdung (at one level an expression of hierarchy between divinity and man) is explicitly regarded as an affirmation of amity between the participants . . . [Babb, 1970: 300].

20. Our speculations concerning the sex of sacrificial victims are based on the fact that villagers regard sons as more important to family welfare than daughters. However, among the Khonds of Orissa, who once practiced human sacrifice, most of the victims appear to have been males (Russell and Lal, 1916: 474–480). We thank D. Jacobson for calling this description to our attention. See also the article on human sacrifice in Walker, 1983, 1: 463–466.

21. We write masan/Masani Mata without diacritics, but they are the same as masán/Masáni.

22. One of our assistants noted that a few Sweepers lit lamps at the shrine. None of our photographs show lamps. Lamps are a feature of many rituals and so it would not be surprising if a few were used on Sili Sat. However, the authors saw scores of offerings, and our observations were supplemented by many interviews. We neither saw lamps nor heard of anyone using them. We never try to "improve" our fieldnotes, but in this case the mention of lamps seems to be an anomaly.

23. Udhyapan is a ritual performed on the completion of an observance. Nayudu (letter to authors, July 22, 1996) wrote:

> It is the termination of the Sixteenth Monday Fast (Solar Somwar Udhyapan) done on behalf of improving the health of any relative who isn't well. You vow to the God Shiva to do this fast in order to cure the relative. A woman fasts for 16 Mondays, excepting the days when she's impure. On the last Monday, she fasts, does a big puja, gives *sidha* to

the Brahman, nice food for relatives, and receives gifts from these relatives. The final day is called Udhyapan.

4: FESTIVALS HONORING THE DEITIES

24. *Arati* is a ceremony of worshipping a deity with a lighted lamp. A lamp is placed on a brass tray, often with other paraphernalia, and the tray is rotated before the representation of the deity (see fig. 50).

25. Dalit now is the preferred term for low-caste disadvantaged persons. The term was coined in Maharashtra and simply means "oppressed." It has replaced Harijan, which in turn replaced earlier, somewhat pejorative terms such as outcaste and untouchable. The Dalits and the "backward classes" are both regarded as "socially underprivileged groups," but they are separate and may be in conflict, as in rural Uttar Pradesh (Rangarajan, 1996).

26. Wadley (letter to authors, July, 2, 1996) called our attention to another interpretation. "Crossing" in songs commonly means crossing the travails of worldly existence, the ocean of life itself. The song honors Krishna and Rama. Since one of the epithets of Rama is "bridge to cross the ocean of life" (Growse, 1989: 431), this interpretation of "crossing" would fit the song. Our interpretation emphasizes the singer's wish not to be left "in between." One interpretation does not necessarily exclude the other.

27. Although Rama and Ravana can be spelled with or without the final *a*, the normal Hindi pronunciation is Ram and Ravan. Both spellings appear to be equally common, and we have not tried to adopt a consistent orthography.

28. Sometimes the festival is said to commemorate the birthday of Lord Shiva (Bhatia, 1961: 64).

5: HOLI AND DULHENDI

29. *Kabaddi* is now an international sport, having found a place in the Asian Games. It is becoming popular in Britain. *Kabaddi* is played between two teams, which alternately send a lone raider into the other's territory. The raider has a brief period of time to touch an opponent and return to his side. If he is captured in enemy territory, he "dies" and temporarily drops out of the game. In Britain the game is "circular" *kabaddi* in which only one player can take on a raider. The village game in the 1950s was "rectangular" *kabaddi*, in which more than one player could try to catch a raider. In the village game, the allotted period was a single breath. The raider had to keep saying *"kabaddi"* without drawing a breath (Majumdar, 1958: 306). Although as played in Britain, a 30-second limit replaces the technique of holding one's breath, the Asian game apparently retains the one-breath rule. (Kunju, 1994; Suri, 1995.)

30. The myth about Holi is different in South India. Gnanambal (1969: 20) recounted, "In South India, specially in Madras and Kerala States, it is believed that Kama Deva (Indian Cupid) who was impudent enough to aim his flower darts to kindle love and passion at the mighty ascetic Siva, was reduced to ashes by the fire emanating from the third eye of the enraged god."

31. We recorded *alha* as *allah*, but this was an error that Wadley corrected. She wrote:
     The tune that you mark as *allah* is actually *alha*. *Alha* is the melody associated with the epic Alha [Blackburn et al., 1989: 197–202] and is commonly used as a specific melody in other places. . . . I am sure that I am right. I have never heard of a melody called *allah*, and the rest you

list I know from my work on performance [Wadley, letter to authors, July 2, 1996].

32. In the older currency, three pie equal one pice. Two pice equal one *taka*. Two *taka*s (four pice) equal one anna. Sixteen annas equal one rupee.

33. Henry provided additional information about this type of performance (letter to authors, Feb. 15, 1996):

> In my field work in eastern U. P. [Uttar Pradesh] a comparable performance was that of the Alha. The reciter used different spoken and sung meters for different segments of the Alha. He accompanied all with his *dholak* [small two-headed drum] and also used it to provide dramatic punctuation of and in between stanzas. All of these differences help to signal development in the story, to highlight drama and to maintain audience attention. Whether the Alha performers I interviewed had names for the different melodies and meters they used did not emerge in our conversations. . . . In summary, epic performers in North India commonly use different melodies for sung portions, different meters for chanted portions, and instrumental accompaniment and interlude to dramatize and enliven their performances.

> Henry called our attention to Wadley (1989: 79–93), who presented in detail a Dhola performance [a series of songs and chants tied together by a narrative theme] that in general form closely resembles the *holi* of the Leatherworkers of Shanti Nagar.

34. The people of Shanti Nagar in the 1950s and 1970s observed Holi and Dulhendi differently than did the villagers of Nimkhera, Madhya Pradesh, in the 1960s (Jacobson, 1970: 399–402). Jacobson commented (letter to authors, July 22, 1996), "This [observance] contrasts sharply with Madhya Pradesh, where the [three] days of Holi are clearly linked with color-playing, pujas, roughhousing, and a grand sacred finale with sacrifice of a goat to Mata. It's one of the most beautiful rituals I've ever seen— clearly very ancient."

35. A lambardar was a village official appointed by the British Government in India who was responsible for collecting land revenue from individual farmers. After Independence, the office was stripped of its functions, but the title retained honorific value in the 1950s.

36. Jacobson (letter to authors, July 22, 1996) pointed out that there are villages of prostitutes in Madhya Pradesh, not to mention the "amateurs" who are everywhere, perhaps earning a few rupees. Nonetheless, when we mentioned syphilis to villagers in Shanti Nagar, they replied, "Syphilis is not common here." They said that villagers were not likely to have venereal diseases, which are more characteristic of cities than villages (R. Freed and S. Freed, 1993: 143). Prostitutes play a significant role in the spread of venereal disease. Just as venereal disease is more common in cities than in villages, so too are prostitutes. Of course, a village man can frequent city prostitutes.

6: FESTIVALS OF INTERACTION AND HONORING THE DEAD

37. "Unmarried" in this context probably means a married virgin daughter who has not yet had her Gauna ceremony and is still living with her parents.

38. The reference may be to the sixth month of pregnancy. A fetus is believed to acquire a soul in the sixth month. This event is not marked with a rite in Shanti Nagar. One woman, who lived in her parent's house during her first pregnancy, vaguely remembered a ceremony in the seventh month for which her parents did

little other than to distribute balls of coconut and sugar to relatives and to send some to her husband's relatives (R. Freed and S. Freed, 1980: 351). Any such prenatal rituals, if they were ever practiced in Shanti Nagar, have long since fallen into desuetude, but traces may survive in folksongs.

39.   We are indebted to Jacobson (letter to authors, July 22, 1996) for this explanation.

40.   Wadley (letter to authors, July 2, 1996) gave us the title of the song, remarking that this version "is really a nice one too."

41.   Williams offered a similar interpretation, involving benefits for descendants and the honoring and nourishing of ancestors. However, he added a nuance. The value of Shraddhas for ancestors is more to increase their merit rather than to nourish them with offerings of food and water. Williams wrote:

> Shraddhas are intended both as acts of homage and as means of ministering to the welfare of deceased relatives . . . . And the Shraddhas do this, not so much by supplying them with nutriment . . . as by accumulating merit (punya) for them and so accelerating their progress through heaven to future births and final union with the Supreme. . . . But a Shraddha is also performed on one's own account. Propitiation and gratification of the Manes are acts fraught with reflex benefits to any one who performs them properly . . . [Williams, 1883: 304].

42.   Lewis (1958: 214) gave an interpretation of the rule that would lead to far fewer problems for housewives than the version of our informants. The prohibition is observed only on the day of a Shraddha rather than for the entire 16-day period. Even then, he noted that the custom is being abandoned.

43.   Jacobson (letter to authors, July 22, 1996) called our attention to this custom.

44.   The festival of Jhonjhi-Tesu in Nandana village, Kanpur District, Uttar Pradesh, is comparable to Simara-Simariya in Karimpur. The festival features the wedding of Tesu, a mythical folk hero, to a girl named Jhonjhi. After the ceremony, the images of Tesu and Jhonjhi are thrown into the village tank (Tewari, 1982: 224).

45.   The name, Teshu-Sanjhi, is equivalent to Jhonjhi-Tesu in Nandana village. Sanjhi is rendered sometimes as Jhanjhi (Jhonjhi).

46.   On this point Malville and Singh (1994: 4) reported, "Throughout India, the Hindu calendar is primarily a lunar device with only occasional solar markers. . . . In Varanasi there are 563 scheduled festivals each year . . . of which only three are established exclusively by the sun."

CONCLUSION

47.   Summarizing the important place of Hinduism and festivals in Senapur, a large village in north-central India, Opler wrote:

> This may be due . . . to the links between all aspects of the culture which Hinduism has historically come to provide. To live a very full and estimable life, a villager has to participate in the religious round. Religion justifies the existence of his line, the tie between his ancestors and his sons. It holds his kin together in family rituals. It provides travel, adventure . . . and connects his village with others. It makes possible the rewarding of servants and dependents . . . . It offers a means of keeping in touch with married daughters. The presence of the protective godlings of the villages strengthens group consciousness. The agricultural rites, the worship of the disease goddesses . . . awaken courage and hope in areas of life where uncertainty and anxiety are most prevalent [Opler, 1959a: 226].

References

BABB, L. A.
1970. The food of the gods in Chhattisgarh: some structural features of Hindu ritual. Southwest. J. Anthrop. 26: 287–304.
1975. The divine hierarchy: popular Hinduism in central India. New York: Columbia Univ. Press.
1995. Introduction. In L. A. Babb and S. S. Wadley (eds.), Media and the transformation of religion in South Asia, pp. 1–18. Philadelphia: Univ. Pennsylvania Press.

BABB, L. A., AND S. S. WADLEY (EDS.)
1995. Media and the transformation of religion in South Asia. Philadelphia: Univ. Pennsylvania Press.

BAHADUR, O. L.
1995. The book of Hindu festivals and ceremonies. New Delhi: UBS Publishers' Distributors.

BALFOUR, E.
1885. The cyclopaedia of India and of eastern and southern Asia, 3rd ed. Vols. 1–3. London: Bernard Quaritch.

BANERJEA, J. N.
1953. The Hindu concept of God. In K. W. Morgan (ed.), The religion of the Hindus, pp. 48–82. New York: Ronald Press.

BASHAM, A. L.
1954. The wonder that was India. London: Sidgwick and Jackson.

BEAMES, J. (TRANSLATOR)
1869. The nineteenth book of the gestes of Prithiraj by Chand Bardai, entitled, "The marriage with Padmavati," literally translated from the old Hindi by John Beames, Esq. B. C. S. J. Asiatic Soc. Bengal 38: 145–60.

BECK, B. E. F., P. J. CLAUS, P. GOSWAMI, AND J. HANDOO (EDS.)
1987. Folktales of India. Chicago: Univ. Chicago Press.

BHATIA, J. C.
1961. Socio-economic survey of village Kharkhari Nahar. Census of India, 1961: 19, pt. 6(13), India. Delhi: Gov. of India Press.

BHATIA, M. S.
1958. Sanjhi in folklore. Nav Bharat Times (Hindi). Oct. 5.

BHATTACHARYYA, S.
1953. Religious practices of the Hindus. In K. W. Morgan (ed.), The religion of the Hindus, pp. 154–205. New York: Ronald Press.

BLACKBURN, S. H., P. J. CLAUS, J. B. FLUECKIGER, AND S. S. WADLEY (EDS.)
1989. Oral epics in India. Berkeley: Univ. California Press.

BONNER, J. P.
1986. When Rahu swallowed the Sun. Discovery (St. Louis Science Center) 6(2): 4–8.

BOUILLIER, V.
1982. Si les femmes faisaient la fête . . . A propos des fêtes féminines dans les hautes castes indo-népalaises. Homme 22(3): 91–118.

BOULANGER, C.
1987. La prêtrise dans les temples çivaïtes de Kanchipuram, Inde du sud. Paris: Librairie de l'Inde Editeur.

BRAHA, J. T.
1986. Ancient Hindu astrology for the modern western astrologer. Miami, FL: Hermetician Press.

BUTTAR, H. S.
1988. Origins and meaning of Sikhism. India Abroad, April 8: 3.

BUCK, C. H.
1917. Faiths, fairs, and festivals of India. Calcutta: Thacker, Spink.

CHAMBARD, J.-L.
1961. Mariages secondaires et froires aux femmes en Inde centrale. Homme 1(2): 72.

CHANNA, V. C.
1984. Hinduism. New Delhi: National.

CHATTERJEE, S. C.
1953. Hindu religious thought. In K. W. Morgan (ed.), The religion of the Hindus, pp. 206–261. New York: Ronald Press.

CRAVEN, T.
1893. The royal dictionary. Lucknow: Methodist Publishing House.

CROOKE, W. C.
1915. The Dasahra: an autumn festival of the Hindus. Folk-Lore 26: 28–59.
1968. The popular religion and folk-lore of northern India. Vols. 1–2. [2nd ed. 1896.] Delhi: Munshiram Manoharlal.
1989. A glossary of north Indian peasant life. Delhi: Oxford Univ. Press.

DANIÉLOU, A.
1964. Hindu polytheism. Bollingen series 73. New York: Pantheon.

DONIGER O'FLAHERTY, W.
1980.   The origins of evil in Hindu mytholo-
        gy. [Original ed. 1976.] Berkeley: Univ.
        California Press.
DOWSON, J.
1891.   A classical dictionary of Hindu
        mythology and religion, geography,
        history, and literature. London: Rout-
        ledge & Kegan Paul.
DUBE, S. C.
1955.   Indian village. Ithaca: Cornell Univ.
        Press.
EDGERTON, F. (TRANSLATOR, INTERPRETER)
1965.   The Bhagavad Gita. [Original ed.
        1944.] Harvard Oriental Series 38.
        New York: Harper Torchbooks.
EMBREE, A. T. (ED.)
1972.   The Hindu tradition: readings in ori-
        ental thought. New York: Vintage
        Books.
ENCYCLOPAEDIA BRITANNICA
1992.   The New Encyclopaedia Britannica.
        Chicago: Encyclopaedia Britannica.
FARQUHAR, J. N.
1915.   Modern religious movements in India.
        New York: Macmillan.
FORBES, D.
1861.   A smaller Hindustani and English dic-
        tionary. London: Sampson Low,
        Marston.
FREED, R. S., AND S. A. FREED
1964.   Calendars, ceremonies and festivals in
        a north Indian village: necessary cal-
        endric information for fieldwork.
        Southwest. J. Anthrop. 20(1): 67–90.
1966.   Unity in diversity in the celebration
        of cattle-curing rites in a north Indian
        village: a study in the resolution of
        conflict. Am. Anthrop. 68(3): 673–692.
1979.   Shanti Nagar: the effects of urbaniza-
        tion in a village in north India. 3. Sick-
        ness and health. Anthrop. Pap. Am.
        Mus. Nat. Hist. 55(2): 285–348.
1980.   Rites of passage in Shanti Nagar. Ibid.
        56(3): 323–554.
1981.   Enculturation and education in Shan-
        ti Nagar. Ibid. 57(2): 51–156.
1985.   The psychomedical case history of a
        low-caste woman of north India. Ibid.
        60(2): 101–228.
1993.   Ghosts: life and death in north India.
        Ibid. 72: 1–396.
FREED, S. A.
1963.   Fictive kinship in a north Indian vil-
        lage. Ethnology 2(1): 86–103.
1970.   Caste ranking and the exchange of

food and water in a north Indian village. Anthrop. Q. 43(1): 1–13.
FREED, S. A., AND R. S. FREED
1976.   Shanti Nagar: the effects of urbaniza-
        tion in a village in north India. 1.
        Social organization. Anthrop. Pap.
        Am. Mus. Nat. Hist. 53(1): 1–254.
1978.   Shanti Nagar: the effects of urbaniza-
        tion in a village in north India. 2.
        Aspects of economy, technology, and
        ecology. Ibid. 55(1): 1–153.
1980a. Origin of the swastika: ceremonies in
        India have shed new light on an
        ancient symbol. Nat. Hist. 89(1): 68–
        75.
1980b. Swastika: a new symbolic interpreta-
        tion. In C. M. Sakumoto Drake (ed.),
        The cultural context: essays in honor
        of Edward Norbeck. Rice Univ. Stud.
        66(1): 87–105.
1982.   Changing family types in India. Eth-
        nology 21: 189–202.
1985.   Fertility, sterilization, and population
        growth in Shanti Nagar, India: a longi-
        tudinal   ethnographic   approach.
        Anthrop. Pap. Am. Mus. Nat. Hist.
        60(3): 229–286.
1987.   Uncertain revolution: panchayati raj
        and democratic elections in a north
        Indian village. Ibid. 64(1): 1–78.
FULLER, C. J.
1992.   The camphor flame: popular Hin-
        duism and society in India. Princeton,
        NJ: Princeton Univ. Press.
GARRETT. J.
1990.   A classical dictionary of India. [Origi-
        nal ed. 1871.] Delhi: Low Price
        Publications.
GARVER, T. H.
1992.   Keeping time. Am. Heritage of Inven-
        tion & Technology. Fall: 8–16.
GAZETTEER UNIT, DELHI ADM.
1976.   Delhi Gazetteer. Nasik: Gov. India
        Press.
GNANAMBAL, K.
1969.   Festivals of India. Anthrop. Surv.
        India, Mem. no. 19. Delhi: Gov. India
        Press.
GODE, P. K.
1946.   Studies in the history of Hindu festi-
        vals—some notes on the history of
        Divali festival—(between c. A.D. 50
        and 1945). Annals of Bhandarkar Ori-
        ent. Res. Inst.: 216–262.
GOVE, P. B. (ED.)
1986.   Webster's third new international dic-

tionary, unabridged. Springfield, MA.: Merriam-Webster.

GROWSE, F. S.

1883. Mathura: a district memoir; with numerous illustrations. 3rd ed. [Allahabad?]: North-western Provinces and Oudh Gov. Press.

GROWSE, F. S. (TRANSLATOR)

1989. The Ramayana of Tulasidasa, 2nd revised ed. R. C. Prasad (ed.). Delhi: Motilal Banarsidass.

GUPTA, S. M.

1991. Festivals, fairs and fasts of India. New Delhi: Clarion Books.

GUPTE, B. A.

1903. Divali-folklore. Indian Antiquary 32: 237–239.

HANCHETT, S.

1988. Coloured rice: symbolic structure in Hindu family festivals. Delhi: Hindustan Publishing.

HENRY, E. O.

1988. Chant the names of God: music and culture in Bhojpuri-speaking India. San Diego, CA: San Diego State Univ. Press.

HOPKINS, E. W.

1898. The religions of India. Boston: Ginn.

IMPERIAL RECORD DEPARTMENT

1914. An alphabetical list of the feasts and holidays of the Hindus and Muhammadans. Calcutta: Superintendent Gov. Printing, India.

INDIA

1912. Delhi district, with maps. Lahore: "Civil and Military Gazette" Press.

JACOBSON, D.

1970. Hidden faces: Hindu and Muslim purdah in a central Indian village. Ann Arbor: UMI Dissertation Services.

1994. The women of north and central India: goddesses and wives. In D. Jacobson and S. S. Wadley, Women in India: two perspectives: 15–109. New Delhi: Manohar.

JONES, SIR W.

1792. The lunar year of the Hindus. Asiatick Researches (Calcutta) 3: 257–293.

KINSLEY, D.

1988. Hindu goddesses: visions of the devine feminine in the Hindu religious tradition. Berkeley: Univ. California Press.

KOLENDA, PAULINE M.

1982. Pox and the terror of childlessness: images and ideas of the smallpox god-

dess in a north Indian village. In J. J. Preston (ed.), Mother worship: themes and variations, pp. 227–250. Chapel Hill: Univ. of North Carolina.

KUNJU, A.

1994. The unsung heroes of the sport of kabaddi. India Abroad, Dec. 30: 44.

KURTZ, S. N.

1992. All the mothers are one: Hindu India and the cultural reshaping of psychoanalysis. New York: Columbia Univ. Press.

LAL, P. (ED., TRANSLATOR)

1992. The Ramayana of Valmiki, 3rd ed. [Original ed. 1891.] New Delhi: Vikas.

LAPOINT, E. C.

1978. The epic of Guga: a north Indian oral tradition. In S. Vatuk (ed.), American studies in the anthropology of India, pp. 281–308. New Delhi: Manohar.

1981. Solar contagion: eclipse ritual in a north Indian village. Man in India 61: 327–345.

LEWIS, O.

1958. Village life in northern India: studies in a Delhi village. Urbana: Univ. Illinois Press.

LUTHRA, S. K.

1961. A socio-economic study of village Jhatikra. Census of India, 1961: 19, pt. 6(8), Delhi. New Delhi: Gov. of India Press.

MAHESHWARI, J. K.

1976. The flora of Delhi. New Delhi: INSDOC.

MAJUMDAR, D. N.

1958. Caste and communication in an Indian village. Bombay: Asia Publishing House.

MAJUMDAR, R. C., ED.

1966. The struggle for empire. History and culture of the Indian people, vol 5. Bombay: Bharatiya Vidya Bhavan.

MALVILLE, J. McK., AND R. P. B. SINGH

1994. Visual astronomy in the mythology and ritual of India: the sun temples of Varanasi. Paper presented at the Conference "The inspiration of astronomical phenomena" (A conference on the influence upon world culture from observed astronomical events), Vatican Observatory, 27 June–2 July 1994.

MAMORIA, C. B.

1980. Economic and commercial geography of India. Delhi: Shiva Lal Agarwala.

MARRIOTT, M.

1955. Little communities in an indigenous

civilization. *In* M. Marriott (ed.), Village India: studies in the little community: 171–222. Chicago: Univ. Chicago Press.

1966.   The feast of love. *In* M. Singer (ed.), Krishna: myths, rites, and attitudes: 200–212. Honolulu: East-West Center Press.

MORGAN, K. W. (ED.)
1953.   The religion of the Hindus. New York: Ronald Press.

MUKERJI, A. C.
1916.   Hindu fasts and feasts. Allahabad: The Indian Press.

NAUTIYAL, K. C.
1961.   Mandi: socio-economic study of rural folk. Census of India, 1961: 19, pt. 6(9), Delhi. New Delhi: Gov. of India Press.

NEHRU, J.
1946.   The discovery of India. New York: John Day.

OPLER, M. E.
1959a.   The place of religion in a north Indian village. Southwest. J. Anthrop. 15: 219 –226.

1959b.   Family, anxiety, and religion in a community of north India. *In* M. K. Opler (ed.), Culture and mental health: cross-cultural studies, pp. 273–289. New York: Macmillan.

PATHAK, R. C. (ED.)
1976.   Bhargava's standard illustrated dictionary of the Hindi language, Hindi-English edition. Varanasi: Bhargava Bhushan Press.

PLANALP, J. M.
1971.   Heat stress and culture in north India. Natick, MA: U.S. Army Res. Inst. Envir. Med., U.S. Army Med. Res. and Dev. Command.

POSTER, A. G. (*WITH* S. R. CANBY, P. CHANDRA, AND J. M. CUMMINS)
1994.   Realms of heroism: Indian paintings at the Brooklyn Museum. New York: The Brooklyn Museum.

RADHESHYAM, PANDIT (ED.)
n.d.   Santoshi Mata: Shukravar Vrat Katha [The Story of Friday's Fast]. Delhi: Ratan.

RAHEJA, G. G.
1988.   The poison in the gift: ritual, prestation, and the dominant caste in a north Indian village. Chicago: Univ. Chicago Press.

RAI, L.
1967.   A history of the Arya Samaj. [Original ed.

1914.] Revised, expanded and edited by R. Sharma. Bombay: Orient Longmans.

RANGARAJAN, M.
1996.   Rise of the Dalits to political power seen as historic. India Abroad, Dec. 6: 2–3.

RATTA, G. P. M.
1961.   Socio-economic study of village Gokulpur. Census of India, 1961: 19, pt. 6(11), Delhi. New Delhi: Gov. of India Press.

REDFIELD, R.
1941.   The folk culture of Yucatan. Chicago: Univ. Chicago Press.

REDFIELD, R., AND M. B. SINGER
1954.   The cultural role of cities. Econ. Dev. Cult. Change 3: 53–73.

REINICHE, M.-L.
1979.   Les dieux et les hommes: étude des cultes d'un village du Tirunelveli Inde du sud. Cahiers de l'homme, nouv. sér. 18. Paris: Mouton.

ROSE, H. A.
1919.   A Glossary of the tribes and castes of the Punjab and North-West Frontier Province. Vol. 1. Lahore: Superintendent, Gov. Printing, Punjab.

RUSSELL, R. V., AND R. B. H. LAL
1916.   The tribes and castes of the Central Provinces of India. Vol. 3. London: Macmillan.

SARASWATI, D. SWAMI.
1956.   The light of truth. G. P. Upadhyaya (translator). Allahabad: Kala Press.

SCHAUSS, H.
1938.   The Jewish festivals, from their beginnings to our own day. New York: Union of Am. Hebrew Congregations.

SEWELL, R., AND S. B. DIKSHIT
1896.   The Indian calendar. London: Swan Sonnenschein.

SHARMA, B. N.
1978.   Festivals of India. New Delhi: Abhinav Publications.

SHARMA, D.
1959.   Early Chauhan dynasties. Delhi: S. Chand.

SHASTRI, P. D.
1979.   Happy new year, Samvat 2036. Voice of the Holy Land, 22(4): 3–5.

SHIL-PONDE
1993.   Hindu astrology. New Delhi: Sagar Publications.

SINGH, C. C.
1955?   Holi Raja Harishchandra. Meerut: General Publishing House.

SINGH, I. P.
1958.   A Sikh village. J. Am. Folklore 71: 479–503.

SIVANANDA, S.
1993.   Hindu fasts and festivals. Shivanandanagar: The Devine Life Society.

SRINIVAS, M. N.
1952.   Religion and society among the Coorgs of south India. London: Oxford Univ. Press.

SRIVASTAVA, R. P.
1961.   A socio-economic study of village Galibpur. Census of India, 1961: 19, pt. 6(10), Delhi. New Delhi: Gov. of India Press.

STEEL, F. A. (WITH NOTES BY R. C. TEMPLE)
1882.   Folklore in the Panjab. Indian Antiquary 11(129): 32–43.

SURI, S.
1995.   Kabaddi taking hold in Britain. India Abroad, Sept. 22: 52.

SWANTON, J. R.
1928.   Religious beliefs and medical practices of the Creek Indians. Forty-second annual report of the Bureau of American Ethnology, pp. 477–900. Washington, D.C.: U.S. Gov. Printing Office.

TANDON, P.
1968.   Punjabi century, 1857–1947. Berkeley: Univ. California Press.

TEMPLE, R. C. (ED.)
1883–1887.
        Panjab notes & queries. Vols. 1–4. Allahabad: Pioneer Press.

TEMPLE, R. C.
1884–1900.
        The legends of the Panjab. Vols. 1–3. Bombay: Educ. Soc. Press; London: Kegan Paul, Trench, Trübner.

TEWARI, L. G.
1982.   The festival of Jhonjhi-Tesu. Asian Folklore Stud. 41: 217–230.

THAPAR, R.
1976.   A history of India. Vol. 1. [Original ed. 1966.] Harmondsworth, Middlesex, England: Penguin.

TOCQUEVILLE, A. DE
1947.   Democracy in America. [Original ed. De la démocratie en Amérique, 1835 and 1840.] New York: Oxford Univ. Press.

TOFFIN, G.
1982.   Introduction. Homme 22(3): 5–10.

TOLSTOY, L. N.
1978.   Anna Karenin. Translated and with an Introduction by R. Edmonds. New York: Penguin Books.

TOOMEY, P. M.
1990.   Krishna's consuming passions: food as metaphor and metonym for emotion at Mount Govardhan. In O. M. Lynch (ed.), Divine passions: the social construction of emotion in India: 157–181. Berkeley: Univ. California Press.

UNDERHILL, M. M.
1991.   The Hindu religious year. [Original ed. 1921.] New Delhi: Asian Educational Services.

UNIVERSITY SEMINAR
1995.   University seminar on tradition and change in south and southeast Asia, 477. Sept. 26. New York: Columbia Univ.

VAN BUITENEN, J. A. B. (TRANSLATOR, ED.)
1973–78 The Mahabharata. Vols. 1–3. Chicago: Univ. Chicago Press.

VAUDEVILLE, C.
1980.   The Govardhan myth in northern India. Indo-Iranian J. 22(1): 1–45.

WADLEY, S. S.
1975.   Shakti: power in the conceptual structure of Karimpur religion. Univ. Chicago Stud. Anthrop. Ser. Soc. Cult. Linguistic Anthrop. 2. Chicago: Dept. Anthrop., Univ. Chicago.

1980.   Sitala: the cool one. Asian Folklore Stud. 39: 33–62.

1983.   Popular Hinduism and mass literature in north India: a preliminary analysis. In G. R. Gupta (ed.), Religion in modern India, pp. 81–103. New Delhi: Vikas.

1989.   Choosing a path: performance strategies in a north Indian epic. In S. H. Blackburn, P. J. Claus, J. B. Flueckiger, and S. S. Wadley (eds.), Oral epics in India: 75–101. Berkeley: Univ. California Press.

1994a. Women and the Hindu tradition. In D. Jacobson and S. S. Wadley, Women in India: two perspectives: 111–135. New Delhi: Manohar.

1994b. Struggling with destiny in Karimpur, 1925–1984. Berkeley: Univ. California Press.

WALKER, BENJAMIN
1983.   Hindu world: an encyclopedic survey of Hinduism. Vols. 1–2. New Delhi: Munshiram Manoharlal.

WATKINS, H.
1954.   Time counts: the story of the calendar. New York: Philosophical Library.

Wax, R. H.
1971.   Doing fieldwork: warnings and ad-
        vice. Chicago: Univ. Chicago Press.
Williams, M.
1883.   Religious thought and life in India.
        London: John Murray.
Wiser, C. V., and W. H. Wiser
1930.   Behind mud walls. New York: Richard
        R. Smith.
Zimmer, H.
1946.   Myths and symbols in Indian art and
        civilization. (J. Campbell, ed.). Wash-
        ington, D.C.: Bollingen Foundation.

Index and Glossary

NOTE: Hindi and Sanskrit words contained in *Webster's Third New International Dictionary, Unabridged*, are not italicized in the index. Unitalicized words also include ceremonies, deities, and commonly used terms, such as lambardar. Brief definitions are given for all Asian words. Fuller definitions can be found in the text.

See the List of Tables and Illustrations on pp. v–vii for page references to the tables and figures cited below.

purinmanta system (calendric system of
    North India), 19, 25, 192, 256
Purinmashi (Full Moon), 20, 145–147,
    148–158, table 7
    Amavas (new moon) compared, 158–159
    Bairagis, observance by, 156
    Brahmans, worship by, 155–157
    Chamar Leatherworkers, observance by,
        156
    Chhipi Dyers, observance by, 155
    Chuhra Sweepers, observance by, 156–157
    havan (fire ceremony), 149, 150, 155–156,
        162
    Holi on, 219
    katha (ritual story), 145–147
    lighting of lamp, 156
    rice put in water offered to moon, 155
    Sat Narayan fast observance, 148–158
purohit (family priest), 77, 96, 252–253, 254,
    260

Q, R

rabi (winter-spring crop), 91, 113, 184
Raheja, G. G., 75
Rahu (ascending node of the moon), 21, 157,
    161
rakhi (protective charm), 250–256
Raksha Bandhan (Charm Tying), 25, 250–256,
    fig. 79, table 8
Rakshasa (demon), 184
Ram, 5, 34, 104, 178
    Dassehra (Tenth), *see* Dassehra (Tenth)
    Dev Uthani Gyas (Gods' Awakening
        Eleventh) and, 166–167
    Karva Chauth (Pitcher Fourth) festival
        and, 72
    Lakshman (Ram's brother), 94, 104
    Ravana (king of Sri Lanka), fight between
        Ram and, 93, 94
    Sita (Ram's wife), 94
Ramayana, 1, 34, 104
    Dassehra (Tenth), *see* Dassehra
    Diwali, Ram versus Ravana as reason for
        celebrating, 93
    Karva Chauth (Pitcher Fourth) story as
        part of, 66–69
    Ram Lila, *see* Ram Lila
Rameshwar (Lord of Rama), 127
Ram Lila, 184–185
    Dassehra, *see* Dassehra
    in Delhi, 184
    duration of, 184
    performance of drama, 184
    Sanjhi festival and, 184, 188, 189, 190
Ranjha and Hir love story, 59–60

Ratta, G. P. M., 230
Ravana (king of Sri Lanka), 93, 94, 166–167
    Dassehra (Tenth), *see* Dassehra (Tenth)
rawa (a special flour), 103, 290
Redfield, R., 26
Reiniche, M.-L., 28
relatives, interaction with, 33, 34, 240, 294
    Baisakhi, 291–293
    Bhai Duj, 240, 278–283, table 8
    Makar Sankranti, 113, 119, 283–292
    Raksha Bandhan (Charm Tying), 250–256
    Sanjhi festival, *see* Sanjhi festival
    Tijo (Third), 240–250
religious rites of intensification, 2
repentance, 4
Republic Day, 3, 17
rice pudding, *see* khir
rishi (sage, saint, mythological ancestor), 66,
    94
rite, defined, 2
rites of intensification, 2–3
    complexity, 3
    deities, worship of variety of, 3
    family and friends, strengthening of ties
        with, 3
    food, giving, 3
    gifts, 3
    religious, 2
    secular, 2, 3
rites of passage, 2–3
    birth ceremonies, 3
    calendric rites and, 2–3
    community members as protagonists, 3
    complexity, 3
    deities as protagonists, 3
    family and friends, strengthening of ties
        with, 3
    marriage rite, 3
    priests, conducted by, 3
    status transitions concerns, 5
ritual, defined, 2
river, worship at, 36
Rose, Frederick P., 15, 124, 125, 148
roti (flat bread), 56, 205
rot (large, thick bread), 56
Rudra (god of storms), 193
rudraksh (a kind of berry), 199
rural versus urban tradition, debate on, 26–27

S

Sadhya mantra, 98
Sakat, 9, 113, 118–122, table 6
    Bairagi women, observance by, 119
    Baniyas, observance by, 119–120
    Brahmans, worship by, 119, 120